AF592737

asia
Annual 2011

Democracy in Asia
Discourses and Counter-Discourses

Edited by PRIYA SINGH

Associate Editors SUCHANDANA CHATTERJEE
ANITA SENGUPTA
SUSMITA BHATTACHARYA

Ministry of Culture
Government of India

Maulana Abul Kalam Azad Institute of Asian Studies
Kolkata

in association with

KNOWLEDGE WORLD

KW Publishers Pvt Ltd
New Delhi

2011 FPBA BEST PUBLISHERS AWARD (ENGLISH)

The Maulana Abul Kalam Azad Institute of Asian Studies was set up at the joint initiative of the Government of India, Department of Culture, Ministry of Human Resource Development and the Government of West Bengal. Registered as a Society under the West Bengal Registration of Societies' Act of 1961, with Prof. Nurul Hasan, the then Governor of West Bengal, as the President of the Society on the 4th of January 1993. It is funded by the Department of Culture, Government of India. Presently, His Excellency, Governor of West Bengal, is the President of the Society. An acre of land in Bidhannagar (Salt Lake City), Kolkata, was allotted to the Institute by the Government of West Bengal for building the Institute's campus.

The Maulana Abul Kalam Azad Institute of Asian Studies is a centre for research and learning with focus (a) on social, cultural, economic and political / administrative developments in Asia from the middle of the 19th Century onwards with special emphasis on their links with India, and (b) on the life and works of Maulana Abul Kalam Azad.

© 2013, Maulana Abul Kalam Azad Institute of Asian Studies

All rights reserved. No part of this publication may be reproduced, stored in a retrieval system, or transmitted in any form or by any means, electronic, mechanical, photocopying, recording or otherwise, without the prior written permission of the copyright owner.

The views expressed are of the individual authors and do not express the viewpoint of the Institute.

ISBN 978-93-81904-30-5

KNOWLEDGE WORLD

Published in India by

Kalpana Shukla
KW Publishers Pvt Ltd
4676/21, First Floor, Ansari Road, Daryaganj, New Delhi 110002
Phone: +91.11.23263498/43528107
Email: knowledgeworld@vsnl.net • www.kwpub.com

Printed and Bound in India

Contents

Essays

Special Essays

Research Note

Review Essay

Book Review

Contributors

Arpita Basu Roy is Fellow, at the Maulana Abul Kalam Azad Institute of Asian Studies, Kolkata.

Harihar Bhattacharyya is Professor and Head, at the Department of Political Science, University of Burdwan.

Susmita Bhattacharya is Fellow, at the Maulana Abul Kalam Azad Institute of Asian Studies, Kolkata.

Swapna Bhattacharya (Chakraborti) is Professor, at the Department of South & Southeast Asian Studies, University of Calcutta.

Kingshuk Chatterjee is Assistant Professor, at the Department of History, University of Calcutta.

Shibashis Chatterjee is Associate Professor, at the Department of International Relations, Jadavpur University, Kolkata.

Suchandana Chatterjee is Fellow, at the Maulana Abul Kalam Azad Institute of Asian Studies, Kolkata.

Sreemati Ganguli is former Fellow, at the Maulana Abul Kalam Azad Institute of Asian Studies, Kolkata.

P. R. Kumaraswamy is Professor, at the Centre for West Asian Studies, Jawaharlal Nehru University, New Delhi.

Monika Mandal is Fellow, at the Maulana Abul Kalam Azad Institute of Asian Studies, Kolkata.

Binoda Kumar Mishra is former Fellow, at the Maulana Abul Kalam Azad Institute of Asian Studies, Kolkata.

Mohanad Mustafa is Lecturer, at the College for Academic Studies, Or-Yehuda, Israel & As'ad Ghanem is Professor, at the Department of Political Science, University of Haifa, Israel.

Sanjay Pulipaka is Fellow, at the Maulana Abul Kalam Azad Institute of Asian Studies, Kolkata.

Safoora Razeq is former Fellow, at the Maulana Abul Kalam Azad Institute of Asian Studies, Kolkata.

Abhik Samanta is Fellow, at the Maulana Abul Kalam Azad Institute of Asian Studies, Kolkata.

Anita Sengupta is Fellow, at the Maulana Abul Kalam Azad Institute of Asian Studies, Kolkata.

Nadine Sika is Assistant Professor, at the Department of Political Science, American University of Cairo, Egypt.

Priya Singh is Fellow, at the Maulana Abul Kalam Azad Institute of Asian Studies, Kolkata.

1. Introduction

Priya Singh

This edition of the *Asia Annual* aspires to shed light on the notion of democracy and its ruptures in the Asian space/milieu. The chapters in this volume have been written from different perspectives, adopting an interdisciplinary approach, which enrich the discussions and exhibit a multitude of opinions and outlooks. This compilation has been structured primarily in terms of 'regions' (in the geopolitical sense) and the contributions have been categorised accordingly. The volume brings together contributions from leading experts and 'area specialists' who offer special insights and critiques on crucial issues and questions related to the central theme of democracy in their respective 'regions/areas' of specialisation.

The decade of the 1990s witnessed democratic changes proceed at a remarkable pace, as a result, the international landscape was significantly altered as democracy had from being a minority regime-type become the most common type of regime the world over. The number of countries with democratically elected governments had risen and along with it the international legitimacy of democracy as reflected in the approval that it had received from multilateral organisations. From the middle of the decade, a cautionary attitude was adopted, once the initial excitement had died down. There were difficulties being encountered by the new democracies in the process of consolidation. Consequently, the democratic euphoria of the early 1990s, tempered by sobering experience gave way to a more realistic appreciation of the difficulty in building and consolidating new democracies.[1]

At the onset of the new millennium, the problems of democracy building in Iraq, Russia's regression into an autocracy and the global rise of 'anti-Americanism' as she was perceived to have inflicted a 'collateral damage' on the process of democracy promotion, contributed towards a more sombre mood even among the most enthusiastic advocates of democracy. By the end of the first decade of the 21st century, the mood became progressively more negative as new grounds of 'erosion of freedom' were discovered in some instances. In other words, the first decade of the 21st century has not been idyllic for the fortunes of democracy in the international landscape. Larry Diamond [2] termed this period as one of 'democratic recession,' wherein the world's autocratic regimes had begun to exhibit a new *élan,* encouraging other commentators to openly articulate about the emergence of an 'authoritarian capitalist' alternative to democracy. While in the decade of the 1990s, political scientists tended to regard authoritarian regimes as transitory, compelled by the staying power of some of the authoritarian regimes, the next decade saw academics concentrating on 'what has enabled the authoritarian regimes to persist and often display a considerable degree of stability', and what Andrew J. Nathan[3] referred to as 'authoritarian resilience,' in the context of China. A large number of other non-democratic regimes of the former Soviet Union and West Asia/Middle East also displayed an impressive ability to maintain their hold on power; as such, much was and continues to be written about the sources of their survival.

With the onset of the participatory movements for democracy in West Asia/Middle East, in the second decade of the new millennia, a new dimension has been added to the debates on democracy.[4] On the one hand, there is increasing turbulence within the world's most potent authoritarian regimes; on the other hand, there is a growing inability or unwillingness on the part of the world's democracies to meet the challenges of authoritarianism, with important consequences for the state of global freedom.[5] The experiences of the earlier decades, (for instance in post-Soviet Central Asia and Russia) have demonstrated that while the transitions to democracy have for the most part been successful, the process of consolidation of democracy, in most cases has not been as successful. So where does that leave the uprisings that constitute the 'Arab Spring' movement? Or for that matter, what will be the fate of the movements for establishing and consolidating democracy and the attempts at democratisation in the region of South, Southeast Asia and China? There have also been attempts at envisaging models (of democracy) for replication/imitation in connected spaces drawing linkages from the past. The volume endeavours to explore these themes and hypothesise/theorise on related notions/concepts. We hope that the essays that have been compiled in this volume will be able to provide some answers to these questions and in the search for solutions, raise a few more relevant questions.

Essays

The Asian Theatre

Shibashis Chatterjee in his essay, 'Realism and Democracy: Two Stories of the American Engagement with Asia,' attempts to construe and spell out the logic behind the American engagement of Asia in the post 9/11 era. Chatterjee contends that the US engagement in Asia can be explained in terms of a) the standard realism that builds on geo-strategic considerations emphasising the role of power or security; b) norm creation based upon democracy, human rights, freedom and free market institutions; and c) articulations of hegemony straddling both material and ideational dimensions of life. In a precise and articulate exposition, Chatterjee endeavours to make sense of realism and the norms of liberal democracy as the guiding parameters of the US engagement of Asia in the post-Cold war period. The essential argument put forth by the author is that realist discourses have played a pivotal role in the making of US foreign policy in practically every theatre of Asia, though the forms of realism have varied significantly across cases. However, this essay also establishes a considerable role for the notion of democracy as a justificatory tool of US foreign policy engagements in Asia and goes further in identifying an apparent liberal inclination in the realist discourses. The author concludes on the note that in reality, power and democracy are not exclusive images of the US policy on Asia and despite the traditional realist orientation, democracy and free market liberalism cannot be ignored as vital components of the US policy in Asia in current times.

China, Southeast & South Asia

Binoda Kumar Mishra's essay, 'Dots of Democracy on a Socialist Canvas: The History of Democratic Movement in China,' attempts to trace the movements for democracy in China from the chapters of history to the contemporary era. Mishra argues that there have been repeated attempts to establish a democratic system in China but the movements have all failed to make any headway. The article touches upon the divergent strands of opinion that have been offered by varied scholars for China's failure in adopting the democratic form of government, ranging from an inherent deficiency within the Chinese society to the natural inclination of its political system towards authoritarianism. Mishra while emphasising upon the uniqueness of the Chinese position, points out that the idea of democracy espoused by the Chinese democrats did not adhere to the so-called 'universal' concept of democracy or the Western/liberal concept of democracy. As such, the prescribed course to achieve democracy in China is not to follow the Western path. The author is of the opinion that popular protest has been an intrinsic part of Chinese history, however; all movements or rebellions have succeeded in China with the exception of the 'Movement for Democracy'. Regarding the future of democracy in China, Mishra wraps-up his exposition by highlighting both the optimistic and pessimistic prognoses about democracy in China but, in his opinion, unless the economic compulsions give way to a more inclusive form of political order, the intermittent movements for democracy whether inside China or among its diaspora would continue to look like 'small dots in the vast authoritarian canvas.'

In 'Promoting Democracy and Foreign Policy: Major Powers and Myanmar,' Sanjay Pulipaka delves into the policies of the major powers including the US, the ASEAN, India and China towards Myanmar. Pulipaka contends that these powers, albeit with varying levels of intensity and with some degree of variance in their approach have been advocating the necessity for bringing about change in the political processes of Myanmar. The author concisely spells out and elaborates upon the two contending approaches for promoting democratic transition in Myanmar, with the ASEAN and India adopting a 'development first approach'; the US supporting a 'politics first approach', and China focussing on an approach, which espouses 'maintaining stability' in Myanmar. The essay examines a few of the vital dimensions of the policies of major powers towards Myanmar and consequently arrives at the conclusion that while some have exhibited an explicitly political approach, others have adopted a combination of political-developmental approaches and the remaining have refrained from actively advocating democratic change. The author attributes the difference in policies to 'contradictory national interests', which, in his opinion has resulted in the furtherance of differing policies towards Myanmar though attempts have been made to explore the prospects of a coordinated strategy.

Monika Mandal in 'The Democratic Role of Ethnicity in Nepal,' concentrates on the interplay between ethnicity and democracy in an ethnically diverse society and polity. Mandal delves deep into history to unveil the unlimited ethnic diversity that the state of Nepal has to offer and in the process provides a comprehensive narrative of the suppression of this diversity till the Panchayat period as the agenda of the state-sponsored process of national integration was 'exclusive' in character, focussing on the establishment of a homogenous, monolithic and unitary state. In other words, the author contends that prior to the 1990s, ethnic politics was banned in Nepal and ethnic group identity and interest was suppressed. Mandal then proceeds to reveal the transformation that takes place in Nepal's political space with the inauguration of the new Constitution (1990) which brought about fundamental changes in the political system heralding the end of absolute monarchy and the promotion of the status of the people of Nepal from that of a 'subject' to a 'citizen.' Subsequently, the pluralistic character of Nepali society consisting of diverse cultural and linguistic groups was given political recognition. It is at this juncture that the changes in the state-ethnic relations occur and the essay attempts to understand and interpret the changing dynamics of ethnicity and democracy in the Himalayan state.

Harihar Bhattacharyya's essay 'Marxists' Democratic Problematic and the Decline of the Left in West Bengal' begins with a quote "…if *panchayats* fail, the CPM experiment fails" attributed to the first finance minister of the Left Front government in the state of West Bengal, which is significant as it is central to the argument put forth by the author. At the outset, Bhattacharyya manifestly articulates the two questions that he wishes to raise about the 'democratic problematic' and the 'associated question of its approach to and role in representative political institutions' of the Left in Bengal in particular and the Left in the Indian context, in general and he seeks to raise it primarily at the grassroots level because it was at this level that the regime received maximum popular support. The author moves on to link this issue with the other fundamental argument that he seeks to make, namely the apparent paradox, between 'massive electoral mobilisation,' on the one hand, and the near absence of 'democratic institutionalisation,' on the other, which in turn, he attributes to the incorrect interpretation of the theory of democracy. Bhattacharyya then proceeds to critique the very notion of democracy, upheld by the Left, which he terms as 'winners take it all' democracy. In his opinion the Leftist discourse of democracy, or rather, 'the discourse of power', turned out to be anti-democratic and anti-institutional in its implications. Bhattacharya concludes with the assertion that the crux of the contradiction lies in the deep-seated theoretical problems of Marxism in respect of democracy and institutions, as such, the only way out lies in an acceptance of the fact that democracy in our times is far removed from Karl Marx's or Lenin's times and that there is no ideal model of democracy to emulate, therefore, peculiarities should not to be taken as signs of deviation but rather as symbols of innovation.

The West Asian Stage

Anita Sengupta in her essay, 'Crossroads: Democracy and the Turkish Model,' argues that the 'Turkish model' that is identified as 'secular, democratic and liberal' and, is at the centre of debates as a number of states in the Middle East search for social, economic and political options, is at crossroads, yet again, at a juncture from where various alternative futures are possible. She finds this as evocative of the era when the collapse of the Soviet Union encouraged speculations on Turkey's geo-strategic significance and a model was developed that emphasised upon the significance of the Turkish experiment for the post Soviet world. In the author's opinion the argument was basic as Turkey, with the exception of Israel, was the only country in the region that combined parliamentary democracy with a market economy that was able to show significant growth rates. Sengupta elaborates that by referring to the country's Islamic heritage and its ethnic affinity with a large part of the post Soviet states in the Caucasus and Central Asia, it was therefore argued that Turkey was well placed not only to act as a 'model' for the countries but also as a bridge between the 'east' and the 'west'. The author maintains that this was an argument that became prevalent not only within Turkey but also in the international arena and that it was aimed primarily at strengthening Turkey's negotiation with the international community, particularly the EU. For the author, certain parallels with the current scenario in the Middle East can be identified instantly as a somewhat similar situation of 'transition' is being predicted for the Middle East today with the imminent 'collapse' of the ruling regimes and there is similarly a crisis in Turkey's relations with the EU. Sengupta concludes with the statement that the attraction for the 'model' here is being projected in a shared Ottoman past though the Arab world does not look upon this heritage without disapproval.

Kingshuk Chatterjee's essay, 'Arab Spring: Authoritarianism in the Middle East Re-examined,' attempts to view the continuing experience of authoritarianism in the Middle East through the lens of the structuralist approach, which seeks for answers to the question of authoritarianism in the political structures and dispensations of social and political power in the Middle East in the specific context of the 20th century and deems that there is nothing inherent in the region that favours an authoritarian dispensation and consequently that authoritarianism may wither away given changes in the milieu in which it flourishes. Chatterjee refrains from subscribing to the characteristic Marxist position of western interests in the oil economy as the main support for authoritarianism in the region. The essay commences by looking at the historical roots of dispensation of political power in the region before moving on to scrutinize the social basis of authoritarianism in the Middle East. The author subsequently proposes to establish the connection between oil and the willing/reluctant acceptance of authoritarianism prior to indicating the weakening of the structure by the 1990s as a consequence of the changes in the oil economy.

In 'The Arab Spring: Quo Vadis?' P.R. Kumaraswamy succinctly interprets the extensive changes witnessed by the Middle Eastern region since January, 2011. The essay commences with a reference to the plethora of terms used to describe these events/developments, such as: unrest, upheaval, revolution, democratic surge, popular protests, regime change, social change, digital revolution, internet revolution, liberation technology and the revolutionary process/movement or the Arab Spring, some of which have been subject to severe criticism. In a similar vein, according to Kumaraswamy, several reasons have been attributed for this phenomenon, for instance: lack of democracy, oppression, and indifference of the rulers; youth bulge and militarisation of the society. The essay attempts to look into the progress card of the Arab Spring movements and in the process arrives at the conclusion that there have been some perceptible changes, some changes for the better, some weakening of central authority, some open wounds and some financial incentives towards buying temporary peace, the region has also witnessed intense power struggles, with some resilient rulers prepared to fight than leave office and of course, there remain a few islands of stability in the region. Nonetheless, in the endeavour to look into *what has happened so far?* Kumaraswamy reveals the essence of his argument, that is, notwithstanding these developments; on the whole, the changes are merely superficial.

Nadine Sika in 'The Façade of Social Capital and Democracy: The Case of Egypt,' seeks to challenge the social capital theory as propounded by the World Bank, which considers social capital to be an important indicator of growth as well as a facilitator of democracy given that it encourages a vibrant civil society. Sika puts forward the argument that in developing nations, especially those governed by authoritarian regimes; the prevalence of social capital can reinforce authoritarianism, while its absence can help in the democratisation process. The author substantiates her basic contention by stating that civic and political participation might be absent in authoritarian regimes because citizens, especially highly educated individuals do not participate 'deliberately' in civil society organisations, political parties, and in elections that are known to be mired with corruption. Accordingly, she states that trust in the socio-political system is low, and an individual's social networks are the privilege of a few who are entrenched in patron-client relations. By the same token, Sika opines that individuals with low levels of education participate in elections; either in 'obedience' to their managers at work or to help family and friends win office. Consequently, the author contends, the possibilities of networking and trust within the system are based on patron client relations, which reinforce authoritarianism, rather than developing democracy or democratic values. In tune with the essential argument of the author, the essay attempts to underline the importance of revisiting the social capital theory, from the World Bank's perspective, especially in light of the recent Arab uprisings, which were primarily the consequence of the mobilization efforts of the educated citizens and specifically, it endeavours to apply the World Bank indicators to a survey study in Egypt to reveal the dichotomy between the high level of political knowledge of the well educated and their low levels of trust of and participation in civic and political activities.

The principal argument of Mohanad Mustafa & As'ad Ghanem's essay, 'The Muslim Brotherhood Movement Facing the Challenge of Democracy: Political Transition in Post-Revolutionary Egypt,' is that mainstream political Islam, to be precise, the Muslim Brotherhood—has continually endeavoured to find common ground between its fundamentalist ideology and democratic values; its chief goal, before the revolution, was to achieve political legitimacy and a political presence in the public sphere, both local and international. The authors' opine that the movement did not aspire to achieve power through elections, as that was impracticable under the authoritarian regime. Post-revolution, however, they indicate, its participation in the new regime seems very realistic; that is, mainstream political Islam would be responsible for policy in practice, and not only for discourse on the theoretical plane. This, according to them has made it more conservative in its presentation of its political attitude towards democracy and the character of the state and has led it to explicitly highlight its support for retaining its Islamic character. Mustafa and As'ad have arranged their essay in three segments. The first presents political Islam's outlook towards democracy while it was in the opposition; that is, the Islamic rhetoric about democracy before the crumbling of the authoritarian regime. Mustafa and As'ad contend that their analysis will be based chiefly on the Muslim Brotherhood's political platform of the year 2005, the first such document in the movement's history. The second segment attempts to analyse the Islamic rhetoric about democracy after the revolution, based on an assessment of its new political platform, which was published following the revolution. In the concluding segment, the authors' set forth their perceptions on the issue.

The Central Asian and Russian Arena

Sreemati Ganguli's essay, 'Debates on Transition and Democracy in Central Asia: The Post-Soviet Experience,' essentially deliberates upon two fundamental categories of academic debates in the post-Soviet Central Asian space, namely debates on the processes of transition and democratisation in the post-Soviet states of Eurasia. She then proceeds to a brief exposition of the contemporary Central Asian situation. Ganguli contends that the transition debate centres on the process as well as the goal of transition to post-communism that is to say, would it lead to democracy, or another form of authoritarianism or a situation of chaos-uncertainty. The author in her analysis of the debates on the democratisation process in the Central Asian Republics brings forth some of its remarkable features calling it as the first instance of /experience at democratisation for the Central Asian Republics. The composition gives the impression that in the Central Asian space, democracy and political stability may often turn out to be mutually exclusive. Yet, Ganguli concludes on a hopeful note with the assertion that the countries of Eurasia, particularly, the Central Asian states are not even mid-way through the process of democratisation or transition to post-communism as only twenty years have passed since the disintegration of the USSR and as such it would be premature to assess the authenticity and genuineness of the process of democratisation in this unique geographical space with its intrinsic particularities.

In the essay, "Russia: From '*demokratizatsiya*' to '*suverennaya demokratiya*,'" Susmita Bhattacharya builds on the premise that over the last two decades 'democratisation' and 'democracy' have been the most extensively deliberated upon and the central organising concepts in the context of the political evolution of the post-socialist and post-communist regimes. Bhattacharya's essay begins with the period of the late 1990s, when the developments in the domestic political arena followed by the disintegration of the Soviet Union led to wide speculation that post-Soviet Russia was going through a transitional phase towards democracy. However, the author proposes that the euphoria was short-lived due to the changes that took place in the political system of the Russian Federation as a consequence of the federal reforms launched by Putin soon after assuming the presidency of the country in the year 2000. Bhattacharya refers to the existence of a plethora of writings, which have suggested that the democratisation process that started under Yel'tsin was derailed by Putin's reforms and the country was moving towards becoming a 'soft autocracy'. In her essay, Bhattacharya attempts to trace the course of the democratisation process in post-Soviet Russia and explore the impact of the federal reform policies initiated during Putin's presidency on the transitional democratic process of the Russian Federation as well as on matters relating to the regional governors, the Federal Legislature and electoral politics, human rights, and the media in particular.

Others: The Special Essays/Notes and Reviews

From the point of view of its basic theme the volume includes two atypical essays that have been placed in the singular category of 'Community, Individual and Democracy.' In the first essay of this section, 'Islam and Democracy: A Conceptual Analysis,' Abhik Samanta, hypothesises on the concepts of 'Islam' and 'Democracy' in the context of the Asian experience. This is followed by Safoora Razeq's essay on 'Maulana Abul Kalam Azad: The Prophet of Democracy,' which is in the nature of an elucidation on Maulana Abul Kalam Azad as an 'Islamic liberal democrat' and a 'visionary'. The concluding section of the compilation incorporates a *research note* by Suchandana Chatterjee on 'Ulan Ude and Ulaan Baatar: The Mongol space re-visited,' a *review essay* by Arpita Basu Roy on 'Mass Attitudes in Democracy Sustainment: A Case Study of Public Perceptions of Democracy in Afghanistan,' and a *book review* by Swapna Bhattacharya (Chakraborti) of Koh Kim Seng's *Misunderstood Myanmar: An Introspective Study of a Southeast Asian State in Transition.*

Conclusion

This is an attempt at presenting a comprehensive volume on the discussions and deliberations concerning the concept of democracy in Asia. It seeks to offer an in-depth analysis that could prove to be useful for those who are engrossed in Asian studies. The essays envelop a wide range of debates on varied aspects related to the processes of democracy and democratisation from the Asian geopolitical space and ponder over practical problems arising from the tensions associated with movements for democracy. At the same time, the authors in their expositions also raise vital questions regarding the feasibility as well as the implications of external efforts at promoting/imposing democracy and the setting up of imported models of democracy. The underling accent is on both the innate uniqueness/distinctiveness of the regions as well as the considerable overlaps, which encourage comparative analyses in general and in the context of democracy/democratisation in particular.

Notes

1. The period of '1990s' fall within what is commonly described as the third wave of democracy. *Democracy's Third Wave*, refers to the third major surge of democracy in history. The term was coined by Samuel P. Huntington, in his essay published in the *Journal of Democracy* and further expounded in his book *The Third Wave: Democratization in the Late Twentieth Century*. Huntington describes global democratisation as a process which has come in the form of three waves, the first beginning in the early 19th century with the third being a contemporary phenomena. Writing in the *Journal of Democracy*, Huntington identifies three historical waves of democracy. The first began in the early 19th century with the extension of the right to vote to a large proportion of the male population in the United States, and continued until the 1920s. A second wave began with the triumph of the Allies in World War II, cresting in 1962. The third wave commenced from 1974 (with the Carnation Revolution in Portugal) and included the historic democratic transitions in Latin America in the 1980s and Eastern Europe after the collapse of the Soviet Union. Many of the newer democracies are not fully 'consolidated,' however, implying that while they have electoral institutions in place, political democracy remains fragile. The reasons for this fragility include economic instability, continued elite dominance of politics, ongoing military interference in civilian affairs, and others. Many political scientists and theorists believe that the third wave has crested and will soon begin to ebb, just as its predecessors did. See Samuel Huntington. "Democracy's Third Wave," *Journal of Democracy*, vol.2 (Spring 1991), pp. 12-34. For a more elaborate discussion see Samuel Huntington. *The Third Wave: Democratization in the Late Twentieth Century* (Norman: University of Oklahoma Press, 1991).
2. Larry Diamond. "Democracy and Governance Performance: How are the 'Third Wave' Democracies Doing?" in Mark.F. Plattner, "Populism, Pluralism and Liberal Democracy," *Journal of Democracy*, vol. 21 (January 2010), p.82.
3. Andrew. J. Nathan. "China's changing of the Guard: Authoritarian Resilience," *Journal of Democracy*, vol.14 (January 2003), pp. 6-17.

4. Recent events in the Arab World, known as the New Arab Awakening/the Arab Spring, have been projected by some analysts as the beginning of a fourth wave of democratisation, though prospects for the establishment of genuine democracies in the region remain uncertain.
5. See Arch Puddington. "Freedom in the World 2011: The Authoritarian Challenge to Democracy," http://www.freedomhouse.org (12 January 2012).

2. Realism and Democracy: Two Stories of the American Engagement with Asia

Shibashis Chatterjee

The US' engagement with Asia can be explained in diverse ways that make any sweeping generalisation impossible. Despite wide variations on the theme, three broad frameworks explain US engagement in Asia: first, standard realism that builds on geo-strategic considerations emphasising the role of power or security; second, norm creation based upon democracy, human rights, freedom and free market institutions, and third, articulations of hegemony straddling both material and ideational dimensions of life. In this brief exposition, we attempt to make sense of realism and norms of liberal democracy as guiding parameters of US engagement of Asia in the post-Cold war period. This essay builds along conventional lines. It disaggregates Asia into standard regions and traces the broad contours of American role(s) therein. The argument developed in the essay is that the US has sought to pursue conventional realist policies in Asia with mixed results. However, realism cannot explain all aspects of this complex narrative and hence additional tools are necessary. The US has justified its foreign policy in Asia largely in terms of democracy, sometimes as a cover for parochial realist goals but also to export and promote the virtues of liberal democracy. In fact, power and democracy are not exclusive images of the US policy on Asia. Realism and liberalism crisscross and their interactions are messy. However, power and democracy can be separated as analytical categories for their underlying assumptions and basic propositions remain distinct. The essay unfolds in two broad sections, the first looking into power/realism and the second engaging with democracy/liberalism as coordinates of the American imagination of Asia.

The Case for Realism

Realism with its basis in power and security remains perhaps the most abiding and overarching paradigm of international politics and this is amply demonstrated in the US engagement both in Asia and throughout the world.[1] The classical realist tradition has always found a healthy reception in US foreign policy making circles, and from George Kennan to Henry Kissinger, American foreign policy had received strong intellectual support for political realism.[2] In other words, reducing security to essentially political and military terms, identifying security with the nation, upholding the claims of national interest as defined by power, among others, stand out as robust attributes of US foreign policy across space and time. The academic debates concerning realism and the proliferation of its categories as a natural corollary have had little, if at all any, significance in terms of US foreign policy choices.[3] The major debates concerning actual foreign-policy have been over the extensity and depth of America's power projection, nature of alliances and forms of commitment, the relative significance of the various elements of national power, the nature of weapons manufacture and trade, both conventional and non-conventional, and how vital American interests can be served throughout the world.[4]

Realists have essentially claimed vindication of their paradigm as a guide to American foreign policy since its very inception as a sovereign state. Even during the post Cold War period, despite the manifest discomfort for realism over the unanticipated collapse of the Soviet Union, realism has claimed broad success. The American military interventions in Afghanistan and Iraq, her commitment towards Israel, holding on to its special relationship with Japan, calibrating its naval presence in the Asia Pacific region, investing significantly in its relations with states hostile to China, and holding on to its massive armament and national defence programmes, despite considerable economic difficulties, are often used as vindication of the realist grip upon America's conception of the world and its legitimate role in it. The fact that the US has emerged as a self-conscious super power in the post-Cold War period, unrivalled by any military competitor, is reinforced by the trends of US led military interventions across the world. The US has succeeded in preventing the formation of any anti-American military coalition in each of these cases of interventions, although great powers like China and Russia had repeatedly voiced their disagreement over America's role.[5] Moreover, the US has decided to invest militarily strictly in accordance with its national interest. Hence, West Asia remains a theatre of constant American involvement, militarily or otherwise, given the enormous geo-strategic significance of the region for America's vital national interests. Africa, in sharp contrast, despite grave internal turmoil and internecine civil conflicts claiming millions of lives, has hardly drawn American military attention, given the continent's low priority in American calculations. Realists argue that American engagement is solidly predicated on national security considerations, with variable emphasis being laid on power and security on a case by case basis.[6]

America's engagement in Asia would thus apparently fit in very well with this realist narrative. The pre 9/11 period, since the onset of the post Cold War era, saw unprecedented consolidation of US power in Asia. In West Asia, the US altered the regional power equation by militarily humiliating Saddam Hussein, but apart from Saudi Arabia, Israel and Turkey, its relations with the mainstream Arab states remained volatile. The US military victory created renewed impetus on finding a diplomatic solution to the vexed Israel-Palestinian problem, but proactive American initiatives failed to solve the nettlesome issue, given the intransigency of hard line positions across the Israel-Arab divide. The US, despite its military victory, failed to gain any purchase with the Islamist Khomeini regime in Iran, and could neither engineer a domestic coup to topple the theocracy nor prevent Iran from silently building up its nuclear infrastructure. The overall record of US foreign policy in this period shows that the military superiority it had so drastically demonstrated in the first Gulf War did not turn it into a successful hegemonic power in West Asia. Its power and alliance ensured that its vital national interests in an uninterrupted supply of oil and the safety of communications remained in fact. But military power did not translate into anything more tangible – its basis of insecurity in the Arab world remained unaddressed despite its unprecedented concentration of military hardware. To quote Stephen Walt: "Although the majority of Arabs and Muslims reject al-Qaeda's methods, hostility toward the US is widespread in the Arab and the Islamic world. This phenomenon explains why Arab support has been relatively limited and why Afghanistan's neighbours have been reluctant to give the US military forces unqualified access to their territory."[7]

For many analysts, the pre 9/11 period was not a uni-linear realist narrative in US foreign policy. The Clinton administration had taken the ideas of democracy, free markets, human rights, civil society and non-proliferation as central drivers of American foreign policy and undertaken a series of measures highlighting commitment to such themes. We will return to this in greater depth in the following section. Realists nevertheless believed that there was no fundamental course correction during this period, as the crucial theme of vital American interests had gone unscathed. Realist preoccupations apparently came back with a vengeance with the terrorist strikes in the US, whose perpetrators were traced to the Middle East. With the Taliban consolidating its power in Afghanistan, many radical Islamist (as most groups called themselves) terror organisations and loose networks found safe haven and a fertile breeding ground in that state. Most of these groups were staunchly anti-American for both political and cultural reasons. The nuclearisation of Pakistan and the close connection of the Pakistani establishment, especially the military and the ISI with the Taliban regime, had created significant security challenges to American interests in the whole region.

The destruction of the Twin Towers catapulted the US to galvanise a quick retributive and punitive military intervention in Afghanistan, and the US led coalition forces succeeded in removing the Taliban from power in Kabul. The military success in Afghanistan, however, was only apparent; while the Taliban lost power, the organisation did not die. The volatile tribal areas of the then Northwest Frontier Provinces in Pakistan, which bordered the Pashto dominated Southern Afghanistan where the Taliban strongholds became safe havens for the Taliban and Al Qaeda operators, and Pakistan was inextricably drawn into the military operations that largely made the outcome contingent on Pakistan's cooperation and support. Without making any decisive headway in Afghanistan, George Bush unleashed the second Gulf War on the flimsy pretext of destroying weapons of mass destruction allegedly hidden in Iraq by Saddam Hussein, an accusation that even US intelligence subsequently failed to substantiate. The US, nevertheless, took on two military operations in Asia, far away from its borders, and no great power provided any military opposition to these moves. Military force has thus returned to the centre-force of US foreign policy in Asia with a vengeance, and apparently this was a strong corroboration of the realist orthodoxy in US foreign policy.[8] But this policy has divided both realists and their detractors. Most realists strongly criticised Bush's decision to attack Iraq and found it going against all forms of realism. Thus, Van Evera writes, "Specifically, the Bush administration has focused heavily on an offensive campaign against al-Qaeda overseas while neglecting three other critical fronts: bolstering homeland defence, securing weapons and materials of mass destruction from possible theft or purchase by terrorists, and winning the war of ideas. And the administration has sometimes done too little even on the offensive, instead diverting itself into a costly and counterproductive sideshow in Iraq."[9] Jefferey Record finds the nature and parameters of this war to be 'frustratingly unclear', conflating different threats into a monolithic whole, and subordinating strategic clarity to moral objectives of foreign policy.[10] Non realists have questioned the very basis of this approach as being demonstrably counter-productive to US interests. Paul Rogers laments that the US policy is based on the requirement to maintain control in a fractured and unpredictable global environment, increasing rather than decreasing insecurity. This policy has been largely counter-productive, as the continuing problems in Afghanistan and Iraq demonstrate.[11]

US engagements in other Asian theatres provide a mixed picture. Realist considerations certainly prevailed in Southern Asia, particularly in reinventing a vigorous geo-political role for Pakistan under General Pervez Musharraf, despite Islamabad recorded violation of the norms of nuclear proliferation and calibrated support for terrorist organisations. As it has repeatedly happened in the past, US foreign policy chose vital geo-political interests over normative commitments yet again. President Bush's Afghanistan strategy was pivoted upon Pakistan and therefore the nature of Islamabad's political regime became inconsequential to Washington's dealings. What more, Bush and key members of his administration were decidedly more comfortable dealing with the General, who apparently championed liberal values and led a crusade against Islamist zealots and terrorists in a vital role reversal for Islamabad since the fundamentalist turn of his predecessor in uniform some years back. There was a general unease in the US administration regarding the future and viability of weak democratic forces in Pakistan and their peculiar vulnerability to radical, Islamist and populist forces. Moreover, US engagement with India, which had started to improve steadily since President Clinton's visit of 2000, reached unprecedented heights under Bush. Despite comparably insignificant geo-political value of India in the US war on terror in Afghanistan, Indo-US relations became incomparably stronger and multifaceted than America's relations with Pakistan.[12] Whatever may be the causes for this manifest difference, realism is ill at ease as a plausible explanation.

Involvement of the US in Central Asia in recent years can also be explained along realist lines. Although Central Asia's energy resources and proximity to Russia, Iran, and China warranted US attention, and the Weapons of Mass Destruction (WMD) infrastructure as a fearful legacy of the Soviet Union's breakup made the region rather alarming, it hardly attracted the attention of the US in the initial post Cold War years. Operation Enduring Freedom in Afghanistan changed all that. Suddenly the Central Asian states were catapulted into significance and the US opened up bases and operations and began to cultivate these states more actively for cooperation. While, the Central Asian republics were dovetailed into US strategy as a consequence of its larger geo-strategic concerns, the intrinsic worth of these states also began to matter over time. Olga Oliker and David A. Shlapak in a RAND Corporation study wrote, "Although US interests in Central Asia before September 11 were focused largely on energy issues, which were deemed to be of lesser importance, they have shifted since that date. Concerns about Russia, China, and Iran; the dangers of proliferation and other transnational threats; and a general desire to support economic reform and democratisation reflect not so much a change in US attitudes as a reassessment of the relative values of each component."[13] According to Robert O. Blake, Jr., the Assistant Secretary of State for South and Central Asian Affairs, the US considers Central Asia as an increasingly vital area. According to Blake, the US pursues five major objectives in Central Asia. In his words, "First, to expand cooperation with Central Asian states to assist coalition efforts in Afghanistan; second, to increase development and diversification of the region's energy resources and supply routes; third, to encourage political liberalization and respect for human rights; fourth, to foster competitive market economies and economic reform and lastly, to prevent the emergence of failed states, or in more positive terms, to increase the capacity of states to govern themselves effectively."[14] It is evident that like all other regions, the US engagement in Central Asia remains plural. However, there is evidence to suggest that the region has ascended in American estimate primarily due to its new found geo-political significance, being strategically located between Chinese, Russian and West Asian spheres of influence and being contiguous to Afghanistan. As relations between the US and Russia have hardened and given China's increasing interest in the region primarily for its energy resources, the US has began to rivet far more attention to this region than it did in the past. While stability, democratisation, development of market institutions and insulation from radical Islamist influence remain critical drivers of this change, the strategic significance of Central Asia as a possible gateway to Afghanistan has certainly been the most important factor that has motivated the US to redirect its policy towards this region.

The US policy in the Asia Pacific provides the most difficult challenge to realism according to its detractors. Liberals are insistent that US policy in this region clearly betrays a different set of policy priorities – the demands of globalised free market institutions, concerns for soft power, the appeal of democracy and human rights seem to outweigh the cumulative effects of military balances, shift in alliances and arms spending patterns. President Barack Obama's administration wants to pivot the US foreign policy away from the Middle East and toward East Asia. Secretary of State Hillary Clinton's recent Foreign Policy piece exemplified this thinking. "The future of the United States is intimately intertwined with the future of the Asia-Pacific," she wrote, touting Washington's 'irreplaceable role in the Pacific'. We shall engage with the liberal case in the following section. But does Asia Pacific offer an unsolvable puzzle for realism? Realists will certainly disagree. There is surely no dearth of strategic compulsions as drivers of the US foreign policy in this region. In fact, the central role of the region in the US thinking came through standard realist concerns. Japan's bellicosity during the Second World War historically transformed the contours of America's Asia Pacific policy. The ideological polarisation of the region got translated in terms of the US alliance patterns during the Cold War. While the collapse of the Cold War took away the basis for the existing alliance pattern, and the US did withdraw from a number of bases and operations, the unresolved problem of Taiwan and the nuclear adventurism of North Korea kept it strategically engaged in the region. The ascension of China and the deterioration in Sino-Japanese ties have complicated the strategic predicament of the US. The Cold War European syndrome is getting replicated in the Asia Pacific. Countries in the region have expressed considerable anxiety about China's growing power and seek US military presence as a counterweight. Chinese provocations in the South China Sea led the Philippines and Japan to promulgate a new 'Strategic Partnership' expressing 'common strategic interests' such as 'ensuring the safety of sea lines of communication'. More recently, the Japanese Prime Minister Yoshihiko Noda cautioned that Japan's security environment had grown 'increasingly murky due to China's stepped-up activities in local waters and its rapid military expansion'. The US, however, finds itself in a paradox. As Justin Logan puts it, "The desire to focus on the Asia-Pacific is sound, but the administration's policies there are not. The impulse to reassure America's Asian allies that the US commitment to their security is rock solid perversely makes it likely that they will continue to free-ride on America's exertions – in an era when Washington has less and less money to spend."[15]

The new US policy highlights several priorities. First, bolstering friendship and alliances with Japan, South Korea, Thailand, the Philippines and Australia continues to be America's chief policy concern. Alliance relationships are the cornerstone of US regional involvement, Clinton had emphasised. Second, addressing global challenges with China remains Washington's top most concern. According to Clinton, Obama administration is committed to strengthening relationship with China and other key players in the region. Other aspects include strengthening the US-India relationship; building cooperation with Southeast Asia; curbing proliferation; engaging directly with people beyond governments; engaging with Myanmar, and pursuing shared interests through multilateral engagement.[16] The US inability to spend more in alliance building operations in an area traditionally held to be crucial to her vital strategic interests despite the steady rise of a great power competitor is indeed problematic for a paradigm that prioritises national security over everything else. However, realists generally tend to argue that there is hardly any evidence that suggests the US insensitivity to power calculations in this region or manifest neglect of her security interests. Most forms of realism would endorse imaginative policy mixes and America's complex intermixing of hard and soft power in the Asia Pacific would therefore reinforce rather than weaken a realist reading.

The US-China relations would demand a separate essay and I would desist from that temptation here. The fact remains that while the US seems to be a declining global power, China is poised as a rising superpower that may well evolve as the most potent contender to the US hegemony in near future. Most realists and proponents of power transition theory would by and large agree though disagreeing about the irreversibility of the US decline and China's ascension and the possible implications this might have within the international order. However, unlike the great power transitions of the past, there are several critical points of departure to this great game – unlike the past, political economy plays a disproportionately significant role in this transition. Two essential components of this deserve mention – first, the US-China economic relations are exceedingly complex and densely intertwined, which induces cautious moderation in their interactions. Their economies are virtually mutually mortgaged as the Chinese buy up most of US treasury bonds as Washington's deficit piles up every year, and China ends up selling most of its industrial and consumer products in the US market, and second, unlike the Cold War system, where two economic systems existed in parallel without any meaningful coordination between them, corresponding to their political and military polarisation, the post-Cold War political economy is distinctively integrated and global, with no insulation for large economies like that of the US and China to cut off trade and commercial exchanges between themselves. Sentiments expressed by recent the US administration bear this out as clearly as possible. Witness for example, Secretary Clinton's remark on May 9, 2011, "We both have much more to gain from cooperation than from conflict. The fact is that a thriving America is good for China and a thriving China is good for America. Earlier this year, on January 19, President Obama categorically stated, At a time when some doubt the benefits of cooperation between the United States and China, this visit is also a chance to demonstrate a simple truth. We have an enormous stake in each other's success. In an interconnected world, in a global economy, nations – including our own – will be more prosperous and more secure when we work together."[17]

This does not suggest that US-China relations are bereft of complications. Uncomfortable strategic issues divide them in the Asia Pacific theatre. As Asia becomes increasingly important for the US in economic terms, these differences are expected to be thrown in bolder reliefs. However, as William J. Burns, US Deputy Secretary, in his speech of November 04, 2011 made it clear, the US and China can ill afford to lock horns in Asian waters at this stage. In his words: "In a complex relationship like this one, neither conflict nor cooperation is preordained. As China's role in world affairs grows, keeping this relationship on a productive track will be a defining challenge – for both sides – for many years to come. For all our differences, we have a lot more to gain by working together than by working apart. And no bilateral relationship is likely to matter more to the interests of each of our countries, or to the future of international order, in the new century unfolding before us."[18] The US policy so far had thus been cautious. While it has rejuvenated its Pacific relations with traditional allies like Japan, Australia, South Korea, The Philippines, and Taiwan, it has taken care not to get into any overt rivalry with China. That the US believes that China will challenge its domination of the Pacific over time is clear from Washington's investment vis-a-vis India and the ASEAN states, particularly Vietnam, both in strategic and economic terms. But the US has categorically ruled out the position of being a ring holder in the regional struggles between China and her neighbours.

The US has certainly not being oblivious of balance of power considerations in the Asia Pacific; but it has refrained from pursuing any aggressive and overt strategy of containment against China. Most realists do not find this as anomalous to the theory's prediction since the US still retains a decisive military superiority over China that does not necessitate any drastic course correction in its security policies. Power transition theorists have identified a period of transformation at work as the US economy has slowed down considerably over the years, which far predates the recent economic downturn unleashed by the global recession, while the Chinese have consistently recorded double digit GDP growth rate over two decades. There are many prognostications based upon extrapolations of such trends over the *longue durée*, but time has certainly not arrived to test their veracity as yet.

The Narrative of Democracy

While realism seems to be the guiding paradigm for America's role in Asia, democracy remains a vitally important norm of US foreign policy. Democracy promotion has intermittently shaped the US attitude towards many Asian states although geopolitical considerations have prevailed over it in cases of conflicting interests. This section analyses why democracy promotion is considered important in the US foreign policy, and two cases where the role of democracy seems pivotal in constructing ties of friendship in Asia – the US relations with India and Israel respectively.

The realists and liberals have long battled over the salience of democracy as a guiding norm of US foreign policy. John Ikenberry sums up the issue brilliantly: "To hear critics tell it, the American preoccupation with promoting democracy around the world is the product of a dangerous idealistic impulse… At best, in their view, the American democratic impulse is a distraction, a nettlesome inconvenience that forces the nation's leaders to dress up needed measures in democratic rhetoric. At worst, it unleashes a dangerous and overweening moralistic zeal, oblivious to or ignorant of how international politics really operates."[19] According to Sean M. Lynn-Jones, there are four reasons that critics urge against democracy promotion as a tool of foreign policy – (1) the claim that the democratic peace is a myth, (2) the argument that the process of democratisation increases the risk of war, (3) arguments that democratic elections are harmful in societies that are not fully liberal, and (4) claims that 'Asian values' can undergird polities based on 'soft authoritarianism' that are superior to liberal democracies.[20]

Theoretically, none of these claims are sustainable. Democracies are peaceful towards each other for both normative and institutional reasons.

To put things as briefly as possible, democracies believe in debate and moderation and settle differences peacefully within themselves and usually externalise this norm in their dealings with other democracies. Institutions offer transparency, build trust, reduce arbitrariness in decision-making, and signal intensions with clarity. There is overwhelming historical evidence that upholds the plausibility of these arguments. Ikenberry makes the point that this peace is best on rational calculation of interests and not some woolly trust. He explains, "It occurs because they are accustomed to relations based on the rule of law rather than on political expediency, and because their openness provides their potential international partners with a set of something like verification tools. The partners can see their internal workings and judge for themselves whether promises and commitments are being kept. They can even hope to influence the other's policies. And they can be assured that the complicated political life of a democracy makes abrupt and unwelcome changes of policy unlikely."[21]

In brief, the liberals have strongly maintained that spreading democracy benefits the inhabitants of newly democratising states, promotes peace in the international system, and in the process advances US interests. These factors are closely interrelated. Thus, democracy is supposed to improve the living standards of the people since democracy in a procedural sense is based upon the wishes of the people and is committed to liberty, which is an intrinsic good. As people acquire the right to vote, they are expected to keep their governments in check, deter against misuse of power, and remove ineffective politicians if they fail to perform. Democracy guarantees civil liberties and in turn is strengthened by it. As people enjoy liberty, they come to value the worth of free expression in life. This automatically invests in reason, moderation and peaceful negotiation of differences. Democratic states are not bereft of differences; but what makes them unique is the way these differences are negotiated. Democracies try not to eliminate differences but to arrive at settlements, whereby, people with vastly different points of view can peacefully live together. The fallibility of power is a built-in presupposition of a democracy. Hence, political contestation and dissent are not expected to degenerate into violence in a democracy. A state that is internally peaceful and recognises peace as a positive virtue and an essential precondition to its way in life will seek peace with similar societies. Relations between democracies can thus rely upon a high degree of mutual trust that builds on similar interests and values. These ties are deeper and far more reliable to withstand periodic differences of interests than ones based upon the thin and slippery grounds of military or strategic convenience. The more there are democratic states, the more peaceful the US foreign policy is expected to be with them. The US then can be expected to devote attention elsewhere – to rebuild its beleaguered economy, to fashion a far more relaxed foreign policy appropriate to her national interests, to allow the cost of subsidising the global commons be shared more evenly, and help people all over the world to lead happy and secured lives.[22]

When it comes to Asia, as it is also true elsewhere, the US foreign policy has not necessarily followed these liberal prescriptions consistently and, in cases where it has sought to export democracy or stand by democratic forces, the result has been mixed. The lack of consistency in the US stance is more easily explained. It brings back the abiding relevance of realism in US foreign policy. In cases where vital US interests are concerned, be it in West Asia, South Asia or Southeast Asia, often military dictators, dynastic rulers and authoritarian proto-democratic forces have done the US bidding far better than democratic governments and forces. In all such cases, the US has unequivocally prioritised what it considers to be vital national interests rather than promoting democracy. Promoting liberal democracy therefore is not a vital national interest by itself. The US policies vis-a-vis Pakistan, Turkey, South Korea and Saudi Arabia are common illustrations. Comparing the allocation of American foreign aid (total, economic and military) provided to democratic and dictatorial regimes in Pakistan (in terms of total, average annual, and per capita per year), one finds that the US aid shows a consistent pattern of high flows for military dictatorships and low or negligible flows for democratic governments, indicating that the US aid has not been used to promote democracy in Pakistan; in fact, it has often undermined it. The US has maintained warm cooperative relationships with military dictators to use Pakistan to pursue its own political, security and geo-strategic goals. For instance, the US economic aid to Pakistan (2006) was a paltry 22.4 in 2000 which shoot up to 212.1 in 2001, and 878 in 2002.[23] Pakistan has oscillated between democratic and military rule. But it certainly does not help the cause of Pakistani democracy when the US views every coup d'etat with studied indifference, and then welcomes the military dictator. The message Washington has repeatedly given to Pakistan is that the US is unconcerned about *who* rules in Islamabad, as long as he is amenable to the American agenda.

In cases where the US has sought to put democracy as a key determinant of its foreign policy, the results seem mixed. The matter is complex and no simple explanation will hold. Critics feel that democracy promotion does not work as internal conditions are beyond American control. Thus, to support democracy can mean standing by democratic forces or urging governments to operationalise democratic procedures, most notably holding regular elections. In a prominent article, Robert Kaplan has argued that holding democratic elections in many countries may actually hinder efforts to maintain ethnic peace, social stability, and economic development.[24] Fareed Zakaria feels that elections in countries without liberal values produce illiberal democracies, which pose serious threats to freedom.[25] While democracy can undoubtedly assume a plebiscitary character and press the game of numbers more than rules in some societies, there is neither any theoretical case for autocracies functioning better in this case, and nor is there sustained empirical evidence of democracies leading to war because of ethnic violence. Zakaria is persuasive in his argument that democracies may produce illiberal regimes that can threaten war rather than making peace. However, his case deliberately overplays the significance of civil liberties over that of political freedom. People who have tested democracy will seldom relinquish it easily, and external support can be critically significant during the period of transition. Many Asian states are not liberal in the sense of believing in the autonomy of the individual and their right to radical revision of the conceptions of life. Most Asian societies remain deeply communitarian. But their priority for society/community does not invalidate their candidature as procedural democracies. While, the US will provoke opposition if it imposes Western values and culture on the Asian states, this is surely not a theoretically indispensable part of the democratisation project. The relation between democracy and liberalism remains complex. While societies may not subscribe to comprehensive liberalism, they may continue to function as successful democracies in their public life.

The manifest opposition to the US in West Asia and the Asia Pacific has been over particular traits of American culture and not over the relevance of democratic rights. The Asian values debate is a case in point. Those who argued in favour of Asian values and therefore in support of soft authoritarianism were ultimately exposed of their banality; the centre-piece of their claims rested on the evidence of the Asian tiger economies that failed to insulate themselves from the Asian financial crisis of the late 1990s. The US did not push their case hard enough as they correctly understood the impulse. They allowed the Asian value debate to fizzle out as its promoters got exposed of their iron-fisted policies and were discredited by non-performance in vital economic matters. In West Asia on the other hand, Obama's consistent support for the pro-democratic forces of the Arab Spring has not translated into rich dividend for the US foreign policy as yet. The reason for this remains the American position on the Arab-Israeli conflict that shows no evidence of any fundamental transformation over these years. There has been an enormous credibility crisis for the US in West Asia, given their solid cast iron support for ruthless autocratic regimes throughout the GCC states. America's constant military interventions in West Asia has further diminished it acceptability as a genuine pro-democracy agent. As Ambassador Chas W. Freeman, Jr. cautions: "Americans concerned with the capacity of the United States to shape events in the Middle East should, however, hold the elation. Self-determination is, by definition, a rejection of subservience. This means, among other things, that Arab rulers are considerably less inclined to do America's bidding than in the past. They are starting to do things they see as in their interests even when these things are not in ours."[26] Since the US has found dealing with autocratic rulers easier than democratic ones on several occasions, its self-image as a just and democratic great power carries little legitimacy in theatres where it has traditionally considered its geo-political interests paramount over regime character.

China and Vietnam impose a very different sort of challenge to the liberal understanding of democracy. Both these autocracies have been able to produce well-founded economic growth for decades. But more crucially the governing institutions of these Socialist states managed a long-term stable political succession. Since the late 1970s, they have managed transitions to new generations of leadership every five years with very little disruption. In part this is due to practices within these parties that provide for some level of internal democracy, and deal with factional competition at a low cost. Their success in recruiting new cadres, ensuring upward mobility, filling top leadership positions without systemic crisis, and phasing out generations of leadership, without being swamped by nepotism or personality cults, separate such autocracy from the weak dynastic, personality-centric formations or military fronts that have run or are running autocratic shows in Indonesia, South Korea, Syria, Iraq, Myanmar and so on. Most importantly, these states operate flourishing market economies, and thus, are not stunted by economic malaise of the classical Soviet type of regimes.[27]

While the internal contradictions of these societies, the rising number and importance of their middle classes, and the demand of the younger generations for more substantive freedom of expression, may implode them from within in the long run. Yet, there is little to deny that they remain sustainable models of governance, albeit based on very different principles of informal accountability and internal competition. The appeal of liberal democracy has thus far been largely ineffective in China, though the nature of existing mass disaffection and the capacity of the monolithic party to meet its manifold challenges remain obscure to the outside world.

While the US is engaged in exporting its model of liberal democracy in Asia, the Chinese have no such inclinations, saving them both economic and political capital. Asia is witness to a clash of soft powers of the US and PRC; and the chief attraction of the US model remains its values of liberal democracy, human rights and free markets, multiculturalism, freedom of choice and transparency, and a rich panoply of cultural iconography. Against this the Chinese insists the model of 'peaceful development' and emphasises investment, humanitarian aid, exchange programmes, diplomacy, multilateralism, promoting regional economic integration and security mechanism, supporting the UN role and opposing the US hegemony, and committing itself to the principles of sovereignty and non-interference. To many analysts, China possesses advantages in Asia that the US lacks. [28] These include the physical presence of a sizeable Chinese immigrant population throughout Southeast Asia and a largely non-committal and untainted image in the Arab world that makes Beijing far more attractive compared to Washington. If economic performance is considered a vital aspect of soft power of a state, the Chinese have surely done better than the Americans in the last twenty year's. But what China lacks is political capital as a tool of soft power; and the triumvirate of democracy, liberty and human rights gives unique opportunity to the US to re/model its modes of engagement in Asia.

The two cases where democracy seems to have made a critical difference are America's ties with Israel and India respectively. India and the US had always been democratic states and yet till rather recent times their relations varied between cold and bitter for much of the past. While the reasons for this are many and too well known to demand a recital, it shows that while democracies may not exchange fire but may stay away from a friendly embrace. It also shows that open, diverse and democratic societies may have substantive ideational disagreements. Democracy in brief is necessary but not a sufficient condition of friendship between states. And yet, as Daniel Twining and Richard Fontaine argues, "Differences between India and the United States – on issues from climate change to the Doha trade talks to managing Iran's nuclear challenge – are real. But so is the promise, if not yet the reality, of Indo-American ideational cooperation, with common values serving as a bridge rather than a wedge between the countries as they pursue their national interests."[29] The remarkable transformation in Indo-US relations can be explained in realist terms since the collapse of the Soviet Union had robbed India of its traditional security partner and the post-Cold War international system forced India to mend her ties with the sole superpower of the world. But realism alone cannot explain the depth and extensity of this new found partnership that builds on shared values and a generic commitment to democratic norms. The efflorescence in Indo-US ties owe as much to security considerations as it does on shared ideational factors and interest in an open, liberal, free trade economy. If strategic significance explains everything, why does the US make a distinction between India and Pakistan over nuclear issues and partnership in developing sensitive dual technology? The trust and reliability that the US attests to India in sharp contrast to Pakistan, which has far more geo-strategic value for the US in the context of its military objectives in Afghanistan, is powerful evidence favouring the role and significance of democracy as a factor in Washington's South Asia policy.[30]

The special relation between Israel and the US can also be explained along different lines. Analysts have often used variants of realism, domestic politics/pressure group, and common interests as explanations for their abiding ties. But the role of identity and values in cementing their ties has also been noted and deserves more attention. Of all places in Asia, the US policy in West Asia remains most ineffective despite its disproportionate attention to this region. Its failure to support the just demands of the Palestinians as a result of its unconditional and uninterrupted support for Israel explains this tragic denouement. The point is simple. There are advantages to be gained for the US to redirect its West Asia policy, and these are not merely intangible virtues like goodwill and trust, but hard economic and even military benefits. But the US slant for Israel rules out any change. What is so special about Israel that the Arabs and others in this region lack? The answer is to be found in Israel's self-identity as a modern, democratic state, no matter how different it otherwise is from standard secular liberal societies. As Michael Barnett argues, more than religion, nationalism, and the Holocaust, which make the three elements of Israel's national identity, liberal democracy is peculiarly responsible to embed the Jewish state in the West and forge close relations with the US. At every critical juncture, when Israel has met with grave difficulties selling its repressive Arab policies, Israeli leaders and partisans began to accentuate and promote Israel's 'Western' and democratic character and identity in order to reproduce the US-Israeli alliance and to distinguish Israel from its neighbouring Arab states.[31] Even in the charged context of political cataclysm and social upheaval throughout the Arab world, the US thinking remains largely unchanged. For six months we have witnessed extraordinary change, noted President Obama. The people have risen up to demand their basic human rights. Two leaders have stepped aside. More may follow. In other words, America's wars in the Muslim world are bearing fruit. But this optimism is suitably tempered by hectoring born out of mistrust. Thus, Obama complained about the 'lack of personal self determination' for individuals in the Middle East. Too many leaders in the region tried to direct their people's grievances elsewhere, he explained. The West was blamed as the source of all ills a half century after the end of colonialism. Antagonism toward Israel became the only acceptable outlet for political expression.... [S]trategies of repression and diversion will not work anymore. To characterise Arab antagonism as diversionary tactics of a failed elite sums up the US attitude vis-a-vis the Arab states as does the cast-iron pledge for standing up for Israel's security.

Conclusion

This essay is an attempt to make sense of the US' engagement of Asia in the post-9/11 times. The central argument advanced here is that realist discourses have played a pivotal role in the making of US foreign policy in virtually every theatre of Asia, though the forms of realism have varied considerably across cases. This essay has refrained from characterising the US policies in IR theory terms, or more precisely, by invoking academic categories of realism popularised by a closed community of IR theory scholars. Instead, I have used realism to mean priority to geo-strategic interests and the idea of a national security state that advances its national interests through a combination of military, economic, political and even cultural means. The US has continued to engage with Asia primarily in realist terms, though its recent economic downturn is adding inflections to this mode. Realist policies have provided Washington with mixed success – while it has been more successful in the

Asia Pacific, Southeast Asia and perhaps Central Asia, where it has followed a more mixed policy, it has underperformed considerably in West Asia and Southern Asia. The failures are less explicable in realist terms. For in South Asia, it has defeated and removed the Taliban from power, killed Osama Bin Laden, redrawn its strategic alignments, and prevented any major terrorist strike to its vital interests since 9/11. In West Asia again, it has defeated Iraq, retained its alliances despite innumerable difficulties, and prevented any strategic transformation of the region. It has sustained its reputation as the primary military power of the world throughout Asia and prevented any direct military challenge to its pre-eminence. Yet, most realists argue that its power is declining, though they differ about its reversibility, time and strategic consequences. While the US policy still remains militarily overburdened and stretched beyond its economic means, a calibrated retrenchment is underway that does not seem inconsistent with standard realist canons of foreign policy.

However, this essay also finds a big enough role for the idea of democracy as a justificatory tool of US foreign policy engagements in Asia and goes further in identifying a clear liberal inflection to the realist discourses. There are opportunities and problems in exporting democracy in Asia. And America's experience of playing the democratic card has not necessarily yielded desired policy outcomes. Yet, democracy, liberty and human rights remain the most potent soft powers of an economically weakened the US. In fact, Asia is witness to a soft power contest between the US and China, and the trajectories of the US policy in Asia in the days ahead will largely hinge on its outcome. In this vein, it seems that the US policy towards PRC employs a mix of realist-liberal strategies, with liberal concerns becoming increasingly pressing as the US struggles to kick-start its economy from the global recession and its dependence on China continues to grow. It seems that the real difficulty that the US faces is not about upholding democracy but about additional liberal baggage and its studied indifference to injustice that delegitimises its claim to champion democratic values. Nowhere is this clearer than in West Asia, which refuses to accept America's interventions for the Arab Spring as evidence of Washington's newfound goodwill to resolve the Palestinian case. In cases like India and Israel on the other hand, democratic values have cemented ties with the US and explain far better America's commitments despite the absence of any abiding or compelling geo-strategic compulsions. Hence, despite the traditional realist orientation, which retains its explanatory value, democracy and free market liberalism cannot be ignored as vital components of the US policy in Asia in contemporary times.

Notes

1. For a useful summary of various models of US foreign policy in the post Cold war period, see Charles Krauthammer, Democratic Realism: An American Foreign Policy for a Unipolar World, Biot Report 141: November 20, 2004/ Source: http://www.semp.us/publications/biot_reader.php?BiotID=141
2. For details, see George F. Kennan, *American Diplomacy, 1900–1950*, University of Chicago Press, Chicago, 1951; George F. Kennan, *Realities of American Foreign Policy*, (Princeton: Princeton University Press, 1954); George F. Kennan, *Memoirs: 1925–1950*, (Boston: Little, Brown and Company 1967); Henry Kissinger, *Diplomacy*, Simon & Schuster, (New York: Highlighting edition 1995); Henry Kissinger, *The White House Years*, (Boston: Little, Brown and Company, 1st edition, 1979).
3. The primary texts in contention are Hans J. Morgenthau, *Politics Among Nations: The Struggle for Power and Peace*, (New York: Alfred Knof, 1948); Hans J. Morgenthau, *Scientific Man Versus Power Politics*, Chicago: Chicago University Press, 1947); Kenneth W. Waltz, Theory *of International Politics*, (Reading, Massachusetts: Addison-Wesley, 1979); Robert Gilpin, *War and Change in World Politics*, (Massachusetts: Cambridge University Press 1981); John J. Mearsheimer, *The Tragedy of Great Power Politics*, (New York, London: W.W. Norton and Company, 2001). For a good summary see, *Stephen* G. *Brooks*, "*Dueling Realisms* (Realism in International Relations)," *International Organisation*, vol. 51, no. 3 (Summer 1997), pp. 445-477. Also useful is Glenn H. Snyder, "Mearsheimer's World-Offensive Realism and the Struggle for Security", *International Security*, vol. 27, no. 1, Summer 2002.
4. For an excellent analysis of the sudden transformation of American foreign policy, see Stephen M. Walt, "Beyond bin Laden: Reshaping US Foreign Policy", *International Security*, vol. 26, no. 3, 2002,pp. 56-78.
5. On this, see Matthew Sussex, "Cultures in Conflict? Re-evaluating the 'Clash of Civilizations' Thesis after 9/11," in Peter Shearnan and Matthew Sussex (eds.), *European Security after 9/11*, Ashgate, Aldershot, UK/Burlington, USA, 2004.
6. On various interpretations of US foreign policy in the post-Cold War period, see Barry R. Posen and Andrew L. Ross, "Competing Visions for US Grand Strategy", *International Security*, vol.21, no.3, (Winter 1996/97); Kenneth Waltz, "Structural Realism after the Cold War", *International Security*, vol. 25, no. I, (Summer 2000); Samuel Huntington, "The Lonely Superpower", *Foreign Affairs*, vol.78, no.2, March/April 1999; Charles Kupchan, "After Pay American : Benign Power, Regional Integration, and the Sources of a Stable Multipolarity", *International Security*, vol.23, no. 2, Fall 1998; Michael Mastanduno, "Preserving the Unipolar Movement", *International Security*, vol.21, no. 4, Spring 1994; Christopher Layne, "The Unipolar Illusion: Why New Great Powers Will Rise", *International Security*, vol. 17, no. 4, Spring 1993.

7. Stephen Walt, "Beyond bin Laden: Reshaping US Foreign Policy", *International Security*, vol. 26, no. 3, 2002, p. 60.
8. President George W, Bush's speeches and writings are reliable guides to American action. Among others, particularly germane are George, W. Bush, (1999) A Distinctly American Internationalism, Reagan National Library, Simi Valley, California, November 19. Available from http://www.lcrga.com. (Accessed on November 11, 2011); (2001) Address to a Joint Session of Congress and to the American People. September 20. Available from http://www.whitehouse.gov/news/releases/2001. (Accessed on November 11, 2011); George, W. Bush, (2002a) Graduation Address at West Point. June 1. Available from http://www.white house.gov/news/releases/2002/06/20020601-3.html. (Accessed on November 14, 2011); George, W. Bush, (2002b) President Bush Outlines Iraqi Threat, Remarks by the President on Iraq. Available from http://www.whitehouse.gov.news/releases/2002/10/20021007-8.html. (Accessed on November 14, 2011); George, W. Bush, (2002c) Iraq Must Disarm Says President in South Dakota Speech. Available from http://www.whitehouse.gov/news/releases/2002/11/20021105-1.html. (Accessed on November 14, 2011)
9. Stephen Van Evera, "Assessing US Strategy in the War on Terror", July 01, 2006. Source: http://moelabs.org/b37/Teoria_das_ri_I-Rafael_Pons/I_Semestre/extras/Assessing_US_Strategy_in_the_War_on_Terror_Evera.pdf (accessed on November 11, 2011)
10. Jefferey Record, *Bounding the Global War on Terrorism*, Strategic Studies Institute, US Army War College, Carlisle, 2003, p. V.
11. Paul Rogers, *Global Security and the War on Terror: Elite Power and the Illusion of Control*, (London: Routledge, 2007).
12. For a standard summary from the Us side, see K. A. Kronstadt, "India-US Relations", Library of Congress Washington DC Congressional Research Service, 2009. Source: http://www.dtic.mil/cgi-bin/GetTRDoc?AD=ADA494880&Location=U2&doc=GetTRDoc.pdf (accessed on November 14, 2011). On Pakistan, an excellent account is C. Christine Fair, "US-Pakistan Relations: Assassination, Instability, and the Future of US Policy", Testimony presented before the House Foreign Affairs Committee, Sub-committee on the Middle East and South Asia on January 16, 2008, (Santa Monica: Rand Corporation, 2008). Source: http://www.foreignaffairs.house.gov/110/fai011608.pdf (accessed on November 12, 2011)
13. Olga Oliker, David A. Shlapak, "US Interests in Central Asia: Policy Priorities and Military Roles", (Santa Monica: Rand Corporation, 2005), pp. 20-21.
14. *US policy towards Central Asia*, Carnegie Endowment for Peace Event, Washington, D.C. Source: http://www.state.gov/p/sca/rls/rmks/2010/145463.htm (accessed on November 13, 2011).
15. Justin Logan, "Asia's Free Riders, *Foreign Policy*, November 10, 2011.
16. http://news.xinhuanet.com/english/2010-01/13/content_12801629.htm
17. These speeches are accessed at http://www.uspolicy.be/dossier/china-united-states-policy-toward-china-dossier on November 14, 2011
18. William J. Burns, *Asia, the Americas, and US Strategy for a New Century*. Source: http://www.uspolicy.be/headline/asia-americas-and-us-strategy-new-century(accessed on

November 14, 2011).

19. G. John Ikenberry, "Why Export Democracy? The 'Hidden Grand Strategy' of American Foreign Policy"' *The Wilson Quarterly*, vol. 23, no. 2 (Spring 1999). Source: http://www.mtholyoke.edu/acad/intrel/exdem.htm (accessed on November 15, 2011).
20. Sean M. Lynn-Jones, "Why the United States Should Spread Democracy", ISP Discussion Paper Series, (Harvard University: Centre for Science and International Affairs, March 1998). Source: http://belfercenter.ksg.harvard.edu/publication/2830/why_the_united_states_should_spread_democracy.html (accessed on November 15, 2011).
21. John Ikenberry, n. 18.
22. The literature on democratic peace is vast. For a standard account of most of the important writings, see Michael E. Brown, Jean M. Lynn-Jones and Steven E. Miller (eds.), *Debating the Democratic Peace (An International Security Reader)*, (Cambridge, Massachusetts: The MIT Press, 1996).
23. Sources: *US Overseas Loans and Grants [Greenbook]* and *US Assistance per Capita by Year*. Source: http://gbk.eads.usaidallnet.gov/about/ (accessed on November 14, 2011).
24. Robert D. Kaplan, "Was Democracy Just a Moment?", *Atlantic Monthly*, December 1997, pp. 55-80.
25. Fareed Zakaria, "The Rise of Illiberal Democracy," *Foreign Affairs*, vol. 76, no. 6 (November-December 1997), pp. 22-43.
26. Chas W. Freeman, Jr. (USFS, Ret.), "The Mess in the Middle East", *Middle East Policy Council*, Washington D.C., October 27, 2011.
27. "What China Challenges", *The Economist*, July 11, 2011. Source: http://www.economist.com/blogs/democracyinamerica/2011/07/democracy-v-china (accessed on November 14, 2011).
28. For a detailed study of China's soft power, see Carola McGifert, *Chinese Soft Power and its Implications for the The US: Competition and Cooperation in the Developing World*, (Washington D.C.: A Report of the CSIS Smart Power Initiative, 2009). Source: http://csis.org/files/media/csis/pubs/090305_mcgiffert_chinesesoftpower_web.pd (accessed on November 15, 2011).
29. Daniel Twining and Richard Fontaine, "The Ties that Bind: US-Indian Value-based Cooperation", *The Washington Quarterly*, vol. 34, no. 2, 2011, pp. 193-205.
30. For a balanced account, see S. Paul Kapur and Sumit Ganguly, "The Transformation of US-India Relations: An Explanation for the Rapprochement and Prospects for the Future", *Asian Survey*, vol. 47, Issue 4, 2007, pp. 642-656.
31. Michael Barnett, "Identity and Alliances in the Middle East", in Peter Katzenstein, ed., *Culture of National Security: Norms and Identity in World Politics*, (New York: Columbia University Press, 1996), p. 346.

3. Dots of Democracy on a Socialist Canvas: The History of Democratic Movement in China

Binoda Kumar Mishra

Though 'the Chinese quest for democracy can be dated back to the second half of the nineteenth century when concerned scholars spoke of the need for representative institutions to check the powers of the absolutist monarchy,[1] they got their first taste of democracy in late 1912 and early 1913 when selected sections of the Chinese population participated in a so-called national election to elect a national government. From there onwards, there have been repeated attempts to establish China as a democratic system but the movements have all failed to make any headway. One view of the failure of democratic movements in China is that the Chinese society is not fit for a democratic form of governance. Based on Barrington Moore Jr.'s idea of social origins of modern political arrangements, one can say that democracy did not take root in the Chinese society because of a weak bourgeois class and a lack of a strong industrial base.[2] Others argue that the Chinese society is inherently inclined towards authoritarian form of political system as it best suits the Confucian tradition that forms the basis of the Chinese social fabric.[3] There is another extreme position taken by few who believe that the Chinese society has been deprived of democracy not because of any intrinsic fault in the Chinese social and value system; rather, a combination of various factors has delayed the arrival of democracy in China. It is now high time for China to become democratic irrespective of people's likes and dislikes.[4] It is difficult to agree with any of these views as it is not logical to think that any society can be inherently and permanently averse to a particular idea no matter how alien that might be to that society. It is particularly true for the idea of democracy as evident from it being accepted by societies having diverse characteristics and value systems.

Since the general elections of the 1913, China has experienced trouble with the concept of democracy. While the Chinese intellectuals have kept on advocating for the establishment of democracy by arguing in favour of individualism in opposition to the society and state, they have constantly faced the necessity of maintaining state solidarity for its survival. From then on, it has always been the case that nationalism has pushed the cause of democracy to the secondary position, and scholars have been compelled to support statism; as a result, nationalism has been victorious till date. The Chinese experience of its own brand of democracy during the nationalist period was unique. The nationalist movement that began as an opposition to the autocratic rule of the Qing Dynasty and a celebration of individual freedom, soon turned out to be an autocracy of one political party, the *Guomindang* or the GMD. But the democratic movement did not stop at any point of time during the nationalistic period. It needs to be remembered that part of the problem of democracy not taking roots in the Chinese society is the different interpretation of this concept by its various Chinese protagonists at this point of time. The idea of democracy as it struck to the prominent Chinese democrats did not match either with the so-called 'universal' concept, or the liberal concept, or the Western concept of democracy. Similarly, the path to achieve democracy in China is not to follow the Western path. According to the ideas of Sun Yat-Sen, democracy has to be established in phases – a phase of military rule needed to unite the country by force, followed by 'a phase of political tutelage during which the GMD would prepare the people for constitutionalism'.[5] This was essential as Lian Qichao argues, "They (Chinese) must be trained as citizens first; until then, freedom would lead only to disorder."[6] This then will be followed by the democratic phase of constitutionalism. Analysing these three principles or stages in line with Sun Yat-Sen's idea of democracy and individual rights, one would be tempted to conclude that he preferred harmony (as emphasised by the Confucian tradition to natural equality). Though Sun talked about people exercising four political rights – election, initiative, recall, and referendum – he rejected the concept of natural rights and argued that 'political rights are created by circumstances of the time and [historical] tides'.[7] Further, instead of talking about equality, Sun emphasised on the 'spirit of equality' wherein he recognised the natural inequality of individuals and called for realisation of this inequality based on particular qualities of individuals and each serving the other.[8] This laid the foundation of elite governance, which was turned into a party dictatorship by Chiang kai-shek. In essence, Sun's political tutelage never ended and rather ended in dictatorship of Chiang Kai-shek.

The dictatorship of GMD and its head Chiang Kai-shek was seen as a negation of the spirit of science and democracy, which were the calls of the 'new culture movement' or the 'May Fourth Movement' of 1919. The rule of the Chiang and the GMD were branded as replication of the old culture and demands of liberation again surfaced from 1929. Before the demands for democracy and the revival of the new culture could gather momentum, China faced a national emergency in the form of the Manchurian crisis, and further, Japanese threat to China's security and territory. Therefore, the spirit of nationalism took precedence over the spirit of democracy. Thus, the entire period under the GMD, nationalism was used as a pretext to suppress democratic aspirations of the population though there was no dearth of democratic thought. Kunming emerged as a hub of political dissidents who had assembled there when Beijing University, Qinghua University and Nankai University were moved to form the Southwest Associated University. But their voice could not overcome the spirit of nationalism advocated by the GMD rulers despite the fact that the democrats identified the GMD rule as part of the crisis that was created by the external aggression and internal inefficiency during that period. Describing the state of affairs during the nationalist period, Chen Qitian, a democrat of that period wrote, There is a party state, but no people's state. There are party rights but no civil rights; there are party members, but no citizens; and there is party strife, but no national politics. ... Only when one-party dictatorship is abolished can the national emergency be resolved.[9] Despite strong democratic views expressed by the scholars during the nationalistic period, China, according to Lloyd Eastman, could not be transformed into a democratic system as the democrats 'lacked a sophisticated understanding of the true character of liberal democracy.[10] However, if one scans the democratic literature that managed to enter the public domain, it would be clear that the concept of democracy did not rule out the role and rule of the elite. The concept of democratic government meant a government by an elite minority but popularly elected and accountable to the public in general, and the people would exercise control over the government by enjoying their basic rights of freedom of thought and expression. Apart from the domestic crisis in China, there seemed to be an international trend against Western democratic form of governance as the USSR, Italy, Germany were rising as powers without democracy rather with some form of authoritarian rule that kept those countries united and provided a boost to the spirit of nationalism which was used by the GMD to ignore democratic aspirations of the population. It must be emphasised that during the period from 1911 till the establishment of the Peoples' Republic, China saw glimpses of democracy in the form of participation of many political parties and temporary enjoyment of freedom of speech and expression by the citizens.

The Communist Regime and the Democratic Movement

The dictatorial regime of the Nationalist period was brought to an end by the establishment of the Communist regime under the leadership of Mao Zedong after a long civil war. The communist revolution that gained legitimacy for being a force of liberation against the autocracy of the GM, brought to power the regime that would prove to be most antithetical to the ideas of liberty and freedom. Even before the success of the revolution, the Communists had shown signs of things to come. In the name of rectification of the Communist Party of China (CCP), Mao had adopted brutal methods to silence his and the party's critics. The famous execution of dissident writer Wang Shiwei in the year 1947 for his views against the official CCP approach was the testimony of CCP's intolerance towards freedom of thought and expression. In his famous lecture of May 1942 Mao had advanced the argument that the task of literature is 'not to light the dark side of revolutionary society but reflect on its bright side and extol the masses'.[11] For the fact that Wang Shiwei was emphasising on democratic content and protection off civil rights, he can be traced as the forerunner of the subsequent democratic movements that followed in China.[12] The second democratic movement in China is said to have been instigated by Mao himself. The brutal suppression of freedom of thought and expression by the CCP had alienated the intellectuals of the Chinese society. Mao feared the possibility of democratic uprising in the Chinese society. He had in mind the examples of risings against party rules in Poland and in Hungary in 1956. So he decided to tackle the situation in a controlled manner before things go out of hand. Thus he began the 'Hundred Flowers Campaign'. Though it seemed to be a period of relaxation of the authoritarian rule of the CCP and a move to reduce the gap between the government and the society by allowing the intellectuals to express their opinion against the Party and the government, it turned out to be a move to identify critics and deal with them in a way to reassert complete control over the Chinese society. Mao's idea that the intellectuals can be wooed to the party and would criticise only the policies of the government with an intent to develop the economy and the society within the communist ideology. But soon this license resulted in the production of huge amount of literature against CCP and its method of rule. Cries of democracy were heard all over China. Students took the leading part by installing a 'Democracy Wall' inside Beijing University. Terrified by these undesirable effects of the license, Mao resorted to CCP's effective method of clampdown. The License was turned into sentences. Nearly half a million intellectuals were punished though jail, reformative labour and internal exile. This had a demonstration effect on the Chinese society that prevented the democrats of that period to continue their pursuance of democracy. Those who dared to exercise their rights to freedom of thought and expression were termed as enemies of flourishing Socialist China and were dealt with severely. This was followed by the famous cultural revolution that aimed at establishing Mao's leadership and getting rid of opposition within the party through violent means. The chaos of this period is an over told story. However, Mao's Red Guards quickly realised that what they had believed so far was not true. Their blind faith in Marxism and Maoism was replaced by the regret of doing so. And this paved the way for the next democratic movement of 1979, the first in the post Mao era.

In 1976, Deng Xiaoping succeeded Mao with modernisation and democratic agenda. He reinstated most of the millions tormented and exiled during the Mao era. Deng being one of the victims of the Cultural Revolution, there were expectations that the four great freedoms enshrined in the Chinese constitution such as: to contend; to bloom; to put up wall posters; and to debate will be enjoyed by the Chinese citizens in their real senses. Tortured and disillusioned intellectuals of the Cultural Revolution period tried to raise the democratic movement once again as it seemed to be the right opportunity. Deng seemingly lacked Mao's authority and also initially allowed the citizens the space to express their opinion. Deng's objective was to use the skill and knowledge of the scientists and intellectuals but only within the limits allowed by him. Victims of Cultural Revolution and rural peasants started voicing their troubles by writing on the Democracy Wall in Beijing and activists copied these statements and published them in journals for wider dissemination.[13] This became famous as the *Democracy Wall Movement* and with students joining this movement, it became militant and took distinct political form. Though Deng saw the *Democracy Wall Movement* as useful – since it primarily exposed the dark side of Mao era, he was apprehensive of the Movement going out of hand and threatening his regime. He quickly started curbing the freedom of expression and set the limit by arguing that the intellectuals must respect the Party power. Those who opposed Deng's effort of curbing freedom of expression were jailed. The Democracy Wall was closed down and in 1980, Deng removed the Four Great Freedoms from the Chinese constitution resulting in censorship and prohibition of publication of unofficial journals and imposition of various other restrictions on independent political activities. Thus, the democracy movement failed to achieve democracy, clearly showing the CCP's intolerance towards public dissent and challenge to CCP's authority.

The Democracy Wall Movement of 1979 was followed by the biggest agitation for democracy in the Chinese political system namely, the 'Democracy Square' or the famous 'Tiananmen Square' of 1989. It was special in many senses. It came on the tenth anniversary of the *Democracy Wall Movement*, 20th anniversary of the Cultural Revolution, fortieth anniversary of the Founding of Peoples' Republic and seventieth anniversary of the May Fourth Movement that marked the beginning of modern China.[14] The Tiananmen Square Movement was the most mature of the democracy movements in China. It can be argued that it was the culmination of the experiences of all the previous democracy movements. It had a direct connection with the *Democracy Wall Movement* of 1979. The 1989 movement began with the demand for releasing the most prominent victim of the *Democracy Wall Movement*, Wei Jingseng. The petition was filed by Fang Lizhi, one of the tree members expelled from the party in 1987. Before 1987, Hu Yaobang a leader who was accused of failing to crackdown on the protesting students was expelled. On April 15, 1989, Hu Yaobang died and that was the beginning of mass protest by students at Tiananmen Square demanding democracy. This was the biggest and most widespread demonstration in China in favour of democracy after the May 4, 1919 Movement. The 'uprising gripped the nation for six weeks in the spring of 1989, spreading to an estimated 341 of China's 400 cities'.[15] Statistics vary but it is believed that 5,000 students were killed. Describing the CCP response to the Tiananmen Square Movement, Lucian Pye observes, "Once again China's political leaders [sic] acted in a way that would keep China from regaining the qualities of greatness for which it has strived so hard in modern times. The Chinese style of politics has again obstructed national progress, and all the great hopes of the Beijing Spring have turned to despair."[16] The massacre intimidated the Chinese population. The control of the CCP was retained and the protesters were branded as counter revolutionaries and hooligans being instigated by foreign powers to overthrow the government and the party.

The horrors of the massacre at Tiananmen, though was attempted to terrify anyone thinking of raising a voice for democracy, did not have the impact for long. Within few years, new democratic movements erupted all over China. The CCP was concerned about China's international image and was also slowly realising the importance of international finance for China's economic development. As the political climate cooled down substantially for the CCP to loosen the tight control over the population, Deng took the initiative to revive China's image. In January-February 1992, Deng undertook the famous 'southern tour' and 'called for rapid economic liberalisation and international opening'.[17] To make the Chinese appreciation of liberalism look real, the CCP took certain steps. It freed some prominent leaders of the Democracy Square 1989 and Democracy Wall 1979 Movements. This was needed as China saw two international prospects in that year namely the possibility of entering into GATT (General Agreement on Tariffs and Trade) and winning the rights to host the summer Olympics of 2000.[18] The released leaders regrouped and tried to mobilise support for democracy. By 1995 the CCP got worried about their activities and rearrested most of the prominent leaders and some managed to flee to the US to avoid arrest. The Movement lost visibility for some time and emerged in a new political situation created by the death of Deng Xiaoping in 1997. Around this time the new leadership in China signed two important international Covenants in order to improve China's international image. In 1997 China signed the International Covenant on Economic, Social and Cultural Rights (ICESCR) and a year later the International Covenant on Civil and Political Rights (ICCPR). Seeing this as an opportunity, the veterans of previous movements for democracy began to organise and restart the Democracy Movement in various ways. The activists tried to expose the CCP rule and applied to register organisations that would highlight the failures of the CCP government in matters of human rights. All over China, activists applied to register organisations such as 'Human Rights Watch', and there were applications seeking permission to publish newsletters, such as 'China Human Rights News', 'Corruption Watch', 'Peasant Watch', 'Religion Watch', 'Law Relief Hotline'. Of these, 'Corruption Watch' published three issues reaching ten provinces.[19] The political exiles of previous movements mobilised the Chinese Diaspora and formed 'The Chinese Democracy and Justice Party' in the United States. Some of the exiled leaders sneaked into China and tried to form political parties in opposition to the CCP. Idea of 'Justice Party' was floated and finally in June 1998 'China Democracy Party' was formed by the victims of previous democracy movements and some student leaders. Taking the cover of China's commitment to international human rights covenants, the political activists took legal measures to register the opposition parties in various parts of China. The CCP reacted violently, arresting most of the leaders of this newly formed party and sentencing them to long imprisonment. By mid 1999, the party vanished in its visibility from the Chinese soil but continues to operate from the US by the exiles.

The brief discussion of the Democracy Movements in China points to the fact that popular protest has been an intrinsic part of Chinese history. Describing the importance of protests in Chinese history Elizabeth J. Perry writes:

> No country boasts a more enduring and more colo[u]rful history of rebellion and revolution than China. The Chinese tradition of popular upheaval stretches back well beyond this century; indeed, records allow us to trace it as far back as 209 BCE ... Over the ensuing millennia, popular protest has formed a constant and consequential theme in Chinese political history.[20]

A long history of rebellion indicates that the Chinese society has also been subject to continuous oppression as "oppression and resistance are symbiotic – one almost never occurs without the other".[21] All the movements or rebellions have succeeded in China except the Movement for Democracy. If May 04, 1919 is taken as the beginning of the Movement for Democracy then it is almost a century that there has been no sign of success of this Movement in China. One naturally needs to ponder over the causes as to what prevents democracy from being accepted as a form of political system in China? One can easily avoid any deeper analysis by agreeing with Barrington Moore's argument that it is the social and economic fabric of China that is not conducive to democracy. But the weakness of such conclusion lies in the fact that all democratic societies in the world are not industrial economies and do not have social equality. India is an example of thriving democracy with low economic development and large-scale social inequality. Also, the Chinese society has turned into a fairly industrialised society but still democracy is not being entertained as a political idea.

The second plausible explanation often cited by Sinologists is the Chinese love for social harmony. It is believed that by tradition (Confucian), the "Chinese seek harmony through benevolence and rightness",[22] whereas, democracy is based on the concept of individual rights, which runs counter to the Chinese tradition. In the words of Xia Young:

> The more individuals are isolated, the more they are in opposition to the society, and the more they run into conflict with others. The more rights are made absolute, the more they are guaranteed and the more we talk about human rights. The basis of duty and obligations is carried out in order to protect rights. The implementation of rights is not based upon any internally generated love or benevolence. Rather, it emanates from contrary demands founded on divine and legal order.[23]

This lends support to the argument that the Chinese society remains hostage to its Confucian tradition and it would never be possible to establish an order that is based on rights and equality. But Confucian order is not anti-democratic. There are traits in Confucianism that accommodate values of democracy. Its emphasis on ruler's accountability and rule of law are features supporting the democratic system. But yet only Confucian emphasis on authority, hierarchy, harmony, order and stability are brought forward to make democracy look an alien idea to the Chinese soil.

The third possible reason is what has been discussed earlier – this is the juxtaposition of the spirit of nationalism and the spirit of democracy. Theoretically, democracy is based on the concept of liberal order and individual freedom, while nationalism entails subservience of the individual to the nation. In the words of Fukuyama, "Nationalism and liberalism cannot coexist in a democracy unless national identity is pushed off into the realm of private life and culture".[24] In China, authorities have conveniently brought nationalism to the public domain during times of crisis and particularly to suppress the spirit of democracy. This is a partial explanation for failure of democratic movement in China and thus cannot be identified as the sole factor preventing democracy from succeeding.

The other and arguably the most important factor is the role of the military which has been decisive in many, almost all, occasions in restoring the rule of the elite. It is the army that has preserved the mandate of heaven for the rulers, it has upheld the stability and order of the Chinese political system and protected the politically hierarchical harmony in the Chinese society. In carrying out this task, the Chinese army has mastered the art of suppressing movements that threaten the rule of the elite and the so-called (hierarchical) harmony of the society. In this regard, the Chinese army's "record stands clear: from Taiping Rebellion to Chiang Kai-shek's troops slaughtering the workers of Shanghai, the KMT army's arrival in Formosa..., to the killing of landlords, right down to the People's Liberation Army (PLA) shooting the Tibetan monks only a year before Tiananmen",[25] and the most brutal Tiananmen. Lamenting over the role of the Chinese army as far back as in 1919, Hunnan shanhou xiehui (Human Rehabilitation Association) reported that '[a] nation establishes as army to protect its people. Today, because of the army, the people have no way to protect themselves'.[26] Till date the Chinese elites have prevented democracy from succeeding in China with the active participation of the army. "Six key figures – warlord Yuan Shikai, Nationalist leader Chiang Kai-shek, Communist leader Mao Zedong and his three successors as paramount leader, deng Xioping, Jiang Zemin and Hu Jintao – have chosen to subvert democracy".[27]

How good are democratic prospects in China in the 21st century? China stepped into the 21st century as a confident looking nation with high economic growth and strong military power. It attempts to spread its acceptance all over the globe by generously contributing towards the requirements of other countries through economic engagement or through aid. China achieved this status in the face of "dramatic increases in spatial and class inequality, environmental destruction, the explosive growth of a migrant labour underclass, mounting ethnic unrest, loss of security, jobs and benefits for tens of millions of state sector employees".[28] The country that can boast of its superpower status is viewed by some as a 'Fragile Super power'. Going with the international trend since the last failed major democratic movement in China, the Tiananmen, democrats all over the world see it to be China's turn after the fall of the Berlin Wall, the overthrow of Romanian communist dictator Nicolai Ceausescu and the implosion of the mighty Soviet communist empire.[29] But universal trends are hardly applicable to China. There are both optimistic and pessimistic prognoses about democracy in China. Optimists count upon the economic rise of China. Barrington Moore blamed lack of bourgeois class and economic backwardness as the principal hindrance to democracy in China. In the 21st century, China takes pride in its industrial development. It ranks second only to the United States in industrial development. Therefore, in Moore's line one can argue that the economic condition of contemporary China is now ready to accept democracy as a political form. Refuting the economic logic of democratisation in China,

Jianjun Zhang shows that the Chinese economic development has produced distinct local level social and political configurations not all of which are conducive to the promotion of democracy. He further argues that if economic development leads to concentration of wealth in the hands of few, democracy is unlikely to gain ground.[30]

The optimists again point to the growing dissatisfaction among the Chinese citizens towards their government as an indication of the boiling situation in China which may anytime turn into a mass protest directed against the CCP and demand for an inclusive system as a solution to the problems of the common Chinese. According to China's police, 'the number of mass incidents (over one hundred people) has surged from 8,700 in 1993, to approximately 10,000 in 1994, 32,000 in 1999, 58,000 in 2003, and 74,000 in 2004. More than 200 protests on average occur every day. The number of people involved in protests in 2004 reached 3.76 million, compared with 730,000 a decade earlier'.[31] This figure to some is an indication that the Chinese communist system has failed and thus it is natural that democracy based on liberal order will be the cry of the masses. Identifying this failure back in 1998 Li Shenzhi argued, "After the largest-scale totalitarian experiment ever undertaken in human history... liberalism has convincingly been proven to be the most desirable and universal system of values".[32] If public protests are any indication, then, as reports suggest, on an average, "there are over 100,000 protests every year in China not because the pollution is terrible (which it is) but rather because there is a lack of transparency, official accountability and the rule of law that make it difficult for public grievances to be effectively addressed".[33] But to expect these movements to result in a movement demanding democracy and more importantly succeeding would be too optimistic.

The pessimism about the prospect of democracy in China stems from the fact that the party-state adopts strategies to prevent these democratic protests to expand their base and create an impact on China's politics. The regime ensures that the protestors against the regime remain 'primitive rebels'[34] by preventing the transition of 'class in itself' to 'class for itself'. By not allowing independent political parties to function, the regime makes sure that the 'grievances of the masses' do not get aggregated into 'mass grievances'. Control over means of communication prevents intra-class communications. The much talked about role of the internet as a tool for social communication enabling masses to share grievances and mobilise opinion is extremely limited. In the words of Tamara Shie, "Arguments for the emancipatory power of Internet are merely utopian political rhetoric"[35] in China. The expectation that the enlarging middle class will put pressure on the ruling elite demanding more participatory system of governance is turning out to be a wishful thinking as the party-state controlled economic development is strengthening the political elite enabling them to co-opt the potential harbingers of democracy in the society.[36] The middle class, instead of challenging the status quo, getting increasingly dependent on the ruling elite, thus has strengthened the ruling elite. By creating a controlled and dependent middle class, the regime has just expanded the ruling class without making the system inclusive or democratic. The ruling elite in China "composed of three major elements: the roughly 300 members of the Central Committee, several dozen Communist Party elders, and the top offices of the PLA" co-opted new "entrepreneurs drawn from ruling and working-class background" that is acting as a defence for the regime rather than a force for democratic change.[37]

As far as the increasing numbers of protests are concerned, the regime adopts all possible measures such as co-option, paying hush money, and the physical intimidation by imprisonment. And if all these fail, the regime does not hesitate to use its consistently loyal PLA to crush belligerent protestors without mercy. As a result those who sympathise with the victims of the dictatorship do not dare to come out in support of the victims fearing the fate of the victims to befall them. Therefore, though China can boast of a long history of rebellion and most of them succeeding in registering victory against the regimes they emerged, the democratic rebellion is not destined to yield desirable result owing to cleaver manipulation of the new middle class by the ruling elite and keeping the loyalty of the army to the regime by ensuring the military enjoys a share of the spoils of party-state dictatorship. Unless the economic deprivation caused by guided capitalism in China reaches a critical mass putting intense pressure on the system to collapse and give way to more inclusive form of political order, the sporadic movements for democracy either inside China or among its diaspora are going to look like small dots in the vast authoritarian canvas.

Notes

1. Xiong Yuezhi, *Zhongguo jindai minzhu sixiang shi* (History of modern Chinese democratic thought), (Shanghai: Shanghai renmin chubanshe, 1986), pp. 134-157. Cited in Edmund S. K. Fung, *In Search of Chinese Democracy: Civil Opposition in Nationalist China, 1929-*

49, (Cambridge: Cambridge University Press, 2006), p. 3.

2. For a detailed discussion on Barrington Moore Jr.'s arguments, see Barrington Moore Jr. *Social Origins of dictatorship and Democracy*, (Boston: Beacon Press, 1966).
3. Samuel P. Huntington sees a correlation between Confucianism and authoritarianism. See Samuel P. Huntington, *Third Wave: Democratization in the Late Twentieth Century*, (Normal: university of Oklahoma Press, 1991).
4. Leong H. Liew and Shaoguang Wang, *Nationalism, Democracy and National Integration in China*, (London: Routledge Curzon, 2004).
5. Edmund S. K. Fung, op. cit., p. 30.
6. Liang Qichao quoted by Andrew J. Nathan, *Chinese Democracy*, (London: IB Tauris, 1986), pp. 62-63.
7. Sun Yat-Sen's sixth lecture on *minquan zhuyi* delivered on April 26, 1924, in *Guofu quanji*,I, pp. 151-55. Cited in Edmund S. K. Fung, op. cit., p. 33.
8. Sun divided people into categories such as 'inventors', 'publicists', and 'doers' and made a case for elite rule in the best interest of the society. Edmund S. K. Fung, op. cit. For details on Sun Yat-Sen's concept of inequality see Lecture 3, *Guofu quanji*, I, pp. 127-128 and lecture 5, *Guofu quanji*, I, pp. 91-105.
9. Chen Qitian, "Guonan yu dangzhi" (The national emergency and one-party rule) *Minsheng Zhoubao 21*, April 01, 1932, cited in Edmund S. K. Fung, op. cit., pp. 87-88.
10. Lioyd Eastman, *The Abortive Revolution: China Under the Nationalist Rule: 1927-37*, (Berkeley: University of California Press, 1986), p. 197.
11. Gregor Benton and Alan Hunter (eds.), *Wild Lily, Prairie Fire: China's Road to Democracy, Yan'an to Tian'anmen, 1942-89*, (Princeton, New Jersey: Princeton University Press, 1995), p. 11.
12. Ibid, p. 13.
13. Gregor Benton and Alan Hunter (eds.), "Introduction," *Wild Lily and Prairie Fire: China's Road to Democracy, Yan'an To Tian'anmen, 1942-89*, (Princeton, New Jersey: Princeton University Press, 1995), p. 23.
14. Ibid, p.29.
15. Bruce Gilley, *China' S Democratic Future: How it Will Happen and Where it Will Lead*, (New York: Columbia University Press, 2004), p. 4.
16. Lucian W. Pye, "Tiananmen and the Chinese Political Culture: The Escalation of Confrontation from Moralizing to Revenge," *Asian Survey*, vol. 30, no. 4, April 1990, p. 347.
17. Teresa Wright, "The China Democracy Party and the Politics of Protest in the 1080s-1990s," *The China Quarterly*, vol. 172, 2002, p. 907.
18. Ibid.
19. Ibid., p. 908.
20. Elizabeth J. Perry, Challenging the mandate of Heaven," *Critical Asian Studies*, vol. 33, no. 2, 2001, p. 163.
21. Minxiin Pei, "Rights and Resistance: The Changing Contexts of the Dissent Movement," in Elizabeth J. Perry and Mark Seldon (eds.), *Chinese Society: Change, Conflict and Resistance, 3rd Edn.*, (London, New York: Routledge, 2010), p. 31.
22. Yingjie Guo, "Barking up the Wrong Tree: The Liberal-Nationalist Debate on Democracy

and Identity," in Leong H. Liew and Shaoguang Wang, op.cit., p. 31.

23. Xia Yong, "Human rights and Chinese traditions", in Michael Dutton (ed.), *Streetlife China*, (Cambridge: Cambridge University Press, 1998), p. 24. Cited in Yingjie Guo, ibid., p. 31.
24. Fransis Fukuyama, "Comments of Nationalism and Democracy," in Larry Diamond and Marc Platner (eds.), *Nationalism, Ethnic Conflict and Democracy*, (Baltimore: John Hopkins University Press, 1994), p. 24. Cited in Yingjie Guo, ibid., p. 36
25. Lucian Pye, op.cit. p. 332.
26. *Hunnan shanhou xiehui (Human Rehabilitation Association)* (ed.), 1919, p. 95. Quoted in Edward A. McCord, "Cries that Shake the Earth: Military Atrocities and Popular Protests in Warlord China," *Modern China*, vol. 31, no. 1, January 2005, p. 3.
27. Bruce Gilley, op.cit., p. 14
28. Mark Selden and Elizabeth J. Perry, "Reform, conflict and resistance in contemporary China", in Elizabeth J. Perry and Mark Selden, *Chinese Society: Change, conflict and resistance (Third edition)*, (London and New York: Routledge, 2010), p. 2.
29. Susan L. Shirk, *China: Fragile Superpower*, (Oxford, New York: Oxford University Press, 2007), p. 38.
30. For details on China's Economic development and the co-relationship with the probability of democratic political order, see Jianjun Zhang, M*arketization and Democracy in China*, (Oxon: Routledge, 2008).
31. Public Security Minister Zhou Yongkang's Report to the Chinese People's Political Consultative Congress, quoted in Ta Kung Pao (Hong Kong) and reported in Reuters, July 27, 2005. Cited in Susan L. Shirk, op.cit., p. 56.
32. Li Shenzhi, 'Preface', in Liu Junning (ed.) *Beida chuantong yu jindao Zhongguo (Beijing University and Liberalism in Modern China)*, Beijing: Zhongguo renshi chubanshe, 1998. Cited in Yingjie Guo, op.cit. p. 25.
33. Elizabeth C. Economy, "Why China Is More Like the Middle East Than We Think", available at http://blogs.cfr.org/asia/2011/03/03/why-china-is-more-like-the-middle-east-than-we-think/
34. The term was used by Hobsbawm to describe people who mount a protest without any organizational backup. For details see, Eric J. Hobsbawm, *Primitive Rebels: Studies in Archaic Forms of Social movements in the 19th and 20th Centuries*, (New York: W.W. Norton, 1959).
35. Tamara Shie quoted in Robert K. Schaeffer, *Red Inc.: Dictatorship and the Development of Capitalism in China, 1949 to the Present*, (Boulder, London: Paradigm Publishers, 2011), p. 173.
36. Minxin Pei, "The dark side of China's dazzling economic boom / Hype conceals often sordid reality of government corruption and cronyism", April 09, 2006. Available at http://articles.sfgate.com/2006-04-09/opinion/17290539_1_china-s-gross-domestic-product-the Chinese-internet-the Chinese-communist-party.
37. James Shinn, "Emerging China: Exploiting the Fissures in the Façade," *Current History*, September 1996, p. 242. Cited in Robert K. Schaeffer, *op.cit*, p. 169.

4. Promoting Democracy and Foreign Policy: Major Powers and Myanmar

Sanjay Pulipaka

The recent protests in West Asia have questioned the legitimacy of non-democratic regimes in the region. These protests have also highlighted new challenges that are confronting foreign policies of various countries, as they have prompted many to look at efficient ways to promote democracy in different parts of the world. It appears that the efforts aimed at the promotion of democracy are being guided by stated and unstated belief in the modernisation processes. The notion of modernity is located in the tectonic changes, which England witnessed during the 18th century. These changes were rapid technological growth, significant changes in the economy due to technological changes and a movement towards democratic/participatory forms of government. These developments brought in fundamental changes in the society, as traditional kinship ties, rank-order and collective notions took a back seat and society tended to become individualistic. It was often assumed that the above technological and economic changes will result in more or less similar social organisations (first in Europe and later in other parts of the world) and it was also implicit that societies should become 'modern' to ensure faster economic development. It was also understood that most nation-states over time will have democratic forms of government because of economic development. This movement from traditional society to modern society is often defined as the process of modernisation. For the propounders of modernisation, all societies evolve sequentially viz., from traditional to modern.[1] This meant that over time all societies would evolve sequentially from non-democratic to democratic forms of government. Different scholars emphasised different variables such as education, leaders as agents of change, technology and urbanisation for faster modernisation (democratisation) and often there was a debate as to which of the variables should be prioritized for better results.[2] So, for many developing countries a menu of attitudinal/value changes or institutional changes required for faster development/democratisation were advanced. Scholars such as Lipset argued that the economic growth, more specifically increase in per capita GDP, would usher in participatory political processes.[3] Przeworski and others have argued that there is no causal relationship between economic growth and democracy, however, added that the sustainability/consolidation of a new democracy is determined by the economic conditions.[4] In a similar vein Jack A. Goldstone and Jay Ulfelder argued that a country does not have to be rich to be a democracy.[5] Guillermo O'Donnell and Philippe C. Schmitter also rejected the notion of economic or cultural prerequisites, and emphasised elite 'interaction and strategic choice' as significant variables facilitating political transitions.[6] Guillermo O'Donnell contends that 'popular upsurge' and the 'resurrection of civil society' may play a significant role in facilitating transitions.[7] On the other hand, David L. Epstein et al, after examining a data-set of 169 countries, reiterated Lipset's argument that economic growth is a significant variable in ushering democracy.[8] This debate about the relative importance of 'economy/culture' and 'political interactions/choices of political actors' in the emergence of democratic political order has quite naturally impacted the policies aimed at promoting democracy in other countries. The policies aimed at promoting democracy can be classified into 'politics first' and 'development first' approaches. The political approach focuses on elections, political parties and sees democratisation as a struggle between democrats and non-democrats marked by key junctures such as breakthroughs and reversals.[9] On the other hand, the developmental approach sees transition to democracy as a slow iterative process involving long-term change encompassing political and socio-economic sectors.[10]

This paper will examine the policies of the major powers (such as the US, ASEAN, India and China) towards Myanmar. China, India, the US, and the ASEAN, have been advocating the need (with varying levels of intensity) for bringing about change in the political processes of Myanmar. While there seems to be a broad acceptance on the need for change in Myanmar among important players, their policies are at variance. If we draw a continuum between the two contending approaches for promoting democratic transition, ASEAN and India can be placed closer to the 'development first approach' and the US can be placed closer to the 'politics first approach.' China's approach, on the other hand, was more focused on maintain stability in Myanmar.

China: From Exporting Revolution to Maintaining Stability

China shares approximately a 2,204 km border with Myanmar. China's relations with Myanmar have waxed and waned over the past six decades. During the Second World War, Myanmar (then Burma) was used by the Allied powers as a transit territory to facilitate supplies to the Chiang Kai-shek led Kuomintang (KMT) troops to resist Japanese occupation. In the subsequent civil war in China, due to the sustained onslaught of the Communist forces, KMT forces moved into Myanmar. The KMT forces established bases in Myanmar, without the consent from authorities in Yangon (then Rangoon), and reportedly received assistance from the US.[11] Much to the discomfiture of Myanmar, it became the playground for the Cold War politics between the US and China. However, it was during the 1960s and 1970s that the China-Myanmar relations witnessed a significant downturn. This was largely a consequence of the Cultural Revolution initiated by Mao Zedong, which had a significant impact on China's policy towards Myanmar.[12] The Chinese leadership believed that the Maoist Revolution can be exported to various countries in different parts of the world. Myanmar became an important destination for the Chinese export of 'Maoist Revolution'. In 1967, Burmese nationals of Chinese descent in Yangon started wearing badges signifying their allegiance to Mao. The active participation of the Burmese nationals of Chinese descent in the programmes and activities of the 'Cultural Revolution' triggered anti-Chinese riots in Myanmar. The anti-Chinese riots, in 1967, also resulted in an attack on the Embassy of People's Republic of China and the death of an embassy official. The anti-Chinese riots became a convenient pretext for China to scale up its assistance to the Communist Party of Burma (CPB) aggressively. According to some reports, volunteers from the China-Red Guards of Cultural Revolution and instructors of the regular People's Liberation Army (PLA) were included in the operations of the Communist Party of Burma (CPB).[13] For instance, there were reportedly 5,000 PLA troops operating in Northern Myanmar in support of CPB.[14] Further, the Chinese media also unleashed a propaganda war by constantly referring to the government of Myanmar as a 'reactionary band of fascist killers'.[15] In 1967, the Chinese Communist Party's Central Committee referring its support to CPB stated: We regard such support as our bounden proletarian international duty. ... It is our firm conviction that the CPB headed by Comrade Thakin Than Tun, which persists in the revolutionary line to win the war and seize political power.[16] The government of Myanmar, which was battling many insurgencies, had to confront insurgency initiated by the Communist Party of Burma (CPB).[17] The constant propaganda of Peking Radio against the Myanmar government and the insurgency of CPB strengthened General Ne Win's regime since his military takeover in 1962.[18] The belief among Chinese authorities that 'revolution' can be exported to different countries such as Myanmar actually strengthened the government led by the military in Myanmar as people rallied to support the government.

Attempts were made by the Chinese premier Chou En-Lai to repair the relations with Myanmar in late 1960s and early 1970s by trying to balance the support to CPB with attempts to establish cordial relations with the government of Myanmar. Given the inherent contradiction of such an approach, it failed to yield any results. Chinese support to CPB insurgency in Myanmar waned after 1978. This was because the CPB was facing setbacks in Myanmar, which demonstrated the limits and the costs associated with the export of revolution. CPB also made a significant mistake by supporting the anti-Deng Xiaoping faction in the power struggle in China. Once Deng Xiaoping came to power, he altered the Chinese policy of supporting insurgency of the CPB in Myanmar. Deng Xiaoping retracted the policy of supporting insurgencies and examined multiple ways of expanding China's influence in the Southeast Asian region. The change in China's Myanmar policy was also guided by the realization that Myanmar can play a significant role in ensuring the faster development of Southwest China, specifically the province of Yunnan.

The changes in China's policy, along with erosion in the fighting capabilities of the CPB, facilitated rapid improvement in relations with Myanmar. China emerged as an important trading partner for Myanmar. Some of the main Myanmar-China border trade points are Muse, Lwejei, Laizar, Chinshwehaw, Kambaiti, and a proposed new township Yan Lone Chai township in Kokang Region (12.8 km from Laukkai, capital of Kokang region).[19] Muse Trade Zone has emerged as a major border trade point between China-Myanmar. According to the statistics of the Government of Myanmar, China emerged as the largest exporter of goods and commodities to Myanmar in 2007-08 (see table below). This bilateral trade relationship between China and Myanmar is favourable to China. While, Myanmar exports raw materials such as rubber, mineral, agricultural and aquatic products to China, it imports finished products such as electric machinery, steel, chemicals and pharmaceutical products from China.[20]

Table 4.1

	Imports							
	Country	**2005-06**		**Country**	**2006-07**		**Country**	**2007-08**
1	Singapore	3240.18	1	Singapore	5928.03	1	China	5472.54
2	China	2716.01	2	China	4185.75	2	Singapore	4489.83
3	Thailand	1376.24	3	Thailand	1749.4	3	Thailand	2110.66

Source: Kyat – million Source: Directorate of Trade, Government of Myanmar, available at http://www.commerce.gov.mm/eng/dot/statistics.html

Myanmar is emerging as an important source of energy resources for China. Currently, approximately 80 per cent of Chinese energy requirements are transported through the Straits of Malacca, which has considerable US presence. In order to secure energy supply lines, China is working on multiple energy corridors/pipelines.[21] As a part of diversifying the energy supply lines, China is building two pipelines (oil and natural gas) from the Kyaukryu port in Myanmar to Yunnan province in China.[22] The crude oil pipeline will reportedly carry some 22 million tons of crude oil per year.[23] As a forward integration measure, an oil refinery is scheduled to be completed by 2013 in Kunming, Yunnan province.[24]

For China, closer ties with Myanmar are also critical, as it ensures greater strategic space. Myanmar is a critical component in China's pursuit of the Two Ocean Strategy as it gives access to Indian Ocean. There are also growing concerns, especially in India, that Myanmar may have given China the permission to operate military listening posts in Coco-Islands (in Bay of Bengal).[25] On August 29, 2010, two Chinese naval ships docked at the Yangon harbour on a five day mission.[26] On August 31, 2010, Indian Foreign Minister SM Krishna stated in the Indian Parliament, "India has come to realise that China has been showing more than the normal interest in the Indian Ocean affairs. So we are closely monitoring the Chinese intentions".[27] The possibility of a China-Myanmar military relationship, which will give China greater manoeuvrability in the Indian Ocean, is being perceived as an attempt to contain the emerging Indo-US cooperation in the Indian Ocean.[28] Given the above economic and strategic considerations, China actively supported the military regime in Myanmar and even vetoed the US and the UK's resolution in UN on Myanmar in 2007 stating that problems in Myanmar were largely the internal affairs of a sovereign State.[29]

Moreover, there are a fairly large number of people with shared ethnic identities and economic interests along the China-Myanmar border. Political instability or armed conflict involving ethnic groups in Myanmar will have a spill-over effect in the Chinese province of Yunnan. Therefore, China's interests in Myanmar (along with economic and strategic issues), involve an ethnic dimension. China has been working hard to prevent the ethnic conflict from spiralling out of control in Myanmar. China has three reasons for such an approach – first, the internal ethnic diversity in the Chinese provinces bordering Myanmar is also high. Hence, ethnic conflict in Myanmar will also have a significant impact on the ethnic politics in provinces such as Yunnan; second, constant political uncertainty in Myanmar is not preferable for China, as China has made massive investments in Myanmar, and third, the Chinese presence in Myanmar has registered a significant increase in the political, economic and social realms. It is being estimated that in places such as Northern Myanmar and specifically Mandalay, the Chinese population has increased substantially in the recent past.[30] These changes have been accompanied by anxieties of demographic and economic onslaught from China.[31] Reportedly, there is also a growing discontent among cross-sections of people about the increasing Chinese political influence.[32] In this context, an escalation of civil conflict will also impact the ethnic Chinese in Myanmar, as the trajectory of such conflict is difficult to predict. In order to prevent any adverse impact of ethnic conflict in Myanmar, China has been prevailing on ethnic armed groups and also on the Myanmar military not to escalate the conflict in the border regions of China. In the recent past, China has reportedly advised United Wa State Army (UWSA) and National Democratic Alliance Army (NDAA) not to band together with other armed groups opposed to Myanmar military.[33]

It would be tempting to characterise the Chinese approach to political transition in the last two decades as a largely status-quoist approach. In various regional and international forums China often came to the rescue of Myanmar by referring to the concerns on human rights as an 'internal affair' of a nation-state. However, a closer examination reveals that the necessity of maintaining stability in Myanmar in general and peace along the China-Myanmar border in particular, may have prompted China to nudge the regime in Myanmar on a couple of occasions to make cautious movements towards change. Perceptions that China may be spending substantial diplomatic capital on supporting Myanmar in international forums may have prompted the Chinese authorities to occasionally experiment with new approaches. For instance, in the run-up to Beijing Olympics, various human rights groups demanded that the US should refrain from participating in the Games in order to register protest against the Chinese policies towards Myanmar. Such instances of sustained pressure may have prompted the Chinese authorities to reportedly arrange a meeting (in 2007) between the US government officials and Myanmar government representatives to explore the possibility for having sustained dialogue.[34]

The 2010 election and the functioning of the new government in Myanmar are generating new pressures in the China and Myanmar relationship. The new government has stopped the construction of a Hydro-electric project in northern Myanmar, which would have supplied electricity to China. Moreover, the new government headed by President Thein Sein has been making efforts to ensure political reconciliation at home and is also reaching out to the western powers such as the US. Given the extensive networks that Chinese businesspersons have within Myanmar, rapid deterioration in the relations between the countries may not happen in the immediate future. Often, political transitions tend to be long, arduous and contentious. Therefore, the current Myanmar government will require continuous Chinese support to ward-off international pressure for a faster political reform process. Further, China has close ties with some of the armed groups and may provoke them to protect its interests.

To sum up, China's policy towards Myanmar went through two phases. During the first phase, China aided and abetted Maoist insurgency in Myanmar. Such an approach was adopted based on the belief that political systems can be transplanted through sustained action by local and international actors. This is very much akin to modernisation theories that believed standardised political systems can be created in varied ethnic and cultural landscapes. However, the changing ground realities and the costs associated with such an approach prompted a rethink. During the second phase, China focused on its economic and strategic interests in Myanmar. Given the fact that China has often been criticised for its less than satisfactory record in the realm of human rights, it has been reluctant to adopt similar stance with respect to Myanmar. Further, over the years, China has been advocating that the notion of 'human rights' should be culture specific. For instance a Chinese government report titled 'Human Rights in China (1991)' stated: "...no country in its effort to realise and protect human rights can take a route that is divorced from its history and its economic, political and cultural realities......... Consideration should be given to the differing views on human rights held by countries with different political, economic and social systems, as well as different historical, religious and cultural backgrounds."[35] So, during the first phase, the Chinese believed in exporting communist political system and in the second phase the Chinese adopted a very conservative approach towards export of liberal-democratic political systems to other countries. This is also due to the fact that the Chinese themselves were at the receiving end of democracy promotion and human rights activism. The Chinese approach of emphasising upon the local context and local cultures with respect to human rights and democracy, provided space to the military regime in Myanmar to conceptualise and implement the seven-step road map according its own time-frame.

India: Capacity Building for Democracy

Myanmar was one of the provinces of British India till 1937. The common state apparatus and the economic policies of the colonial masters prompted significant movement of Indian population into Myanmar. Myanmar had substantial presence of People of Indian Origin (PIO) before the Second World War.[36] According to some sources ,the number of Indians in Burma was at 10,17,825 according to 1931 census.[37] However, the exact figures during the colonial period are not certain as many may have listed themselves under the category 'Burmese speaking'.[38] Therefore, by 1940, the number of PIOs would have been way above the number suggested. The presence of a large number of PIOs in Myanmar was a significant factor in Indian foreign policy towards Myanmar.

During the early years of independence, Myanmar was beset by insurgency and the writ of the government was often confined to the capital city of Yangon. It was during those trying times that India extended military assistance to then government of Myanmar. The nationalisation of policies of General Ne Win in 1960s and the movement of PIOs from Myanmar into India generated strain in the relationship between the two countries. However, compared to the relations with its western neighbour, India's relationship with Myanmar went through significant shifts without substantial deterioration over extended periods of time. During the late 1980s and early 1990s, India strongly supported the movement for democracy in Myanmar. Referring to the pro-democracy student protest, the Indian Ministry of External Affairs' statement reportedly stated: "Undaunted resolve of the Burmese [Myanmar] people to achieve their democracy....be able to fulfill their legitimate aspirations for a representative government".[39] Further, Aung San Suu Kyi was given the Jawaharlal Nehru Award in 1993, demonstrating India's support for the democracy movement in Myanmar.

However, since the mid-1990s, India adopted a more nuanced approach in its relations with Myanmar because of geopolitical, ethnic and economic considerations. The belief that India needs sustained cooperation from Myanmar to combat militancy in the North-East India prompted India to engage the military regime in Myanmar. India has a 1,643 km long border with Myanmar, and large tracts of it are unguarded because of difficult terrain. This makes it easy for many rebel groups to operate from bases inside Myanmar. Reports indicate that insurgent groups from Nagaland and Manipur are also operating from Myanmar and the Indian government is seeking active cooperation from Myanmar to flush out militants.[40] It has also been reported that India has been supplying military equipment to garner greater cooperation from Myanmar authorities to combat cross-border militancy.[41]

Table 4.2

India-Myanmar Trade		**(Rs. Crores)**
	1997-98	**2007-08**
Exports to Myanmar	183.26	746.19
Imports from Myanmar	832.53	3259.28

Source: DGFT, India.

To ensure that Northeast India registers sustained growth rates, India has been making efforts to enhance economic interactions with Myanmar. The overall two-way trade between India and Myanmar has been increasing and there is scope for significant increase in the trade relations. For instance, according to Directorate General of Foreign Trade (DGFT) statistics, India's Trade with Myanmar in 2007-08 amounts to approximately 0.24 per cent of India's over all international trade.[42] In order to give an impetus to trade relations, India has been seeking to open more trade centres along the India-Myanmar border. Currently, Moreh in Manipur is the official trading point and India has proposed additional trade centres in Nagaland and Mizoram.[43] India is involved in developing infrastructure projects in Myanmar. For instance, India is involved in developing a multi-million dollar seaport, in the city of Sittwe, which has the potential to become an oil and gas industrial hub.[44]

In the recent past, Indian and Chinese engagements with Myanmar have come under intense scrutiny. Both countries have been criticised for not pushing the current government of Myanmar to speed up the transition process. The scale of Indian engagement may not match the Chinese engagement and at the same time, the nature of the Indian engagement in Myanmar is also qualitatively different from that of China. Placing the Indian and Chinese engagement of Myanmar in the same category may not be appropriate for the following reasons. First, compared to China, the commercial benefit that India received because of its engagement with Myanmar is miniscule. On the other hand, India's capacity building activities in Myanmar have received little attention. Second, unlike the China-Myanmar relationship, India-Myanmar relationship reportedly has not accomplished the fullness it should have achieved. For instance, while Indian President and Vice-President visited Myanmar, the Indian Prime Minister is yet to visit Myanmar. The absence of such a visit is being interpreted in some sections of Myanmar as an indication of the hesitancy in New Delhi in engaging full-steam with Myanmar. On the other hand, India's engagement with Myanmar has been multidimensional. It should be noted that India has been actively engaging Myanmar in the realms of education and business training. The Indian approach has been substantially developmental and the Indian engagement has been aimed at enhancing the capacities of many youngsters to access the fruits of development. For instance, India has set up a host of institutions such as Myanmar India Entrepreneurial Development Centre, India Myanmar Industrial Training Centre, and Myanmar Centre for English Training. These institutions are working to enhance capacities of the citizens of Myanmar in various fields such as entrepreneurship and basic skills required for industrial growth among other areas. Moreover, in the recent past India has been training journalists from Myanmar.

In the political realm, India has not questioned the credibility of the 2010 Elections. In the run up to 2010 Elections India's National Security Adviser Shivshankar Menon said: "We've tried to engage with Myanmar [Burma] and to encourage Myanmar in what they themselves say is their attempt to rebuild democracy and to come back to the international mainstream........ [Election]could be one step and a significant step in their transition, but I think we all have to work at it with the Myanmarese [Burmese] to see that it comes out right".[45] As one can see, India has been urging Myanmar with great subtly to move forward along the stated path of political transition.

At the same time, India has been involved in various capacity development programmes in Myanmar. India's approach has been a classic developmental approach towards democracy promotion. India's advocacy for democracy in Myanmar in various international platforms has been low-key. On the other hand, India has been involved in developing capacities that are required for the effective functioning of a transitional government. India needs to scale up its capacity developmental programmes in Myanmar to ensure that the necessary prerequisites for democracy are strengthened in Myanmar.

The United States: Sanctions for Democracy

It is well known that the US was using Myanmar as a transit route in its support for the Chinese Kuomintang Forces (KMT) in late 1940s and 1950s. The US was deeply concerned about the possibility of Myanmar coming under a communist onslaught and conceptualised aid programmes to strengthen the military in that country.[46] However, Myanmar given its geo-strategic location decided to follow the policy of non-alignment. In fact, Myanmar was one of the founder-members of the Non-Aligned Movement. Interestingly, Myanmar withdrew from Non-Aligned Movement in 1979, as it felt that the NAM was moving closer to the Soviet bloc. Myanmar's foreign minister at the Sixth NAM Conference in Cuba observed that 'the principles of the movement are not recognisable anymore: they are not merely dim, but they are dying'.[47] Because of its fixation to be recognised as a genuine non-aligned country, Myanmar made efforts to ensure that the military aid programmes it receives from the US remain modest. In 1970s, the US gave humanitarian assistance and basic military assistance to Myanmar to address the opium production. For instance, approximately 255 military officers from Myanmar were trained under the International Military Education and Training programme (IMET) in the US between 1980 and 1988.[48] During the late 1980s, there was anticipation among some of the senior policy-makers in the US that relations with Myanmar will witness an upswing in the near future and the US should aid the Myanmar military to meet multiple challenges.[49]

Such positive assessment did not materialise as the US-Myanmar relations experienced severe stress after the suppression of the 1988 student protests by the then Myanmar government. The relations between the two countries nose-dived in 1990 following Aung San Suu Kyi's house arrest after her party secured a majority in the national elections and the US downgraded its diplomatic representation to Charge d'Affaires. In 1997, the US President,

Bill Clinton, through an executive order prohibited new investments and facilitation of new investments by the US citizens in Myanmar. However, the executive order had a 'grandfather clause' which exempted all investments which were agreed to before May 21, 1997.[50] After the Depayin incident, where Aung San Suu Kyi and her supporters were attacked, the US in 2003 enacted the 'Burmese Freedom and Democracy Act' (BFDA), which mandated[51] ban on products of Burma, ban on import from certain companies [such as those owned by SPDC and Myanmar Economic Corporation (MEC)], freeze of assets of the regime in the US, denial of visas to members associated with SPDC and also the necessity of opposing loans from international financial institutions to Myanmar. The US along with Great Britain and Northern Ireland, in 2007 proposed a UN Security Council Resolution to call on Myanmar to 'cease military attacks against civilians in ethnic minority regions', and 'to take concrete steps to unconditionally releasing Daw Aung San Suu Kyi and all political prisoners, lifting all constraints on all political leaders and citizens, and allowing the National League for Democracy (NLD) and other political parties to operate freely'.[52] However, Russia and China vetoed the resolution as they perceived that passage of the resolution would result in an infringement of the principle of non-involvement in the internal affairs of a nation-state. In response to Myanmar government's crackdown on protesting monks, the US government expanded sanctions in 2007. Through successive Executive Orders (in 2007 and 2008), the US expanded the list of individuals and companies with whom the US citizens/organisation are prohibited from having financial/business transactions. The US also made efforts to deny the revenues to the government of Myanmar by making business dealing with precious stones difficult. Through the Tom Lantos Block Burmese JADE (Junta's Anti-Democratic Efforts) Act of 2008, the US banned the importation of 'jadeite and rubies, including jewellery containing such articles (covered articles)' from Myanmar.[53] As one can see that, over the years, the US has been demanding the establishment of a democratic political system in Myanmar and to achieve this objective it had adopted a three-pronged strategy. First, the US sought to isolate Myanmar internationally and drastically reduced its diplomatic interactions with the regime in Myanmar; second, the US, along with some of its allies imposed economic sanctions on Myanmar for its failure to move towards democracy, and third, the US continued emphasising the release of political prisoners, and making them active partners in the political transition to democracy.

With the advent of the Obama administration, there were perceptions that the US was making changes in its foreign policy towards Myanmar by making it more nuanced. The statements and actions of the US government and its representatives indicated that they are actively working towards greater engagement with Myanmar. In February 2009, the US Secretary for State, Hillary Clinton, stated that the US is re-looking at its Myanmar policy, and is exploring ways to influence the government in Myanmar. In continuation with the policy shift a month later (in March), the Director of the Office for Mainland Southeast Asia, the US State Department, Stephen Blake visited Naypyidaw, the capital of Myanmar, to interact with senior government officials. Incidentally, this was the first visit by a senior US government official to Myanmar's new capital. While there was no formal statement from the US officials, news reports speculated that Stephen Blake had suggested the possible withdrawal of some economic sanctions while continuing other targeted sanctions. A few months later in 2009, Assistant Secretary of State for Pacific and East Asian Affairs stated that the while 'the goals of the US policy in Burma remain the same....a policy of pragmatic engagement with Burmese authorities holds the best hope for advancing our goals'.[54] However, the extension of Aung San Suu Kyi's detention and the perceptions that the processes aimed at conducting elections did not measure up to the acceptable standards prompted the US administration to criticise the then government in Myanmar. The political changes in Myanmar after the 2010 elections (such as release of Aung San Suu Kyi and some progressive legislation) has improved the relations between the US and Myanmar. American President, Barrack Obama referred to the developments in Myanmar as flickers of progress,[55] and the US Secretary of the State visited Myanmar in November 2011.

The US interactions with Myanmar have been substantially political in nature and were aimed to aggressively push Myanmar on the path to democracy. The US sanctions on Myanmar received support from Aung San Suu Kyi. For instance, she reportedly told a news agency: "We very much appreciate the U.S. sanctions because they have been a tremendous psychological boost for the democracy movement and also they have made businesses think carefully about what is really going on in Burma."[56] On the other hand, there was also criticism of the US' sanctions policy towards Myanmar. The aggressive sanctions approach coupled with calls for a more active intervention from the expatriate community may have produced nationalist reaction and grave concerns among the senior leadership of the military, [57] which may have delayed the transition process.

There were also concerns that the sanctions approach instead of punishing the military leadership ended up preventing the emergence of a vibrant business class, which could have played a significant role in the establishment of an open and pluralistic political order.

To sum up, the end of the Cold War did not result in improved relations between Myanmar and the US. On the contrary, the relations deteriorated substantially. During the initial years of the post-Cold War, the US placed significant emphasis on promoting democracy and human rights in its foreign policy. It is precisely during these years that the democratic movement in Myanmar experienced severe setbacks. Myanmar was not as strategically significant as West Asia and yet it received considerable attention of the US policy-makers. While the US had to turn a blind eye to the movements for democracy in other parts of the world due to security considerations, in the case of Myanmar the US perceived no such constraints.[58] As a consequence, Myanmar became a test case for promoting democracy and the US adopted a forceful 'political first approach' to promote democracy.

ASEAN: Constructive Engagement and Transition to Democracy

It was in 1967 that five Southeast Asian countries – Indonesia, Malaysia, the Philippines, Singapore and Thailand – signed the Bangkok Declaration thereby forming the Association of Southeast Asian Nations (ASEAN). It should be noted that in 1967, Myanmar was approached to be a part of the ASEAN. However, the then prevailing Cold War dynamics prompted Myanmar to stay away from the grouping. The end of the Cold War and the rise of China prompted many Southeast Asian countries to have a relook at the regional security architecture. Soon other countries such as Brunei Darussalam (in 1984), Vietnam (1995), Lao PDR (1997), Cambodia (1999) joined ASEAN.[59] Myanmar became a member of ASEAN in 1997 much to the discomfiture of western countries such as the US. Becoming a member of ASEAN provided an opportunity for Myanmar to break free from the isolation caused by the sanctions of the western countries. ASEAN incorporated Myanmar into its fold hoping that 'constructive engagement' and sustained interaction will bring about political transition in Myanmar.[60] Instead of sanctions (economic and political), quiet diplomacy and friendly persuasion were central to the policy of constructive engagement.

The policy of 'constructive engagement' was seen as an attempt to wean Myanmar away from the growing Chinese influence. ASEAN policy towards

Myanmar has also been dictated by economics. Many ASEAN members are economically engaged with Myanmar. Around 20 per cent of Thailand's electricity comes from natural gas supplied by Myanmar. Further, Thailand shares approximately 2,400 km boundary with Myanmar, which witnesses' considerable formal and informal trade. There is also considerable refugee movement along the Thailand-Myanmar border and the political instability in Myanmar will have an immediate impact on Thailand. Singapore is one of the largest investors in Myanmar; moreover, Singapore and Malaysia aggressively source minerals from Myanmar.[61] ASEAN is a significant trade partner of Myanmar. By 2005, Myanmar's exports to ASEAN amounted to 51.6 per cent of its total exports.[62] The jump in trade demonstrates Myanmar's growing interaction with the ASEAN.

Many Southeast Asian countries adopted the policy of 'constructive engagement' even when Myanmar was not a full member of ASEAN. In 1994, Indonesian Foreign Minister Ali Alatas reportedly stated, "The best approach was constructive engagement by encouraging Rangoon to modify its policies through frequent contacts and quiet diplomacy rather than isolating the country or imposing economic sanctions". After Myanmar became a full member, one of the core principles of ASEAN viz., 'non-interference in the internal affairs of one another'[63] further reinforced the policy of 'constructive engagement.' Further, some of the ASEAN countries experienced a long road to democracy. In some cases the military continues to be a major player in the decision-making. For instance, Malaysian Prime Minister Mahathir

Table 4.3

Country	Freedom Status
Brunei	Not Free
Cambodia	Not Free
Indonesia	Free
Malaysia	Partly Free
Philippines	Partly Free
Singapore	Partly Free
Thailand	Partly Free
Vietnam	Not Free
Laos	Not Free

Source: Freedom in the World 2011: The Authoritarian Challenge to Democracy, Table of Independent Countries

Source: www.freedomhouse.org

Mohamad in 1997 stated: "We too have been guilty of the same things these other countries are accused of. For example, during the Ferdinand Marcos period, there was no democracy in the Philippines, but we never asked them to leave ASEAN. There was a time in Thailand when there was a military leadership, yet we did not ask them to leave. And our democracies are not the same. We have different concepts of democracy".[64] According to Freedom House rankings, most of the Southeast Asian countries even in 2011 were categorised as 'partly free' or 'not free.'[65] The necessity to adhere to the 'principle of non-interference,' the ASEAN countries' experience with transition to democracy, and the geographic proximity of Myanmar, prompted ASEAN to maintain a distance from the sanctions approach adopted by the US and the European Union (EU) in its interactions with Myanmar. The policy of constructive engagement and principle of non-interference came in for substantial criticism from various quarters. Two years after Myanmar became a member of ASEAN, in 1999, ASEAN's policy of constructive engagement was sharply criticised by Aung San Suu Kyi. In an article in 'The Nation' she observed:

> "ASEAN also invokes the principle of non-interference with the internal affairs of member-countries, though not with a clear conscience. Rather, they are afraid that there may be some aspects of their countries that might invite criticism. Our position is that if they have problems that invite legitimate criticism, let there be criticism. If not, they have nothing to fear. Because of its policy of non-interference, ASEAN has rejected calls from other governments outside the region to nudge the Burmese government into allowing greater freedom for its people. Instead, it has opted for a non-confrontational 'constructive engagement' stance in relation to Rangoon. This has not worked. This policy of non-interference is just an excuse for not helping. In this day and age, you cannot avoid interference in the matters of other countries."[66]

A few days later, responding to Aung San Suu Kyi's views, Thailand's then Deputy Foreign Minister MR Sukhumbhand Paribatra elucidated ASEAN's approach to democracy promotion: first, economic sanctions will work only if there is unanimity among all the major powers and all the neighbours, which is not the case with Myanmar; second, it is necessary for the principle of non-interference to evolve over time to meet the changing needs. This should not result in complete abandonment of the principle of non-interference; third, the capacity of ASEAN states to be proactive promoters of democracy is limited; fourth, the exclusion approach may reinforce status quo and may increase the suffering of the people.[67] While the overall approach of the ASEAN has been to refrain from active intervention in Myanmar, some of the individual ASEAN states had divergent opinions on 'interference in the internal affairs' of the member states.[68] Adherence to the principle of non-interference did not prevent ASEAN members to constantly prod Myanmar to change its domestic policies. Often displeasure with Myanmar prompted some of its staunchest supporters such as Malaysian Prime Minister Mahathir Mohamad, in 2003, to suggest that Myanmar may have to be expelled from ASEAN.[69] Over the years, ASEAN has consistently called for national reconciliation, release of and dialogue with Aung San Suu Kyi and also expressed support to the UNSG Special Representative.[70] Often ASEAN's 'constructive engagement' policy was opposed by the US in various international platforms. For instance, in July 2005, the then Secretary of the State of the US, Condoleezza Rice refrained from attending the meeting of ASEAN Regional Forum (ARF) to convey displeasure with the possible ASEAN chairmanship for Myanmar in 2006.[71] Some of the individual member countries of ASEAN were also reportedly unwilling to damage the economic relationship with the US and the EU over the chairmanship issue.[72] Due to sustained pressure from the US, and also from some of the individual member countries of ASEAN, Myanmar relinquished the Chairmanship of ASEAN in 2006 stating that it needs to focus on the national reconciliation process.[73] As Paribatra noted above, the ASEAN principle of non-interference evolved over time. In consonance with the principle of 'non-interference in internal affairs', ASEAN refrained from supporting specific political groups in the member states. However, the principle of non-interference did not prevent ASEAN from conveying displeasure over internal issues of member states. In one of its strongest statements, in 2007, the ASEAN criticised the government of Myanmar for its handling of the protests by the Buddhists monks. The then Foreign Minister of Singapore and the Chair of ASEAN in a statement on September 27, 2007, stated, "They [ASEAN Foreign Ministers] expressed their revulsion to Myanmar Foreign Minister Nyan Win over reports that the demonstrations in Myanmar are being suppressed by violent force and that there has been a number of fatalities..... They called upon Myanmar to resume its efforts at national reconciliation with all parties concerned, and work towards a ***peaceful transition to democracy*** [emphasis added]".[74] The above statement while expressing revulsion at the use of violence did not specify a time-line for transition to democracy. Further, as Donald K Emmerson notes, transitioning to democracy could be based on 'relativist' and 'absolutist' positions and the statement fails to mention the higher end which such transition should serve.[75]

The fears that Myanmar and its democracy/human rights record will adversely impact the functioning of the ASEAN seem to have been partially addressed by the November 2010 elections in Myanmar. ASEAN recognised the election process in Myanmar and called for hastening of the Seven Step Road Map for National Reconciliation and Democracy. In the run up to elections, while many western countries were expressing concerns about the election process, the Secretary-General of ASEAN Dr. Surin Pitsuwan stated: "I hope that Myanmar will prove the skeptics wrong and Myanmar will respond positively to appeal for freedom of mobility and expression during the lead up to the elections scheduled for November 07".[76] After the elections in November 2010 in Myanmar, ASEAN officials termed the November 07, 2010 elections as a landmark event and 'as a significant step forward in the implementation of the 7-point Roadmap for Democracy'.[77]

Myanmar witnessed significant political developments after the November 2011 elections. Aung San Suu Kyi was released from prison and subsequently many political prisoners were also released. Sustained efforts are being made to ensure greater dialogue between Aung San Suu Kyi and the government of Myanmar. There have been reports which indicate that National League for Democracy (NLD) will be allowed to contest elections and Aung San Suu Kyi may contest elections in an upcoming by-poll.[78] All these developments opened the possibility of Myanmar assuming the leadership of ASEAN in 2014.[79] ASEAN, in spite of pressures from within and from outside, refrained from advocating immediate regime change in Myanmar. Given its member states experience with political transition, overall, the ASEAN believed in giving space to Myanmar to sequence the political transition process.

Conclusion

The above arguments demonstrate that major international actors have adopted different approaches to facilitate transition in Myanmar. While attempts have been made to explore the possibility of a coordinated strategy, often the different national interests resulted in the continuation of divergent policies towards Myanmar. This paper has made an attempt to plot some of the significant dimensions of the policies of major powers towards Myanmar. While some have explicitly political approaches, others have adopted a combination of political-developmental approaches and some have refrained from actively advocating for democratic change. How were the policies of the above mentioned countries/organisations perceived within the political and administrative frameworks in Myanmar would require further study. Such a study will help us in gauging the impact of external policies on the decision-making apparatus in countries experiencing a transition towards democracy.

Notes

1. For instance see Gilbert Winham, "Political Development and Lerner's Theory: Further Test of a Causal Model," *The American Political Science Review*, vol. 64, no. 3, September 1970, pp. 810-818.
2. See Myron Weiner, *Modernisation: The Dynamics of Growth*, (New York: Basic Books, 1966).
3. Seymour Martin Lipset, "Some Social Requisites of Democracy," *American Political Science Review*, vol. 53. no.1, March 1959.
4. Przeworski, Adam, Michael E. Alvarez, Jose Cheibub, and Fernando Limongi. *Democracy and Development,* (New York: Cambridge University Press, 2000).
5. Jack A. Goldstone and Jay Ulfelder, "How to Construct Stable Democracies," *The Washington Quarterly*, vol. 28, no.1, Winter 2004-05.
6. Guillermo O'Donnell and Philippe C. Schmitter, *Transitions from Authoritarian Rule: Tentative Conclusions about Uncertain Democracies* (Baltimore: John Hopkins University Press, 1986) as cited in Philippe C. Schmitter, "Twenty-Five Years, Fifteen Findings," *Journal of Democracy,* vol. 21, no. 1 January 2010
7. Guillermo O'Donnell, "Schmitter's Retrospective: A Few Dissenting Notes," *Journal of Democracy,* vol. 21, no.1, January 2010.
8. David, L . Epstein, RoberBtates, Jack Goldstone, IdaK ristensen, and Sharyn, O'Halloran, "Democratic Transitions," *American Journal of Political Science*, vol. 50, no. 3, July 2006, pp. 551-569.
9. Thomas Carothers, "Democracy Assistance: Political vs. Developmental?" *Journal of Democracy*, vol. 20, no. 1, January, 2009, pp. 5-9.
10. Ibid.
11. See Bertil Lintner, *Burma in Revolution: Opium and Insurgency Since 1948*, (Chiangmai: Silkworm, 2003), pp. 125-157.
12. For an interesting discussion on the impact of Cultural Revolution on China's Foreign policy see "Intelligence Report: The Failure of Maoist Ideology in Foreign Policy," (Reference Title: Polo XLIII), RSS No. 0053/71, November 1971, Directorate of

Intelligence, Government of the United States of America.

13. See Bertil Lintner, Op.Cit., n.xi.
14. Robert A. Holmes, "China-Burma Relations since the Rift," *Asian Survey*, vol. 12, no. 8, August 1972, pp. 688-689.
15. Ibid.
16 Frank N. Trager, "Burma: 1967-A Better Ending than Beginning," *Asian Survey*, vol. 8, no. 2, February 1968, p. 114.
17. It should be noted that CPB came into existence in 1948. However, the support from China Communist Party gave it momentum in late 1960s.
18. John H Badgley, "Burma's China Crisis: The Choices Ahead," *Asian Survey*, vol. 7, no. 11, November 1967, p. 687.
19. "Myanmar to Add Another Border Trade Zone in N Shan State," *Xinhuanet*, October 15, 2009, available at http://news.xinhuanet.com/english/2009-10/15/content_12238127.htm
20. "Myanmar-China Border Trade Fair to be Held in Muse this Year", *Xinhuanet*, September 29, 2008, available at http://news.xinhuanet.com/english/2008-09/29/content_10132109.htm
21. Currently China is constructing Sino-Kazakhstan pipeline, China-Pakistan pipeline and Sino-Russian pipeline. See, Li Woke, "Myanmar Pipeline to Diversify Energy Sources," *Global Times*, September 14, 2010, available at http://business.globaltimes.cn/industries/2010-09/572820.html
22. Eric Watkins, "CNPC Starts Construction of Refinery, Pipeline System," *Oil& Gas Journal*, September 13, 2010, available at http://www.ogj.com/index/article-display/5406950539/articles/oil-gas-journal/processing-2/2010/09/cnpc-starts_construction.html
23. Clifford McCoy, "China, Myanmar Reaffirm Strategic Vows," *Asia Times*, September 16, 2010, available at http://www.atimes.com/atimes/China/LI16Ad03.html
24. Eric Watkins, "CNPC Starts Construction of Refinery, Pipeline System," *Oil& Gas Journal*, September 13, 2010, available at http://www.ogj.com/index/article-display/5406950539/articles/oil-gas-journal/processing-2/2010/09/cnpc-starts_construction.html
25. Indrani Bagchi, "China Eyeing Base in Bay of Bengal?", *Times of India*, August 09, 2008, availableat http://timesofindia.indiatimes.com/articleshow/msid-3343799,prtpage-1.cms
26. "Chinese Warships Dock in Myanmar," *AFP*, August 30, 2010, available at http://www.google.com/hostednews/afp/article/ALeqM5jj0CLGPmwjtRV5AR7U7mZYjHm0NQ
27. "Delhi Concerned at China's 'Interest' in Indian Ocean," *Daily Times*, September 01, 2010, available at http://www.dailytimes.com.pk/default.asp?page=2010\09\01\story_1-9-2010_pg20_3
28. "Myanmar-China Border Trade Fair to be Held in Muse this Year", *Xinhuanet*, September 29, 2008, available at http://news.xinhuanet.com/english/2008-09/29/content_10132109.htm
29. "China and Russia Veto US/UK-Backed Security Council Draft Resolution on Myanmar", *UN News Centre*, January 12, 2007, available at http://www.un.org/apps/news/story.asp?NewsID=21228&Cr=myanmar&Cr1
30. Min Lwin Mar, "The Chinese Road to Mandalay," *Irrawaddy*, vol. 17, no. 2, March-April,

2009 available at http://www.irrawaddy.org/article.php?art_id=15404

31. Sai Zom Hseng, "Wa People Rely on Chinese Wages for Survival," *Irrawaddy*, April 18, 2011, available at http://irrawaddy.org/article.php?art_id=21127
32. Kyi Wai, "Dangerous Anti-Chinese Discontent Growing in Mandalay," *Irrawaddy*, July 08, 2011, available at http://irrawaddy.org/print_article.php?art_id=21656
33. Zin Linn, "China Moves to Prevent Ethnic Conflicts on Burma border," *Asian Correspondent*, March 24, 2011, available at http://asiancorrespondent.com/51092/is-china-worrying-over-ethnic-conflicts-on-burma-boundary/ (Downloaded on November 04, 2011).
34. Larry A. Niksch, "*CRS Report for Congress: Burma-U.S. Relations*," Code RL33479, October 04, 2007.
35. "Human Rights in China," *Report of the Information Office of the State Council of The People of Republic of China*, November 1991, Beijing, China, available at http://sangle.web.wesleyan.edu/chrr/governments/91wp/91hr-wp.html
36. The Indian population in Myanmar registered a decrease in 1960s due to General Ne Win's nationalisation policy.
37. John L. Christian, "Burma," *Annals of the American Academy of Political and Social Science*, vol. 226, March 1943, pp. 120-121.
38. Ibid.
39. Sanjoy Hazarika, "India, Breaking Its Silence, Backs Government Opponents in Burma," *New York Times*, September 13, 1988, available at http://www.nytimes.com/1988/09/13/world/india-breaking-its-silence-backs-government-opponents-in-burma.html (Downloaded on November 30, 2011)
40. "New Effort: India-Myanmar to Begin Talks", *Times of India*, September 12, 2006, available at http://timesofindia.indiatimes.com/articleshow/1984115.cms
41. "Myanmar Deal: Right Neighbourly of India", *Asia Times*, January 11, 2008, http://www.atimes.com/atimes/Southeast_Asia/JA11Ae01.html
42. See Export-Import Data Bank of Directorate General of Foreign Trade (DGFT), available at http://dgft.delhi.nic.in/
43. "India for More Trade Centres with Myanmar", *The Economic Times*, October 13, 2008, http://economictimes.indiatimes.com/articleshow/msid-3591225,prtpage-1.cms
44. Bappa Majumdar, "India Rushes Aid to Myanmar, Helping Warming Ties", *Reuters*, May 05, 2008 http://in.reuters.com/article/topNews/idINIndia-33415220080505?sp=true
45. Lalit K. Jha, "India Says Burma Election Offers Hope," *Irrawaddy*, October 01, 2010, http://www.irrawaddy.org/article.php?art_id=19600
46. The Pentagon Papers, Volume 1, Document 9, *Summary of Existing Policy on Indochina for the Joint Chiefs of Staff*, July 25, 1950, pp. 373-374, available at http://www.mtholyoke.edu/acad/intrel/pentagon/doc9.htm (Downloaded on November 23, 2011).
47. William L. Scully and Frank N. Trager, "Burma 1979: Reversing the Trend," *Asian Survey*, vol. 20, no. 2, (Feb., 1980), pp. 172-173.
48. David I Steinberg, "The United States and Myanmar: 'a Boutique Issue'?" *International Affairs*, vol. 86, no.1, 2010, p. 180.
49. Gaston J. Sigur, Jr, "FY 1989 Assistance Requests for East Asia and the Pacific," *Department*

of State Bulletin, July 1988, vol. 88, no. 2136, p. 37.

50. "Current Realities and Future Possibilities in Burma/Myanmar: Options for U.S. Policy," *Asia Society Task Force Report*, Washington: March 2010, p. 61.
51. "Burmese Freedom and Democracy Act of 2003," Public Law 108–61, July 28, 2003 available at http://www.treasury.gov/resource-center/sanctions/Documents/bfda_2003.pdf
52. "United Kingdom of Great Britain and Northern Ireland and United States of America: Draft Resolution," January 12, 2007, *Security Council Report*, United Nations, S/2007/14, http://www.securitycouncilreport.org/atf/cf/percent7B65BFCF9B-6D27-4E9C-8CD3-CF6E4FF96FF9per cent7D/Myanper cent20S2007per cent2014.pdf
53. "H.R. 3890: Tom Lantos Block Burmese JADE (Junta's Anti-Democratic Efforts) Act of 2008," available at http://www.govtrack.us/congress/bill.xpd?bill=h110-3890&tab=summary
54. Priscilla Clapp, "Burma's Political Transition: Implications for US Policy," in Nick Cheesman, Monique Skidmore and Trevor Wilson (edt.,), "*Ruling Myanmar: From Cyclone Nargis to National Elections*," (Singapore: ISEAS Publishing, 2010).
55. "Obama sees "flickers of progress" in Myanmar, to send Clinton in December," *The Hindu*, November 18, 2011, available at http://www.thehindu.com/news/international/article2638672.ece
56. "Can sanctions bring democracy to Burma?" *Irrawaddy*, vol. 6, no. 2, April 1998 available at http://www.irrawaddy.org/article.php?art_id=7564&page=1
57. David I Steinberg, "The United States and Myanmar: 'a Boutique Issue'?" *International Affairs*, vol. 86. Issue. 1, 2010, p. 186.
58. Ibid.
59. "Overview," *ASEAN*, 2009, available at http://www.aseansec.org/about_ASEAN.html
60. Amitav Acharya , "ASEAN at 40: Mid-Life Rejuvenation?" *Foreign Affairs*, August 15, 2007, available at http://www.foreignaffairs.org/20070815faupdate86481/amitav-acharya/asean-at-40-mid-liferejuvenation.html?mode=print
61. Lee Hudson Teslik, "The ASEAN Bloc's Myanmar Dilemma", *Council on Foreign Relations*, October 02, 2007, available at http://www.cfr.org/publication/14353/asean_blocs_myanmar_dilemma.html
62. Clive Parker, "Unhappy Anniversary for ASEAN, Myanmar," *Asia Times*, July 26, 2007, available at http://www.atimes.com/atimes/Southeast_Asia/IG26Ae02.html
63. For details see "Treaty of Amity and Cooperation in Southeast Asia," *ASEAN*, February 24, 1976, available at http://www.aseansec.org/1217.htm
64. "I am Still Here," *Asiaweek*, 1997, available at http://www-cgi.cnn.com/ASIANOW/asiaweek/97/0509/cs2.html
65. "Freedom in the World 2011: The Authoritarian Challenge to Democracy," *Report of Freedom House, 2011*, available at http://www.freedomhouse.org/images/File/fiw/Tablespercent2Cpercent20Graphspercent2Cpercent20etcpercent2Cpercent20FIWpercent202011_Revisedpercent201_11_11.pdf
66. Aung San Suu Kyi, "Nudge Burma Toward Democracy," *The Nation*, July 13, 1999, available at http://www.burmafund.org/Pathfinders/nld/ASSK/

Nudgepercent20Burmapercent20towardpercent20democracy.htm

67. Sukhumbhand Paribatra, "Burma, Asean, Democracy, Dreams and Realities," *The Nation*, July 15, 1999, http://www.ibiblio.org/obl/reg.burma/archives/199907/msg00458.html
68. "Forcing Help on Myanmar", *Economist*, May 22, 2008, available at http://www.economist.com/opinion/displaystory.cfm?story_id=11412481
69. Phar Kim Beng , Myanmar: ASEAN's Thorn in the Flesh, *Asia Times*, July 25, 2003, available at http://www.atimes.com/atimes/Southeast_Asia/EG25Ae01.html
70. "Joint Communiqué of the 36th ASEAN Ministerial Meeting," *ASEAN*, June 16-17, 2003, available at http://www.aseansec.org/14833.htm ; also see "ASEAN Chairman's Statement on Myanmar," *Ministry of Foreign Affairs of Thailand*, May 19, 2009, available at http://www.aseansec.org/PR-ASEANChairmanStatementonMyanmar.pdf ; "*ASEAN Chairman Statement on Myanmar*," ASEAN, 2007, available at http://www.aseansec.org/21057.htm;
71. C. S. Kuppuswamy, "Myanmar: ASEAN'S Problem Child," *South Asia Analysis Group*, Paper no. 1478, July 27, 2005, available at http://www.southasiaanalysis.org/percent5Cpapers15percent5Cpaper1478.html
72. "Myanmar Gives Up 2006 ASEAN chairmanship," *New York Times*, July 26, 2005, available at http://www.nytimes.com/2005/07/26/world/asia/26iht-web.0726asean.html
73. "Burma will not take Asean Chair," *BBC*, July 26, 2005, available at http://news.bbc.co.uk/2/hi/asia-pacific/4715283.stm
74. Statement by ASEAN Chair: Singapore's Minister for Foreign Affairs George Yeo, New York, September 27, 2007, available at http://www.aseansec.org/20974.htm ; Reportedly, Philippines Foreign Minister Alberto Romulo and Indonesian President Susilo Yudhoyono expressed frustration at the "constructive engagement policy" not giving necessary dividends. See Myanmar, *Security Council Report*, United Nations, November 22, 2006, available at http://www.securitycouncilreport.org/site/c.glKWLeMTIsG/b.2263725/k.9F86/Update_No_3_br_Myanmar_br_22_November_2006.htm
75. Donald K. Emmerson, "ASEAN's "Black Swans", *Journal of Democracy*, vol. 19, no. 3, July 2008, pp. 70-84.
76. "ASEAN SG Welcomes News of Myanmar Elections," *ASEAN*, August 26, 2010, available at http://www.asean.org/25088.htm
77. "ASEAN Chair Issues Statement on Myanmar Elections," *ASEAN*, November 11, 2010, available at http://www.asean.org/25580.htm
78. "Aung San Suu Kyi to Stand for Parliament in Burma," *BBC*, November 18, 2011, available at http://www.bbc.co.uk/news/world-asia-15787605
79. "Asean Leaders Approve Burma Chairmanship Bd," *BBC*, November 17, 2011, available at http://www.bbc.co.uk/news/world-asia-15771531

5. The Democratic Role of Ethnicity in Nepal

Monika Mandal

Ethnic parties and ethnic politics more broadly, have often been viewed as being incompatible with democracy, even though they frequently emerge in new democracies. Horowitz, for example, argues that the ethnic parties encourage people to identify in narrow and exclusive ways rather than with the whole society. Political systems in which ethnic parties operate become less democratic because people vote, not as individuals who are concerned with the common good, but rather as groups concerned only with group needs. Since these categories are ascribed, politics take on a fixed character, reduced to a struggle between unchanging ethnic groups, rather than operating as democracies should – competitions between fluid interest groups that coalesce around a variety of issues.[1] Ethnic parties often claim that the identities of the people they represent are given at birth and have ancient roots; however, most social scientists would disagree. As anthropologists and other social scientists have argued for several decades, ethnic identities are not primordial or fixed; rather, they are constructed in particular social contexts. Ethnic identification is a highly fluid process. Power relations structure the formation and definition of ethnic identities, including relationships between different groups, and the relations between ethnic groups and the state. New political contexts in which power relations are altered often bring about efforts to redefine ethnic identities. Ethnic movements and ethnic parties can also be catalysed by the ideas of equality in the discourse of democracy. Chantal Mouffe argues that identity-based social movement arises within democracies because the discourse of democracy constructs political subjects as citizens who should all be equal. There is a disjuncture between this democratic discourse of equality and the ways in which other hegemonic discourses of gender, ethnicity or race construct some political subjects as subordinate to other. People begin to question these discourses and struggle for equality 'because they have been constructed as subjects in a democratic tradition that puts those values at the centre of social life'.[2]

The Discourse

This paper attempts to address a couple of questions, which draw greater attention for public discourse in Nepal in the post-1990 period. Democracy was restored in Nepal in 1990, after a 30-year absence. People hoped for development, stability, and good governance in the democratic era. A new Constitution was enacted, ensuring most fundamental rights and freedoms for the people. Three general elections have since been held, leading to democratic governments. Two local elections have also been held, which institutionalised democracy at the local level. People are increasingly aware about democracy, and they have participated in democratic practices. Some laws have been changed in accordance with the Constitution. The government, legislature and courts have applied the new Constitution to deal with day-to-day problems.

Yes, democracy has brought some change, but since 1990 other problems have increased. The Parliament does not work properly. It only forms and dissolves governments. Political instability has become the norm. Parties factionalise over personal interests. Human rights violators from the earlier Panchayat regime have obtained immunity from prosecution. People's concerns are ignored; governments are only concerned with how to hold a majority in parliament. The judiciary is also the subject of criticism that it is corrupt and losing its neutrality. Political leaders have lost their previous popularity and become corrupt commission takers. People have not had an opportunity to realise democracy in their day-to-day lives. Social problems – poverty, underdevelopment, unequal distribution of resources, social injustice, exploitation, untouchability and gender inequality – have all continued in the democratic era. Inflation is high; black-marketeering and bribery increase day by day; unemployment is growing among literate youths; poor people are dying of disease and hunger. The government has not been able to eliminate these social evils.

The Nepal Communist Party was established in 1950. In the beginning, there was no debate on policy within the communist party. In the 1960s there was a big debate on the monarchy within the communist party, and later it brokedown into several factions. Seven left-wing parties and the Nepali Congress party led the democratic movement. After the establishment of democracy, two major communist factions united into the United Marxist-Leninist party (UML). It became the main communist party and took second position in parliament in the first general election, in 1990. Meanwhile, the

Nepal Communist Party (Maoist) started its 'People's War' in 1996. It is strongest in the remote and underdeveloped mid-western districts.

Discourse on ethnicity in Nepal has been developing with conflicting views on three major subjects: conceptual framework, definition of dominant and minority groups, and understanding and interpretation of caste-ethnic relations. Opinions among the native scholars are generally divided in line with one's belongingness to a particular group. This paper covers the representative ideas and thoughts of both native and foreign experts. To capture the emerging ethnic movement in Nepal in a conceptual framework, few observe in the primordialist line that it is a quest for identity; others, particularly those belonging to hill Bahun-Chhetri, take an instrumentalist stand that ethnic upsurge is motivated to gain some political and economic advantages. The opinions of many scholars, both native and foreigner, are close to what Prayag Raj Sharma states, "The ethnic politics of Nepal in the 1990s seems to have elements conforming with both the primordialists and the instrumentalists models".[3] It is, however, interesting to note that foreign scholars observe – without mentioning explicitly but indicating the elitist nature of such movement[4] and its relevance to the interest of the masses of the ethnic groups – that the ethnic activism in Nepal has greater elements of instrumentalism and less of primordialism. For instance, David Gellner is of the opinion, "One should not assume that ethnic activists and ordinary people share the same agenda".[5] Scholars from ethnic groups discard the instrumentalist and primordialist model and urge to perceive the ethnic movement of Nepal from the perspective of the principles of equality and struggle against discrimination.[6] Ganesh M. Gurung's opinion could be a representative of one set of argument, "Ethnic movements in Nepal are a natural outcome of age old suppression through the imposition of stratified hierarchical model by the Hindu rulers of Nepal, which needs to be removed with a view to making the hitherto deprived ethnic groups equal partners in the development of a single territorial Nepalese nation-state".[7]

The ethnic issue of Nepal from a particular conceptual angle–principle of equality and struggle against discrimination – has its own relevance in defining the dominant group and minority group. Numerically, all groups are minorities in Nepal and the largest one, Chhetri, constitutes 15.8 per cent. The combined strength of hill Bahun and Chhetri is 28.54 per cent. They (including hill low castes) have, however, long been treated as the majority group, because the people identified with Nepali language and Hindu religion are in majority, 48.61 and 80.6 per cent respectively, according to the 2001 census. Nepali language and Hindu religion are closely associated with hill Bahun-Chhetri identity, and presently the tarai castes also share a common identity. However, *madhesi* is a minority group since the majority population of the country are inhabitants of the hill region. The *janjatis* are also a minority group, because they are originally neither Hindu nor Nepali speaking people. So culturally, the majority-minority division has already been shaped as superior-inferior groups. Recently, such a division has been reformulated into 'dominant group and minority group'. Hill Bahuns-Chhetris are considered as a dominant group because of their dominant position in the power structure of the country; others, who have been historically 'discriminated', are treated as minorities. This is a widely accepted and adopted approach to the study of ethnicity in Nepal. The division of groups in line with dominant and minority is mostly used in dealing with the question of inclusion and exclusion.

Richard Burghart finds a systematic exclusion of minorities in the nation building process since the post-unification period. Harka Gurung has played with a number of statistical data projecting hill Bahun-Chhetri as the dominant group and the others, that is, *janajati*, *dalit* and *madhesi* as marginalised groups in all the social, economic and political spheres of the country. He, therefore, argues that the country has not yet been integrated in a way of multicultural nationalism. Mahendra Lawati points out an intrinsic nuisance of the majoritarian democracy – what Nepal adopted in the post-1990 period – and concludes that the Westminister model is unsuitable to the pluralistic society of Nepal, and so, contributing for the contentious exclusion of numerous socio-cultural groups. As the situation remains unchanged even after a decade long exercise of multiparty democracy, Krishna Bahadur Bhattachan predicts 'ethnic insurgency' in a 'predatory unitary Hindu state' on two grounds – one, the structure of political opportunities in Nepal is unduly favourable to Bahauns-Chhetris but unfavourable to other groups, and the other is the strength of the Federation of Nepali Nationalities (FENNA) constituting of 48 janajati organisations at present. Dilli Ram Dahal counters that the prevailing ethnic politics could hardly pose any threat to political stability and national integration due to two major reasons – one is the lack of base of ethnic activism at the grass-roots level and the other is heterogeneity within and among the various janajati groups in culture, tradition, language and religion.

Moreover, Dahal challenges the validity of the most used approach – hill Bahun-Chhjetri as dominant and the rest as minorities – while making the argument that distribution of economic and political power does not strictly follow the line with caste and ethnic division.[8] Giving an account of the historical pattern of elite formation in Nepal, he rather formulates a thesis of 'dominant individuals' against the most common used concept of 'dominant caste'. Dahal's argument, particularly on the question of dominant group in terms of wealth, seems valid while linking the issue of development and regional disparity. The people of mountain regions and mid-west and far-west regions are more excluded from development. 17 out of 22 districts in which Chhetris – considered as one of the dominant groups – constitute as the majority or the largest group of district population – are below the standard of national human development index.[9] The poverty index also shows Chhetris's position, marginally better than Rai, Magar and Limbu but slightly worse than Gurungs and Tharus.[10]

Differences of opinions are reflected in the understanding and interpretation of relations among different groups of Nepal. Based on caste, ethnic, regional, cultural and linguistic cleavages, the Nepali population can be broadly classified into three major groups: 'pahadi '(hill people) and 'madheshya' (plain people); 'jat' (caste groups) and 'janajati' (ethnic/ tribal groups), and high caste and low caste Hindus (within jat). Inter-group relations in a pluralistic and diversified society may be complementary or conflicting or mixed of both types. In Nepal, some argue, relations between diverse groups of society are harmonious and free of tension and violence. Based on her study on Humla district, Nancy E. Levine generalises, "Models of ethnicity in Nepal stress, on the one hand, unlimited ethnic diversity and, on the other, a rather limited set of ethnic contrasts … ethnic relations … are characterised more by interaction, interdependence, and mobility than contrasts and boundaries between groups".[11] Disagreement to such views are expressed, 'the ethnic harmony may have been exaggerated'[12] and, to the extreme, it is 'blatantly manufactured myth'.[13] Even those taking the position of harmonious relations among different groups of Nepal, consider the case of madhesi as an exception. Frederick H. Gaige is the pioneer author who explores regional conflicts between hill and plain groups on issues of language, citizenship and land ownership. The native scholars from Bahun caste conform to his findings and perceive the tarai as a vulnerable area.[14] Its geographical proximity with India and ethnic affinity with the people across the border area are additional reasons behind the anxiety of disintegration. But the relations between other groups (caste and janajati of hill, and high caste and low caste Hindus) have long been seen as harmonious. Nevertheless, Lionel Caplan's studies, done in the late 1960s and the early 1970s, reveal conflict between hill high caste and hill ethnic groups, and tension between hill high caste and low caste Hindus.[15] These parts of conflict have received prominence since Dor Bahadur Bista pin points "Bahaunbad' as an obstacle for development in Nepal.[16]

The exchange of heated words in recent discourse make both Bahun and janajati scholars more rigid in their stand. For instance, Prayag Raj Sharma, who showed his sympathy to the problems of exclusion in his early writings,[17] asserts to accept the foundation of Hindu state as a hard reality of history while expressing it bluntly, Weaker groups and weaker powers have always been overrun by stronger powers and groups. While retaliating to the climbing up of harsh opinions coming from ethnic scholars and leaders, Sharma has switched his position from being a part of the moderate camp to being a member of the conservative camp now, and pleads for the continuation of the age-long tradition of Nepali nationalism based on monarchy, Hindu religion and Nepali language; otherwise, he warns the birth of 'Bahun ethnicity'. At the other extreme, Krishna Bahadur Bhattachan blatantly depicts Bahuns-Chhetris as 'exploiters, oppressors, and internal colonisers', and provokes the excluded groups to wage zero-sum struggles against the Bahun-Chhetri.[18] The making of a particular group, instead of state, as the target of struggle may lead to the degeneration of the ethnic movement into communal politics. The ethnic upsurge will remain ethnic so long as the target is state but it gives it a flavour of communalism if the target is a particular group. Perhaps, Bhattachan is aware of it and has consciously indicated to the characteristics of South Asian states that they have always been insensitive to the ethnic problem unless the ethnic tension turns into communal violence between two groups. In fact, ethnic relation has been changing rapidly towards a greater degree of discord, conflict and tension. The root of problems lies in history.

Historical Background

The monarchy has played a central role in the unification and evolution of the Nepali state. Prithvi Narayan Shah, the king of Gorkha principality, established a modern unified Nepal by conquest. He, thus, introduced the Shah regime based on the right of sword. The utility of sword for territorial expansion was, however, effectively blocked following the end of war with British-India in 1816 and demarcation of the political territory of the Kingdom. Hence, the legitimacy of sword was confined to and symbolised with the royal army, which was, however, significant to retain control in conquered areas. But the symbol of the sword was not sufficient to establish legitimacy among the people of vanquished lands. Absolute control in political authority, monopolisation of economic resources, and penetration and expansion of social value systems of the victorious groups in vanquished areas were some of the mechanisms the Shah rulers and the subsequent Rana rulers bestowed to consolidate their respective regimes. It was, as one critic observed, an 'empire model' of national integration.[19]

Prithvi Narayan Shah is rated differently from his successors so far as the state's designed national integration is concerned. Some of the points highlighted are: Gorkhali army had a multi-ethnic character, comprised of hill castes and tribal groups;[20] Magars and Gurungs were found among the ruling elite of Gorkha House;[21] 'I (P.N. Shah) am the King of Magarant';[22] 'Prithvi Narayan Shah gave internal autonomy to Limbu';[23] and 'King respected the customs of a country in the tenurial administration of his possessions'.[24] All these statements have some meaning with what Shah said about Nepal, *A garden of four varnas and thirty-six jats*. This famous quotation has frequently been used to defend that the Shah dynasty respected the pluralistic characteristics of the Nepali state. But it seems contradictory to another version and motto of the same unifier king about Nepal, asli Hindustan (pure Hindu state). The balance between respect to diversity and imposition of the ruling value system was changed in favour of the latter soon after the unification of the country.

For the successors of Shah, Nepal as asli Hindustan had become the mul mantra in the state-designed project of national integration. It also manifested the source of legitimacy of the Hindu king, derived from divine right. The Shah monarch, as a hereditary institution, was enforced by the traditional Hindu view of the nobility of birth, as it was an accepted tradition all through the ancient and the medieval times. The Hindu polity places the king as a sovereign lord, a protector of territory and subjects, a guardian of moral order, an upholder of traditions, and the source of all spiritual and temporal power.[25] As the ideology of Hindu religion and polity provided legitimacy to the Shah regime, the rulers tried their best to spread Hinduism all over the country. In the post-unification period, 'the process of Hinduisation was intensified'.[26] So kingship, along with Hindu religion, played a key role in the construction of Nepali state and identity.

The Hindu polity – in which monarchy and religion have a decisive role – was further enacted more rigidly during the Rana period (1846-1951). The Rana prime ministers were also monarchs by title (Shree Tin Maharaj, king of Kaski and Lamjung) and by an authority they enjoyed. Jung Bahadur Rana, founder of the Rana regime, promulgated a Civil Code 1854, providing a legal framework to the Vedic prescription of social order in a hierarchical caste society. In fact, the Hinduisation process in Nepal followed casteism. Jaisthiti Malla (king of Kathmandu valley in 1382-95) and Ram Shah (king of Gorkha principality in 1603-36) are generally regarded as the protagonists for the introduction of caste system in their own respective territory. The caste system was, however, regulated largely by the *hukum* of the king and the *bachan* of the priests. The contribution of Jung Bahadur was providing the legal framework to such practices. The Civil Code of 1854 classified the people in three broader categories in ascendancy order: (a) Tagadhari (scared-thread wearing castes) at the top; (b) Matwali (alcohol drinking castes and ethnic groups) in the middle, and (c) 1. Sudra (impure but touchable castes) and 2. Acchut (impure and untouchable castes) at the lowest position. A scholar appreciated the Civil Code of 1854 as 'the historical solution to the problem of cultural diversity' and 'worked more in the spirit of inclusion'.[27] This view could be considered, in one perspective, as the states' conscious attempt at integration by bringing all the prajas (subjects) of the country into the fold of one rule. But the Code violated the very notion of national integration – that is equality among the people of a given territory, state. The Code discriminated the people of different caste hierarchy in the judicial system and in the distribution of the state resources. By putting ethnic groups into the fold of Hindu based hierarchical caste system, the Code translated diversity into inequality. Since inequality is the source of all kind of conflicts, the Civil Code of 1854 contributed negatively to the national integration of Nepal.

The partyless Panchayat system under absolute monarchy (1960-90) upheld the old symbols and practices, though the new Civil Code 1963 is a radical departure from the past as it recognises the universal principal of equality of people. The legal abolition of caste discrimination was/is, however, hardly translated into practice because of the self-contradiction of the value system which the state ushered. The Hindu religion and caste system is complementary and the ruler's adherence to Hindu religion was well reflected in the late king Birendra's perception of the source of legitimacy of monarchy.

He said, "In Nepal, the monarchy and his subjects have been governed by Dharma, a system drawn from the Hindu religion. The King cannot change this value system".[28] His predecessor king Mahendra, the founder of Panchayat regime, legally identified Nepal as a Hindu state as it was explicitly mentioned in the Constitution of Nepal of 1962 for the first time, unlike the previous constitutions. So, the king and Hindu religion were/are retained as the core components of Nepali nationalism.

The Panchayat system spread Nepali language, which had already received the status of official language since 1930. Even before the introduction of the Panchayat system, the state took a policy of promotion of Nepali language at the cost of other languages. Here, recommendations made by Nepal National Education Planning Commission (1955) are worthwhile to mention: "Nepali should be the medium of education, exclusively from third grade onwards, and as much as possible in the first two grades. No other languages should be taught even optionally, in the primary school because few children will have need for them; they would hinder the reaching of Nepali…other language will gradually disappear and greater national strength and unity will result".[29]

With state protection and promotion, Nepali language – being the official language and medium of education as well – has increasingly received prominence with the development of infrastructure, particularly in education, media, transportation and communication. Internal migration also contributed to developing Nepali as the lingua franca of the country, and so, as a powerful means of national integration. The dominant trend of migration in the pre-1990 period was from the west hills (original homeland of Khas/Nepali speaking people) to the east hills (janjati dominated area) and later from north (hill) to south (plain tarai). The migration of hill people in tarai – a traditional homeland of tribal people and the people of Indian origin – led to a change in its demography. At present, nearly one-thirds of the total tarai population consists of hill migrants, mostly Nepali speaking people.

Centralisation of politics and administration was another instrument of the state's project of national integration. The independent principalities of the pre-unification time were later integrated into administrative units of the country. The administration during the Shah and the Rana period was confined to two jobs – maintenance of law and order, and collection of revenue – by centrally deputed elites and or local elites co-opted by the government.

The division of the country into 35 districts by the Rana regime was done mainly for extraction of revenues and distribution of belief, value and culture of the ruling class/caste. The old revenue-based administration – shaped in the form of tenants-local chiefs' relations – was modernised by the Panchayat system introducing a uniform administration system. The Panchayat regime revised the administrative units into 5 development regions, 14 zones and 75 districts. Decentralisation, balanced regional development, and people's participation are some of the buzz words the Panchayat regime propagated in seeking development legitimacy, what the previous Shah and Rana rulers did not feel it necessary. As the system itself was highly centralised, the objective set in the decentralisation project was largely confined to paperwork, which obviously had adverse impact on national integration in a real sense and also to the survival of the regime itself. The model of national integration which the Panchayat system prescribed was homogenisation and assimilation of diverse groups into the fold of parbatiya Hindu culture. Disregard to pluralism was expressed in slogans, like 'our king, our country' and 'one language, one dress, and one culture'. In sum, the Panchayat system upheld and espoused traditional components, that is, kingship, Hindu religion, and Nepali language, and added new contents like decentralisation, development and coexistence in the state- designed scheme of national integration.

Since the time of unification of Nepal, the rulers – Shahs, Ranas and Panchas – had tried to develop Nepal as a homogeneous, monolithic and unitary state providing protection to one language (Nepali), one caste group (hill Bahun-Chhetri), and one religion (Hindu), ignoring the reality of the diversified and pluralistic character of Nepali society. Besides, the state-designed 'Nepalisation' process – through Hinduisation, spread of the parbatiya's culture, institutionalisation of caste system converting separate identity of ethnic groups into caste structures, and centralisation of politics and administration – had led to increased disparity among different social groups. The hill high caste Brahmin-Chhetri and Newar have long been in privileged positions. Other groups, that is, *janajati*, *madhesi* and *dalits* are generally marginalised. The legacy of history is well reflected in an unequal distribution of socio-economic resources of the country and in the representation of the political power structure of the country.

Table 5.1(A): Human Development by Caste and Ethnicity, 1996

Dominant Groups					Marginal Groups			
Bahun			chhetri	Newar	Madhesi	Janajati	Dalit	Nepal
1	Life Expectancy	60.8	5603	62.2	58.4	53.0	50.3	55.0
2	Adult Literacy rate %	58.00	42.00	54.80	27.50	35.20	23.80	36.27
3	Means years of schooling	4.4647	2.786	4.370	1.700	2.021	1.228	2.254
4	Per capita income Nrs	9,921	7,744	11,953	6,911	6,607	4,940	7,673
5	Per capita PPP income US$	1,533	1,197	1,848	1,068	1,021	764	1,186
6	Life Expectancy Index	0.957	0.522	0.620	0.557	0.467	0.422	0.500
7	Educational Attainment index	0.490	0.342	0.462	0.221	0.280	0.186	0.295
8	Income index	0.237	0.181	0.289	0.160	0.152	0.110	0.179
9	Human development index	0.441	0.348	0.457	0.313	0.299	0.239	0.325
10	Ration to HDI Nepal = 100	135.87	107.31	140.73	96.28	92.21	73.62	100.00

Source: NESAC. 1998. *Nepal: Human Development Report 1998*. Kathmandu: Nepal South Asia Centre.

Table 5.1(B): Integrated National Index of Governance, 1999

Dominant Groups				Marginalised Groups				
Bahun/Chhetri			Newar	Madhesi	Janajati	Dalit	Other	Total
1	Court	77	13.6	7.6	1.7	0	0	235
2	Constitutional Bodies	56	24	12	2.8	0	0	25
3	Cabinet	62.5	9.4	15.6	12.5	0	0	32
4	Parliament	60	7.6	17.4	13.6	1.5	0	265
5	Public Administration	77.6	17.6	3.7	1.2	0	0	245
6	Party Leadership	58.8	10.9	15.8	15.2	0	0	165
7	Leadership: local elected bodies	55.5	15.7	16.2	12	0	0	191
8	Leadership: Commerce and Industry	16.7	47.6	35.7	0	0	0	42
9	Leadership: Educational arena	77.3	11.3	7.2	2.1	1	1	97
10	Leadership: cultural arena	69.1	17.9	0	4.9	0	0	123
11	Science/technology	58.1	29	9.7	3.2	0	0	62
12	Civil society leadership	75.9	14.8	7.4	1.9	0	0	54
Total		66.5	15.2	11.2	7.1	0.3	1	
Population %		31.6	5.6	30.9	22.2	8.7	1	
Difference with population %		+ 34. 9	+9.6	- 19.7	- 15.1	- 8.4	-1	

Source: Neupane, Govinda. 2000. *Nepalko Jatiya Prasana* (Question of Caste/Ethnicity in Nepal). Kathmandu: Centre for Development Studies.

In retrospect, the inequality between dominant group (hill Bahun-Chhetri, and Newar) and minority group (madhesi, janajati and dalits) is a by-product of the legacy of the historical process of national integration in Nepal. That process occurred under the absolute regimes, except for a short experience of multiparty system in interregnum (1951-60). All types of non-democratic regimes – whatever names and forms – are, by nature, exclusionary as they generally prohibit and discourage people's participation. Nepal had long been under a patrimonial system and the king was at the apex of the power structure and those who received the palace's favour were the only ones with a chance to become members of elites. On this ground, Dilli Ram Dahal brings out the thesis of 'dominant individuals' against the most common used concept of 'dominant caste'.[30] Of course, being a member of the high caste group alone is not adequate for political fortunes, but history shows overlapping of dominant individuals and dominant caste, and economic elite and political elite. The reduction of bhardars from that of Chha thar ghar (six-family linage) of the Gorkha palace to four families (Shah, Thapa, Basnet and Pandey) in the post-unification period was evidence of the exclusion of ethnic groups from and monopoly of twice-born hill high castes in the power structure of the country. Till the end of the Rana regime, the ethnic groups were completely out from the composition of central elites, though some from non-hill high castes were found in the local elite structure as mukhiya, jimalwal, talukdar, etc. The family networking of high castes is extensive and the culture of afno manche, long upheld by the state itself, has contributed to the retaining of the broader alliance of privileged castes and their domination in the power structure of the country. There is a Nepali proverb, *goru bechheko saino,* which refers to the skills of Bahun-Chhetri to cultivate connection for their own benefit. The hill high caste domination was also explained by the overlapping of economic elite and political elite in the past under the patrimonial and feudal system. Dahal himself wrote, "Historically, land ownership in Nepal is closely and systematically tied to the hierarchical caste framework; the higher the caste status of a family, the larger its landownership and vice versa".[31]

Exploring reasons for the domination of hill high castes, one needs to explore the other side of story. Unlike the present tendency of keeping the ethnic groups away from the parbatiya culture, the dominant trend in the past was to accept the culture of the hill high caste people as a model for one's upliftment and enhancement. The process by which a low caste Hindu, or tribe or any other group, changes its customs, ritual, ideology and way of life in the direction of a high and frequently twice born caste has been popularised as Sanskritisation by M.N. Shrinivas.[32] In the past, Sanskritisation was a model followed by a number of hill and tarai ethnic groups of Nepal for their upward mobility and status under the prevailing patron-client culture and system. In the given culture and system, the elites – from Rana rulers at the centre to the local notables at the village level – distributed jagir (job), conducted pajani (annual reshuffling of service personnel), granted baksis (gift and reward), solely on their own discretion, to their own clients and sub-clients. A commoner received material and other benefits by demonstrating his loyalty, obedience, submission through Chakari (obsequious attendance) to his respective patrons. The reasons to opt for Sanskritisation and Hinduisation might be beyond the factor of material benefit. The perception of status upgrade also motivated the non-caste groups to follow the habit and custom of the hill high caste groups. The recent social history of Nepal is the active adoption and adaptation of Nepali language, parbatiya culture and symbols of those in power by the ethnic mass in general and ethnic elites in particular.[33]

As parbatiya culture was adopted as a model by the ethnic groups, there was absence of resistance against the Bahaun-Chhetri's domination in the power structure of the country. Only a subdued ethnic feeling was observed within the regional (Tarai) and hill communities.[34] The Panchayat system restricted the fundamental rights of the people to speak and to organise against its ideology and value system. The dominant issue for oppositional politics in the pre-1990 period was multiparty democracy not the ethnic question. Ethnic politics was banned as party politics, thus, the voices of ethnic groups so far as their group identity and interest was concerned were suppressed. Democracy – reinstated in April 1990 – has provided an outlet to the needs and interests of the excluded groups.

State Ideology and Ethnicity

The 1990 mass movement ended the Panchayat regime and restored democracy. The new Constitution brought out fundamental changes in the political system of the country – from a partyless to a multiparty system, reduction of king's position from absolute to constitutional monarchy, and promotion of people's status from subject to citizen. The newly established democratic regime is associated with the principles of popular sovereignty, fundamental and human rights of the citizen, representative government, and independent judiciary. Are such changes significant to reset the state's ideology vis-a-vis ethnicity? To what extent, the new political system is different from the past regimes vis-a-vis the grievances of the excluded groups? Considering the constitution as a mirror of the state's goal, the table below shows a comparative picture of the state ideology under different regimes (constitutions) related to the questions of national integration.

Table 5.2: Constitutions and Ethnicity

Nation/ State	
1990	1. King, symbol of Nepalese nationality and the unity of the Nepalese people 2. Nation, constitute of people irrespective of religion, race, caste or tribe 3. Strengthen national unity and harmony amongst various religious, castes, tribes, language, race and communities 4. Multiethnic, multilingual, democratic, independent, indivisible, sovereign Hindu, and Constitutional Monarchical Kingdom
1962	1. Nation, constitute of people irrespective of religion, race, caste or tribe 2. Common aspirations and united by the common bond of allegiance to the crown 3. Maintain national unity with due regard to existing mutual harmonious tolerance 4. Monarchical Hindu Kingdom
1959	Monarchical Kingdom
1951	Monarchical Kingdom
Citizen/Ethnicity	
1990	1. All citizens are equal before law; no discrimination on grounds of religion, race, sex, caste, tribe 2. Eliminate all types of economic and social inequalities 3. Maintain cultural diversity 4. Promotion of language, literature, scripts, arts and culture of different groups
1962	1. All citizens are equal before law; no discrimination on grounds of religion, race, sex, caste, tribe 2. Establish exploitation-less society
1959	1. All citizens are equal before law; no discrimination on grounds of religion, race, sex, caste, tribe
1951	1. All citizens are equal before law; no discrimination on grounds of religion, race, sex, caste, etc.

Religion	
1990	1. Hindu kingdom 2. Freedom to profess and practice own religious and to protect religion places and trust 3. Prohibit to convert another person from one religion to another
1962	1. Hindu kingdom 2. Freedom to profess and practice own religion 3. Prohibit to convert another person from one religion to another
1959	1. Freedom to profess and practice one's own religion 2. Prohibit to convert another person from one religion to another
1951	Freedom to profess and practice own religion
Language	
1990	1. Nepali: national and official language; 2. Mother tongue: national languages of Nepal
1962	Nepali: national language
1959	Nepali: national language
1951	-

The Constitution of the Kingdom of Nepal of 1990 upheld a number of features of Nepali nationalism adopted since 1951 and before. Particularly from the end of the Rana regime in 1951, the components like kingship, Hindu religion, and Nepali language, and the concepts of citizenship, equality, and unity and harmony of different social groups have been adopted as ingredients of the nation-state of Nepal. Though, Nepali language and Hindu religion were not mentioned in the 1951 Constitution and the 1959 Constitution was also salient on the religious identity of Nepal, secular or Hindu state. These two constitutions were relatively less pro-Hindu and pro-parbatiya in comparison to the succeeding 1962 and 1990 constitutions. As the 1990 Constitution recognised Nepal as a unitary, Hindu, and monarchical state, and Nepali as official language as before, many things remained unchanged in the basic characteristics of the Nepali state. The National symbols – crown, scepter, royal crest, royal standard, coat-of arms, cow, national flag, rhododendron, and red blob – set up by the Panchayat, and most of them associated with the monarchy and Hindu religion[35] and national anthem (phrased in a way equating patriotism with worship of king) were retained without any change.

The 1990 Constitution does not recognise the existence of inequality and discrimination on caste/ethnic, linguistic and religious lines – except for the consideration of women and dalits as marginalised groups deserving to get special treatment from the state in education, health and employment sectors. It, therefore, does not provide provisions for state's protection, promotion and affirmative action's to the excluded and marginalised groups. Besides, the Constitution separates politics from ethnicity by a provision prohibiting the formation of political party on the basis of religion, community, caste, tribe and region. This provision was, however, implemented loosely and flexibly.

What are the new things that the 1990 Constitution provides for the cause of ethnic groups? It recognises the pluralistic character of Nepali society consisting of diverse cultural and linguistic groups. Such a constitutional recognition of Nepal as a state of diverse cultural groups comes for the first time in its history. The constitutional commitment to 'maintain cultural diversity', right 'to promote literature, scripts, arts and culture of different groups', freedom 'to protect religious places and trust' and recognition of other than Nepali (language of the nation) as 'languages of nationalities' are certainly new contents, which were not found in the previous constitutions. The inclusion of words multiethnic and multilingual in the identification of the Nepali state is widely appreciated as a major departure from the historical model of national integration.[36]

More significantly, democracy has provided space for the excluded groups to organise and mobilise themselves to promote their interests. Though the 1990 Constitution gives continuity to a number of traditional contents and symbols of nationalism set previously by the Panchayat regime, one could not help but notice a change in the state's behaviour vis-a-vis ethnicity following the restoration of a multiparty democracy. It is because of the change in the political system from absolute to liberal that led to changes in state-ethnic relations. The post-1990 governments are, by all means and standard, relatively progressive and responsive to ethnic pressures. In fact, the origin and evolution of ethnic movements have been closely associated with the history of democracy in Nepal.

Ethnic activism was first noticed with the dawn of democracy in 1951. The 1959 general elections to parliament brought out the hill ethnic groups and madhesi community from complete exclusion in the past under the Shah and the Rana regimes. In 1959, their representation was 26.3 and 15.5 per cent in the government and 15.6 and 22.0 per cent in parliament respectively.[37] Hence, their representation continued – 14-21 per cent of hill ethnic groups and 11-18 per cent of madhesi community – in legislature throughout the Panchayat period despite the regime being highly tilted to the hill high castes, the Chhetris in particular. The ethnic activism was revived as Panchayat politics appeared flexible following the announcement of referendum in 1979 (held in 1980) to choose one between a multiparty system and a partyless Panchayat system. The elections of Rastriya Panchayat (national legislature) in the post-referendum period were noticed as successful assertion by the backward groups of *madhesi* community.[38] Particularly after the end of the Panchayat system and the restoration of multiparty democracy in 1990, ethnic movements are accelerating and gaining in momentum.

Ethnic Movement

Ethnic upsurge is inevitable in Nepal as the historical process of national integration is exclusionary. The restoration of democracy with the principles of popular sovereignty, equality, freedom and cultural rights has provided a platform for ethnic activism. The advent of democracy has, therefore, been followed with the rise of ethnic consciousness and awareness. The ethnic issue has gained a new weight and strength because of the impact of the Maoist's armed insurgency. Of course, the Maoist party has ethnic contents, that is, secular state and ethnic autonomy, but it could be simply overridden by the communist principle of 'democratic centralism'. Experiences of other communist countries show that autonomy is limited to the paper only. However, it is generally perceived – particularly by the Western media, academia and diplomats – that the Maoist succeeded to capitalise the psyche of alienation and frustration of the excluded groups, dalit and janajati in particular, in escalating their armed insurgency. In coming years the ethnic problems of Nepal is likely to be addressed at a greater level by the donor countries in their much-awaited scheme of 'conflict management' in Nepal. The ethnic activism of Nepal has already been internationalised. The international environment, particularly UN declaration of 1994-2003 as a decade of indigenous people, has provided additional imputes to highlight the problems of ethnic groups within the country and also to link the local initiative as a part of the global movement.

Among the ethnic groups of Nepal, the largest groups are janajati, madhesi and dalit. There are many forums championing the cause of such different ethnic groups. The FENNA and its member organisations have focused more on the problems of janajati. Dalit activism has largely been expediting as the NGO movement having link with INGOs and backed by several donors. There are about 150 dalit NGOs,[39] and the Dalit NGO Federation is an umbrella organisation of 102 NGOs. The problem of Madheshya is more addressed by the Nepal Sadbhabana Party (NSP), a tarai based regional party.

The demands of ethnic groups can broadly be categorised into three areas: quest for identity, sharing of national resources, and greater representation in the political structure. The janajatis' assertion for cultural identity is mainly based on the rights of indigenous nationalities; madhesis stress on regional identity; and dalits focus against the practice of untouchability. The dalit movement is highly tied up with its demand of sharing national resources and representation in the governmental structures. Madhesi activism is also directed to the same purpose but in a different context and shape. Ethnic demands of janajati have naturally geared up over time and the focus changed from the issues related to identity to sharing of resources and more representation in political structures. The volume of demands of the janajatis has increased and is embodied in the NEFNA's 27-point recommendations for the amendment to the Constitution. The suggestions covered a wide range of issues from respect to minorities' language and religion to reservation in governance. The demands for federalism, ethnic autonomy, and proportional representation in political structures on the basis of the size of population of janajati and dalits are also included.

The question of sharing of economic resources and political power has always been problematic. Bhattachan, while referring to the core thoughts of Habermas and Foucault, states, 'Knowledge serves interest and yields power'. This explains why the minorities of Nepal are marginalised, because they are far behind the dominant Bahun-Chhetri and Newar in the knowledge industry.[40] This logic is very close to agglutination theory of elite formation as it considers education, wealth, and social status as 'political resources'.[41] So beyond historical reasons, some points need to be highlighted to understand the problems of equality and power sharing in Nepal. Bahun, Chhetri and Newar are in better position than any other group in Nepal in educational attainment.[42] Hill Bahuns are relatively more affluent and adaptable to the changing needs and situations of the society. A study done in the mid-1990s found the minority groups politically less articulate.[43] One of the ways of accumulating ethnic capital is to overcome one's shortcomings and to adopt selective qualities of other groups. Irrespective of their disadvantaged position vis-a-vis sources of power, the logic of justice provides the minorities strength to fight against the state. Reservation in education, employment and government is invariably included in the ethnic movements. To reduce the possibility of reproduction of the dominant class within the ethnic groups, reservation and other policies should be blended with class factor – poverty, illiteracy and underdevelopment within the groups – in ethnic contents. This will serve more the purpose of masses than that of elites of the minority groups.

The ethnic groups' quest for identity, sharing of national resources, and greater representations in the political structure, naturally contend against the hill Bahun-Chhetri domination. Inserting some issues concerning dalits as well in its agendas, the NEFNA has sought to forge an alliance with other minorities and broaden the scope of the ethnic movement. At once, the language activists crossed the pahadi (ethnic)-madhesi division while protesting against the Supreme Court decision of barring the use of mother tongues in local government. The NSP also – particularly in election times – appealed to have a unity between madheshyas and janajatis against the domination of hill Bahun-Chhetri. The target was to cash in the votes of janajati migrants in tarai.

Though janajati, madheshi and dalit have a common target to shift the prevailing balance of power, their destination is different. The issues, that is, language, religion, culture, etc., related to janajati's identity have nothing to do with the dalits as they are part of parbatiya Hindu culture. For dalits, both the high caste groups and non-caste janajati are exploiters so long as the practice of untouchablity remains unchanged. The objective of dalit movements is social justice so the questions of saha bhoj (mealing together with non-dalits), refusal to throw bodies of dead animals, and entry in Hindu temples are its key agendas and activities. Madhesi hardly distinguish between pahadi caste groups and pahadi janajatis so far as its regional identity, language and culture are concerned. So, the unity among the three largest ethnic groups is hard to achieve.

Divisions within each of the three largest ethnic groups are another bitter truth. Within dalits, there is a hierarchy of upper and lower castes. The day-to-day life of tarai is affected more by the internal division of madheshyas themselves into the backward and forward groups than the distinction between pahadi and madhesi. The Tharu shares a common identity with the hill ethnic groups as janajati and as a member of FENNA. But community specific demand, agenda, and priority make them different. Rise of consciousness among the Tharu community is invariably linked with their fight for the liberation from bonded labour system and land to sukumbasi. The hill janajati movements are taking up the questions of language and culture as priority areas.

Ethnic mobilisation is another problem, though dalit and Tharu activism are visible at the grass roots level. Tharu movements (in Bake, Bardiya, Kailali, Kanchanpur, and Dang) for ending the bonded labour system, refusal to throw dead bodies of animals by Chamar of Siraha and Saptari, and entry of dalits into Hindu temples of different parts of the country are a few of the successful struggles. The dominant trend is the establishment of the organisation, involvement in advocacy, and running after donors for fund. Ethnic mobilisation and launching of movements are noticed least. The FENNA is a fat body consisting of 48 organisations but the dominants are those already known as SETAMAGURALI (Sherpa, Tamang, Magar Gurung, Rai and Limbu). Those who are actively involved in ethnic politics are educated intellectuals employed in government, university and NGOs/INGOs, entrepreneurs, ex-Gurkha soldiers, politicians etc. So the ethnic mobilisers constitute the 'dominant class' of the minority groups.

The ethnic movements are largely educated middle class-based and their activities are mainly concentrated in the capital of the country. Besides, many leaders and activists of ethnic organisations are affiliated with political parties, particularly with communist parties; their individual vested interests has led them to be in proximity with the power structure; and they have been co-opted and collaborated by the government – all these factors have influenced in shaping the minorities' struggle as mainly an elitist movement. At the grass-roots level the existence of ethnic activism is displayed only in the signboards of their own respective organisations in the district headquarters and ethnic content mattered only if the researcher provoked the respondents to say something about ethnic problems. The absence of ethnic movements at grass-roots level is also reflected in the results of elections. The parties that contested elections on ethnic and regional basis failed to gain any seat in parliament except the NSP, which gained 3-6 seats in the last three parliamentary elections. The Rashtriya Jan Mukti Party and the Jan Mukti Party obtained only 1.06 and 0.10 per cent respectively in the 1999 parliamentary election.

Ethnic movements that have emerged since the restoration of democracy in 1990 is, till now, largely limited in bringing out alternative ideas and exerting pressure politics. However, despite several limitations and constraints, the movement is earning ethnic capitals, and gaining something, particularly in sensitising the political institutions of the country.

Ethnic Demands for a New Nepal

Since April 2006, the indigenous nationalities movement has come closer to seeing its goals being realised as mainstream political discourse increasingly addresses issues that the movement has raised. During the 19-day popular movement that month, which forced the king to relinquish his control of the government and reinstate the parliament that he dissolved in 2002, people across the country demanded changes that once only radical ethnic and leftist political groups had voiced: the end of the monarchy, a secular state, and a new constitution. Since then, the government has made many key decisions that converge with long-term demands of the indigenous nationalities. Upon being reinstated, the parliament repealed the political power of the monarchy, declared Nepal a secular state, and pledged to hold elections to a constituent assembly. The comprehensive peace accord and Interim Constitution have further implemented these changes. However, these documents have failed to meet the demands of the indigenous nationalities and other marginalised groups. Indigenous nationalities activists charge the interim government with paying inadequate attention to their demands, which they had clearly expressed.

The Comprehensive Peace Accord, which the Maoists and the Seven Party Alliance signed on November 8, 2006, officially ended the decade long war. In addition to reaching a settlement about managing the arms and armies of the government and the Maoists, the Maoists and the SPA made many agreements relating to ethnic issues. They agreed to hold elections to a constituent assembly that will draft a new permanent constitution, and that these elections would employ a mixed electoral system, with 205 members elected through the first-past-the-post system and 204 members elected by proportional representation, on the basis of votes won by political parties. 16 members would be appointed. The accord did not guarantee proportional representation for marginalised groups but suggested that political parties should implement it when choosing their candidates. It restricted the power of the king, nationalised royal property, and stated that the constituent assembly would decide the fate of the monarchy. It proposed that the interim government consist of 209 members of the Seven Party Alliance, 73 Maoists, and 48 members from 'sister organisations and professional bodies, oppressed ethnic communities and regions, and political personalities'. Regarding the structure of the state, the agreement recommended that the centralised and unitary structure of the state be deconstructed and that an inclusive and democratic state be established, but it also stated that the final decision would be made by the constituent assembly.[44]

Nepal Federation of Indigenous Nationalities (NEFIN) and other organisations critiqued the peace accord for not addressing the interests and demands of the indigenous nationalities.[45] In a public letter issued on November 18, 2006, NEFIN General Secretary Om Gurung forwarded 15 demands, and warned that NEFIN would begin a series of protests if the Maoists and the Seven Party Alliance failed to comply. NEFIN demanded (1) clarification on how the state would be restructured, (2) proportional representation for indigenous nationalities in the constituent assembly and in all levels of the interim government, and (3) a referendum on the monarchy to be held along with the constituent assembly elections, among other issues. Furthermore, the letter stated that the documents failure to include the term adibasi janajati suggests that the political parties do not respect and recognise this identity.[46]

The Interim Constitution was finalised on December 16, 2006, and adopted on January 15, 2007. This constitution upholds many of the decisions of the peace accord. While it represents a significant advance over the 1990 Constitution with respect to ethnic issues, it failed to meet the demands of the indigenous nationalities.

In its demands to the Interim Constitution Drafting Committee in July 2006, NEFIN requested that the Interim Constitution to express Nepal's status as a secular state, provisions guaranteeing the right to use ethnic languages in education and government offices, the restructuring of the state into ethnic and regional autonomous regions, the right to ethnic self-determination, and proportional representation for indigenous nationalities in all sectors of the state.[47] The Interim Constitution does not include any of these demands, aside from the statement that Nepal is a secular state, leaving these issues to be resolved by the constituent assembly. Proportional representation, reservations, and federalism are the issues on which there is the biggest discrepancy between ethnic demands and the Interim Constitution. Indigenous nationalities want these changes made through amendments to the Interim Constitution, before the constituent assembly elections, so that they have a better chance of being well represented in the assembly.

From NEFIN's perspective, political leaders must explicitly include ethnic issues in state documents rather than merely calling for broad changes and assuming that ethnic aspirations are subsumed within these statements. Indigenous nationalities want their demands to be at the centre of efforts to revise the political system. While they welcome the symbolic changes that the lawmakers have adopted, such as the declaration that Nepal is a secular state, these changes are not sufficient. Furthermore, they want to be included in the decision making process and want their community acknowledged by having it named in official documents.

Conclusion

Recent political developments along with emerging ethnic assertions have been leading the country towards a new direction/destination different from the past. The decade of 1990s and the following years will be recalled as a transitional phase characterised by the breaking of some major traditional ingredients of nationalism and building of new values and systems for national unity and integration. At present, these foreseeable changes largely exist as alternative ideas pushed forward by janajati and other minority groups, civil society and advocacy groups, and small political parties. Considering multiple factors – merit of issues, increase of public opinion and pressure for restructuring political institutions to promote inclusive democracy, the Maoist's pressing for radical change, and increasing sensitivity of the larger parties to the issues of minorities concerned the thought of alternative model of national integration, as suggested above, will certainly turn into reality. The important question is 'timing', when will the proposal of the restructuring of the state into the project of national integration, translate into practice. As the politics is heading towards the restructuring of the state, either through constitutional reform or an election of the constituent assembly, it is high time to intervene and exert pressure for a consensual/inclusive democracy that definitely opens up a new horizon for national unity and integration.

Notes

1. Donald Horowitz, *Ethnic Groups in Conflict.* (Berkeley: University of California Press), pp. 296-298.
2. Chantal Mouffe, "Hegemony and New Political Subjects: Toward a New Concept of Democracy", in *Marxism and the Interpretation of Culture,* L. Grossberg and C. Nelson (eds). (Chicago: University of Illinois Press, 1988), p. 95.
3. Priya Raj Sharma, "Nation Building, Muti-Ethnicity, and the Hindu State." In David N. Gellner, Jonna Pfaff-Czarnecka, and John Whelpton. (eds). 1997. *Nationalism and Ethnicity in a Hindu Kingdom: The Politics of Culture in Contemporary Nepal.* (Amsterdam: Harwood academic publishers, 1997), pp. 483.

4. The elitist nature of ethnic movement is reflected in composition of its leaders/activists, not 'frustrated middle class' but elites, as observed by one foreign scholar, "At present among the promoters of 'cultural politics' are many prominent politicians, parliamentarians and intellectuals employed in key positions, entrepreneurs, highly regarded priests and religious leaders, and even government officials'. Jonna Pfaff-Czarnecka, "Debating the State if the Nation: Ethinization of Politics in Nepal" – A Position Paper, in Jonna Pfaff-Czarnecka, Damini Rajsingham-Senanayake, Ashis Nandy and Edmund Terence Gomex, *Ethnic Future: The State and Identity Politics in Asia*, (New Delhi: Sage, 1999), p.77).
5. David N. Gellner, "How should One Study Ethnicity and Nationalism". *Contributions to Nepalese Studies*, 2001, 28:1, p. 5.
6. Krishna Bahadur Bhattachan, "Making No Heads or Tails of the Ethnic "Conundrum" by Scholars with European Head and Nepalese Tail". *Contributions to Nepalese Studies*, 1998, 23:1, pp. 111-130.
7. Ganesh M. Gurung, "Ethnic Identity and the Politics of Ethnographic Museum in Nepal". In Ram B. Chhetri and Om P. Gurung (eds.). *Anthropology and Sociology of Nepal: Cultures, Societies, Ecology and Development*. (Kathmandu: Sociological and Anthropological Society of Nepal, 1999), p. 81.
8. Dahal states, "Historically those involved in trans-Himaliyan trade, i.e. Byansi of Darchula, Thakalis of Thakkhola, Manangbasi of Manag, Sherpas of Solkhumbu, Bhotiyas of Olangchunggola, Newars of Kathmandu valley, though they hold little cultivable land, are the most prosperous groups. Taking an isolated case of the result of 1991 general election, Dahal argued that it is not only the hill Bahun and Chhetri but also Newar, Thakali, Limbu, Gurung and Tharu were over represented in parliament than the size of their population. Dilli Ram Dahal, "Ethnic Cauldron, Demography and Minority Politics: The Case of Nepal", in Dhruba Kumar (ed.), *State, Leadership and Politics in Nepal*, (Kathmandu: Centre for Nepal and Asian Studies (CNAS), 1995), p.159.
9. NESAC. *Nepal: Human Development Report 1998*. (Kathmandu: Nepal South Asia Centre, 1998), p. 264-265
10. Harka Gurung, "Janajati and Dalit: The Subjugated in Governance". *Reading on governance and Development*, 2003, 2, p. 7.
11. Nancy E. Levine, "Caste, State, and Ethnic Boundaries in Nepal". *Journal of Asian Studies*, 1987, 46:1, p. 71.
12. David N. Gellner, "Ethnicity and Nationalism in the World's Only Hindu State". In David N. Gellner Jonna Pfaff-Czarnecka, and John Whelpton (eds). *Nationalism and Ethnicity in a Hindu Kingdom: The Politics of Culture in Contemporary Nepal*. (Amsterdam: Harwood academic publishers, 1997), p. 6.
13. Krishna Bahadur Bhattachan, "Ethnopolitics and Ethnodevelopment: An Emerging Paradigm". In Dhruba Kumar (ed.) *State, Leadership and Politics in Nepal*. (Kathmandu: CNAS, 1995), p. 125.
14. P. R. Sharma views, "The rigid attitudes which divide the Pahades and Madhesiyas indicates an ethnic conflict of explosive potential which could well engulf Nepal in fugure. (P. R. Sharma, "How to Tend this Garden", *Himal*, 1992, p.9). Similarly Dilli Ram Dahal expresses "If there is one area of the Himalaya that is simmering with ethnic discontent,

it is the Tarai." (D. R. Dahal, "Grasping the Tarai Identity", *Himal*, 1992, p.17).

15. Lionel Caplan, *Land and Social Change in East Nepal: A Study of Hindu-tribal relations.* London: Routledge and Kegan Paul Limited. --. 1975. Administration and Politics in a Nepalese Town: A Study of a District Capital and its Environs. (London: Oxford University Press, 1970).
16. Dor Bahadur Bista, *Fatalism and Development: Nepal's Struggle for Modernization.* (Calcutta: Orient Longman, 1991).
17. P.R. Sharma's sympathy to the problems of minorities is reflected in sentences, like, "...need of time is to accord other languages a meaningful place in national life". "...the cultural rights of the different communities were not recognised by the old state". "Modern states are based on the newer values of democracy, human rights, minority rights, equality and social justice" (1992).
18. Krishna Bahadur Bhattachan, "Ethnopolitics and Ethnodevelopment: An Emerging Paradigm". In Dhruba Kumar (ed.) *State, Leadership and Politics in Nepal.* (Kathmandu: CNAS, 1995).
19. Jonna Pfaff-Czarnecka, "Vestiges and Visions: Cultural Change in the Process of Nation-Building in Nepal". In David N. Gellner Jonna Pfaff-Czarnecka, and John Whelpton (eds). *Nationalism and Ethnicity in a Hindu Kingdom: The Politics of Culture in Contemporary Nepal.* (Amsterdam: Harwood academic publishers, 1997), p. 421.
20. Priyag Raj Sharma, "Nation Building, Muti-Ethnicity, and the Hindu State." In David N. Gellner, Jonna Pfaff-Czarnecka, and John Whelpton. (eds). 1997. *Nationalism and Ethnicity in a Hindu Kingdom: The Politics of Culture in Contemporary Nepal.* (Amsterdam: Harwood academic publishers, 1997), p. 477.
21. John Whelpton, "Political Identity in Nepal: State, Nation and Community". In David N. Gellner Jonna Pfaff-Czarnecka, and John Whelpton (eds). *Nationalism and Ethnicity in a Hindu Kingdom: The Politics of Culture in Contemporary Nepal.* (Amsterdam: Harwood academic publishers), p. 43.
22. Harka Gurung, "Nepali Nationalism: A Matter of Consolidation". *Himal*, 2001, 14:3, p. 19.
23. Krishna Bahadur Bhattachan, "Ethnopolitics and Ethnodevelopment: An Emerging Paradigm". In Dhruba Kumar (ed.) *State, Leadership and Politics in Nepal.* (Kathmandu: CNAS, 1995), p. 137.
24. Richard Burghat, *The Conditions of Listening: Essays on Religion, History and Politics in South Asia.* (Delhi: Oxford University Press, 1996), p. 24.
25. Priyag Raj Sharma, "Nation Building, Muti-Ethnicity, and the Hindu State." In David N. Gellner, Jonna Pfaff-Czarnecka, and John Whelpton. (eds). 1997. *Nationalism and Ethnicity in a Hindu Kingdom: The Politics of Culture in Contemporary Nepal.* (Amsterdam: Harwood academic publishers, 1997), p.475.
26. Lok Raj Baral, "Minority Groups in the Kingdom of Nepal: Status, Dynamic and International Implications". *Ethnic Studies Report*, 1991, 9:1, pp. 56.
27. Priyag Raj Sharma, "Nation Building, Muti-Ethnicity, and the Hindu State." In David N. Gellner, Jonna Pfaff-Czarnecka, and John Whelpton. (eds). 1997. *Nationalism and Ethnicity in a Hindu Kingdom: The Politics of Culture in Contemporary Nepal.* (Amsterdam:

Harwood academic publishers, 1997), p.481.

28. Rishikesh Shaha, *Nepali Politics: Retrospect and Prospect*, (Delhi: Oxford University Press, 1975), p. 7.
29. Krishna Bahadur Bhattachan, "Minority Rights: Country Report-Nepal", 2003 (A report under publication). pp. 26-27.
30. Dilli Ram Dahal, "Nepal's Governing Elite: Their Composition and Role in Constituting the State." In Dhruba Kumar (ed.) *Domestic Conflict and Crisis of Governability in Nepal.* (Kathmandu: CNAS, 2000).
31. Dilli Ram Dahal, "Ethnic Cauldron, Demography and Minority Politics: The Case of Nepal." In Dhruba Kumar (ed.) *State, Leadership and Politics in Nepal.* (Kathmandu: CNAS, 1995), p. 159.
32. Rishikesh Shaha, *Nepali Politics: Retrospect and Prospect,* (Delhi: Oxford University Press, 1975), p. 19.
33. Jonna Pfaff-Czarnecka, "Debating the State of the Nation: Ethnization of Politics in Nepal – A Position Paper". In Jonna Pfaff-Czarnecka, Darini Rajsingham-Senanayake, Ashis Nandy and Edmund Terence Gomex. *Ethnic Future: The State and Identity Politics in Asia.* (New Delhi: Sage, 1999), p. 53.
34. Lok Raj Baral, "Ethnicity and Constitutional Reforms in Nepal". In Iftekharuzzman. *Ethnicity and Constitutional Reform in South Asia.* (New Delhi: Manohar, 1998), p. 84.
35. Harka Gurung, "State and Society in Nepal". In David N. Gellner Jonna Pfaff-Czarnecka, and John Whelpton (eds), *Nationalism and Ethnicity in a Hindu Kingdom: The Politics of Culture in Contemporary Nepal.* (Amsterdam: Harwood academic publishers, 1997), p. 505.
36. Ibid., p. 502.
37. DREFDEN. Report on the Study and Research on the Local Elections in Nepal 1992. (Kathmandu DREFDEN, 1992).
38. Rishikesh Shaha, *Essays in the Practice of Government in Nepal*, (New Delhi: Manohar Publishing House, 1982), pp. 205-206.
39. Hira Biswakarma, "Nepalko Dalit Andolan ra Dalit Sangthanko Bhumika (Dalit Movement in Nepal and role of Dalit Organisations). In Pratyoush Onta, Promod Bhatta, Vidya Nath Koirala, Khegendra Sangrola and C.K. Lal (eds.) *Chhapa ma Dali* (Dalit in Prinet Media). (Kathmandu: Yaketa Books, 2001), p. 269.
40. Krishna Bahadur Bhattachan, "Possible Ethnic Revolution or Insurgency in a Predatory Unitary Hindu State, Nepal." In Dhruba Kumar (ed) *Domectic Conflict and crisis of Governability in Nepal.* (Kathmandu: CNAS, 2001).
41. Lok Raj Baral, Krishna Hachhethu and Hari Sharma. *Leadership in Nepal.* (Delhi: Adroit Publishers, 2001), p. 19.
42. The literacy rate of Bahun, Newar and Chhetri is 58, 55 and 42 per cent respectively but for *Janajati, Madheshi* and *Dalit* the figure of literacy rate goes down to 35, 27 and 23 per cent respectively. Similarly among the graduates of Nepal, Bahun constitutes 44 per cent, followed by Newar's 31 per cent and Chhetri's 14 per cent. Such figure for *Janajati, Madheshi and dalit* is 2, 11, and 0.2 percent respectively (Gurung: 1998, 121).
43. Krishna Hachhethu, *Party Building in Nepal: Organisation, Leadership and People.*

(Kathmandu: Mandala Book Point, 2002), p. 91.

44. "Full text of the decisions of the SPA-Maoist summit meeting." www.nepalnews.com/archive/2006/nov/nov08/Full-_text_summit_meeting.php.
45. "Historic Agreement Fails to Woo Janajatis." *Himalayan Times.* November 09, 2006.
46. The letter, dated November 16, 2006, is posted at http://nefin.org.np
47. "NEFIN wants due berth in statute draft," *Himalayan Times,* July 13, 2006.

6. Marxists' Democratic Problematic and the Decline of the Left in West Bengal*

Harihar Bhattacharyya

"…..if *Panchayats* fail, the CPM experiment fails"
— Asoke Mitra, 1987[1]

Introduction

It is now almost common political knowledge for those concerned about the left regime in West Bengal (1977-2001), and its dramatic decline in 2011 that the indications of such an impasse were being gradually clear from 2008 when the then ruling Left Front comprising a host of Marxist and leftist parties under the dominance of the CPI-M had to concede about half the political ground to the opposition at the Gram Panchayat (lowest tier of the three tier rural self-governing bodies) level. The significant cracks in the grassroots were followed in urban grass root institutions such as Municipalities through to 2009 and 2010. In the Lok Sabha elections in 2009, the left was almost swept! Students of political change might discern the logic of political transition in the above, a subject that remains understudied in political scientific accounts, which seems to take place like successive earthquakes in the seismic scale. Our purpose here is different. Keeping in mind the forewarning made by Mr Asoke Mitra, the first former Finance Minister of Left Front Government in West Bengal, we seek to raise basically two questions about the Bengal left's, or for that matter, the Indian Left's – democratic problematic and the associated question of its approach to and role in representative political institutions. We seek to raise such questions at the grassroots of the regime because it was at that level that the level of popular mandate had usually been quite high, hardly below 80 per cent. We also need to keep in mind that had been the scenario for many elections since the late 1970s in West Bengal. That leads to another apparent paradox, namely, the gap, nay, opposition between massive electoral mobilisation, on the one hand, and the near absence of democratic institutionalisation, which is a complex process itself, but which received at best a left handed compliment, if not total neglect, by the then left alliance dominated by the CPI-M in power, on the other. The result has been predictable – a somewhat primitive control over such institutions by inner party mechanisms, as we will explore below soon, has taken the place of any serious attempt at democratic institutionalisation[2], a process and method of institutionally involving the people, and the elected ordinary members in the process of decision-taking and implementation, as endurable bases of social support of the socially underprivileged around the representative bodies, and the movement and the party beyond it, if at all.[3] So, the left's decline was both democratic and institutional at the same time. Despite the wishes of the party to do otherwise, the malaise is rooted in the poverty of theory itself as far as democracy and the running of democratic institutions are concerned.

Before we move on, we must make it clear that if the Left thought that democracy meant winning elections and securing a majority at the representative bodies, they must have been wrong, or at best, expressing only a half truth regarding democracy. The standard theoretical prejudice of the Left has since Karl Marx's times been, as we will examine shortly, that there could be either a liberal (capitalist), or a 'socialist' democracy. But for all practical purpose, the Left held (and perhaps still continues to hold) a very old-fashioned notion of democracy, which is otherwise called, condescendingly, 'winners take it all' democracy.[4] As Kaviraj has rightly and forcefully argued, winning elections is only the beginning, not the end; of democracy since democracy has much deeper meaning and significance, and possibilities, moral and political.[5] If one is a dogmatist protagonist of the Left, especially of the CPI-M, who refuses to read writings on the walls since Marx's times, one could parade the election of the vast majority of the poor, illiterate and poverty-stricken to the representative bodies as a proof enough of democracy! The official reports of the functioning of the Panchayats since 1978 in West Bengal, and many empirically-based academic studies of the same[6] seem to suggest otherwise. A total lack of any idea of self-government was noted quite early on among Panchayat functionaries in the State, to give but one example; many academic studies have shown clearly that a nearly total lack of any regard for the sanctity of the institutional and formal democratic aspects of the representative bodies in respect of properly holding meetings, allowing the voice of the elected ones, let alone differing ones, adequate political literacy for running such bodies and so on reigned supreme because party majority saw to it that those 'institutional formalities' could be subverted at ease. Otherwise, one could not explain a near total rout of the Left from Bengal after decades of an 'experiment'; one would ponder over how long it requires for such bodies to become truly the popular platform of the people, a public space, so to say, in an open competitive multi-party democratic system, unlike the former USSR. From this, one should not jump to the conclusion that the Left was ill-motivated to misuse such institutional space for some evil purposes. On the contrary, it was thanks to the Left that 'democratic process' in the sense of multi-party and free electoral competition, was properly re-introduced at the State and the grassroots in the post-Emergency period (1975-77); the Left was also to be credited for holding regular elections to representative bodies at different levels; they must also be given good marks for carrying through land reforms, which are yet to be carried out in many States in India. The point that is driven home here is theoretical, in the democratic and institutional sense of the term. The argument that is being made is that the Left, especially the CPI-M, has got a faulty theoretical understanding of the above two phenomena. Or, to put it differently, perhaps it does not have any theory at all! The following sections take up those issues for further examination.

CPI-M's Discourse of Democracy

The party has seldom undertaken any serious exercise in fully stating its theoretical position on democracy and democratic institutions except indicating, in its pragammatic statements that the party would take an instrumentalist position on them as part of its strategy of People's Democratic Revolution, an idea rooted in the Comintern debates in the 1920s. When understood in the Indian context, it meant for the party to take part in the constitutional democratic process including elections at all levels of the polity, and even forming governments at State levels within the Indian federation (under Article 112 of the old Constitution of the Party; dropped since 2000!). The rationale of such an exercise, according to the party's understanding, was to make use of all available space within the constitutional democracy of India, and thus, to complete the incomplete 'bourgeois revolution' in India. It was thought that as a result of forming such governments, which would be used, the working classes would be inspired, and made conscious of the need for a fundamental transformation.[7] Since the party termed the existing state in India as 'bourgeois-landlord', the party's special paradox was the question of primacy between the party and the government or administration, which Nossiter called 'the cart and the horses' problem'.[8] What is being argued here is that those ministry-movement dialectics is but the symptom of the deeply-rooted theoretical problem of not having any creative approach to democratic and representative institutions as far as the communist parties in India are concerned.

We now turn our attention for a while to a book titled 'Marxism and Democracy' (1993) edited by two CPI-M leaders, which is but a collection of articles penned by higher level party leaders including late Jyoti Basu, and E. M. S Nambudripad plus Appendices on excerpts from the writings on democracy by Marx, Engels, Lenin and Stalin on democracy, and so on. This collection can be accepted to be an authoritative text of the CPI-M's discourse on democracy. In the very Foreword to the book, late Sailen Das Gupta (then Secretary of the West Bengal State Committee of the CPI-M, and later Chairman of the Left Front) stated the obvious that the conventional Marxists have been stating over the last one century and a half:

Democracy is not a new invention of the bourgeoisie. From the early days of the Greek city states to the present age, democracy has meant different things to different people. But none of the theoretical postulate or practices has been devoid of class content.[9]

In the very introductory chapter titled 'Democracy and Marxism', the conventional and somewhat mechanical Marxist position is stated in greater detail with suitable quotes from the founders and Lenin and Stalin. The fundamental contribution of Karl Marx to the concept of democracy, it is believed, consisted in pointing out the class content, or essence of democracy. Retaining the old dogmatic label 'bourgeois democracy', it was asserted: "Most features of bourgeois democracy – constitutionalism, universal suffrage, parliament, jury, the system of local self-government bodies, the official personal freedom – are resulted from the struggle of the masses."[10]

That democracy was a form of the state; that 'bourgeois democracy' was organically linked with the rise and fall of capitalism, from its progressive to reactionary forms; that the capitalists endangered their own democracy; and that 'democracy can only be guaranteed in a socialist state with the dictatorship of the proletariat'...[11], and so on and so forth are restated without an inch of any critical faculty exercised about the historical specificity of the phenomenon of democracy in a country such as India, as perhaps elsewhere, as Kaviraj[12] has well argued.

Further on, Biswas and Bera[13] felt tempted to quote from Stalin ('Concerning Questions of Leninism') in order to make the party's, or the

Marxists' 'theoretical' position on democracy clearer: "(a) Although the party carried out the dictatorship of the proletariat and in this sense the dictatorship of the proletariat is, in essence, the dictatorship of the party, this does not mean that the dictatorship of the party (its leading role) is identical with the dictatorship of the proletariat.... (b) Not a single important decision is arrived at by the mass organizations of the proletariat without guiding directives from the party..., and (c) The party exercises the dictatorship of the proletariat. The party is the direct governing vanguard of the proletariat...In this sense, the party takes power, that the party governs the country".[14]

The readers perhaps cannot take anything more along the lines depicted regarding the party's understanding of democracy. Shorn of all shibboleths, it was hard, if not impossible, to digest, the ideas that 'dictatorship' (whether of the angles or of the devils) could be democracy, and second, a party (in this case the Communist Party of course) is nearly equal to the state form, and governs the whole country, etc. The cynicism and criticality that the founders of Marxism reserved for democracy and the highly context-bound nature of their many concepts including 'dictatorship of the proletariat' (which was hardly ever made equal to the party dictatorship by Marx and Engels, and much less theorised by them as such).[15]

The Party's Discourse on Running the Representative Institutions and its Effects

Given the above understanding of the party about democracy and representative institutions, it would not perhaps be surprising at all to understand the operative discourse of the party in running the elected governing bodies within the so-called 'bourgeois' democratic edifice in India. I will pay attention, in particular, to rural representative institutions known in India as Panchayats. In running such institutions, the CPI-M developed its own inner party mechanisms: Party Directives (on a regular basis), Party Letters; and above all parallel Party Sub-Committees to that of the institutions they were and are still in charge, electorally speaking. In one such West Bengal State Committee level 'Directives', the party 'political objective' was explained at some length: "This does not mean acting at will. It means activation of Panchayats in accordance with the principles and ideals of the party. The basic issue involved here is giving party leadership to Panchayats. This leadership consists of (a) political leadership, and (b) Organisational leadership. The political leadership of the party is established only when people in their own experience accept the political perspective of the party as their own.... The party has a definite aim. Panchayat activities should be conducted in such a way that they conform to the basic goals of the party.[16] "Accordingly, the thee-tier Panchayats are to be run like this. Since there is Panchayat Sub-Committees at each level: all elected party members of Panchayat Samiti, and Zilla Parishad will act under the respective committees. Generally, the local and zonal committees of the party will look after the Gram Panchayats and Samitis respectively. The final decision at each level will be taken by *Parichalan* ('Guide' in literal rendering) Committee (read Sub-Committee) of the party although the elected members may offer recommendations".[17]

Now, let us take a look at how the above State level 'directives' could be taken down the distinct level. To give some evidences from inner party sources from the district of (Bardhaman/Burdwan):

- The party has clear directives about the way a revolutionary party should use and utilise these Panchayats. [emphasis is added]
- We have absolute control over the three-tier Panchayats (emphasis added) in this district. The District Committee has definite directions. They have been sent to all zonal and local committees. The District Panchayat Sub-Committee regular meets to direct the Panchayats. It is the District Committee and the Secretariat which take all the important decisions regarding the Panchayats. On the whole, the District, Zonal and Local Committees have control and vigilance over Panchayats.
- In running the Gram Panchayats, the decisions of the Sub-Committee are final. As a result, the ordinary members of the Panchayats do not feel encouraged to attend meetings. They lose all interest in attending any meeting. Their voice is not heard and reflected in the Panchayats. Many think it is the duty of the Prodhan (Sarpanch) to involve the people with the Panchayats. These create difficulties.
- That the activities of the Panchayats will be performed by elected members of Panchayats alone is the outlook which is opposed to the long-term political objective of the party. In order to transform Panchayats into weapons of struggle against vested interests, and to utilise them in further developing class struggle, what is necessary is strong party control over Panchayats (emphasis added), collective discussion and leadership, and regular check up of Panchayat activities in party committee meetings.[18]

Such inner party documentary sources could be mentioned ad infinitum. In other writings of mine on the Panchayats, I have given some further evidences.[19]

Before we return to the theoretical question that we began with, a few comments are here in order to highlight the effects of the party's discourse on running representative institutions, as described above. Michel Foucault asserted that power and its exercise is always accompanied by some discourses of truth; he also said that exercise of power produces its effects. In my 'Micro-Foundations of Bengal Communism' (1998), I emphasised the point that the party's (CPI-M) mode of exercise of power was modernist because it entailed external control over institutions and societies. I also pointed out, on the basis of many empirical studies of the working of Panchayats in West Bengal since the 1990s the nearly little or no role of the poorer sections of society elected to Panchayats on the party's tickets. But personal discussion with Sudipta Kaviraj, a leading political theorist today, over the last few years about the findings of my work, and his own writings, especially 'The Enchantment of Democracy and India' (2011) seem to confirm that the party's 'primitive control' over such democratic bodies should be read not as 'socialist' but of a pre-modern variety[20], an effect once again of having no a theory of democracy as far as the party, or conventional Marxism in India, is concerned. Ironically, the party's inner party sources show that the above 'directives' of the party have not worked the way they were intended, and the party itself was self-critical of many blemishes. Consider the academic assessment of a western academic study: It is one thing to create decentralised institutions; it is another for those institutions genuinely to become the vehicles for the majority interest, the mass of the poor villagers and to facilitate a qualitative transformation of both the political and condition.[21]

In most western, in particular, Scandinavian, academic accounts of West Bengal Panchayats, the role of Panchayats as programme implementing agency of the government, that is, its developmental role, has received more attention than its self-governance aspect.[22] Even there the picture was found much to be desired. We have noticed above that in the party's understanding, the constitutional aspects, or obligations, in particular, pertaining to the provisions of the 73rd Amendment Act 1992 did not figure at all, which sought to develop Panchayats as institutions of self-government for the villagers.

Reading through the inner party sources carefully, one will notice that the activities of the Panchayats as well as of other such bodies at higher and lower levels, have been discussed and examined, and some self-criticisms have also been undertaken. Consider the following:

- We must involve the people irrespective of all classes and creed in the activities of the Panchayats. The people of the area must be made aware that it is their money and work. They will decide upon the priority of expenditure and implementation of development work.
- If everything is concentrated in the hands of a few and people are kept in the dark, then even honest operation will also arouse suspicion in the eyes of the people.
- We cannot expect those who do take part in decisions to carry out decisions. The process of decisions must start from the people.[23]

The passage from another state committee level inner party source titled 'Panchayat Parichalanona Samparkei Parjyalochona' (in Bengali) is even more candid: There is even indifference in involving in decision-taking and Panchayat activities those elected on CPI-M party ticket, let alone the common people of the area. Decisions are at best kept at the level of merely information. Regarding women, no progress has been noticed in their participation at all. There are complaints regarding opposition members not taken into consideration in matters of purchase committee or beneficiary committee; maintaining contractorship in fictitious names; lack of transparency; and even corruption by the party or a group within it...[24]

Gram Sansad and Civic Participation: Party's Instrumentalisation

Since 1994, a novel institutional platform, an assembly of all eligible voters of each Constituency of Gram Panchayats, was introduced in West Bengal, as a truly grassroots self-governing body. It was designed to act as a kind of village parliament, which is to hold two meetings a year, one half-yearly (May) and one annually (November), to approve the activities of the Panchayats (or not); such as budget and accounts, proposed planning, and so on. As distinguished from the Panchayats, which is after all a case of representative body, Gram Sansad is an instance of a grassroots body at the lowest level of the village, and a training ground for civic participation by the villagers. Since I have examined its effectiveness elsewhere,[25] as above, here I will only refer to its limitations following from the externally imposed control by the party which have grossly discouraged the common citizen voters of the village from taking part in it who have tended to take it as a party platform, and hence to be avoided![26]

Two caveats here are in order – first, representative democracy per se does not guarantee civic participation which is so essential, as Putnam et al [1993][27] said, for the working of democratic institutions, and therefore, a grassroots corporate body of the kind of Gram Sansad could ensure civic participation in making Panchayat work,[28] and second, unlike the now desiccated modernisation theories, we need to give up the idea of the civic to be associated with the urban and the industrial only; instead we should rethink our community resources and re-assess their implications for democracy.

In this connection, I am tempted to quote a passage from Nelson Mandela's now classic Long Walk to Freedom (1994). Describing the features and democratic elements in the tribal tradition to which he belongs in South Africa, and referring, in particular to village level meetings, he said, "Everyone who wanted to speak did so. It was democracy in the purest form. There may be hierarchy of importance among the speakers, but everyone was heard, chief and subject, warrior and medicine man, shopkeeper and farmer, landowner and labourer. People spoke without interruption and lasted for many hours. The foundation of self-government was that all men were free to voice their opinions and equal in their value as citizens."[29] He also said, "The meetings would continue until some kind of consensus was reached. They ended in unanimity or not at all. Unanimity, however, might be an agreement to disagree, to wait for a more propitious time to propose a solution. Democracy meant all were to be heard and a decision was taken as a people. Majority rule was a foreign notion. A minority was not to be crushed by a majority."[30]

These lines of Mandela give us indications enough about the need to rethink our categories of democracy, and also the rural/tribal community resources for the making of a civic life.

What then has happened to our Gram Sansad? How effective has it been for the purpose for which it was constitutionally and politically designed? Within the space available and the fact that I have examined it elsewhere, I shall very briefly touch upon the subject. Despite the CPI-M's operational guidelines for the working of the Gram Sansad[31] to involve the common people, to make it transparent, and the party's emphasis on its regular functioning, the party's political motive seemed to have nonetheless stood in the way of its full-form functioning so much so that such bodies, in the party's own inner party assessment, have turned out to be merely a political ritual, and very often violative of the constitutional stipulations. First, in many cases, regular Sansad meetings are not held the way it should have been held. Second, in most cases, as per official records,[32] 10 per cent requirements of quorum have been found to be difficult to achieve, and if achieved at all, it has been so done by merely collecting signatures subsequently. Third, the common villagers are also not aware of the existence and importance of such bodies; and little efforts have been made to make them so. Consider the official statement on the issue: "The main issue is that people in general are not interested in the affairs of Panchayats, except for election, when on average around 85-90 per cent vote. On the contrary, only 10-12 per cent of these voters usually attend a Gram Sansad meeting. This indicates the aversion of the common people towards these meetings".[33]

In my earlier assessment of the failure of Gram Sansads in West Bengal,[34] I pointed out that the main reason was organisational, to be more precise, the vexed question of the party's relation with democratic institutions such as Panchayats, or Gram Sansads. To put it differently, it was the party's 'political theory' that recognises the party as the fundamental agency of social transformation, and its corollary, the notion of subservience and subordination of the representative institutions to the authority of the omnipotent party. When compared with the exclusionary limits of the so-called Athenian democracy[35] that had flourished in ancient Greece, the Gram Sansads in West Bengal were better designed, institutionally speaking, as an assembly of all citizens irrespective of caste, colour or creed. But the detailed empirical studies of such institutions suggest that could have been possible only when these are free from the overarching control of the party in power[36]. In other words, these institutions are to be allowed to work freely, without external control and interference, for creating the real basis of civic participation, something that was hard to achieve given the political theoretical neglect of the issue as such in the CPI-M's democracy discourse. No wonder, Neil Harding aptly remarked that 'one of the principal factors for the discrediting of communism was its neglect of meaningful democracy'.[37]

Conclusion: Poverty of Theory

From the above discussion of the CPI-M's discourse of democracy, to be more exact, of the operational dynamics of running the representative bodies – in other words, the discourse of power, to follow Michel Foucault – has turned out to be anti-democratic and anti-institutional in implications. The question is: Why is this so? We can raise this question because the party and its movements in India have fought for democracy, civil rights, ethnic rights, and so on in different parts of India at different times. Then why this happens that when the party was elected for more than three decades to run a state level administration in India and also the levels below, neither democracy nor the representative bodies developed and flourished? Of course, a full-length examination of this complex issue cannot be taken up here. But it is possible within the space available to indicate and highlight some of the deep-seated theoretical problems of Marxism in respect of democracy and institutions. For Kaviraj (2011), the problem is historical in the sense that democracy has different trajectories, and developed unevenly across different historical settings.[38] He argues that democracy in India has evolved and become successful in 'unrecognised forms'.[39] In other words, democracy in India has become successful, he argues, as a peculiar case, which means not as something unique, because all cases of successes of democracy are peculiar.[40] So, the theoretical point that can be made here, following Kaviraj (2011), is that Marxism as such is skeptical about the prospect of democracy, and Marx's views on the subject smack of his reading of the nineteenth century Europe of private property-based liberal constitutionalism',[41] the reason why Marx preferred to call it, condescendingly, 'bourgeois democracy'. Marxism, especially classical Marxism's theoretical unease with the issue of democracy,[42] as was being manifest at his times with such features as universal suffrage, civil rights, limited government, and the rule of law, was pointed out by other scholars too.[43] Lukes, for instance argued, that there was evolution in Marx's attitude to democracy, for Marx in his earliest writings was more committed to direct democracy, and a Rousseauesque critique of the principle of representation.[44] Lukes also observed 'contradictory possibilities' in Marx's assessment of 'bourgeois democracy' in his later writings.[45] In my investigations of the issue (1997), I attempted to show that Marx was trying to give shape to an alternative notion of democracy, called 'social republic', based on the experience of the Paris Commune of the 1870s, but then his statist orientation in respect of democracy seemed to have co-existed with his anti-state political theory.[46]

Leninist notion of democracy was no better in this regard because he followed in the footsteps of Marx without the former's skeptical attitude and more open-endedness towards democracy and institutions though holding on to the same statist and instrumentalist notion of democracy. In other words, democracy for the classical founders remained 'real people's power' without the state (or better on its abolition!) and without institutions, by implications. The more pertinent issues that modernity has thrown for us, namely, power and its exercise, bureaucracy's unavoidable omnipotence, individualism, liberty, human rights, protection of the environment, sustainable development, gender equality, ethnic conflicts, social hierarchies of sorts, media, communications revolutions and so on vis-a-vis democracy. Democracy's relations with them is too complex and its role there too unpredictable. What the Marxists have since Marx's times failed to understand is the power of democracy, and its consequences. Democracy in our times (Anthony Giddens calls 'reflexive society'[47]) is far removed from Karl Marx's or Lenin's times. Finally, even though Antonio Gramsci (1971)[48] sought to rescue and revise classical Marxist position on democracy and institutions, to some extent, by highlighting, in some original way, the importance of consent in civil society, and the feelings and common sense of the masses, something to which the party-centred and statist Marxism so far had hardly paid any attention, today's world has moved farther on. Finally, drawing on the notion of 'peculiarities' that Kaviraj has emphasised in his critical and original reflections on democracy worldwide, and in particular on India, it may be argued that such peculiarities are not to be taken as the sign of deviation of democracy, as there is no ideal model of democracy to emulate. Democracy rethinking in the twenty-first century and beyond needs to look for the innovations that such 'peculiarities' have brought forth for the welfare of most, if not all, members of society, especially the underprivileged. This can alone be done when such efforts do not leave out for considerations the societal/communitarian resources to build on for a living link with the people. The Marxists, however, can ignore only at their peril the question of efficacy of their deep-rooted belief in the omnipotence of the Communist Party vis-a-vis democracy today

Notes

1. Quoted in Atul Kohli, *The State and Poverty in India*, (Cambridge: Cambridge University Press), 1987, p. 109.
2. By the expression, 'social institutionalisation', as institutionalisation, as is generally understood in standard political science writings (e.g., Samuel P. Huntington, *Political Order in Changing Societies*, 1968), the attention is drawn here to the social bases of this process so that wider sections of societies are made aware of the institutional dimension, norms and conventions that are demanded of in running democratically elected governing bodies. Once this is done, a basis is created for an organic link between the people and the institutions, which the people can take as their own. This requires further theoretical

reflections which I reserve for another writings due to lack of space here.

3. Harihar Bhattacharyya, Communism in Tripura, (Delhi: Ajanta Books International, 1998); Harihar Bhattacharyya, "Democracy and Rural Governance in West Bengal since 1978" in *India Politics and Society: Today and Tomorrow (Essays in Honour of Professor Amal Kumar Mukhopadhyay)* edited by Sobhanlal Datta Gupta, (Calcutta: K. P. Bagchi and Co, 1998), pp. 198-227. Harihar Bhattacharyya, *Making Local Democracy Work in India: Social Capital, Politics and Governance in West Bengal*, (New Delhi: Vedams Bookts Ltd., 2002); Harihar Bhattacharyya, "Approaches to Local Government: Arguing a Case for Human Rights", *The West Bengal Political Science Review*, 10 (2), July-December 2007, pp. 1-14.
4. A. Lijphart, *Democracies*, (Westfort, Mass: Yale University Press, 1984), for a detailed examination of some 21 democratic countries, and the many pitfalls of majoritarian rule across the globe.
5. Sudipta Kaviraj, *The Enchantment of Democracy and India*, (New Delhi: Permanent Black, 2011). See Introduction, pp. 1-25.
6. For the first official report on West Bengal Panchayats, see Nirmal Mukerjee and D. Bandopadhyay, "New Horizons of West Bengal Panchayats", (1993) in *Decentralization: Panchayats in the Nineties* edited by Amitava Mukherjee, (New Delhi: Vikash Publishing House, 1994), pp. 214-262.
7. See Harihar Bhattacharyya, *Communism in Tripura*, (Delhi: Ajanta, 1999), pp. 234-35 for further elaboration.
8. The so-called 'cart and the horses problem' have differentially stood in the way of smooth functioning of the Marxist-led State governments in India, and in many cases served to produce effects to cripple the party and the movement. To cite one example from the case of Tripura, only surviving Marxist led State level government in India: 'In this state, the Communist Party organization is not the determinant of the Ministry. The Ministry, on the other hand, is the determinant of policy, government and party. The result is excessive dependence on the administrative-bureaucratic-police apparatus, and the reduction of the importance of the party'. (One political commentator of Tripura) (Bhattacharyya 1999: 235). The State Party's understanding in its 12th Party Congress in 1985 corroborated the above observation. The inner party source wrote: 'We must keep in mind that not dependence on government but its *use* as an important instrument of struggle of the people is the correct policy.' [Bhattacharyya 1999: 235] Interestingly enough, to make the ministry more effective in the second term, 7 out of 8 State Secretariat members were made ministers in Tripura. The party's explanation was that although it had strained the organisational resources, 'but this step was required to instill confidence in the people about the government'. (Bhattacharyya 1999: 235] Rather than halting the process, it had continued unabated. In the 1988 State Assembly elections, "practically the entire leadership" were "fighting the election as candidates", and as I have argued [Bhattacharyya 1999: 245], as a result, the state level leadership failed to provide guidance and co-ordination during the critical time after the deployment of the Army and the Congress (I) offensive. This was one major instance of the debilitating effect of the 'marxist ministry' on the movement, and also the consequence of the communist movement had to suffer in

the wake of its near total immersion in electoral politics. [Bhattacharyya 1999: 235]. My 'Micro-Foundations of Bengal Communism' (1998) contains micro level empirical and organisational data to prove the same point more poignantly of the so-called 'the cart and the horse problem'. But we will discuss it later in the article. The Kerala experiment which T. J. Nossiter (1982) has discussed at length did not show any different picture.

9. Anil Biswas and Anjan Bera eds. *Marxism and Democracy*: (National Book Agency Pvt. Ltd., : 1993), p: 1
10. Biswas and Bera 1993, p. 3.
11. Biswas and Bera, 1993, p. 5.
12. Kaviraj 2011, pp. 1-24.
13. Biswas and Bera, 1993, pp. 8-9.
14. The excerpts, appended to the book 'Marxism and Democracy' referred to above edited by Biswas and Bera (1993), especially those of Marx, Engels and Lenin, are a testimony to the party's reading of the issue of democracy in India, or West Bengal, in the light of what has happened in Europe, and what the founders said about them. One wonders if the elected members of local self-governing bodies, or today's 'Marxist' Members of Legislative Assembly, would be able to read his or her understanding of democracy that way, and also whether that would be the right thing to do today. (For further details, see Biswas and Bera 1993, p. 8).
15. Interestingly enough, even Lenin in his famous *The State and Revolution* (1917) did indeed try to visualize the rule by the proletariat after the revolution as a makeshift arrangement far removed from the one the former USSR experienced subsequently at its great peril though. Also, in Marx's conceptualization of the dictatorship of the proletariat first in his letter to his friend Joseph Wedemeyer (dated London March 5, 1852) did not mention even for once the party, let alone its all pervasive role. [*Marx-Engels Selected Correspondence*, 1975/1955, p. 64].
16. Quoted in Bhattacharyya, "Democracy and Rural Governance in West Bengal since 1978", 1998, p. 230.
17. Quoted in Ibid., 1998: 230.
18. Quoted in Ibid., p. 231.
19. Harihar Bhattacharyya, *Communism in Tripura*, 1999; Harihar Bhattacharyya: 2002; Harihar Bhattacharyya, *Micro-Foundations of Bengal Communism*, Delhi: Ajanta, 1998; Harihar Bhattacharyya *India as a Multicultural Federation: Asian Values, Democracy and Decentralization (In Comparison with Swiss Federalism)*, (Fribourg: Institute of Federalism, 2001).
20. Commenting on the consequences of power-change in the wake of democratic transformation, Kaviraj (2011) said that as a result of the belief of the radicals that 'once there is a new class of holders, there is nothing more to worry about in political life' (p. 22). And when this is the case, he argues that "[T]his leads often to a relapse into pre-modern forms of political control, and to their misleading defence as a post-bourgeois form' (p. 22).
21 Neil Webster, *Panchayati Raj and the Decentralization of Development Planning in West Bengal,* (Calcutta: K. P. Bagchi & Co., 1992), p. 36.

22. Webster, 1992; G. K. Lieten, *Devolution, Development and Democracy: Village Discourse in West Bengal*, (New Delhi: Sage Publications, 1996); Kohli 1987 & *Democracy and Discontent: India's Growing Crisis of Governability*,(Cambridge: Cambridge University Press, 1990); Harihar Bhattacharyya (1998; 1999; 2001; 2005 and 2007).
23. Harihar Bhattacharya, "Democracy and Rural Governance in West Bengal since 1978" in *India: Politics and Society: Today and Tomorrow (Essays in Honour of Professor Amol Kumar Mukhopadhyay)*, edited by S. Datta Gupta, (Calcutta: K.P. Bagchi and Co., 1998), pp..230-31.
24. CPI-M State Committee, *Party Chithi Sankalan* (Compilation of party Letters) (in Bengali) (Unpublished), 1998, p. 229.
25. Harihar Bhattacharyya, "Grass-roots Democracy and Civic Participation in Rural West Bengal: The Case of Gram Sansad", in *Theme India: Essay in Honour of Late Prof Prasanta Kr Ghosh* edited by D. Sen Gupta and S. Ganguly, (Kolkata: Arambag Book House, 2005), pp. 63-76.
26. The empirical studies of the districts of West Bengal confirm that in many cases the people coming to attend the Sansad meetings come with the respective flags of the parties they belong to.
27. Robert Putnam et al eds. *Making Democracy Work: Civic Traditions in Modern Italy*, (New Jersey: Princeton University Press, 1993).
28. Bhattacharyya (2002).
29. Nelson Mandela, *Long Walk to Freedom*, (London: The Little, Brown and Company: 1994, p. 34.
30. Mandela 1994, p. 35.
31. Bhattacharyya 2005, p. 69.
32. Data furnished by the State Institute for Panchayat and Rural Development (SIPRD), Kalayni, 2002-03 & SIPRD 2011.
33. SIPRD 2011.
34. Bhattacharyya 2005, pp. 73-74.
35. Simon Hornblower, "Creation and Development of Democratic Institutions in Ancient Greece", in *Democracy: The Unfinished Journey (508 BC to AD 1993)* edited John Dunn, (Oxford: Oxford University Press, 1992), p. 12.
36. Harihar Bhattacharyya, *Making Local Democracy Work….* 2002 and " The CPI-M: From rebellion to Governance" in *Political Parties in South Asia* edited Subrata K Mitra, Myke Enskat and Clemens Spiess, Westport, CT: Prager, 2004, pp. 76-103.
37. Neil Harding, "The Marxist-Leninist Detour", in *Democracy: The Unfinished Journey (508 BC to 1993 AD)* edited John Dunn, (Oxford: Oxford University Press, 1993), p. 155.
38. Kaviraj, 2011, p. 8.
39. Kaviraj 2011, p. 22.
40. Kaviraj 2011, p. 13-23
41. Kaviraj 2011, p. 6.
42. Christopher Pierson in his *Marxist Theory and Democratic Politics*, (Oxford: Polity, 1986) brings out a detailed critical examination of the Marxist tradition on the subject, and identified the limitations and weaknesses in the same in developing a coherent theory

of democracy. From his account too, the historical context-bound reading of Marx of developing democratic institutions in the West, especially Europe, are clear too.

43. The theoretical exploration of Marxism's relation to democracy is still limited. See for some knowledge, Alan Hunt, ed. *Marxism and Democracy*, London: Lawrence and Wishart, 1980; Ralph Miliband, *Marxism and Politics*, (Oxford: Oxford University Press, 1977); Steven Lukes, "Democracy" in *A Dictionary of Marxist Thought* edited Tom Bottomore et al, (Oxford: Basil Blackwell, 1983), pp. 114-115.
44. Lukes 1983, p. 114.
45. Lukes 1983, p. 114.
46. Harihar Bhattacharyya, "Rethinking Democracy: Marx's Concept of Social Republic", in *Perspectives in Political Science*, (Burdwan: Academic Staff College, Burdwan University, 1997), p. 134.
47. Anthony Giddens, *Beyond Left and Right: The Future of radical Politics*, (Cambridge: Polity Press, 1994).
48. A. Gramsci, *Selections from Prison Notebooks* (London: Lawrence and Wishart, 1971). His special emphasis on the issues of consent, national-popular, people-nation, hegemony, civil society and so was indicative of the shifts in his thinking on the relation of democracy and society and from the conventional statist notion of the same.

* The author wishes to thank Professor Sobhanlal Datta Gupta for reading an initial draft of the paper and offering comments, which helped improve the draft.

7. Crossroads: Democracy and the Turkish Model

Anita Sengupta

In the aftermath of the events in Egypt and other Middle Eastern countries in February-March 2011, expectations were once again raised that Turkey would serve as a moderate 'democratic' model that would be emulated by these states.[1] There was speculation that the 'Turkish Model' was being studied by those seeking reform and a change of regime in Egypt. Projection of the model as 'moderate' and 'useful' was made from divergent viewpoints and by actors with very varied understanding of the model. As an useful alternative strategy that is put forward by the West as a counterbalance in the face of initiatives that could prove to be detrimental to their interests in the region, the model was projected as an alternative in the face of the specter of the success of the Muslim Brotherhood in Egypt. Representatives of the Muslim Brotherhood, on the other hand, stated that the 'moderation' of the Turkish AKP represented a model for the Egyptian Islamic Movement.[2] This was followed by the comment of Namik Tan, the Turkish Ambassador in Washington, that Turkey was unique in the Muslim world to have a parliamentary system and a functioning free market adding that the country might be an 'inspiration' for the Middle Eastern countries.[3] Tan went on to note that Turkey always had close relations with its immediate region. This has been supported by the fact that the Turkish Prime Minister Recep Tayyip Erdogan and President Abdullah Gul had publicly urged the Egyptian President Hosni Mubarak to resign. Also Turkey's attack on Israel over the last two years has made Erdogan the most popular leader on the 'Arab streets', and there is a renewed Turkish interest in its Middle Eastern neighbourhood.

Turkey's position, of course, has not been without criticism. It has been noted that Turkey's main aim has been to improve relations with countries in the Middle East in the course of a policy of 'zero-problems' with neighbouring countries through improving dialogue, commercial ties and acting as a mediator. As a result Turkey's foreign policy has prioritised rapprochement in its neighbourhood and support for human rights and 'democracy' has not been unconditional.[4] For instance, it is being argued that the Turkish Prime Minister's celebration of democracy in Egypt lacks credibility, since the Turkish leadership had displayed no concern for democratic reform when mass protests were suppressed in Iran after the elections in 2009. The concern seems to be in cases where the Islamists are in opposition, contrary to expectations of a 'democratic' pulse as the principle motivating factor. Similarly, Turkey has abstained from publicly condemning Colonel Qaddafi's position and has been opposed to the imposition of sanctions and military measures.[5] Turkish diplomacy towards the Libya crisis ended with the evacuation of a majority of its citizens from Libya and extending help to the US and other countries in the evacuation operations. Turkey's position in Libya is rooted in its significant investments in the country and the fact that a large number of Turkish citizens are working and doing business in Libya.[6] The expanding domestic economic interests and regional dynamism represented by business constituencies that support the ruling AKP has seen the emergence of new Anatolian businesses competing against the traditional metropolitan businesses in western Turkey. These have acted as strong advocates for further Turkish expansion into the Middle East rather than European markets. And, it has been noted, Turkey was mindful of these interests and investments when Ankara's stand towards Libya was formulated.[7]

However, it can be argued that irrespective of the country's record of support for democracy abroad, Turkey constitutes a model due to its own democratic record and level of economic success in recent years. The representation of Turkey as a model of democracy within Islam is not new. The Bush administration presented Turkey as a model within the framework of the Greater Middle East initiative. This image is supported by the AKP which portrays itself as a 'conservative democratic' party which is politically and economically liberal while being sensitive to certain societal values and traditions. There is a tendency to read the current experiment in Turkey as the successful political integration of an Islamic movement within democracy. This has, however, raised questions about whether the AKP's denial of its Islamic connection is simply a compromise between the state and the AKP, or whether it indicates the ability of the Turkish system to transform political Islam.[8] The political opposition within Turkey, however, disputes this image and there is a debate on the 'moderation' of the AKP regime particularly with the arrest and implication of a large number of individuals in what is termed as the 'Ergenekon' affair.[9] This has brought into question Turkey's commitment to 'democratic ideals', a commitment that is being increasingly stressed upon by the European Union.

Despite such contradictions, however, an interesting analogy is being made based on the fact that just as Kemal Ataturk had once been the inspiration for mid-twentieth century Middle Eastern modernizers like the Egyptian President Gamal Nasser and Anwar Sadat or Tunisia's first President Habib Bourgiba, the current Turkish Prime Minister, who has claimed success as a modernizer with significant economic progress during his tenure and the success of the policies of the AKP, are being cited as suitable examples for emulation. Pro-government commentators in the Turkish media have argued that what is happening in North Africa, which is popular uprisings against authoritarian 'secularist' states, is another version of what has recently happened in Turkey, where a popular Islamic force represented by the AKP defeated an 'authoritarian' state structure. This in its turn has given rise to the apprehension that rather than acting as a 'moderating' agent, events in the Middle East may actually radicalize Islam within Turkey. What is undoubted is the fact that a remake of the Middle East is inevitable. What remains debated is whether in this emerging Middle East Turkey would project itself in a leadership role.

Turkish foreign policy, under the AKP, has come to articulate a vision for improving relations with all neighbours, particularly by privileging the former Ottoman space in the Middle East where agreements are being negotiated for a free trade zone and an eventual Middle Eastern Union. The growing economic and political engagement of Turkey with the Middle East has already led to significant realignment in the region. In order to come to an understanding of this it would be necessary to take note not just of Turkey's current strategy towards its neighbourhood but also Turkey's position within the broader global arena and particularly in the EU accession process. At the present moment Turkey's relations with the EU has reached an all time low with Belgium's six month presidency of the EU closing, on December 2010, without any chapters in Turkey's membership negotiations being debated. This is the first time that an EU presidency has been concluded without the opening of any chapters since Turkey's accession process was launched in October 2005. Issues of human rights, democracy and Islam continue to mire the accession process in controversy. Incidentally, it is 'success' in these fields that is being projected by the US in its current designation of Turkey as a 'model' in the Middle East.

This essay argues that what is generally defined as the 'Turkish model' is once again at crossroads, at a juncture from where various alternative futures are possible. Its identification as 'secular, democratic and liberal' is at the heart of debates as a number of states in the Middle East search for social, economic and political options. This is reminiscent of the era when the collapse of the Soviet Union prompted speculations on Turkey's geo-strategic significance and a model was developed that asserted the significance of the Turkish experiment for the post Soviet world. The argument was simple. Turkey, with the exception of Israel, was the only country in the region that combined parliamentary democracy with a market economy that was able to show significant growth rates. Referring to the country's Islamic heritage and its ethnic affinity with a large part of the post Soviet states in the Caucasus and Central Asia, it was argued that Turkey was well placed not only to act as a 'model' for the countries but also as a bridge between the 'east' and the 'west'. This was an argument that became prevalent not only within Turkey but also in the international arena and it has been argued that it was aimed primarily at strengthening Turkey's negotiation with the international community, particularly the European Union. Certain parallels with the current scenario in the Middle East are immediately discernable. A somewhat similar situation of 'transition' is being predicted for the Middle East today with the imminent 'collapse' of the ruling regimes. There is similarly a crisis in Turkey's relations with the EU. The attraction for the 'model' here is being projected in a shared Ottoman past though the Arab world does not look upon this heritage without criticism.

The Debate

The viability of the Turkish 'model' has thus re-emerged in transition debates. This viability needs to be examined at two levels, at the level of domestic compulsions faced by Turkey and at the international level where the model is being projected as a 'democratic' alternative by the US. A very large part of the domestic debate is around issues involving 'negation' of a heterogeneous past and attempts at homogenisation of Turkish society, and the subsequent aspiration of some of its citizens to a distinctive religious or ethnic identity. This debate includes within itself the Kurdish policy of the state and the attitude of the state towards other minorities, the question of the headscarf, attitudes towards Islamic institutions and organisations, the position of women, the question of human rights, etc. At the international level the debate is centered around the acceptability of Turkey as an international player and here the issues include the projection of Turkey as the link between the 'east' and the 'west' in a post cold war scenario, the long denied EU membership, Turkey's position within the global economy, the question of Armenia and Cyprus, transformation of Turkish policy towards its neighbourhood, and a change in Turkish stance towards its old allies, the US and Israel. A detailed analysis of all of these issues will be beyond the scope of the essay, though it is important to point out that most of the issues are in some way inter-related and all have a bearing on the principal debate that has dominated Turkish politics for a long time, that is, the EU accession.

While perceptions and connotations have differed there is a broad consensus on the fact that the Turkish Model is essentially based on its secular character. It has been argued that Turkish secularism was not about the separation of state and religion but about the submission of religion to the reason of the state, promotion of an acceptable 'state Islam' and the judgment of non-conforming Islams as potential threats to the 'secular' regime.[10] Hence, secularism in Turkey involved not only the disestablishment of Islam, but also its different establishment in accordance with the new basis of legitimacy of separation of religion and state. The AKP's interpretation of this has been identified as 'new Islamism'. For the AKP, Islamisation is not to be achieved through the state. The state is important only for opening new spaces for individuals and society as a whole by assuring basic rights and liberties. The state should not impose its ideology on society. 'New Islamism' aims to engage in politics on the basis of social legitimacy and socio-economic compromise. Change is achieved by liberating societal dynamics` and allowing them to be reflected in politics. With respect to world politics, 'new Islamism' reflects a reevaluation that sees civilisational dialogue between the Islamic and the western worlds as essential. Globalization has become a constant point of reference for the AKP leadership and the European Union is seen as its embodiment. Domestically, 'new Islamism' has developed a culture of compromise. As a result the leadership has refrained from political polarisation and has distanced itself from insisting on solving issues that that could generate strong polarisation. As such, the AKP represents a compromise between democracy and Islamic identity, and the management of tensions by peaceful means.

A new term 'conservative democracy' is being used to define the 'new Islamism' of the AKP.[11] Since its foundation the AKP leadership has argued that that politicisation of religion is dangerous for democracy and religion. This is based on the awareness that the majority of the Turkish population is as strongly attached to democracy and secularism as they are attached to religious values; the 'new politics' is the search for a new social contract between different sectors of the Turkish society. It is based on a synthesis between liberal desires for reform and conservative cultural sensitivities. This was based on a three layered strategy: first, the adoption of a 'language of human rights and democracy as a discursive shield'; second, mobilisation of 'public support as a form of democratic legitimacy', and third, the construction of a 'liberal democratic coalition with modern/secular sectors that recognise the AKP as the legitimate political actor'. This enabled the AKP to bring together business, urban poor and conservative religious electoral constituencies.[12]

Conservative democracy has defined the expression of the AKP's will to internalise international norms. Having accepted human rights, democracy and the rule of law as universal values the AKP embraced dominant western values while remaining committed to conservative Islamic roots. The AKP has realized that an anti-western Islamist group would not have the opportunity to continue to hold political power in Turkey. Therefore a pro European foreign policy is seen as the instrument of legitimisation for the party not only in the eyes of the Turkish state elite but also in the eyes of the international system. During its term in government the AKP has introduced significant political and economic reforms to consolidate Turkish democracy on the Copenhagen Criteria.[13] Despite difficulties in the process of integration, the AKP has taken steps to ensure the implementation of reforms in line with European standards. In a number of instances these reforms address issues related to the core elements of Turkey's political structures and dynamics. These include reducing the influence of the military in politics, eradicating the death penalty, abolishing the State Security Courts, strengthening gender equality, broadening the freedom of the press, aligning the judiciary with the European standards and establishing the supremacy of international agreements in the area of fundamental freedoms over internal legislation.[14]

However, it is argued that the Turkish model has become dysfunctional for Turkey's long standing aim to join the EU as a full member.[15] Since the signing of the Association (Ankara) Agreement of 1964, Turkey's relations with the European Union, then referred to as the European Economic Community, has passed through various phases. Turkey took over twelve years from its March 1987 accession application to the achievement of formal candidate status at Helsinki in December 1999. A further six years elapsed before the official opening of entry negotiations in October 2005. Accession negotiations were restarted by the AKP Prime Minister Erdogan in 2005. An air of crisis seems to be hanging over the accession process where ambitious plans for political deepening have run into trouble while monetary cooperation has not opened the door to political union.[16] The debate on the possibilities of Turkey's membership in the EU is centered around two groups of issues; the EU requirement for modernising economic, political and legal systems and adjusting them to EU membership and a second group of factors that are subjective in nature, the civilisational, cultural, historical and geographical specifics and the complexity of the EU domestic situation. It is argued that while Turkey is moving towards compliance with regard to many of the first group of requirements, the situation will be more complicated with regard to the second group. Membership within the EU requires recognition of a system of values shared by all members and there is widespread opinion that Turkey as a 'Muslim' country has a different set of traditions and values and a different mentality.[17]

In parallel with its economic deepening and the acquisition of a broader public policy remit, the European integration project, has since the early 1970s sought to develop a collective identity based on shared civilisational values. Central to this has been what is described as the 'democratic tradition' of European integration, an image of the EC/EU as the repository of a historical tradition of devotion to democracy.[18] The expression of this was found in the Laeken Declaration of 2001 and it found concrete expression in the growing emphasis of democracy as criteria for membership. It is being argued that the EU is increasingly pursuing a foreign policy of its own, rather than a sum of its member states'.[19] It also has an agenda of its own starting with the promotion of regional stability, democracy and human rights. The declaration of the Copenhagen criteria as condition for membership and the decision for incorporating a 'human rights' clause into all trade and association agreements that the EU concludes were the first legal instruments that the EU initiated to force third parties willing to join the Union, or increase trade links with the EU to respect human rights and promote democracy and good governance.

With the growing emphasis on democracy as the primary defining characteristic of a European state, Turkey's classification in this category came increasingly into question. Since 1960 Turkish political life has experienced direct or indirect intervention of the military in civilian political life every ten years. The country's democratic image was set back three times by military coups in 1960, 1971 and 1980. Then in 1997 a 'post-modern' military intervention led to the fall of an 'Islamist' government opposed by the military. The privileged position of the Turkish military has been challenged by the pre-accession process whose compliance requires diminishing the control of the military over civilian life. The challenge of 'security sector reform' and 'democratic oversight' has brought into question the extensive influence that the military preserved in Turkish politics. However, the military retains significant political and economic control. In the 1990's a new element was added to the picture with the growing international concern with 'Islamic' militancy across a vast geographical region. This also began to influence perceptions about Turkey. The fact that Turkish society was predominantly Muslim gained a new and negative prominence.

A significant part of the changes within Turkey has been reflected in the process of constitutional amendment which was prioritised by the AKP in its second term in power. Although the AKP asked a panel of legal experts to draft a constitution its inability to garner broader support for constitutional reform and resistance from the opposition put the issue on a back burner. Instead it opted for limited revisions mainly intended to remove restrictions encountered by female students wearing headscarf. This initiative led to a closure case against the AKP and allegations that it had become the focal point of anti-secular activities.[20] In March 2011, the government announced that instead of rewriting the constitution it would opt for a smaller package of amendments that would redefine the powers and composition of state agencies. The AKP's problems in the so called 'Kurdish opening' also forced it to reconceptualise the issue of giving greater rights to Turkish citizens of different backgrounds and present it as a broad based 'democratic opening'.

It is in this context that the June 12, 2011 Parliamentary elections assume importance. In the course of the campaign, both the AKP as well as the main opposition party the CHP committed themselves to introducing a democratic 'civilian constitution' after the elections. Although on the surface there exist a broad consensus on the need to draft a new constitution, contradictory opinions dominate on the issues of contention that have plagued Turkish politics over the years--- the Kurdish issue, the question of the place of religion in society and the role of the military. There has been apprehension that there remains the possibility that the issues that severely polarise Turkish society would reassert themselves even more during the electoral process. The AKP launched its election campaign with the slogan, "Vote for AK. Write your own Constitution" a clear reference to the AKP agenda for a new constitution to replace the one that came into force in 1982 during a period of military rule and which has been widely criticised for limiting individual rights. The new constitution is expected to strengthen democracy and pluralism. Among the changes that would be sought for are a directly elected President of seven years, restriction of the political role of the military, and a change in the headscarf policy, all issues that have led to debates between the government and the opposition. The headscarf remains at the core of the continuing battle between overtly pious and pro-secular Turks. The former insist that it is an expression of faith. The latter retort that it is a symbol of political Islam and contrary to the secular policies of Ataturk's republic. The EU has also repeatedly called on the AKP to reform the Turkish legal system, including restructuring the Supreme Board of Prosecutors and Judges (HSYK). This is one of the twenty six proposed changes that the AKP has proposed for the new constitution. However, the constitutional reform package has been criticised by the opposition who has complained that it increases the power of the government and President Gul over the choice of members of the HSYK and the Constitutional Court and thus reduces the independence of the Judiciary.[21]

The AKP required 367 out of a total of 550 seats to approve a new constitution on its own. The 49.9 per cent vote that it received gave it 326 seats, requiring it to seek agreement from other parties.[22] Mr. Erdogan admitted that the election results indicated that the new constitution should be created through agreement and negotiation and that the AKP would be respectful towards the rights of all sections of the state. The CHP has won 26 per cent of the vote and the MHP 13 per cent. This becomes all the more significant given the strong showing by Kurdish independent candidates. Thirty five have won seats and this will give them a voice in the Parliament and also put pressure on Erdogan to address their grievances. Without a 'supermajority' a referendum on a new constitution with a Presidential system is likely to trigger debate. The CHP also admits that there is need to modernize the constitution but it is deeply suspicious of Erdogan and the AKP. Kurdish nationalists want a redefinition of the citizenship clauses which could provoke a backlash from the nationalists. And any attempt to amend the first four clauses of the constitution, which describes Turkey as a secular state, would galvanise secularists, who in 2008 had organised mass protests against the AKP's attempt to lift a ban on headscarf in universities.

Key domestic elements of concern today remain issues like gender role within the state exemplified by the debate around the headscarf and the rights of minorities along with related questions of democracy and human rights. This debate goes beyond the necessity of conforming to the political criteria of Copenhagen to the challenge of identity related arguments. Identity related arguments are best exemplified through an examination of what is referred to as the 'Kurdish question' in Turkey. The question of the Kurds in Turkey has both domestic and international dimensions, and over the years, it has exemplified both the identification of the state as less than 'democratic' and the efforts by the state to move beyond this identification. It also portrays the complexities within Turkish society and brings to the forefront debates around the nature of the Turkish model and the rhetoric that has been built around it. As a consequence it also throws light on whether the model would remain a 'myth' or transcend into reality.

The Issue

With its policies of a 'democratic opening' the Justice and Development Party (*Adalet ve Kalkinma Partisi*, AKP) government in Turkey has embarked on an enterprise that will attempt a rethinking on a number of issues, including the dilemma of establishing a secure foundation for the state in a setting of societal heterogeneity and particularly the state's policy towards the Kurds or the *Kurt Sorunu*, the issue of the headscarf and 'Islamic' education particularly the case of the *imam-hatip* schools. This is part of the broader rethinking on the Kemalist modernity project which was oriented towards a particular vision of a 'modern' Turkish state which had attempted the transformation of a multicultural multilingual society into a nation 'happy to call itself Turkish'.[23] The attempt was to transcend the monarchical and imperial structures of the Ottoman society and replace them with rational bureaucratic institutions under the rule of law within a nation-state. However, it has been argued, the insistence on modernisation proved to be an ideological handicap both from a conceptual as well as a pragmatic point of view.[24].

On the other hand there have also been debates on whether the Kurdish people could have been included within the new stage of Turkish modernisation by addressing Kurdish claims in ethnic-cultural, national, political and socio-economic areas without undermining social harmony and territorial integrity.[25]Andrew Mango argues strongly against the opinion that it was the Kemalist failure to accommodate Kurdish nationalism that led to the alienation and subsequent dissident movements among the Kurds.[26] He argues that Kurdish nationalism could not have been accommodated without endangering law and order and the construction of the modern state. Kurdish nationalism first appeared among malcontents among the feudal leadership of the fragmented Kurdish tribal society. It was inseparable from the threat to law and order that the tribes had always posed. The Kemalists sought to solve it by co-opting part of the feudal leadership in order to isolate the malcontents and by modern development of the area. Mango goes on to argue that the Kemalists are also accused of exacerbating the Kurdish problem by disestablishing Islam and then by using force to subdue Kurdish disaffection. But, he argues, the disestablishment of Islam was a precondition to the country's modernisation process, irrespective of its effects on the Kurdish society. In any case, there is broad agreement on the fact that the Kurdish question is closely connected to the Turkish question, to the question of how a more inclusive formulation of 'Turkishness' can be adopted. The Turkish perception of social-political diversity is still affected by the so called 'Sevres syndrome' which refers to the dominant ways in which Turks interpret how they lost their Empire and came to the brink of colonisation in the early 20th century. These interpretations attribute the Ottoman meltdown to the unbridled spiraling of hostile minority nationalisms that foreign powers fostered and liberal Ottoman-Turkish elites endorsed. This has inculcated skepticism towards minority movements.

A plethora of debates exists on the viability of the Kemalist project, that focus on how the transformation of the traditional Ottoman cosmopolitan ethos in the course of a project of creating a 'modern' Turkey lead to denial of diversity within the state and subsequent attempts at neutralising heterogeneity. Critical rethinking of this project of modernity in recent times has sought to come to terms with the cultural plurality of a society that had traditionally imbibed within itself varied groups with multiple religious and ethnic identities. Sponsored by a government whose own 'Islamic' background remains an anathema to the Kemalists, it has brought to the forefront policies of assimilation that fell short of transforming a majority of Kurds into 'Turks'. It has been suggested that just as the first modernizers of the Ottoman Empire, the Tanzimat reformers, attempted to forestall the collapse of the state by incorporating Christian minorities as equal citizens the AKP government is planning an 'opening' that seeks to bring to an end the Kurdish question by setting the stage for the assertion of societal autonomy.[27]

It has been noted that the conflict between the 'old Turkey' represented by the Kemalist establishment and the 'new Turkey' represented by civil society has to be resolved through the establishment of a more inclusive social contract that addresses the cultural diversity of Turkish society. Here, it has been argued that a neo Ottoman ethos would be more pluralistic and cosmopolitan. It is undeniable that compared to the Ottoman system Kemalism was essentially exclusivist and attempted to create a uniform Turkish citizen, which resulted in the denial of Turkey's 'true' cosmopolitan identity.

In fact, it was the creation of a 'Turkish' identity and the non-recognition or 'denial' of the existence of other communities/identities along with a denial of the 'pre-modern'/Ottoman past of Turkey that leads to the creation of the 'other' within society. It is interesting that that this 'other', which in this case is the Kurdish population of Turkey, also imbibes within itself various cleavages. It is not uncommon to come across a Kurd who considers himself to be a member of a particular tribe, holds Kurdish ethnic identity, but also feels himself to be a Turkish citizen. In certain instances, there are also elements of this 'other' who sympathize with the majority cause and in fact the ideologue of the new Republic, Ziya Gokalp had eastern Anatolian origins. Similarly, the current leader of the CHP Kemal Kilicdaroglu was born into a family speaking Zaza, a Turkish Kurdish dialect. However, he rarely refers to the Kurdish problem in the course of his speeches.[28] In a way, this is inevitable and in many ways a universal process. However, in the Turkish case there are certain peculiarities. Given the process of the emergence of the state it was the intensity of focus on secularism as well as non-recognition or denial of the existence of groups other than the 'Turk' that becomes significant. Here one would have to keep in mind not just the complex mosaic of people who constituted the new state but also the fact that a pan Turkic thinking was also in existence at this time influenced by men who were more often than not from outside the boundaries of Anatolia.

While many scholars ascribe the current politicisation of Kurdish identity to the uneven and incomplete modernisation of south eastern Anatolia, it has been argued that the Kemalist conception of statist modernity and a state led social and cultural transformation was in fact a major cause of the phenomenon.[29] Kurdish intellectuals used the economic and social gap between the western and eastern parts of the country to construct Kurdish ethno nationalism. Thus excessive state centric development along with an increase in literacy, led to the rise of Kurdish ethnopolitics. As the Republic moved away from a 'civic' nationalism to an ethnic-based Turkishness, between 1970 and 1980, Kurdish people were further alienated. The state's refusal to recognise Kurdish cultural identity and its political repercussions during the 1980s military coup and its aftermath further reinforced the impression of the Kurdish people that the state of Turkey is a state for the Turks not for the Kurds. This perception in turn undermined the legitimacy of the state. The 'other' of the Kemalist modernisation project has always been a politicised Islamic identity. The powerful Kurdish representation within the pro-Islamic National Outlook Movement which was institutionalised as the *National Salvation Party* and the (1973-80) and then as the *Welfare Party* (1983-98) brought the state in direct opposition to both its enemies, Kurds and Islamists.

It also has to be kept in mind that the Kurdish question cannot be understood in isolation. The monolithic nature of Turkey's political culture, the military's role in politics, the uneven development of parts of the state and the incomplete integration of the country's Kurdish regions are all part of a complex phenomenon. Part of the 'democratic opening' is also in response to EU requirements. In fact, recognition by the EU of Turkey's candidacy for membership within the EU has made democratization a practical necessity.[30] Similarly, the 'Kurdish opening' has important foreign policy implications. With US troops scheduled to complete their withdrawal by summer 2010, Turkey is set to indirectly fill in the vacuum in northern Iraq. Developments in Kurdish controlled northern Iraq will provide Turkey with an opportunity to neutralize the PKK. Similarly Turkey's policy of rapprochement with Syria and Iran, seen as part of a neo Ottomanist foreign policy is also in part aimed at dealing with the PKK as the two states' support for the Kurdish separatist movement is well known.[31]

2009 opened with some major steps towards the politics of recognition. At the beginning of the year, the state broadcasting agency TRT launched a 24-hour Kurdish language channel, TRT 6. Also the Higher Education Board resolved to establish Kurdish language and literature departments in Universities. These are radical gestures on the road to the recognition of Kurdish identity in Turkish history. Additionally the AKP government announced in July 2009 that it was preparing a comprehensive plan to provide a solution for the Kurdish question. Whether these will be successful, still remain to be seen. In any case, the fundamental dilemma of identity within the state will remain as long as the ideal is perceived in terms of a homogeneous monolingual political community. With its policies of 'democratic opening', the AKP government has embarked on an enterprise that will ultimately challenge the core identity of the Republic as a specifically 'Turkish' state.

Turkey's June 12, 2011 elections saw the pro-Kurdish movement score its biggest ever Parliamentary victory, with an increase from 20 to 36 seats. The victory by the pro-Kurdish Peace and Democracy Party (BDP) which primarily backed the independent Kurdish candidates came at the expense of the AKP. In two of Turkey's predominant Kurdish provinces, the BDP secured 90 per cent of the votes. The election results reflect the Kurds' despondency over the postponement of the AKP's promises. In the 2007 general elections, Prime Minister Erdogan had campaigned on a platform of addressing Kurdish demands for greater cultural freedom. However Erdogan's efforts to end the conflict with the Kurdistan Workers' Party resulted in failure. Prior to the 2011 elections, Erdogan declared that there is 'no longer a Kurdish problem' campaigned on a nationalist platform, and dismissed key Kurdish demands for political autonomy and Kurdish language schools. The writing of a new constitution is now identified as the only vehicle to address key Kurdish demands and as the new Parliament begins the drafting of the new constitution the Kurdish issue and its constitutional ramifications will occupy centre stage.[32] Unfortunately, since the election results did not give the AKP the number of seats required to change the constitution without referendum or taking the views of the other parties into account, the process of constitutional amendment has now become complex. While the CHP has also been in favour of amendments the extent to which it would amenable to change the Kemalist foundations of the state remains to be seen. The pressure for a new liberal constitution will come from the new middle class in Anatolia that does not owe its ascendancy to the state. It will also come from the Kurdish minority. In his June 12 victory speech, Erdogan promised that the writing of the Constitution will be an inclusive process. The degree of political accommodation during the process will determine the extent to which the process of framing a 'civilian', 'democratic' constitution will be successful.

In Lieu of Conclusions

It is an undoubted fact that a large part of the 'democratic opening' initiated by the AKP was impelled by the EU accession process. There is apprehension, however, that the recent disillusion with the process could mean a slowdown of many of the measures that had been underway bringing back to the forefront the question of the viability of the 'Turkish model'. Also, since Turkey has not solved significant problems regarding the integration of political Islam into its system by accommodating it but has transformed it to the point where the movement denies its past, it is problematic to propose Turkey as a model for 'Islamic' democracy. However, the projection of the model as an alternative in the Middle East in recent times has emphasised the rhetoric surrounding the myth of the model and has once again raised questions about whether the Turkish world as an alternative makes sense both from a historical as well as contemporary perspective. As new political landscapes emerge in the Middle East debates on the Turkish model also assumes various forms ranging from those to point to its fragility to others who focus on its advantages. What remains unchanged is the rhetoric of a myth that reemerges in the face of transitions and then recedes as alternatives emerge from within.

Notes

1. See for instance, Mathew Brunwasser, "Turkey as a Model Democracy for Middle East" The World, Global Perspectives for an American Audience, February 21, 2011, http://www.theworld.org/2011/02/turkey-as-model-democracy-for -middle-east/ where he cites Hugh Pope, Turkey/Cyprus director at the International Crisis Group as pointing to the projection of Turkey as a model. See also Karem Oktem, "Turkey remains an 'Angry Nation' but could still serve as a democratic inspiration", *The Turkey Analyst*, vol 4, no 5, March 07, 2011.
2. See Halil M. Karaveli and Svante Cornell, "Turkey and the Middle Eastern Revolts: Democracy or Islamism?" *Turkey Analyst*, vol. 4 no. 3, February 07,2011 where they cite Tariq Ramadan (the grandson of Hasan al-Banna, the founder of the Muslim Brotherhood).
3. Comment made by Namik Tan at a panel discussion at the John Hopkins School of Advanced International Studies, cited from 'US ambassador: Turkey may be an Inspiration for Middle Eastern countries', *Trend*, March 08, 2011, http://en.trend.az/regions/met/turkey/1841736.html.
4. See for instance Paula Sandrin, "Unrest in the Middle East, the Turkish Response and the Turkish Model", *Political Reflection Quarterly*, , vol 2, no. 1, March-April-May 2011.
5. More recently however, there are reports that Turkey has established contacts with the Libyan opposition. The main concern is that Libya should not become a second Iraq.
6. For details see Joshua Walker, "Turkey's Regional Leadership in the Middle East: Principle or Realpolitik?" *Turkey Analyst*, vol. 4, no. 6, March 21, 2011.
7. Walker "Turkey's Regional Leadership in the Middle East: Principle or Realpolitik?"
8. See for instance, M. Hakan Yavuz, "The Role of the New Bourgeoisie in the Transformation of the Turkish Islamic Movement", in *The Emergence of a New Turkey, Democracy and the*

AKP Party, (Salt Lake City: The University of Utah Press, 2006).

9. The Ergenekon affair involves investigations against a group of people who were accused of alleged involvement in a plot to overthrow the AKP government and includes hundreds of senior military officials, journalists and academics.
10. Menderes Cinar and Burhanettin Duran, "The specific evolution of contemporary Political Islam in Turkey and its 'difference'", in Umit Cizre (ed) *Secular and Islamic Politics In Turkey, The making of the Justice and Development Party*, (Abingdon, Oxon: Routledge, 2008).
11. The AKP developed its normative framework through its official publication, *Conservative Democracy*. The book defines the AKP's conservatism as an ideology that stresses common sense, prudence, and gradual change. It rejects rationalist utopias, Jacobinism and social engineering. At a conference organised to elaborate on the Party's conservative and democratic stand, Erdogan emphasised that the AKP's understanding of conservatism did not mean the conservation of established institutions and relations but implied the protection of important values and principles while pursuing progress. The attempt was to synthesize local and universal values, tradition and modernity and morality and religion. For details see Ahmet Kuru, "From Islamism to Conservative Democracy: The Justice and Development Party in Turkey", Paper presented at the annual meeting of the American Political Science Association, Marriot, Loews, Philadelphia and the Pennsylvania Convention Centre, Philadelphia, PA, August 31, 2006, http://www.allacademic.com/meta/p151181_index.html
12. I. D. Dagi, "The Justice and Development Party: Identity, Politics and Human Rights Discourse in the Search for Security and Legitimacy", in M.H. Yavuz (ed) *The Emergence of a New Turkey: Democracy and the AK Party,* (Salt Lake City: The University of Utah Press, 2006).
13. The EU's Copenhagen Criteria requires stability of institutions guaranteeing democratic governance, human rights and a functioning market economy.
14. Burhanettin Duran, "The Justice and Development Party's New Politics'; Steering towards Conservative Democracy, a Revised Islamic Agenda or Management of New Crisis?" in Cizre (ed) *Secular and Islamic Politics in Turkey, The Making of the Justice and Development Party.*
15. See Mehmet Ugur and Nergis Canefe, "Turkey and the European Integration, Conclusions", in Mehmet Ugur and Nergis Canefe (eds.) *Turkey and the European Integration, Accession Prospects and Issues*, (London and New York: Routledge, 2004).
16. Susannah Verney, "The dynamics of EU Accession: Turkish Travails in Comparative Perspective", in Susannah Verney and Kostas Ifantis (eds) *Turkey's Road to European Union Membership, National Identity and Political Change,* (London and New York: Routledge, 2009).
17. Pavel Varbanets, "A Turkic Alliance: Possible Alternative to Turkey's Unrealized EU Membership?" *Central Asia and the Caucasus,* no. 1(55), 2009.
18. Susannah Verney, "National identity and Political Change on Turkey's Road to EU membership" in Verney and Ifantis (eds) *Turkey's Road to European Union Membership, National Identity and Political Change,* (London and New York: Routledge, 2009)

19. Ozlem Terzi, "Introduction: Is it Possible to Speak of a Process of Europeanization in Turkish Foreign Policy?" in *The Influence of the European Union on Turkish Foreign Policy*, (Surrey and Burlington: Ashgate, 2010).
20. Saban Kardas, "Constitutional Amendments Further Polarise Turkish Politics", *Eurasia Daily Monitor*, vol. 7 issue 87, May 05, 2010.
21. For details of the proposed changes see Gareth H Jenkins, "Turkey's Constitutional Amendments: One Step Forward, Two Steps Back?", *Turkey Analyst*, vol. 3 no. 6, March 29, 2010.
22. The AKP required 367 seats to pass the constitutional amendment on its own. With more that 330 seats it would be possible for the AKP to make the changes with a public referendum. With less than 330 seats it is now bound to seek consensus among other parties in the parliament.
23. There are alternative interpretations of this that claim that the phrase prioritised a personal identification with "Turkishness" rather than an ethnic or racial scrutiny of individual citizens. See Omar Taspinar, ,*Kurdish Nationalism and Political Islam in Turkey,* (New York and London: Routledge, 2005).
24. Sinan Ciddi, *Kemalism in Turkish Politics, The Republican People's Party, Secularism and Nationalism,* (London and New York: Routledge, 2009).
25. Murat Somner, "Defensive and Liberal Nationalisms: The Kurdish Question and Modernisation/Democratization", in E. Fuat Keyman (ed*) Remaking Turkey, Globalization, Alternative Modernities and Democracy,* (Lanham: Lexington Books, 2008).
26. Andrew Mango, "Introduction: Ataturk and Kemalism throughout the Twentieth Century", in Celia Kerslake, Kerem Oktem and Philip Robins (eds) *Turkey's Engagement with Modernity: Conflict and Change in the Twentieth Century*, (Basingstoke, Hampshire: Palgrave Macmillan in association with St Antony's College Oxford, 2010).
27. Halil M. Karaveli, "Could Turkey's Glasnost Establish Equality as the Founding Principle of the State?" *Turkey Analyst*, vol. 2, no. 23, December 21, 2009.
28. Nicholas Birch, "Turkey: Traditionalist Opposition Party Attempts Radical Makeover", *Eurasianet,* November 15, 2010, www.eurasianet.org.
29. M Hakan Yavuz, "Search for a New Social Contract in Turkey: Fethullah Gulen, the Virtue Party and the Kurds", *SAIS Review* vol. 19, no. 1, 1999.
30. For details see, Fotios Moustakis and Rudra Chaudhuri, "The Turkish Kurdish Relations and the European Union: An Unprecedented Shift in the Kemalist Paradigm?", *Mediterranean Quarterly,* Fall 2005.
31. M. K. Kaya, "The AKP Seeking To Reinvent Turkey, Is Forced To Tread Carefully', *Turkey Analyst*, vol. 2, no. 21, November 23, 2009.
32. Dorian Jones, "Turkey: Time Up for a Kurdish Compromise", *Eurasianet Weekly Digest*, June 16, 2011.

8. Arab Spring: Authoritarianism in the Middle East Re-examined

Kingshuk Chatterjee

The ubiquitous banners screaming 'Irhal' (Go!) that had mushroomed all over Egypt during the heady days of January and February 2011, would probably go down in the history of the Middle East as the iconic visual of the year. As the so-called Arab Spring begins to mellow (somewhat) and rolls over through the summer to usher in the autumn, the head count seems far more impressive than at any other time in the history of the region. The ouster of Mubarak, Zain al-Abedine ben Ali and Muammar Ghaddafi, the virtually certain departure of Ali Abdullah Saleh, and the embattled nature of the hitherto iron-fisted Assad regime in Syria has begun to hold out the greatest promise of change in the region since the Nasserite coup of 1953. Indeed, the momentum has ebbed somewhat given the very decisive crackdown in Bahrain, and the determined discourse of resistance to reforms that Riyadh seemed to be broadcasting. Nevertheless, the edifice of authoritarianism in the Middle East has been badly dented, even though it might be premature to celebrate any definitive victory for the forces of democracy just yet. It is, however, opportune to revisit the question of authoritarianism in the Middle East.

The question of authoritarianism in the Middle East usually revolves around three positions that can loosely be called behaviouralist, cultural exceptionalist and structuralist. Long before embarking on his contentious theory about clash of civilisations, Samuel Huntington gave expression to the behaviouralist argument, maintaining that the predominance of Islam was the principal reason behind the absence of democracy in the Middle East. He argued, Cultures (such as Islam) which are consummatory in character, that is, where the intermediate and ultimate ends are closely connected – seem to be less favourable to democracy. Looking at the state of democracies around the world, Huntington showed that in 1984, of the thirty-one countries with Muslim majorities, twenty one were listed by the Freedom House as 'not free', fifteen as 'partially free', and none as 'free'. The one Muslim majority country that turned out to be intermittently democratic, Turkey, had repudiated its Islamic credentials; the only Arab country that had sustained democracy over a period of time happened to be Lebanon, having 40-50 per cent Christian population, and this too imploded when the Muslim majority asserted itself.[1] Such arguments have often gained support from scholars working on Islam, who have often argued that in Islam, no distinction exists between religion and politics, between the spiritual and the secular, and political participation was historically an alien concept.[2]

The cultural exceptionalist argument does not hold Islam as necessarily conducive to authoritarianism, although it does not forcefully refute such arguments either. This approach contends that the political culture of the Middle East is distinctive, owing to its historical peculiarities in the realm of dispensation of power. Hisham Sharabi, for instance, makes the case that a sort of traditional neo-patriarchy characterises the Arab world, and by extension the Middle East. According to him, "The neo-patriarchal state, regardless of its legal and political forms and structures, is in many ways no more than a modernized version of the traditional patriarchal sultanate."[3] In its substance, Sharabi's argument embraces authoritarian regimes of military (Egypt, Iraq, Libya), party (Syria) and tribal monarchical (Jordan, Saudi Arabia, Kuwait, UAE, Bahrain, Qatar) vintage alike. He sees little to distinguish the essential character of power enjoyed by Nasser, Sadat, Mubarak, Ghaddafi, Saddam, Hafiz and Bashar al-Assad on the one hand and the houses of al-Saud, al-Sabah, al-Thani, al-Khalifa, etc. on the other hand. The powers of all of this rest on the presumed conceptualisation of the state as one giant family, where the head of the family enjoys virtually untrammelled authority. Michael Hudson modified this argument somewhat by admitting powerful modernising dynamics as a defining feature of the politics of the region, for 'they do not conform precisely to the classical Middle Eastern patriarchy'. Nevertheless, he accepts, "[T]their legitimizing values are essentially rooted in kinship, tradition and religion".[4]

The structuralist argument dismisses theories of both Islamic and cultural exceptionalist, and looks for answers in the political structures and dispensations of social and political power in the Middle East in the specific context of the 20th century. Scholars such as Lisa Anderson, Roger Owen, and F. Gregory Gause III are among the finest exemplars of this position; they argue that the problem of authoritarian propensity was factored into the process of state-formation in the Middle East in the 20th century – sometimes owing to the manner of colonial dispensation of power, sometimes owing to post-colonial power struggles; occasionally on account of the rentier nature of the state, frequently on account of the early 20th structures atop which subsequent state-formation took place. The substratum of such argument is, of course, that there is nothing intrinsic to the region that favours an authoritarian dispensation, and the corollary therefore that authoritarianism may wither away given changes in the backdrop in which it flourishes in the region.

This essay conforms in the main to the structuralist approach in order to look at the enduring experience of authoritarianism in the Middle East. It avoids the standard Marxist position of western interests in the oil economy as the main prop of authoritarianism in the region. The essay begins by looking at the historical roots of dispensation of political power in the region. It goes on to examine the social basis of authoritarianism in the Middle East. The essay then proposes to establish the connection between oil and the willing/reluctant acceptance of authoritarianism before demonstrating the weakening of the edifice by the 1990s as a result of the changes in the oil economy.

Inventing Patriarchy: The Optical Illusion of Tradition

The notion of unsuitability of democratic politics, and its inevitable corollary of propensity towards authoritarianism, rests on a kind of optical illusion that afflicts commentators quite frequently. Truly speaking, almost all the Middle Eastern states are of considerably recent vintage, coming into being only in course of the second half of the 19th century and the first half of the 20th. If one leaves aside the kingdom of Morocco, virtually none of the Arab countries today had any independent existence before the disintegration of the Ottoman Empire began around the time of the First World War – Egypt being the only Ottoman province to effectively detach itself from the Empire and chart its own political journey in the 19th century. The only country to have enjoyed roughly the territorial frontiers in 20th that it did in the 19th was Iran, as the erstwhile kingdom of Persia. Hence, the exercise of identifying a 'regional' political culture, at a time when the existing contours of the region could not even be said to have existed is fraught with a kind of optical illusion.

The extended region of the Middle East and North Africa comprises of at least three distinctive sub-regions – the region around the Persian Gulf (comprising of Iran, Iraq, Bahrain, Kuwait, Qatar, and the countries of the

Arabian peninsula, viz. Saudi Arabia, the UAE, Oman, and Yemen); the Levantine areas of Asia and Africa (Turkey, Syria, Lebanon, Israel-Palestine, Jordan and Egypt), and the region of North Africa west of Egypt (Tunisia, Libya, etc). Of the three regions, the whole of the Levantine area used to be the core of Ottoman Empire in Asia, constituted as the vilayats of Syria and Misr, from about the 16th century. In the Persian Gulf region, only Iraq and Kuwait used to be parts of the Ottoman Empire (divided into the sanjaks of Baghdad, Basra, Mosul and Kuwait). Along the northern coastline of the Gulf, stretching as far north as the Caspian lay the kingdom of Persia, held together by a kind of loose central authority of Shahs of different tribal dynasties during 18th and 19th century. Along the southern shores of the Gulf, the Arabian Peninsula was a land of political fragmentation, with only the Red Sea coastal region of Hejaz (with the twin Holy Cities of Mecca and Medina) under Ottoman control. The desert region of Rub al-Khali, and the desert and mountainous southern region of Nejd were dominated by the Bedouin, while the coastal regions were infested by pirates who plagued shipping in the Gulf and the Arabian Sea before the British brought some order in the region, persuading local elites to contain piracy. The region of North Africa west of Egypt, including Tunis and the region of Cyrenaica and the Sahara were only tenuously associated with Ottoman control.

In the various parts of the Ottoman Empire, authority was seldom found in a concentrated and consolidated manner. Held together by the person of the Ottoman sultan, authority was divided among the Ottoman military functionaries (dominated by the Pashas and the Beys) and the civilian functionaries (viz. Emirs) responsible for maintaining law and order, frequently with the ambits of the two overlapping. For purposes of civil law, the component peoples of the empire were divided into confessional communities of millet. Even in the kingdom of Persia, the central authority was no less tenuous than of the Ottomans, with the Shah holding disparate and loosely held regions together by virtue of a marginal military superiority over the various regional and tribal elites. Given such political fragmentation, a lot of elbow room was available for the regional ashrafiyyah (landed notables) who were able and willing to maintain law and order, on behalf of the central authorities where they existed (viz. in the Ottoman Empire, Kingdom of Persia), and on their own where they did not (viz. the Arabian peninsula). Given the weakness of central authority, as late as the 19th century, neither the Ottoman Sultan, nor the Persian

Shah (and definitely not the smaller Emirs) were strong enough to qualify as authoritarian rulers, even though in absence of any institutional checks on their power, they were despotic in nature.

The First World War was the watershed in the emergence of the political culture of centralised states that characterised the 20th century Middle East. The cardinal development of the period was, of course, the collapse of the Ottoman Empire, and the emergence of Arab nationalism(s). The British and the French, having developed strategic and commercial interests in the Ottoman Empire, actively pursued the programme of breaking the Empire up, and in this their interests converged with the Arab elite, who resented the deadening centralisation attempted by the Young Turk regime in the years leading up to the war. The Arab revolt of 1916 was instigated and aided by the British in a bid to tie down Ottoman forces away from the theatres of war, but the Arabs responded to British initiative only upon the promise of independence. However, once the war was over the Arab provinces were made over to the British and the French, with Mandate from the League of Nations for them to be groomed for self-government.

The French split up the mandated area of Syria into Muslim majority state of Syria and predominantly Christian state of Lebanon, both being organised along republican principles. In neither of the two French mandated states were any 'traditional' institutions of power 'revived'. By contrast, wherever the British gained a toehold, they seemed to prefer to invent 'traditional' forms of authority. In Egypt, after three decades of de facto protectorate, the British had established a de jure protectorate in 1914, but by the end of the war, given the anti-British mood on the streets of Egypt the British decided to reinstate Farouk, the Khedive from the old ruling line, but this time as king. Similarly, they had promised the Hashemite leaders of the Arab Revolt, Faisal and Abdullah, dominion over the Fertile Crescent and the Arabian Peninsula respectively constituted into two kingdoms. While Faisal was denied kingship over the Ottoman province of Syria, he was compensated with the kingdom of Iraq, cobbling together the sanjaks of Baghdad, Mosul and Basra. Upon Abdullah's failure to unite the peninsula behind him, he was given a new kingdom in the Bedouin lands east of river Jordan, carved out of the Ottoman Sanjak of Palestine and called it the kingdom of Transjordan. Neither Faisal nor Abdullah had any roots in their kingdoms, but the British assumed that mere descent from the family of Banu Hashim (from which the Prophet himself had descended), would provide them with some legitimacy and support from kingdoms that were overwhelmingly Muslim by faith. It took the ouster of Faisal to disabuse the British of this illusion.

Even where the British did not enjoy any Mandate, such as in the southern littoral of the Gulf, they lent support to whoever could safeguard British interests. Accordingly, the seven emirates that entered into a truce with the British, pledging to prevent acts of piracy in the Gulf from their realm, came to constitute the Trucial States, which came out of British tutelage in 1961 as the United Arab Emirates. The claims to rulership of the constituent emirates, along with their territorial limits, rested on British recognition of the corresponding house, just like the cases of Bahrain and Qatar. The house of al-Sabah also came to power because the British, meaning to control the access to the Gulf, sequestered the Sunni majority coastal region of Kuwait from the Shi'i majority sanjak of Basra. Each of the ruling houses claimed legitimacy by virtue of leadership of individual tribes that inhabited the corresponding emirates, and British recognition of such claims (conditional upon their prioritising British interests) in turn cemented such claims. Saudi Arabia, the only peninsular Arab kingdom apart from Oman that did not owe its origins to the British, came into being by right of conquest and tribal alignments only as late as the 1920s, consolidating political power in the peninsula for the first time since the fall of Abbasid power in the 13th century. Hence, the notion of the various 'tribal monarchies' of the peninsula (as some observers call them) as being examples of 'traditional' political formation ignores the fact that the 'tradition' is of very recent vintage.

Similarly, the argument that patriarchal power structure of the various emirates, sultanates and imamates constitutes the foundational platform for political power in whole the region is simplistic. Hudson's argument about 'kinship, religion and tradition', as the language of political legitimacy, was derived from the case studies of the Gulf monarchies. Attempts at application of similar principles outside the Arabian Peninsula failed spectacularly, as in Iraq and Egypt. Although various historians have highlighted how tribal and sectarian affiliations have continued to be relevant all through the 20th century (particularly in Iraq, Syria and Libya), it is difficult to argue that the structures of power and society have anything remotely 'traditional' about them. The blanket application of what had been conceived of as 'the Arab tradition' was substantially unmindful of the differences between those Arab societies that were urban in character with settled agricultural economy (viz. Egypt, Iraq, Syria, Palestine, the eastern part of Libya around Benghazi), and those that were not (Saudi Arabia, UAE, Kuwait, Jordan). The ties of 'tradition' were considerably weaker in those parts of the Middle East where settled agricultural economy and urban society had been the norm for ages. Hence, to use a the explanatory variable of a particular political culture favouring authoritarianism pervading the whole of the Middle East is as misleading as it is simplistic. The answer to the riddle has to be sought not in the 'culture' of the region, rather in the process of state-formation in the 20th century.

Authoritarianism and the Social Basis of Power

The transformation of political culture of the Middle East, in the sense of a drive towards centralisation of political authority, began in the 19th century, in response to steady economic penetration by European powers – principally Britain, France and Russia, but eventually others as well. The urge to mobilise greater resources to hold one's own against western penetration impelled attempts at modernisation of the state apparatus in the Ottoman Empire and in Persia (known respectively as 'tanzimat' and the 'nizam-e jadid'), meant to allow better control of the territories. Such reforms fared best in Egypt under Muhammad Ali Pasha, who emerged militarily strong enough to effectively break away from the Ottoman Empire, and set up his own dynasty. The twin impact of western economic penetration and the introduction of western education (a necessary component of the various reform programmes) resulted in the creation of a new social and economic group, the *effendiyah*. Analogous to the bourgeoisie elsewhere, these educated professionals in state and private service and compradorial entrepreneurs played a crucial role in the rise of the spirit of nationalism in the Middle East. Far more importantly, they spearheaded the process of gradual integration of the Middle Eastern economies into the international economic arena, and exerted the internal pressure which created and sustained 'modern' manufacturing sector. Politically, they were the principal movers behind movements to restrict the scope of the power at the disposal of the monarch, and also centralisation of political authority in a reasonably effective manner, cutting into the power of the 'traditional' regional or local elite of the 'ashrafiyyah' (viz. the Constitutional Revolution of Iran in 1906, and the Young Turk revolution in the Ottoman Empire in 1908).

During the period between the two World Wars, most of the newly formed nation-states of the Arab world as much as the Republic of Turkey and the Kingdom of Persia (Iran from 1935), witnessed the steady ascendancy of the 'effendiyah' to political power. In some cases in the newly formed Arab countries, the rise of the effendiyah took place within, and with the support of, the colonial apparatus run by the Mandate authorities (as in Syria and Lebanon). Elsewhere, such as in Iraq and Egypt, the effendiyah ascendancy took the form of nationalist assertion over the economic space of the nation against continued western domination.

The general drift in the politics of the effendiyah was towards the simultaneous processes of integration of the 'national economy' as much as the invention of the 'nation-state', which eventually weakened the protagonists themselves. Pivotal to both of these nation-building agenda was considerable emphasis placed on the public education system, which was secular and following the pedagogic model of the Europe, or at least its Middle Eastern approximations, as in Ataturk's Turkey and Reza Shah's Iran. The number of people gaining access to education increased several-fold, churning out a far larger number of people qualified for the 'modern' sector of economy than the fledgling sector could absorb, particularly as the Great Depression set in. A substantial number of such people, lower-middle class in origin, educated in the new public education system and aspiring for a better standard of living than the traditional sector could provide, left their rural and suburban roots and moved to the big cities (viz. Cairo, Alexandria, Damascus, Beirut, Baghdad, Tehran, Benghazi, Tripoli, etc). Given the failure of the market to absorb such a huge influx of educated labour, social disaffection grew against the incumbent governments all through the 1930s and 1940s. It was in this backdrop that the political programme of Arab nationalism, aspiring towards political (and economic) unity of the Arab world gained considerable popularity, hoping to reconfigure the Ottoman economic space in the eastern Mediterranean.

The definitive trend, however, was to emerge in the Republic of Turkey, and following it in Iran, prioritising the integration of the nation and creation of a state strong enough to ward off foreign influence in the country, to prevent the kind of challenges that the two had encountered from the 19th. The need for the creation of a strong state necessarily involved modernisation and enhancement of the military profiles of the country, particularly as the constitutionalist experiments had failed to rise up to the challenge of resisting western penetration. Turkey under Mustapha Kemal Pasha, aka Ataturk, and Iran under Reza Shah Pahlavi, thus embarked on a process of state-building in which the military occupied a central position. On the one hand, the agenda of expanding military capability enabled the Turkish and Iranian states to absorb a large number of the educated youth churned out by the public education system. On the other hand, the economic demand generated by the state, and particularly the military, helped stimulate industrialisation and the development of the 'modern' economic sector. Consequently, the model of state-led development added to itself the variant of the military functioning as an engine of economic growth.

The success of the Turkish model and its Iranian variant, coupled with the retreat of liberal democracy in Europe during the 1930s, weakened attempts in the Middle Eastern countries to move along the trajectory of democratic governance. At the end of the Second World War, as all the European powers retreated from the region exhausted, the Middle East underwent another process of churning in which the Turkish model held great charm. The man who personified this trend in the Arab world was of course Gamal Abdel Nasser, but the example of a civilian government being toppled by a military leader inspired the imagination of many in the Middle East, resulting in the overthrow of the Hashemite monarchy in Iraq (1958), that of the republican regime in Syria by the Ba'ath party under the leadership of Hafez al-Assad, and that of the Sanussiya monarchy of King Idris I as a result of a revolution led by Colonel Muammar Ghaddafi in Libya (1969).

Although each of these was impelled by different contingent circumstances at different times, they conformed to the pattern set by Nasserite Egypt and inhabited the same discursive space on development. Each of these revolutions were run by a generation made upwardly mobile by access to public education, disappointed by the politics of the effendiyah and determined to broaden the social basis of power. They seized power from governments who had operated within constitutionalist frameworks, and whose failure to deliver the much-promised prosperity was taken as a failure of not merely of constitutional government itself but also liberal market economic principles that these governments had championed. From the 1950s, therefore, a number of Arab states began to tread the path of state-led development, with economies that were tightly regulated, and political systems that denied the kind of freedom that came in the way of such regulation – much in the manner of the Turkey and Iran.

The rise of this upwardly mobile generation to political power took place in simultaneously yet another development that was to transform the economic character of the whole region, and the character of political power that went with it. This was the emergence of the oil economy, to which we turn next.

Authoritarianism and the Oil Economy

Till the beginning of the 20th century, the economy of the Middle East as a region had little of the wealth that now seems to characterise it. In a region that was otherwise very arid and barren, the valleys of the Nile and the Fertile Crescent (comprising in the main of the valleys of Jordan and the Tigris-Euphrates) were the only areas of sustained agricultural activity. Hence major centres of political power centred historically round these regions. Proximity to the Mediterranean Sea made commerce a far more important economic activity in Levantine Middle East than agriculture, quite like the northern reaches of the Persian Gulf which played the crucial role of connecting the sea and overland routes linking the Arabian Sea with the Mediterranean. The poorest of the lot were to be found in the Arabian peninsula, where little agriculture was possible, and coastal commerce, nomadic pastoralism and maritime piracy (till the British curbed it in the 19th century) where the mainstays of the population.

Unlike the former provinces of the Ottoman Empire, where direct colonial presence of Britain, France and Italy expedited the transition to the modern economy and the replacement of the pre-modern with modern state structures, with corresponding new approaches to public finance, governments in the Arabian Peninsula remained poor well into at least the first third of the 20th century. King 'Abd al-Aziz ibn Saud, founder of the kingdom of Saudi Arabia, depended heavily upon British subventions, much in the manner of the much smaller emirs of Kuwait, Bahrain, Qatar and the Trucial States. Such poor governments provided little by way of services, confining themselves to primarily judicial functions, establishing a rudimentary system of courts culminating in the ruler's majlis to adjudicate disputes, and a minimal police power to enforce such adjudication. It was difficult for them (except the Kingdom of Saudi Arabia, given the larger scale of British subvention) to maintain a standing army of any size.

All of this began to change in the early 20th century when European and American companies prospecting for oil found primarily the Persian Gulf but also other parts of the Middle East to be have collectively the richest oil reserve in the world. The earliest of the discoveries were made in Iran (1908), followed by those in Iraq (1927), Bahrain (1932) and Saudi Arabia (1935).

By 1951, it was clear that the Middle East region held more than half (52 per cent) of the world's proven reserve of oil. Royalties from oil exploration concessions and then from the sale of oil provided a steadily increasing source of revenue for the governments. Although initially the western companies who were given concessions to explore the various Middle Eastern countries for oil walked off with the largest share of the profits, leaving behind peanuts to the governments, the share of the states was large enough for them to allow the blatantly exploitative system to continue. This was because of two reasons – first, the concerned governments were unable to explore, extract and export oil on their own because they had no access to the required technology, and were not wealthy enough to acquire such technology from the market, and second, till as late as the Second World War, the proven reserves of the Middle East were not known to be large enough to swing the balance in favour of the countries owning such reserves. The balance began to move away from the oil companies to the states owning such reserves only from the 1950s. By that time, oil revenues accounted for at least 50 per cent of the revenues of most of these governments. Although the attempt at nationalisation of the oil resources in Iran failed in 1951-52, the oil companies gradually began to concede a larger share of the oil revenue to the concerned states. In course of the 1960s, the countries successfully asserted their ownership rights over the resource, and foundation of the OPEC in 1960 marks, truly speaking, the end of the era of domination by the oil companies.

The difference this made in the politics of the oil-rich states was too stark to be ignored, turning these into rentier states. As the government's share of oil exports expanded steadily, the fiscal base of the government expanded substantially. In Iran, where a constitution and an elected legislature were meant to curb the power of the monarch, the oil bounty liberated the ruler, Reza Shah, from financial dependence on taxes voted by the Majlis. As the major drive for industrialisation in Iran had been powered by oil revenue from the 1920s itself, a large body of beneficiaries of the regime emerged who were willing to allow such slide into authoritarianism. This allowed him to circumscribe and ignore the powers of the Majlis pretty effectively. Similar strengthening of state finances in Saudi Arabia, courtesy royalty from the American company ARAMCO, helped hold the Saudi state together, and allowed it to overcome dependency on the British. By the end of the Second World War, while British subvention amounted to £1 million, oil revenue amounted to US$ 10 million out of total government revenue of £13.2 million.

The exponential rise in the price of oil in the 1970s enabled most of the Middle Eastern rentier states not merely to remain independent of their people in seeking resources for running the state, but also enabled the states to spend lavishly in order to develop core constituencies of supporters behind the regimes as they became more authoritarian. Beginning in the 1970s, the share of government expenditure tended to rise between thirty and fifty per cent of the GDP of most of the Gulf states, reaching as high as 74 per cent in Saudi Arabia in 1984. The only exception to this is the government of the UAE, spending on an average between 12 and 15 per cent of GDP, which also happens to be the Gulf state where authoritarianism is least pronounced.

The enhanced ability to extend patronage to the citizens took various forms. By the 1970s, all the oil-exporting states having acquired operational control, considerable ability developed in generating employment among the citizens in the oil industry itself, replacing foreign labourer wherever possible. This was particularly true of the more populous of the oil-rich states, such as Iraq and Iran, with their own pool of engineers and technicians trained abroad at state expense. The state emerged as the single largest employer in almost all the oil-rich states, by means of a bloated bureaucracy that was unprecedented in the history of the region as a whole. Official statistics indicate that 42 per cent of the citizen workforce in Kuwait and well over 50 per cent in Saudi Arabia and Oman were employed in the civil and community services run by the state during 1988-90. Anecdotal evidence suggests that the same figures for UAE around that time were as high as 75 per cent.

Apart from generating employment, the oil-rich states also began to provide the 'substitution effect' required to stimulate the non-oil sector of the economy of these states, creating demand in real estate, construction, infrastructure development, etc. Iran for instance underwent a veritable economic boom between 1962 and 1963 and 1977 and 1978, seeing the construction industry grow from a total output of 14.1 million rials (1962-63) to 179.5 million rials (1977-78). Iraq, in particular, saw a major strengthening of its programme for planned development, which it had undertaken since the overthrow of the Hashemite monarchy by a group of military officers, and then developed in greater earnest under the Ba'athist elements of the military from 1968. Between 1970 and 1974 alone, the Iraqi government's share in total expenditure in the industrial sector stood at a staggering 87 per cent, 76.6 per cent of all infrastructure-related expenditure and 100 per cent in all sectors other than agriculture, industry, transport and infrastructure. Similar quantum transformations were seen in Libya, and each of the Gulf monarchies. The road connectivity that Tripoli enjoyed with Benghazi, Misurata and Sirte (ironically contributing to Ghaddafi's fall in 2011, allowing smooth passage for rebellious troops) was as much a development of the 1970s as much as the highways traversing the kingdom of Saudi Arabia and the cityscapes of the desert-capital of Riyadh, and the businessman's delight that is Dubai. The citizenry of the oil-rich states are, in a way, given plenty of material advantages to encourage silence on matters dealing with the dispensation of power in the state.

However, cost-benefit calculus of the citizenry is not the only prop behind authoritarian tendencies of the oil-rich states of the Middle East. Alongside indulging in the politics of patronage, in the decade and a half preceding the Gulf War, restraints on the power of the ruler, as and when they seemed to have existed, vanished for all practical purposes. Or, at least attempts were made to such end. Thus, in Kuwait, the constitution and the national assembly that were introduced in 1962, began to annoy the Emir to such an extent that several political and civil rights were suspended along with the national assembly. These were restored in 1980, before the national assembly and the constitution as a whole were altogether suspended in 1986. In Saudi Arabia, where much of the legitimacy enjoyed by the ruling house derives from its credentials as 'Khadim al-Haramain' (the custodians of two of the holiest places of Islam, Mecca and Medina), the state's championship of Islam acquired a new dimension from the 1970s. Steadily, the Saudi state had reduced the 'ulema to the status effectively of civil servants by putting them on the state's payroll. Internally, this took the form of enforcement of a much stricter 'Islamic morality', with the appointment of 'mutawwains'; externally, it took the form of export of a very radical Wahhabi ideology by means of export of *'ulema* who could not be easily accommodated at home. With the possibility of any substantial challenge emerging from within the discursive space of Islam effectively pre-empted, the Saudi state had made any legitimate challenge to its authority a virtual impossibility. The best example of this was its success in thwarting demands for the introduction of a constitution, saying Allah being the only sovereign, the notion of a people exercising sovereignty was unIslamic. Such pre-emption of legitimate challenge was one of the reasons why a firebrand dissenter like Osama bin Laden had to veer towards the direction of illegitimate and military challenge to the state.

The most crucial factor in the development of the sinews of the oil-rich states however was the tremendous growth in their military capacity. This was quite tangible in the relatively more populous states of Iran and Iraq. The size of the Iranian military establishment increased from 2,00,000 in 1963 to 4,10,000 in 1977; the annual military budget increased from US$ 293 million in 1963 to US$ 1.8 billion in 1973, and then shot up to US$ 7.3 billion. The build-up of Iraqi military establishment accelerated even more rapidly as a result of the oil bounty. In 1970, Iraqi military strength had stood at 62,000 strong, climbing up to 82,000 in 1973. But by 1980, the armed forces stood at 4,30,000 on the eve of the Iran-Iraq war which began that year. Even in the relatively less populous states, the size of the armed forces and security services saw appreciable increase from the 1970s: Kuwait's armed forces doubled from 10,200 (1975) to 21,800 (1990); that of Oman rose from 16,100 to 29,400 for the same period; that Qatar rose from 4,700 (1980) to 7,000 in 1990, while that of Saudi Arabia jumped from 69,500 to 73,500 in the five years between 1975 and 1980. But the real difference in the capacity of oil-rich states with relatively less population strength is to be found in the amount spent on developing arsenal, particularly military hardware. In Libya, for instance, the armed forces grew from 14,000 strong at the time of independence (1953) to 20,000 when King Idris I was overthrown (1969). Since 1973, the strength of the armed forces has been doubled through conscription, to stand at 50,000 strong when Ghaddafi was overthrown in the revolution of 2011. Far more important was the kind of investment Colonel Ghaddafi was willing to make in defence hardware – Libya's inventory of 500 combat aircraft was roughly equivalent to that of France, although the Libya's population is only 7 per cent of the French population; during 1973-83, Libya acquired US$ 28 billion worth of arms, although the capacity of the personnel required to man the hardware had always been suspect, which was borne out by the precipitate collapse of the regime in 2011. This trend in fact developed into a veritable arms race in the Middle East at the end of the Gulf War of 1991, when almost each of Iraq's neighbours went on a buying spree, given the disclosures about Iraq's WMD programme. While most of the Persian Gulf states embarked on military expenditure ranging up to US$ 5 billion, Saudi Arabia had steadily increased its expenditure to touch US$ 25 billion in 2003, before shooting up to around US$ 43 billion in 2009.

However, while the oil economy had dramatically enhanced the coercive capabilities of the states, it had another completely unanticipated outcome in the transformation of the economic and social dynamics of the Middle East as a whole. The changed dynamics of the region had been long predicted by observers to be a possible factor in the steady erosion of the edifice of authoritarianism in the region that began in the 1990s, and can be said to have bloomed in the Arab spring of 2011.

The Challenge to Authoritarianism and the Arab Spring

For all practical purposes, the so-called Arab Spring of 2011, ousting three of the longest serving rulers in the Middle East (and possibly one or two more by the time this essay is published), has taken the world by surprise. However, a number of observers of the region as a whole, or of individual states, have long been playing Cassandra in predicting the inevitable crumbling of the edifice of authoritarianism.

What is curious about the Arab spring is that it seems to affect states that have oil wealth, as well as those which do not. Till the autumn of 2011, the disaffection which began with the self immolation of a Tunisian spread through Egypt, engulfed Yemen, Bahrain, Libya and Syria, and even left some impact on the Hashemite kingdom of Jordan. Of these, Tunisia, Egypt, Jordan, and Yemen have no oil to export, but Bahrain has oil reserves (albeit declining) and Syria has a small reserve, while Libya sits atop the largest oil reserves in Africa. Among the states only Bahrain and Jordan happen to be monarchical, and the military happens to be the mainstay of the remaining states. By the time this article went to press, three of the longest ruling leaders in the Middle East – Zain al-Abedine Ben Ali of Tunisia, Hosni Mubarak of Egypt and Muammar Ghaddafi of Libya – had been overthrown, Ali Abdullah Saleh of Yemen seems to be looking at virtually certain departure; and the Ba'athist regime of Syria under Bashar al-Asad is faced with a popular movement that is almost as determined to oust him as he is to cling on to power. By the middle of the year, the Doha based satellite television channel al-Jazeera began to gently moot the query, Who next? For the first time in the history of the region, there is a growing optimism (albeit perhaps prematurely) that authoritarianism is on the verge of collapse, because the structural props of authoritarianism appear wobbly.

The chinks began to develop in the edifice of Arab authoritarian regimes from the 1980s, largely as a result of the same oil economy which had once strengthened it. When the oil price revolution began in the 1970s, most of the oil-rich states (particularly Libya and those in the Gulf) were in no position to handle the rapid expansion of the oil-based industrial sector that followed. Determined to shake of dependence on European and American expertise, the Arab states began to bring in skilled labour (engineers, doctors, teachers, technicians, etc.) as well as unskilled (security personnel, drivers, domestics, etc.) from other Arab countries, as well as those further afield (viz. India, Pakistan, Bangladesh, Malaysia, Indonesia). Meanwhile, the Gulf States invested heavily in developing their own human capital by investing in health and public education, over and above the necessary infrastructure. The change this involved was quite dramatic. Better access to public health, drinking water and sanitation provided by the Gulf states resulted in a fairly high growth rate of population, averaging over 4 per cent in most of the states. Better access to higher education guaranteed that a far higher number of the younger generation had formal education than ever before in the history of the peninsula, averaging more than 60 per cent in most states.

The growth rate of the oil industry had been, however, slowing down from 1977 onwards. By the 1980s, the Middle Eastern economies were sliding into recession, the problems of which were accentuated by the dislocation caused by decade long Iran-Iraq war, and then the briefer but frightfully expensive Gulf War of 1991. In the continued recessionary situation of the 1990s, growing population and development of education began to impact on the issue of employment. As structural adjustment policy prescription required governments to contract the public sector wage bill, the governments adopted the policy of hiring less and early retirement, rather than settling for lay-offs.

In this background of economic recession, and the imperative to develop the defence infrastructure in the light of the discovery of Saddam's WMD programme at the end of the Gulf War, the Gulf monarchies came to confront major political disaffection. Exhibiting a firm desire to retain control over their country, all the major Gulf monarchies embarked on a very painfully slow process of political reform from above, in a bid to pre-empt revolution from below.

The country that has probably gone the greatest distance is Kuwait, where the dire financial situation at the end of the Gulf War prompted the government to impose income tax for the first time ever in the history of the kingdom. In return, the house of al-Sabah conceded greater powers to the elected national assembly. Although the Emir continued to wield sweeping powers, gradual devolution continued all through, and emboldened the national assembly to even reject the ruling house's preferred candidate Saad al-Abdullah for succession to the emirate, upon the death of Sheikh Jabar al-Ahmad in 2005, resulting in the succession of the dead emir's half-brother, Sheikh Sabah. The very next year, major grounds were broken with women being given the right to vote in elections to the national assembly.

Consultative systems were strengthened in other Gulf monarchies as well. Oman introduced a Majlis al-Shura (consultative council) in 1991 to review governmental legislation on culture, education, social and economic issues. By the mid-1990s, direct political participation had been introduced quite successfully, followed by the Basic Law of the State, laying down the constitutional structure, culminating in the decision to have a fully elected Shura council in 2000 (where, curiously, women were allowed to run as candidates, but not vote).

Bahrain had reinstituted its Majlis al-Watani (National Assembly, in abeyance since 1975) in 1993, but as a pale shadow of its former self. By 2000, however, the demand for political reform grew so much that further reforms were instituted, turning the Majlis into a bicameral legislature, along with the release of a constitution. Although the Majlis has little actual power, the mere fact of its resuscitation, coupled with the issue of a constitution and introduction of elections at the municipal level indicate weakening of the authoritarian edifice in the kingdom.

Similarly in Qatar, in response to growing demand for political freedom and representative politics culminating in a petition to the Emir signed by 54 prominent Qataris, the house of al-Thani also responded favourably. In 1995, upon the elevation of Sheikh Hamad al-Thani, Qatar committed itself to a constitution. In 1999, elections were introduced at the municipal level in 1999 with women running as candidates, and in 2003 the draft constitution was put to a referendum, and upon approval by 97 per cent of the voters came into force in 2004. Qatar has had regular elections since 1999, and the degree of press freedom it enjoys comes clear from the sharply critical position taken by the al-Jazeera over the past decade.

Even in Saudi Arabia, popularly seen as the bastion of conservatism in the region, concessions came, albeit slowly. Demands for political reforms and a constitution were made in a petition in 1991, followed by another in 1992. Riyadh responded with the introduction of a 'basic system of government' in March 1992 and the creation of its first ever consultative body, the Majlis al-Shura in 1993, alongside introduction of regional governments with their own Shura council, to allow the Saudi citizens some kind of participation in government. The pace of reforms slowed down thereafter, as the Saudi state resorted to heavy handed repression to counter an emerging Islamist opposition, from which Osama bin Laden and the al-Qaeda were to emerge around that time. However, after the launch of the War on Terror, and the worldwide crackdown on the al-Qaeda network, the Saudi state quietly resumed a very slow trek towards reforms, introducing elections at the municipal level in 2005.

It is perhaps too early too comment, but given the relative absence of disquiet in the Gulf monarchies apart from Bahrain during the Arab spring, it is tempting to argue that Bahrain suffers the most because it has advanced the least in terms of grant of political freedom to its citizens, coupled with fewer fresh material sops to bestow on them, particularly as its oil revenue happens to be faced with a terminal decline. By contrast, the Saudis appear to have been spared much discontent so far, despite the lack of political freedom of its citizens, largely because the state still has the deepest pockets in the region. Nevertheless, the government has deemed it prudent to lace its resistance to the notion of reforms under pressure from below (which prompted it to give military assistance to Bahrain to crush the protests in Manama, lest the idea catches on) with reforms from above: its move to allow women to drive by themselves, a longstanding demand, has to be seen in this context.

The other response of the Gulf States, apart from the slow process of liberalisation, was to take a hard look at the question of migrant labour. At the height of the expansion of the oil industry in the 1970s, a massive outflow of surplus labour from Arab countries like Egypt, Jordan, the West Bank, Tunisia, Yemen and Lebanon had taken place, headed for the labour-deficit countries of the Gulf as well as Libya. In 1975, such migrant labour constituted 47 per cent of the labour force in the Gulf countries, and by 1990 the proportion climbed up to 68 per cent. In Kuwait, the proportion was as high as 86 per cent of the entire workforce. All these migrant workers came in on a contractual basis and had to leave at the expiry of such contracts, because they were rarely granted citizenship. These migrant labourers were needed primarily because of two reasons – first, it cost more to employ a citizen, who was entitled to a minimum wage restriction by law, and second, there were some jobs which the educated citizen would not be willing to do, or may not be skilled enough to attend to. However, beginning in the 1990s, the Gulf States felt the imperative of reducing the number of expatriate workers. According to a study by the Economic and Social Commission for West Asia (ESCWA), by 2000 nearly 2 million workers had to return to their land of origin, of whom 7,00,000 were Egyptians, 7,00,000 were Yemenis and the nearly 3,00,000 were Jordanians and Palestinians.

The expatriates who began to return to their countries of origin, in their turn, began a process of change on the rebound. During the heyday of the oil boom, economies like Tunisia, Egypt, Jordan, Yemen and Lebanon became inextricably linked to the oil economy by exporting their surplus labour, and reaping the bounty by way of foreign exchange remittances. The remittances stimulated market demand, and therefore development of the domestic industrial and service sectors as well. The integration of the region's economy, however, had a downside as well. Given the infusion of money into the economy, strong inflationary pressures were generated in the labour-surplus economies, which (with the exception of Lebanon) hitherto tended to be tightly regulated by the tribal and/or military elites ruling them. The inflationary pressures proved too strong for such regulations to survive. While the consociational democracy of Lebanon became engulfed in a civil war that lasted a decade and a half, the authoritarian regimes began to deviate from the Nasserite model of regulated economy, and embark on gradual liberalisation. Egypt under Sadat set the example with its policy of 'infitah', with Syria under Hafiz al-Assad following in the late 1980s, and Hussein following suit.

As the oil economies slid into recession, and expatriates began to return, additional problems of relocating them in the economic life of the country had to be addressed precisely. As the expatriates had become used to a relatively high material standard by way of opportunities and public services in the oil rich states, they began to interrogate the various regimes on their failure deliver. Given the repressive character of the regimes, particularly in Egypt, Syria, Yemen and Tunisia, such interrogation resorted mostly (but not exclusively) to the only institutional apparatus left available by the state – that of Islamic voluntary organisation dispensing public services. In Egypt and Jordan, this involved the infusion of fresh blood to Ikhwan (Muslim Brotherhood), which was dominated no longer by the lower-middle and underclass, rather by the engineers, doctors and other educated and aspiring professionals. By 2000, as the economic situation continued to deteriorate, domestic and international pressure began to mount on most of the regimes to embark on steady political liberalisation as well. While elections at the municipal level began to address this demand, the grip remained fairly tight at the national level in most states. Nevertheless, liberalisation at the level of locality allowed for the emergence of genuine political opposition for the first time in ages in most of the countries.

It is still too early to understand what exactly tipped the scale in 2011 towards open opposition. However, a couple of conjectures would not be entirely out of place. During 2005-08, when oil prices shot up, the principal beneficiaries had been the oil rich states, not the labour surplus ones, owing to the policy of hiring locally encouraged from the 1990s. Once the global economic recession hit in 2008, food prices in Egypt and Tunisia shot up because the states could no longer subsidise adequately in the post-liberalisation set-up, even as economic opportunities kept on shrinking. Also, it is probably no mere coincidence that the turmoil seems to engulf precisely those countries where unemployment, particularly youth unemployment, is the highest in the region (viz. Egypt, Tunisia, Syria), and where mechanism for the redistribution of national wealth are the weakest (Syria, Tunisia, Yemen). Even among the oil rich states, Libya's continuation of hiring expatriate labour from other African countries right down to 2010, without addressing the problem of unemployment at home rendered its redistributive mechanisms the weakest. It is difficult to avoid the conclusion that the agenda of broadening of the social basis of power has finally acquired the critical mass in the Middle East. Hereafter, authoritarianism would have to reinvent itself in order to survive.

Conclusion

Authoritarianism is no more embedded in the society and polity of the Middle East than it is anywhere else in the world. The authoritarian regimes that obtain in the region came into being in the 20th century, without exception. Some of these were the creation of European powers (particularly the British) in the wake of the Great War; others came into being as a result of a power struggle to change the social basis of power in the region after the departure of the colonial powers. The authoritarian propensities of both were strengthened by the transformation of the region's economy by the rising oil revenue of the 1970s, making the regimes less responsive to the people they ruled over. However, the stagnation of the global oil prices in 1990s weakened these regimes somewhat, pushing them down the way of economic and political liberalisation. Since the 1990s, many of the Middle Eastern regimes have tried to (mostly with great reluctance) transform the edifice of authoritarianism by broadening the social basis of power in their realms in such a manner that the ruling elite (military, political, familial or tribal) may continue to wield ultimate power.

The so-called Arab spring seems to mark the dissatisfaction of the people in a large number of countries with the tardy pace of political reform in the backdrop of a languishing economic situation. This in itself is not a guarantee for the eventual triumph of democracy; indeed, it is perfectly possible that attempted redressal in terms of social balance of power degenerates into civil war, as it did in Lebanon in the 1970s. It is equally possible that Saudi Arabia's decision to bankroll resistance to pressures from below, as in Bahrain, gives authoritarianism a lease of life in the Gulf monarchies. However, authoritarianism powered by oil revenues and remittance payments looks increasingly less likely to flourish in the twenty-first century as oil reserves steadily begin to decline. The time for reckoning is fast approaching, if it has not arrived already.

Notes

1. Samuel Huntington, "Will More Countries Become Democratic", *Political Science Quarterly*, vol. 99, No. 2, (Summer 1984), p. 208.
2. Daniel Pipes, *In the Path of God: Islam and Political Power*, (New York: Basic Books, 1983), pp. 48-69, 144-47.
3. Hisham Sharabi, *Neopatriarchy: A Theory of Distorted Change in Arab Society*, (New York: Oxford University Press, 1988), p. 7.
4. Michael Hudson, *Arab Politics: The Search for Legitimacy*, (New Haven: Yale University Press, 1977), p. 165.
5. Lisa Anderson, "Absolutism and Resilience of Monarchy in the Middle East," *Political Science Quarterly*, vol. 106, no. 1, (Spring 1991), pp. 1-15.
6. Roger Owen, *State, Power and Politics in the Making of the Modern Middle East*, (London and New York: Routledge, 2000 [2nd edition]).
7. F. Gregory Gause III, *Oil Monarchies: Doemstic and Security Challenges in the Arab Gulf States*, (New York: Council on Foreign Relations Press, 1992).
8. For a sense of the dispensation of power during the closing years of the Ottoman Empire, see Hasan Kayali, *Arabs and Young Turks: Ottomanism, Arabism, and Islamism in the Ottoman Empire, 1908-1918*, (Berkeley: University of California Press, 1997).
9. See, Ervand Abrahamian, *Iran Between Two Revolutions*, (Princeton, NJ: Princeton University Press, 1982).
10. For the most detailed account of this period and the making of the map of the modern middle east, see David Fromkin, *A Peace to End All Peace: the Fall of the Ottoman Empire*

and the Creation of the Modern Middle East, (New York: Holt Paperbacks, 2001).

11. For a discussion of the French policy, see Michael Province, *The Great Syrian Revolt and the Rise of Arab Nationalism,* (Austin: University of Texas, 2005).
12. See Robert Blythe, *Empire of the Raj: Eastern Africa and the Middle East 1858-1947,* (London: Palgrave Macmillan, 2003. See also, Paul J. Rich, *Creating the Arabian Gulf: British Invasions of the Gulf,* (Lanham: Lexington Books, 2009).
13. However, the resources required for the modernisation of the state apparatus in Egypt could not be generated internally. This prompted the Egyptian state to borrow heavily from Europeans, particularly the British and the French, who accordingly gained considerable leverage in the country. As resentment grew towards such European penetration, the British moved in to safeguard their investments, and established a de facto protectorate in Cairo in 1881.
14. The French policy in both its mandated territories tended to favour the *effendiyah,* which turned out to be a great success in Lebanon where these were the dominant group. By contrast, in Syria, the *ashrafiyyah* being the dominant group, the French witnessed a major uprising in 1926, whereupon they were rehabilitated in an arrangement that more or less survived the remaining period of French Mandate.
15. See for instance, Albert Hourani ; see also Amatzia Baram, "A Case of Imported Identity: The Modernizing Secular Ruling Elites of Iraq and the Concept of Mesopotamian-Inspired Territorial Nationalism, 1922-1992", *Poetics Today,* vol. 15, no. 2, (Summer, 1994), pp. 279-319.
16. The connection with the Ottoman economic space comes out best in the fact that the idea of Arab nationalism did not gain much political appeal in the Arabian Peninsula, which had a different economic sub-system centring round the Persian Gulf.
17. For an exhaustive account of the Turkish phenomenon, see Stanford Shaw and Ezel K. Shaw, *History of the Ottoman Empire and Modern Turkey, vol. II, Reform, Revolution and Republic: The Rise of Modern Turkey (1808-1975),* (Cambridge: Cambridge University Press, 1977). For Iran, see Abrahamian, op. cit.).
18. F. Gregory Gause III, *Oil Monarchies,* p. 44-45.
19. Iran began exporting oil from 1913, Iraq from 1928, Bahrain 1934, Saudi Arabia 1938. Keith McLachlan, "Oil in the Persian Gulf Area," in Alvin J. Cottrell, *Persian Gulf States: A General Survey,* (Baltimore & London: Johns Hopkins University Press, 1980), p. 212.
20. *60 Years BP Statistical Review of World Energy,* p. 3. www.bp.com/liveassets/bp_internet/globalbp/globalbp_uk_english/reports_and_publications/ statistical_energy_review_2011/STAGING/local_assets/pdf/statistical_review_of_world_energy_60_anniversary.pdf
21. The best example of this was the attempt of Reza Shah of Iran in 1933 to renegotiate the original D'Arcy concession given to the Anglo-Persian Oil Company. He managed to reduce the geographical ambit of the original concession made out in 1901, and also pushed for a more favourable revenue mechanism. However, the share of the state could be increased from 16% of all profits to only 20%. 80% of the profits continued to be taken by APOC.
22. The scale of the bounty becomes clear from a study of some basic figures. All through the

1920s, total budgetary allocation of the government of Iran hovered around an average of 350 million rials. After the renegotiation of the revenues, the budgetary allocation increased from 625 million rials in 1934 to 4,174 million rials in 1941, that is, a seven-fold increase in state expenditure in seven years. See, Homa Katouzian, *Political Economy of Modern Iran: Despotism and Pseudo-Modernism 1926-79*, p. 120.

23. Madawi al-Rasheed, *A History of Saudi Arabia*, (Cambridge: Cambridge University Press, 2002), p. 94.
24. The price of crude oil climbed up from US$ 2.83 per barrel in 1973 to US$ 10.41 in 1974. This resulted in a quantum jump in the revenue receipts of the oil exporting countries. In 1973, Iran received revenue worth US$ 5,600 million selling 5.896 million barrels a day. In 1974, selling 6.02 million, its revenue climbed up to US$ 18,871 million. The oil revenue of Iraq during the same period jumped from .219 million to 1.7 billion at a time when out rose only by a factor of two. Fred Halliday, *Iran: Dictatorship and Development*, (Harmondsworth and New York, Penguin, 1979), p. 143. Abbas Alnasrawi, *The Economy of Iraq: Oil, Wars, Destruction of development and Prospects 1950-2010*, (London: Greenwood Press, 2010), p. 12.
25. F.G. Gause III, *Oil Monarchies*, p. 48.
26. Ibid., p. 51.
27. For instance, of the skilled technicians employed in Iranian oil industry in 1958, Iranians numbered 8,139 while foreigners numbered 693. In 1972, the number of Iranian technicians climbed up to 12,831, while foreigners reduced to 497. See Halliday, *Iran*, p. 179.
28. F.G. Gause III, *Oil Monarchies*. 59-60.
29. Source, *Annual Report*, Bank Markazi-ye Iran, cited in Katouzian, op. cit. p. 276.
30. For a detailed treatment of Iraq's attempt at developmental planning See Alnasrawi, op. cit. 35-79.
31. F. G. Gause III, *Oil Monarchies*, p. 90.
32. Abrahamian, op. cit, p. 435.
33. Alnasrawi, op. cit. pp. 91-92.
34. F.G. Gause III, *Oil Monarchies*, p. 67.
35. www.globalsecurity.org/military/world/libya/mod.htm
36. Pieter D. Wezeman, "Conventional Strategic Military Capabilities in the Middle East," www.nonproliferation.eu/documents/backgroundpapers/wezeman.pdf
37. See for instance F. Gregory Gause III, "The Gulf Conundrum: Economic Change, Population Growth, and Political Stability in the GCC states," *The Washington Quarterly*, Winter 1997, 20:1, pp. 145-65; Anoushiravan Ehteshami and Steven Wright, "Political Change in the Arab Oil Monarchies: from Liberalization to Enfranchisement", *International Affairs, 83:5*, 2007, pp. 913-32.
38. During the period 1980-96, Bahrain's population grew at 4%, Kuwait at 4.3%, Oman 4.2%, Saudi Arabia 4.6%, UAE at 5.5%. Valentine Moghadam, "Population Growth, Urbanization and the Challenges of Unemployment", in Deborah J. Gerner, *Understanding the Middle East*, (Boulder and London: Lynne Rienner, 2000), p. 244.
39. The most dramatic change is to be seen in Saudi Arabia and Oman. In Saudi Arabia

the proportion of children with secondary education climbed from 7% (1960) to 63% (1988); in Oman the same figures were 3 (1970) and 75% (1988). Literacy rates in the UAE jumped from 24% (1970) to 90% (1990). In 1969-70, 808 Saudi students graduated, all from foreign universities; in 1985-86, Saudi universities churned out 15,301 students with bachelor's or graduate degree. In UAE, the number of students churned out by University at al-'Ain has grown from 502 (1977) to 12,000 (1994-95). F.G. Gause III, "The Gulf Conundrum", p. 157.

40. Valentine Moghadam, op. cit., p. 250.
41. See, F. G. Gause III, "The Gulf Conundrum"; see also Ehteshami and Wright, "Political Change in the Oil Monarchies".
42. Ehteshami and Wright, op. cit. pp. 924-25.
43. Abdullah Juma al-Haj, "The Politics of Participation in the Gulf Cooperation Council States: the Omani Consultative Council", *Middle East Journal,* 50:4, Autumn 1996, pp. 559-71.
44. Ehteshami and Wright, op. cit pp. 918-20.
45. Ibid., pp. 921-22.
46. Ibid., pp. 926-29.
47. Moghadam, op. cit. p. 248.
48. Ibid., p. 249.
49. For Egypt, see Goldschmidt Jr. op. cit, pp. 196-99. For Syria, see Raymond Hinnebusch, "Syria: The Politics of Economic Liberalisation," *Third World Quarterly,* vol. 18, no. 2, pp. 249-65. Also Angel Joya, "Economic Liberalization and Reform in Syria: 1970-2005", pp. 16-19. www.countdownnet.info/archivio/analisi/altro/511.pdf. For Jordan see, Pete W. Moore, *Doing Business in the Middle East: Political and Economic Crisis in Jordan and Kuwait,* (Cambridge: Cambridge University Press), pp. 145-167.
50. See, Jeremy Jones, *Negotiating Change: The New Politics of the Middle East,* (London: I.B. Tauris, 2007).11-27.
51. The region shows a steady rate of 10.3% of unemployment, the highest regional rate in the world. The rate of youth unemployment stands at four times that. The regional employment to population ration stood at 45.4%, i.e. less than one out of every two people in the Middle East actually work. [Vide, *Global Employment Trends 2011: The Challenge of a Jobs Recovery,* (Geneva: International Labour Organisation, 2011) *p.* 51]. In Egypt, the official unemployment figures stand at 9% of the population in 2009-10, but more than 30% of the total unemployed hold a university degree.

9. The Arab Spring: Quo Vadis?

P R Kumaraswamy

Since early January, the Middle Eastern region has witnessed far-reaching changes. Among others, some terminologies – unrest, upheaval, revolution, democratic surge, popular protests, regime change, social change, digital revolution, internet revolution, liberation technology, revolutionary process/ movement or the Arab Spring – have been used to depict these developments; some of these terminologies have also faced criticism. Noted Lebanese journalist Rami Khouri took exception to the term 'Arab Spring'. He saw it as another manifestation of the western Orientalism.[1]In similar manner, several reasons have been attributed for this phenomenon: lack of democracy, oppression, indifference of the rulers; youth bulge and militarisation of the society. More than nine months after the initial wave of protests in Tunisia, what is the progress card of the Arab Spring? There are some noticeable changes, some improvements, some weakening of central authority, some open wounds and some financial incentives towards buying temporary peace. There are intense power struggles, with some resilient rulers willing to fight than leaving the office. A few islands of stability are also there. Nevertheless, on the whole the changes are only cosmetic. *What has happened so far?*

Leaders' Removal

Since December 2010, two prominent and once strong Arab leaders (Tunisia and Egypt), have been removed by the Arab Spring and the fate of the third (Libya) one is still unclear (The essay was written prior to the fall of Muammar Gaddafi). This is no mean achievement, considering the longevity of Arab rulers. Indeed, the idea of a ruler voluntarily relinquishing office remains alien to the Arab world. Natural deaths or assassinations seemed, till recent events in Tunisia and Egypt, to be the only accepted way to end the rule of an Arab leader. Indeed, since the end of the Second World War, no Arab ruler has voluntarily relinquished office so far. Most were either overthrown in a coup or died in the office. Monarchies were overthrown by republican regimes in Egypt (1952), Iraq (1956) and Libya (1969), while Oman (1970) and Qatar (1995) witnessed fathers being deposed by more ambitious sons. In the early years after world wars, Syrian and Iraqi rulers were changed periodically by men in uniform. The lives of King Abdullah of Jordan (1950) and King Faisal of Saudi Arabia (1975) were cut short by assassins, while some other Arab monarchs died in office. Indeed, despite his debilitating stroke in November 1995, Fahd remained the King of Saudi Arabia until his death in August 2005.

As a result, even republican regimes evolved into life-time presidencies. Muammer Qaddafi ruled Libya since September 1969 (over 41 years); Zine al-Abidine Ben-Ali of Tunisia since November 1987; Hosni Mubarak of Egypt for three decades since November 1981; Ali Abdullah Saleh of Yemen since July 1978 (first as head of North Yemen and since 1990 as the President of the unified Yemen). If one considers the father-son duo, the Assads have ruled Syria since March 1971 i.e. over four decades. [Table 2]

In contrast to their elongated dominance, while the Tunisian President Zine al-Abidine Ben-Ali struggled for 28 days before relinquishing the position, Egyptian President Hosni Mubarak needed only 18 days of public protests to leave office. While the former took political asylum in Saudi Arabia, contrary to widespread speculations during the dying days of his departure, the latter opted to stay in Egypt with his family. Though his sojourn in the sea resort of Sharm al-Sheikh proved short-lived, Mubarak did not wish to soil his reputation by seeking asylum elsewhere.

The situation elsewhere was murkier. Despite serious injuries that he suffered in the blast inside the presidential palace on June 03, Yemeni President Ali Abdullah Saleh was not ready to relinquish powers. His convalescence in Saudi Arabia did not prevent him from continuing to exercise his powers, from hospital bed in Riyadh, for running the government and conducting the civil war. On September 23, he suddenly returned to Sana'a and dispelled any rumours of him accepting the GCC-backed power sharing arrangement and relinquishing office.

In Libya, the political change remains far from certain till early October. Muammar Qaddafi's whereabouts are still unclear and despite the fall of Tripoli to the rebels on August 22, he continued to broadcast defiant speeches for weeks from his hideouts. On October 01, the forces loyal to the National Transition Council (NTC) had encircled the Qaddafi's native town of Sirte. It should not be forgotten that the rebel 'victory' was made possible by the protracted military air campaign by NATO that lasted over six months. Indeed, in early June, the NATO had quietly extended its initial 90-day deadline for the successful completion of the Libyan operations.

There are no signs that other Arab rulers are in a mood to leave. Six months of protests have not resulted in any political change in Syria and President Bashar al-Assad's hold on power has not diminished.

Weakening of Rulers

While only two and a half rulers were changed, many Arab rulers are considerably weakened and have become vulnerable to public protests. The spate of concessions offered by Mubarak since late January clearly indicated that his hold on power was waning. He was ready to offer concessions which were once unthinkable: not to seek re-election in September 2011, and not to appoint his son Gamal as successor or merely to serve in office until orderly transfer of power to a civilian government was completed. Above all, Mubarak sworn in a new government under Omar Suleiman as first vice-president though it proved insufficient to tide over the opposition.

There were similar, although cosmetic, changes introduced by some rulers in other Arab countries that faced public protests and upheavals Unpopularity forced the rulers of Jordan and Syria to dismiss prime ministers and sworn in new governments. On February 01, Samir al-Rifai was replaced by Marouf Bakhit as the Prime Minister of Jordan. Similarly, on April 14, Assad replaced Muhammad Naji al-Otari with Adel Safar as the Prime Minister. Going a step further and responding to criticisms over corruption, in June, Assad was ready to sacrifice a powerful businessman and confidant Rami Makhlouf (Assad's cousin). His decision to quit business and move to charity work was seen as an appeasement towards the opposition who accused Makhlouf of being a symbol of corruption.[2]

New Openness

Serious opposition, especially from the Islamists, forced Jordan and Morocco to go beyond cosmetic changes. Both were not ready to accept the key oppositional demand of constitutional monarchy, yet both rulers made significant concessions to the opposition. While King Mohammed VI settled for the enhancement of powers of the parliament, King Abdullah was prepared to give up some of his powers which were the bone of contention with the opposition. By an overwhelming majority, the Moroccans endorsed the reform package of the King through a referendum held on July 01. Jordan, however, opted for a more rigorous parliamentary procedure and introduced as many as 41 amendments in the Constitution of 1952.[3] Through his address to the Jordanian citizens, the King promised to hold the 'next parliamentary elections according to the compatible political laws that resulted from this dialogue and seek to realise more just representation, to encourage the free and effective participation of national political parties in parliamentary elections and to enable members of Parliament to participate in the government based on their party programmes and the proportion of their representation in the House of Representatives'.[4] A couple of days later, he observed that it would require 'two or three years' for the political parties to become 'mature and well enough established to make gains in legislative elections, and, subsequently, to implement their programmes on the ground'.[5] This is seen by many as a pledge for an elected government to replace the current practice of royally appointed one. Likewise, on March 19, Egyptians went to a referendum to amend the constitution that allowed political parties to take part in the parliamentary elections. It also put certain restrictions upon those who can contest the presidential election, now slated for early 2012.

While many countries pledged for more open legislative accountability, elections were confined to local elections in Saudi Arabia (September 29), by-elections in Bahrain (September 24) and the first partial elections to the advisory council in the UAE (September 24). Responding to popular demands, King Abdullah promised in September that the Saudi women would be allowed to take part and contest in the next local elections scheduled for 2015, and that women would be included in the currently nominated Majlis al-Shura. More critical elections to parliaments in Tunisia, Egypt and Morocco would be held in late 2011 while the Jordanian elections are expected in the second half of 2012. Only when these elections are held, one can make a better assessment of the gains and losses of the Arab Spring.

These small openings have to be seen within the wider context of managed elections in the past. [Table 3] Partly due to the popularity of the idea and partly due to international pressures, some rulers have resorted to elections to justify their continuance in office. Such legitimacy-seeking exercises are often cosmetic and fraudulent. In July 2000, Bashar al-Assad secured 97.29 per cent of the valid votes cast and was elected President; this figure improved to 97.6 per cent in May 2007. The same held true for Hosni Mubarak who secured 97.1 per cent of the valid votes cast in July 1987; 96.3 per cent in October 1993; and 93.8 per cent in October 1999. In September 2005, for the first time, Mubarak faced multiple candidates but he still secured 88.58 per cent of the popular vote. Tunisian ruler Ben-Ali, likewise, secured 99.3 per cent of the votes cast in April 1989; 99.9 per cent in March 1994; 99.5 per cent in October 1999; 94.5 per cent in October 2004 and 89.62 per cent in October 2009. In comparison, the Algerian ruler Bouteflika was better and secured only 73.8 per cent in April 1999; 84.99 per cent in April 2004, and 90.24 per cent in April 2009.

The same story holds true for parliamentary elections. Most monarchies do not have elected representative councils and prefer to deal with nominated bodies. Those who hold periodic elections, such as Egypt, ensure domination of the ruling party and decimation of the rest. In the November 2010 parliamentary election, Mubarak was not ready to concede even a single seat to the opposition Muslim Brotherhood in the first round of elections. Elections in Jordan are relatively fair but are heavily loaded in favour of the Bedouins, the principal backers of the Hashemites. Through effective gerrymandering, the Hashemites have sought to marginalise urban constituencies, inhabited mainly by Jordanians of Palestinian origin.

Financial Package

However, the immediate response of most of the Arab states, especially the rentier economies was to offer financial largess as a way of pacifying the domestic opposition. Both rich and poor countries sought to bribe their citizens.

- The impoverished Jordan was the first to respond to the public protest and in mid-January, the government announced a US$ 125 million financial package that included pay raise for civil servants and increased subsidies for stable food items such as sugar and rice. Speaking at the parliament, the soon-to-be-replaced Prime Minister Samir Rafai put the cost of additional subsidies and raises for 2011 at US$ 425 million.[6]
- In early February, Bahraini ruler promised nearly US$ 2,700 for each family.
- Still in his hospital bed in the US in late February, King Abdullah promised US$ 37 billion worth of aid package to Saudi citizens, which included pay rise, new jobs and reprieve to imprisoned debtors. Upon his return to the kingdom in March, he went for a second round of concessions and on March 18, 2011, King Abdullah promised further US$ 93 billion as welfare measures.
- On February 16, Sultan Qaboos Bin Said announced a hike in the minimum monthly salary from US$ 365 to US$ 520 for private sector workers.

- Since oil reserves of some of the Gulf countries are depleting, in March the GCC pledged to provide US$ 10 billion each to Bahrain and Oman towards job generating measures.[7]
- It would be safe to conclude that if and when Assad adopts a more conciliatory posture or a pro-Saudi regime is installed in Damascus, Riyadh would be more accommodative towards Syria and its needs.

Resilient Rulers

The early departure of Ben-Ali and Mubarak has apparently hardened the attitude of other Arab rulers. The once strong and powerful rulers of Tunisia and Egypt did not live up to their 'reputation' and surrendered rather easily and without a fight. This appears to be the reading of other rulers, especially in the non-monarchical countries such as Libya, Syria and Yemen. There are no signs that other Arab rulers are in any mood to leave. The same holds true for the monarchical Bahrain where the conservatives appear to hold sway over the reformist branch of the ruling dynasty. Prime Minister and ruler's Uncle Shaikh Khalifa bin Salman Al-Khalifa is often held responsible for sabotaging the efforts by the Crown Prince to reach out to the protestors.[8]

As a result, some rulers have plunged their countries into a virtual civil war and the resultant deaths and destructions. In early October, the spokesperson for the UN High Commissioner for Human Rights announced: "Based on our detailed list of individual names that we have been keeping, the total number of people killed in Syria since protests began now stands at more than 2,900."[9] The Syrian government claims that a large number of security personnel were killed since March. There are no reliable estimates of the civilian casualties in Libya and Yemen but it is clear that hundreds have been killed and maimed in both countries. There were widespread human rights violations by both government and security forces. There are suggestions of a large number of mass graves in Libya where the opponents of the regime were brutally killed. There was also retaliation from the other side and in early September, the Human Rights Watch urged the transition NTC government in Libya to 'stop the arbitrary arrests and abuse of African migrant workers and black Libyans assumed to be mercenaries'.[10]

The resilience has resulted in direct external interventions. Two resolutions by the UN Security Council 1970 and 1973 enabled the NATO to launch an air campaign against Libya to enforce a 'no-fly-zone'. This campaign soon became a code-word for regime change and European countries, especially France, took the lead in arming and assisting the Libyan rebels to overthrow the Qaddafi regime. A different kind of external intervention was played out in Bahrain. Led by Saudi Arabia, a 1,000-strong GCC force crossed the King Fahd causeway on March 15 to shore up the beleaguered al-Khalifa regime. Though the bulk of the forces have been withdrawn soon, the message was loud and clear: Saudi Arabia would not allow the overthrow of the al-Khalifa rule in Manama.

The status-quoist Bahraini rulers enjoy Saudi support. Besides providing refuge to Ben-Ali, Saudi rulers disapproved the American reversal on Egypt and Obama's call for Mubarak 'to heed' to the public demand. In a rare public display of Arab solidarity with a beleaguered ruler, King Abdullah cautioned against Mubarak's removal. A similar but less articulated approach is apparent in Yemen. The continuation of Saleh in Yemen would not be possible without Saudi backing, especially when he was rushed to Riyadh following the explosive attack on the presidential palace on June 03. The injured president was treated in Saudi Arabia and his political appetite only increased.

There are suggestions that the invitations to Jordan and Morocco to become members of the Gulf Cooperation Council were primarily aimed at consolidating the gulf monarchies. While Jordan is a proximate to the Gulf, it is not a littoral of the Gulf and such excuse does not apply to Morocco.[11] The desire to transform the regional GCC into a club of monarchies is obvious. There are suggestions that the recent meetings between the Abdullahs of Saudi Arabia and Jordan were primarily aimed at slowing down political reforms in Jordan. The continuation of the Saleh regime in Yemen is also due to Saudi support.

Somewhat different kind of intervention is being played out in Syria. It is widely believed that forces hostile to the Assad regime are smuggling weapons from Lebanon, Turkey, Jordan and Iraq into the country and contributing to the prolonged violence.

Military's Pre-eminence

The popular uprising only brought home the centrality of the military in Arab politics. One of the primary reasons for the popular discontent and protests is the militarised nature of the Arab societies. Since the end of colonialism, the survival of many Arab rulers has rested on the military, especially the notorious internal security services or Mukhabarat. The military not only formed the power base of the rulers but also kept the population under constant check and surveillance. The military flourished at the cost of the development agenda and through excessive military spending, upkeep and modernisation, Arab rulers maintained and retained the support and loyalty of the security establishment. This support has been crucial for the prolongation of the rule of many Arab rulers. (See chart for the longevity of Arab rulers)

Many Arab rulers, especially the republican ones, had strong military background, for example, Mubarak (Egypt), Hafiz al-Assad (Syria), Qaddafi (Libya), and Ben-Ali (Tunisia). The former ophthalmologist Bashar al-Assad of Syria is an exception but his survival rests on the continued loyalty and support of the Alwaite-dominated Syrian army.

The situation of the monarchies is somewhat different. Abdullah, who became the King of Saudi Arabia in August 2005, has been the head of the powerful National Guards since its founding in 1962.[12] The same holds true for the other Abdullah, the King of Jordan, who was trained to be an elite commando before his father, King Hussein, switched the succession line in his favour just days before his death. Arab monarchies, especially the oil rich ones, spend a considerable amount on the military and have been the principal consumers of most modern inventories. Though the usefulness of many of the acquisitions has been periodically questioned, arms trade has become an effective means of cultivating and maintaining strong political contacts with the West.

Hence, for decades the military has been the source of power, patronage, employment and a tool of intimidation. The departure of Ben-Ali happened because the military changed sides and decided to abandon the former military officer. The same holds true for Egypt where the military nudged the reluctant Mubarak, a former air force chief, to leave the presidential palace. The lack of military background was often seen as the primary cause for his son Gamal's failure to take the political plunge. At the same time, the determination of the military to side with the rulers, have prolonged the crises in Libya, Syria and Yemen. Mubarak's survival depended upon the military but the latter could survive independent of Mubarak. Hence, even after Mubarak's departure and eventual trial, the military continues to rule Egypt, while, the former intelligence Chief Omar Suleiman took over the reins from Mubarak, the Supreme Military Council is headed by former general and Defence Minister Field Marshal Mohamed Hussein Tantawi.

The situation is radically different and acute in Syria. While Assad's political survival rests on the military, the latter depends on the former for its continued hold on the country. If Assad were to be toppled, the regime which is dominated by the Alawite minority would crumble and so will the army and the security establishment. The Alawite nature of the regime meant that the ruler and military are somewhat intertwined in Syria and the survival of one rests on the survival of the other.

Hence, whether the status quo continues or changes happen, military has continued to wield considerable influence in the Arab countries and the Arab spring has not diluted the importance of the military or its role in the political arena.

External Interference

The US Role

Until mid-March, when public protests broke out in Syria, the Arab unrest swept countries which are seen to be closer to the US. Not that every pro-US regime has witnessed unrest (for example, Qatar and the UAE), but wherever it happened, the regime is seen to be more pro-Western than necessary. The outbreak of violence in Syria and anti-Hezbollah protests in Lebanon has challenged this interpretation. Simmering discontent in Syria and Iran and anti-Hezbollah protests in Lebanon added regional and all inclusive flavour to the uprising.

Like many other powers, the US has not been quick in responding to the Arab Spring. At one level, anti-regime demonstrations signalled the popular disapproval of autocratic rulers and genuine longing for democracy and freedom. However at the same time, some of the most popular demonstrations took place against rulers who were considered as staunch allies of Washington. For long, various US administrations have sidestepped the widespread discontent over democracy and human rights violations in favour of larger strategic goals. Public alienation of the rulers placed Washington in a quandary and, as happened to the Shah of Iran during the dying days of the monarchy, the US began distancing itself from the unpopular Arab rulers. American calls for dialogue became a codeword for the 'abandonment' of the rulers by their erstwhile patron and significantly strengthened the opposition movements, especially in Egypt and Libya. The US has been muted in its response to events in Bahrain and the Saudi determination to militarily intervene in defence of the al-Khalifa rule. Though it had stepped up its criticisms and imposed sanctions against the Assad regime, the US policy towards Syria has been governed more by stability than democracy.

Conclusion

What began as a protest by a marginalised vegetable vendor Mohamed Bouazizi in Sidi Bouzid in Tunisia, has transformed the Middle East beyond recognition.

The levels of protest and the causes underlying them have been different and are country-specific. What is relevant for an authoritarian republican regime may not be applicable to a benevolent monarchy and vice-versa. Popular resentments against despotic rulers may not be applicable to countries where the rulers are still popular, do not live in caged palaces and freely mingle with their citizens. Uneven levels of popular protests and the relative grip of the rulers highlight the peculiarity of each Arab society. There are a number of local cleavages, such as sectarian discord (Bahrain), national disharmony (Jordan) or rural-urban divide (Egypt) or regional divide (Libya), which have exasperated the tension and public protests.

Despite their widespread nature and vociferous calls for democracy, the uprisings lack recognised leadership and coherent agenda. Besides the common consensus against the rulers they also lack a clear agenda, platform, charter of demands or action plan. Winds of change are visible but the direction still remains unclear.

Table 9.1: Some Basic Data Concerning the Middle East

Country	GDP	Per capita	Defence budget	Population	Active military	Para military	Reserve
Algeria	161	4,714	5.3	34.178	1,47,000	187,000	
Bahrain	20	27,446	697m	728,000[13]	8,200	11,260	
Egypt	186	2,370	3..27[14]	78.866	4,68,500	3,97,000	4,79,000
Iran	359	5,418	9.59[15]	66	5,23,000	40,000	3,50,000
Iraq	76	2,627	-	28.945	5,78,000	-	-
Israel	198	27,390	9.78	7.233	1,76,000	8,000	5,65,000
Jordan	21	3,347	2.31	6.269	1,00,500	10,000	65,000
Kuwait	123	46,027	6.65	2.692[16]	15,500	7,100	23,700
Lebanon	30.7	7,642	911m	4.017	59,100	20,000	-
Libya	37.2	5,880	-	6.324	76,000		40,000
Morocco	95.2	3,043	3.19	31.285	195,000	50,000	1,50,000
Oman	54.2	15,860	4.06	3.418[17]	42,600	4,400	-
Qatar	90	1,08,138	1.75[18]	8,83,000[19]	11,800	-	-
Saudi Arabia	410	14,316	41.2	28.686[20]	2,33,500	15,500	-
Syria	53.3	2,448	1.87	21.762	3,25,000	108,000	3,14,000
Tunisia	39.9	3,800	534[21]	10.486	35,800	-	-

UAE	245	51,220	15.47	4,798[22]	51,000	-	-
Turkey	658	8,561	9.9	76.805	5,10,000	102,000	3,78,700[23]
Yemen	229	1,000	1.55	22.858	?	?	?

Source, Military Balance, 2009 (London: IISS)

Note: Defence Budget In billions US$ 2009; M=millions;

Table 9.2: Arab Rulers for Life

Country	Ruler	Date of ascendance
Algeria	Abdul-Aziz Boute-Flika	April 27, 1999
Bahrain	Sheikh Hamad bin Isa al-Khalifa	March 06, 1999; As King since February 14, 2002
Egypt	Hosni Mubarak	October 13, 1981
Jordan	King Abdullah II	February 07, 1999
Kuwait	Sheikfh Sabah al Ahmad al-Sabah	January 19, 2006
Libya	Col Muammar Qaddafi	September 08, 1969
Morocco	King Muhammad VI	July 23, 1999
Oman	Qaboos bin Said al-Said	July 23, 1970
Qatar	Amir Khalifa ath Thani	June 27, 1995
Saudi Arabia	King Abdullah	August 01, 2005
Tunisia	Zin al Abidine Ben-Ali	November 07, 1987
UAE	Khalifa bin Zayed an nahhiyan	November 02, 2004
Syria	Basher al Assad	July 17, 2000
Yemen	Abdullah Saleh	July 18, 1978 to May 22, 1990 as President of North Yemen; as president of Yemen since May 22, 1990;

Source: Adapted from Europa Year Book, 2010

Table 9.3

Some of the farcical elections in the Middle East and the margin of winners	
Syria	since Bashar Assad became President in 2000 ❍ July 2000 (97.29 per cent); May 2007 (97.6 per cent)
Egypt	since October 1981 when Mubarak became President ❍ July 1987 referendum for President (97.1); ❍ October 1993 (96.3 per cent) ❍ October 1999 (93.8) ❍ September 2005 88.57 popular vote first multi-candidate election

Algeria	since Abdul-Aziz Boute-Flika became President in April 1999 ❍ April 1999 73.8 per cent ❍ April 2004 84.99 per cent ❍ April 2009 90.24 per cent
Tunisia	since November 1987 ❍ April 1989 99.3 per cent ❍ March 1994 99.9 per cent ❍ October 1999 99.5 per cent ❍ October 2004 94.5 per cent ❍ October 2009 89.62 per cent

Source: Adapted from Europa Year Book, 2010

Table 9.4: Raging Age

Country	Population	Under 25
Algeria	35.9	47.5
Bahrain	1.2	43.9
Egypt	84.6	52.3
Iraq	31.4	60.6
Jordan	6.4	54.3
Kuwait	3.5	37.7
Lebanon	4.3	42.7
Libya	18.7	47.4
Morocco	32.4	47.7
Oman	3.3	51.5
Palestinian Authority	4.1	64.4
Qatar	1.7	33.8
Saudi Arabia	27.1	50.8
Sudan	43.2	59.0
Syria	22.5	55.3
Tunisia	10.4	42.1
UAE	6.7	31.8
Yemen	24.3	65.4

Source: *The Economist*, February 05, 2011

Notes

1. Rami G Khouri, "Spring or Revolution?" *The Jordan Times*, August 19, 2011.
2. Anthony Shadid, "Reviled Tycoon, Assad's Cousin Resigns in Syria, *The New York Times*, June 16, 2011. http://www.nytimes.com/2011/06/17/world/middleeast/17syria.html

3. These amendments were approved by both the houses of parliament and ratified by the King on September 30, 2011.
4. Speech of His Majesty King Abdullah II on the Occasion of Arab Revolt, Army Day and Coronation Day, Amman, Jordan, June 12, 2011, http://www.kingabdullah.jo/index.php/en_US/speeches/view/id/478/videoDisplay/0.html, accessed on October 02, 2011.
5. *The Jordan Times*, June 15, 2011.
6. "Jordan Expands Subsidies, Raises Pay", *Arab News*, January 20, 2011, http://arabnews.com/economy/article239071.ece
7. "$20b GCC Aid Package for Oman and Bahrain", *Khaleej Times*, March 10, 2011, http://www.khaleejtimes.com/DisplayArticle09.asp?xfile=data/middleeast/2011/March/middleeast_March192.xml&section=middleeast
8. Caryle Murphy, "How Hardliners Ruined Chance of Compromise in Bahrain", *The National*, April 04, 2011, http://www.thenational.ae/news/world/middle-east/how-hardliners-ruined-chance-of-compromise-in-bahrain
9. "Death Toll in Syria Rises to 2,00: UN", *Reuters*, October 06, 2011, http://www.reuters.com/article/2011/10/06/us-syria-un-idUSTRE7952SH20111006
10. "Libya should Stop Arbitrary Arrests of Black Africans", September 04, 2011, *Human Rights Watch*, http://www.hrw.org/news/2011/09/04/libya-stop-arbitrary-arrests-black-africans
11. For example, the distance between the Moroccan capital Rabat and the Iraqi port city of Basra is 5, 105 kilometres or 2,756 nautical miles. http://www.timeanddate.com/worldclock/distanceresult.html?p1=206&p2=1051, accessed on 2 October 2011.
12. He relinquished this in November 2010 and was succeeded by his son and deputy, Mautaib bin Abdullah.
13. Nationals 64 per cent.
14. 2008 figures.
15. 2008 figures.
16. Nationals 35 per cent.
17. Expatriates 27 per cent.
18. 2008 figures.
19. Nationals 25 per cent.
20. Nationals 73 per cent.
21. 2008 figures.
22. Nationals 24 per cent.
23. Plus 50,000 paramilitary reserve.

10. THE FAÇADE OF SOCIAL CAPITAL AND DEMOCRACY: THE CASE OF EGYPT

Nadine Sika

Social capital has been widely perceived as a positive force for development, by many social scientists. In fact, the World Bank adopted this approach as an important growth indicator through which the poor could be included. The approach comes from liberal theorists who argue that the development of social capital creates a vibrant civil society, which is essential for democracy. According to most researches, thus far, social capital is also highly correlated with education: the higher the education level of an individual, the higher his/her civic participation and consequent trust in the system.[1] However, much of this research failed to identify the dynamics of social capital in authoritarian regimes.[2]

This study seeks to challenge the social capital theory as applied by the World Bank. I hypothesise that in developing nations, especially those governed by authoritarian regimes; the prevalence of social capital can reinforce authoritarianism, while its absence can help in the democratisation process. Civic and political participation might be absent in authoritarian regimes because citizens, individuals do not participate deliberately in civil society organisations, political parties, and in elections that are known to be mired with corruption. Accordingly, trust in the socio-political system is low, and an individual's social networks are the privilege of a few who are entrenched in patron-client relations. By the same token, individuals who do participate in elections; do so either in obedience to their managers at work or to help family and friends win office, regardless of their education standard. Hence, the possibilities of networking and trust within the system are based on patron client relations, which reinforce authoritarianism, rather than developing democracy or democratic values.

This study will highlight the importance of revisiting the social capital theory, especially from the World Bank's perspective, particularly in light of the recent Arab uprisings that were mainly the result of educated citizens' mobilisation efforts. It will first trace the conceptual development of social capital in theory and then its development as indicators, as identified by the World Bank. This will shed light on the negligence of the World Bank to take into consideration counter arguments by only advancing the liberal theoreticians' perspectives on developmental studies and practice. Social capital will only be a mirage if we are to rely on positive indicators alone because they do not necessarily advance knowledge of the dynamics of authoritarian rule and the transition to democracy.

Second, the research will apply World Bank indicators to a survey study in Egypt[3] to show the dichotomy between the high level of political knowledge of the well educated and their low levels of trust and participation in civic and political activities.

Social Capital: From Theory to Indicators

The most important contributors to the development of the concept of Social Capital have been Bourdieu[4], Coleman [5] and Putnam.[6] According to Bourdieu, there are three forms of capital that have a symbolic relationship – economic, cultural and social. While we might be more familiar with the economic and cultural aspects, social capital increases networking among different institutions and between the economic and cultural capital. He emphasises the importance of class distinction in society as an important factor in holding social networks together.[7] For Bourdieu, social capital is "the sum of current and potential resources which are linked to possession of a network of lasting relations, of more or less institutionalised shared acknowledgement and recognition."[8] Even though he addresses both the negative and the positive connotations of social capital, Coleman's and Putnam's more positive perspectives are the ones most cited in development studies.[9]

Unlike Bourdieu, Coleman[10] and Putnam[11] developed the concept from a more classic liberal perspective, by identifying the importance of social capital as a social function, but linking it more with trust and cooperation rather than with social conflict.[12] Here social capital is a concept defined by the social structure, which facilitates the actions of individuals who lie within it. Thus, the social interaction between individuals is an essential aspect of social capital formation.[13] Putnam further develops these ideas, and emphasises the importance of social capital as the 'features of social organisation, such as trust, norms and networks that can improve the efficiency of society by facilitating coordinated action'.[14] He also identifies horizontal networks that develop civic skills, as opposed to vertical ones that promote clientelistic relationships. Horizontal relationships increase norms of reciprocity and facilitate the functioning of communication and the flow of information.[15] Foley and Edwards[16] further emphasised the difference between networks and norms and defined them as the essential aspects of social capital. Portes [17] developed the concept even further by separating an individual's membership in a network or group, as the main source of social capital. Building on this definition, trust becomes an important product of social capital, rather than a reason for it.[18] Giddens[19] identifies trust as 'networks that individuals can draw upon for social support'. It was Putnam,[20] however, who brought this concept out from the micro level of the individual to the macro level of polity. This macro analysis is essential for my study because it looks at social capital at the national level, as well as ways it could enhance the development and consolidation of democracy within a certain polity.

The World Bank identifies 'trust' as an important attribute per se, without developing on Portes' idea of trust as a by-product of social capital. Other thinkers like Paxton,[21] identify trust as a key element to understand the interdependency of both social capital and democracy in various countries. He believes that social capital can help to create democracy in an authoritarian regime, and at the same time can improve an already consolidated democracy. It is important for disseminating knowledge about an authoritarian regime, and is influential in developing a social space that delegitimises this regime. The argument goes that trust is developed by participating in different associations, and individuals can become more democratic on the micro level and help democratisation at the macro level.[22] Nevertheless, the following analysis of the World Bank's indicators for social capital will shed light on the incapability of these indicators to advance sufficient knowledge about the dynamics of citizens' civic and political behaviour in authoritarian regimes.

Social Capital and Education

The link between social capital and education was developed much earlier by John Dewey's perception of civic education and democracy. According to Dewey, Society means association; coming together in joint intercourse and action for the better realisation of any form of experience which is augmented and confirmed by being shared.[23] Thus, education constructs a shared feeling of belonging and binding. Dewey, who believed in participating in school-led activities to increase cooperation between individuals, advanced the idea of cooperative learning. Others, like Dill[24] who built on previous research about civic engagement at the school level[25] linked education with the school environment by showing a close correlation between the latter and the increase in social capital for students. In fact, students who engage in school activities learn to trust their institutions and learn civic and political engagement at school, so when they become young adults they participate effectively in their civic and political environments.

Taking these different views into consideration and believing in the importance of social capital in development, the World Bank identified different indicators based on its identification of the most important concepts of social capital:

- Groups and Networks: civic engagement is essential for its horizontal and vertical ties, and also for bridging and bonding through networks. Political participation, though not essential for the World Bank's indicators, becomes an important tool to understand the macro level of analysis. Rather than concentrating only on the individuals' participation in his/her community, looking at the macro level like participating in elections becomes essential. Thus, in the following analysis the main indicator depends on the extent to which an individual participates in elections (parliamentary and presidential), in addition to membership in political parties, civil society organisations, or syndicates.
- Trust and Solidarity: develop an individual's behaviour, and foster cohesion and collective action in society.
- Collective Action and Cooperation: this indicator is mostly concerned with the capability of people to work together to resolve their communal problems.
- Social Cohesion and Inclusion: by ensuring the inclusion of the poor and marginal in society within the developmental process of a given nation.
- Information and Communication: enables the improvement of social capital by acknowledging the importance of access to information and by breaking down the negative social capital (World Bank 2011).

Except for social cohesion and inclusion[26], by applying these indicators to Egypt the research found a missing link in social capital theory and its indicators based on the World Bank's analysis. The theory states that education is necessary to develop the social capital skills that will effectively lead to democracy. Thus on a depoliticised scale, the World Bank finds social capital accumulation in developing countries to be essential for the inclusion of the poor in the socio-economic development process, and for the development of democracy. Nevertheless, empirical evidence in Egypt, found out that essential parts of social capital, like voting, membership in civil society organisations, collective action and cooperation, are not prevalent, due to the nature of the authoritarian system of the regime. However, the absence of social capital is a result of citizens' increased knowledge, and understanding of the nature of the authoritarian structure they live in, rather than their inability to participate in and trust the system per se. Consequently, social capital is low in general. It is relatively higher amongst the highly educated; however, its prevalence sustained an authoritarian system for three decades, rather than diminishing it. The dichotomy herein, is that highly educated individuals, who did not participate in civil society organisations, or political parties, and rarely voted in any elections, sparked the Egyptian January 25 revolution.[27] Moreover, as will be shown in the following, those who have had high education levels and did indeed have higher social capital levels than the less educated, were doing so for their individual advantage within a highly corrupt regime.

Data and Methodology

The study uses the Socio-Economic Returns of Education survey conducted in five Egyptian governorates from September 2009 to March 2010 by Partners in Development for Research Consultancy and Training. It was based on a multi-phased random sampling from rural and urban governorates in Upper and Lower Egypt, along with Cairo as the major urban governorate.[28] The sample was chosen together with the Central Agency for Public Mobilisation and Statistics in Egypt (CAPMAS) that conducted the sampling from the 2006 population census (the last population census in Egypt). The sample was composed of two parts: The first part was concerned with the socio-economic standards of families and individuals in Egypt. This part was composed of 2,364 families, representing 9,363 individuals.[29] Within this sample, there were 4,516 (48.2 per cent) women respondents and 4,847 (51.8 per cent) men respondents. The second part of the sample, was concerned with the socio-political attitudes of individuals, here, another sample from these 9,363 individuals was taken, amounting to 3,918 individuals, with the same value of 48.2 per cent women and 51.8 per cent men.[30]

Groups and Networks

As argued by social capitalists and the World Bank, civic participation is essential for social capital through vertical and horizontal networks. [31] This section capitalizes on vertical links in civil society organisations and on horizontal links by analysing membership in civil society organisations and voting behaviours.[32] Table 1 shows that participation in political parties, is very low, with only 6.7 per cent membership. Of these, the highly educated constitute the highest percentage, with 9.9 per cent membership. When I asked party members, mainly former NDP members, the reasons behind their membership, the most common answer was to attain better services and to decrease bureaucratic arrangements in government institutions.[33] Hence, party association amongst the highly educated, is for patron-client relations, rather than for the advancement of democratic governance.

Civic participation in nongovernmental organisations is even lower than political participation, with an average of 1.24 per cent membership, as revealed by Table 2. The low participation level is no surprise, given the nature of state security intervention in the proceedings of nongovernmental organisations. For example, according to Tadros,[34] Since the period around mid-2000, the [State Security Investigators] SSI has increasingly moved from exercising hidden power as a secret actor to one which exercises visible power vis-a-vis the civil society arena and public life. Syndicate membership, on the other hand, has the highest membership levels, especially amongst highly educated individuals as shown in Table 3. However, the nature of professional syndicates whose membership is dependent on technocrats is one of the main reasons behind this high percentage of membership. Moreover, syndicates that have higher levels of membership manifest state control. For instance, Law 100/1993 erected major impediments to the electoral process of professional syndicates to counterbalance the Islamic radicals' threat that was able to control them through the ballot box. As a consequence, the law ensured the hegemony of the NDP over these syndicates.[35] Thus, civic engagement through membership in civil society organisations, and political engagement, through voting in these organisations in Egypt does not reflect the 'positive' sequence of social capital Putnam and the World Bank envision, on the other hand, it obstructed the normal proceedings of democracy. On the other hand, state interventionism in these organisations is highly indicative of the precedence of state power over civil society.

Table 10.1: Membership in Political Parties

Are you a member in any Political		Less than Secondary Education	Secondary	Above Secondary Education	Total
Yes	Count	20	46	37	103
	% within education categories	4.2	6.6	9.9	6.7
No	Count	454	650	338	1442
	% within education categories	95.8	93.4	90.1	93.3
Total	Count	474	696	375	1545
	% within education categories	100	100	100	100

Table 10.2: Membership in Non Governmental Organisations[36]

Are you a member of an NGO?		Less than Secondary Education	Secondary	Above Secondary Education	Total
Yes	Count	1	2	2	5
	% within education categories	0.67	1.1	2.67	1.24
No	Count	150	179	73	402
	% within education categories	2	1	3	1.2
Total	Count	151	181	75	407
	% within education categories	100	100	100	100

Table 10.3: Membership in Professional Syndicates

Are you a member in a Political party?		Less than Secondary Education	Secondary	Above Secondary Education	Total
Yes	Count	23	121	568	712
	% within education categories	8.3	12.1	66.8	33.5
No	Count	254	880	282	1416
	% within education categories	91.7	87.9	33.2	66.5
Total	Count	277	1001	850	2128
	% within education categories	100	100	100	100

Civic engagement is an example of vertical links, which lead to bonding on a macro level in this study, and to understand how this engagement can lead to bridging between the civic community and the polity, voting patterns of individuals were analysed. These further identified the problem with social capital in authoritarian regimes. Table 4 shows patterns of voting behaviour in Egypt that indicate very low turnouts in elections. Only 37.8 per cent of all respondents revealed that they have voted at least once in their lifetime. Hence, this is an indication, that the percentages of citizens who actually go to the ballot box and vote regularly are even lower than this number. For example, according to some estimates, no more than 10 per cent of the eligible voters went to vote during the 2010 parliamentary elections in Egypt[37]. This low turnout is an act of dissent, against the authoritarian structure of governance that is known to be marred by corruption, vote rigging and vote buying.[38] Moreover, amongst the higher educated citizens, the main reason for voting was to please the government officials, as revealed in Table 5. Thus, 83.6 per cent of the highly educated individuals who have voted once in their lifetimes do so, not because they believe in the importance of participation for democracy, but rather for pleasing government officials. This shows their submission to the regimes' choice; especially in professional syndicates given that the highest levels of participation among educated individuals are in syndicates, as shown earlier. For instance, the 2010 press syndicate elections showed high scale mobilisation by the former NDP to make Makram Mohamed Ahmed, longtime head of the syndicate, win the election against Al-Tajamu' party's candidate, Diaa' Rashwan.

Table 10.4: Voting Behaviour

Did you vote at least once in your life?		Less than Secondary Education	Secondary	Above Secondary Education	Total
Yes	Count	258	362	183	803
	% within education categories	33.8	39.2	41.6	37.8
No	Count	505	562	257	1324
	% within education categories	66.2	60.8	58.4	62.2
Total	Count	763	924	440	2127
	% within education categories	100	100	100	100

Table 10.5: Reasons for Voting

Did you vote at least once in your life?		Less than Secondary Education	Secondary	Above Secondary Education	Total
Please government officials	Count	117	242	153	512
	% within education categories	45.3	66.9	83.6	
To use my political right to vote	Count	100	140	74	314
	% within education categories	38.8	38.7	40.4	
To help a candidate	Count	51	76	14	141
	% within education categories	19.8	21.0	7.7	
To choose the most appropriate person	Count	86	100	55	241
	% within education categories	33.3	27.6	30.1	
To choose the person which the government wants me to choose	Count	10	22	7	39
	% within education categories	3.9	6.1	3.8	
To imitate my friends	Count	31	24	5	60
	% within education categories	12.0	6.6	2.7	
To help my family and/or friends	Count	49	62	17	128
	% within education categories	19.0	17.1	9.3	
To receive money	Count	8	6	0	14
	% within education categories	3.1	1.7	0.0	
Other	Count	5	3	4	12
	% within education categories	1.9	0.8	2.2	
Total	Count	258	362	183	803
	% within education categories				

Percentages and totals are based on respondents

For the majority of people, the main reason for electing a candidate was most likely because of his/her political affiliation. The second reason was the services of a candidate toward his/her community, with the percentage decreasing with higher levels of education. An official was elected not for religious reasons, but for the public policies promised in his/her campaign, and individuals with lower levels of education showed political participation based on 'competitive clientelism'.[39] In this sense, voters are not interested in the legislative powers of their candidates, but are more interested in a candidate's influence on ministers and bureaucrats to create more jobs and provide more social services to their constitutents.[40]

On the other hand, as shown in Table 6, the main reason for not participating in elections was because they would not receive personal gain from elections, and the second main reason was disbelief that participation would change the outcome of elections. Here personal gain is more important than social benefit. The third reason for not voting was due to the lack of trust in the outcome of elections. It is important to note here that the highest distrust is amongst the lower educated individuals. The dynamics of the voting process here is important to understand these results. Since vote buying, is a tool that is mainly conducted in poor areas, people who have less levels of education, are more likely to encounter this vote buying process, and hence, do not trust the outcome of the elections. On the other hand, higher educated individuals, who are most likely to have better standards of living, are most likely to know about vote rigging and vote buying, however, they also encounter the process of mobilizing individuals in syndicates and public sector services who do not receive money, but who are told to vote for government officials. Hence, the results of the elections, for them may show a true reflection of the voting process, but due to illegitimate abuses of mobilization strategies rather than pure electoral rigging.

Table 10.6: Reasons for not Voting

Why did you never participate in any elections?		Less than Secondary Education	Secondary	Above Secondary Education	Total
No personal gain	Count	444	558	288	1290
	% within education categories	87.9	99.3	112.1	

Don't see any benefit in participation	Count	76	93	36	205
	% within education categories	15.0	16.5	14.0	
Country's political situation does not make it worthwhile	Count	13	15	4	32
	% within education categories	2.6	2.7	1.6	
Don't want any problems	Count	54	73	26	153
	% within education categories	10.7	13.0	10.1	
No trust in the outcome of elections	Count	120	139	48	307
	% within education categories	23.8	24.7	18.7	
Others	Count	89	81	42	212
	% within education categories	17.6	14.4	16.3	
	Count	100	68	22	190
	% within education categories	19.8	12.1	8.6	
Total	Count	505	562	257	1324

Percentages and totals are based on respondents

Tolerance and Trust

As argued by Putnam,[41] trust and tolerance are important to hold a society together, and to form an individual who lives in a community and develops his/her social traits by overcoming barriers to individualism. Religious tolerance is relatively high, with 54.7 per cent respondents arguing that it is normal to have friends from different religious backgrounds, as presented in Table 8. This table also manifests that the higher the education of an individual, the higher his/her tolerance level of others, as shown in Tables 7 and 8. Nevertheless, in this case study tolerance and solidarity do not translate into trust. Trust is prevalent in Egyptian society at very high rates as opposed to other factors of Social Capital. Nevertheless, Table 9 reveals that trust is not highly correlated with education, since lower educated people have shown more trust, than higher educated ones. Accordingly, tolerance is prevalent at a much higher percentage amongst the highly educated people, while lower educated people have more trust. Hence, in authoritarian regimes, individuals can be tolerant, especially highly educated ones, however, the more educated they are, the more knowledge they attain about their regime, and consequently trust in the social system as a whole is less as can be seen in Table 6.

Table 10.7: Tolerance

I can work with people who do not share my attitudes		Less than Secondary Education	Secondary	Above Secondary Education	Total
Yes	Count	393	493	278	1164
	% within education categories	51.5	53.4	63.2	54.7
No	Count	241	290	118	649
	% within education categories	31.6	31.4	26.8	30.5
Don't know	Count	129	141	44	314
	% within education categories	16.9	15.3	10.0	14.8
Total	Count	763	924	440	2127
	% within education categories	100.0	100.0	100.0	100.0

Table 10.8: Religious Tolerance

A person should not have friends who belong to different religious background		Less than Secondary Education	Secondary	Above Secondary Education	Total
Yes	Count	214	241	72	527
	% within education categories	28	26.1	16.4	24.8
No	Count	466	582	339	1387
	% within education categories	61.1	63	77	65.2
Don't know	Count	83	101	29	214
	% within education categories	10.9	10.9	6.6	10
Total	Count	763	924	440	2127
	% within education categories	100	100	100	100

Table 10.9: Trust

I trust people		Less than Secondary Education	Secondary	Above Secondary Education	Total
Yes	Count	502	569	278	1349
	% within education categories	65.8	61.6	63.2	63.4
No	Count	148	170	79	397
	% within education categories	19.4	18.4	18	17.9
Don't Know	Count	113	185	83	381
	% within education categories	14.8	20	18.9	17.9
Total	Count	763	924	440	2127
	% within education categories	100	100	100	100

Collective Action and Cooperation

The capability of people to work together to solve their problems is an essential trait in social capital, as stated by the World Bank's indicators. In this case study, as shown in Table 9 collective action was not highly discerned. The main inquiry about collective action was 'what individuals do when a new law is applied.' The response was not positive: disregarding their educational background, the majority of individuals said that they would rather not do anything and wait until the law was changed. An important aspect in the dynamics of authoritarianism is the absence of interest in contacting the People's Assembly representative in their district to change the law. Thus, the electoral process in which the majority of the less educated individuals participate is dissociated from the capability of holding candidates accountable to their constituents. Hence, competitive clientelism [42] was at the root of the electoral process, without thinking beyond the capability of candidates to directly change the laws according to their constituents' will. There is a clear absence of the social capital sense of individuals working together to solve national problems. These results are revealing and important in the context of the January 25 revolution because prior to this date, collective action was kept at bay, and only a number of small demonstrations used to take place against general political issues, like the Kifaya Movement that was established in 2004, which called for an end to the Mubarak regime and had small number of followers. Nevertheless, the difference between the highly educated versus the lower educated is revealing, where almost 42 per cent of the higher educated argued that they would wait until change happens, while 65 per cent of the less educated would do so. In the same context 51 per cent of the highly educated argued that they would 'publically oppose' a certain legislation which they do not think is proper, compared to 27.9 per cent of the lower educated.

Table 10.10: Cooperation and Solidarity

If you do not agree with a certain law, what is your reaction		Less than Secondary Education	Secondary	Above Secondary Education	Total
Publically oppose	Count	213	353	226	792
	% within education categories	27.9	38.2	51.4	
	Count	6	0	1	7
	% within education categories	.8	.0	.2	
Make public awareness campaigns	Count	11	13	7	31
	% within education categories	1.4	1.4	1.6	
Oppose even when I know that I will not make a difference	Count	6	11	5	22
	% within education categories	0.8	1.2	1.1	
Do not abide by the law	Count	2	8	2	12
	% within education categories	0.3	0.9	0.5	
Wait until change happens	Count	498	508	188	1194
	% within education categories	65.3	55.0	42.7	
I call my Member of Parliament	Count	3	6	3	12
	% within education categories	0.4	0.6	0.7	
Other	Count	28	36	23	87
	% within education categories	3.7	3.9	5.2	
Total	Count	763	924	440	2127

Percentages and totals are based on respondents

Information and Communication

Access to information and communication are crucial in gendering positive social capital and counterbalancing negative social capital (World Bank, 2011). In this respect, respondents were asked about the sources of information they acquired concerning their political life, and they ranged from newspaper readership to knowledge of political party life in Egypt. Even though newspaper readership is not very high, political knowledge is much higher among individuals with higher education, which again draws a cliché in social capital theory. It is generally believed by liberal social capital theorists and the World Bank that the higher the political knowledge, the more likely a citizen participates in civic and political activities of his/her choice. Nevertheless, the higher the education level in Egypt, the higher the political knowledge, however, civic and political participation are considerably low, and are not enacted out of their own choice but rather out of the governments' incentives to do so, as shown before. Almost 40 per cent of higher educated individual read newspapers, compared to only 10 per cent of graduates from lower level education (Table 10).

Table 10.11: Newspaper Readership

Do you read the newspapers?		Less than Secondary Education	Secondary	Above Secondary Education	Total
Yes	Count	39	126	153	318
	% within education categories	5.1	13.6	34.8	15.0
Rarely	Count	29	68	55	152
	% within education categories	3.8	7.4	12.5	7.1
No	Count	695	730	232	1657
	% within education categories	91.1	79.0	52.7	77.9
Total	Count	763	924	440	2127

Percentages and totals are based on respondents

Access to communication through the Internet is prevalent at both the intermediate and higher levels of education. Nevertheless, individuals from all education levels do not use the Internet as a source of communication and information, as shown in Table 11. Access to news was reported to be the highest interest among those who use the Internet.

Table 10.12: Access to the Internet

Do you have access to the internet?		Less than Secondary Education	Secondary	Above Secondary Education	Total
Yes	Count	9	37	93	139
	% within education categories	1.2	4.0	21.1	6.5
No	Count	754	887	347	1988
	% within education categories	98.8	96.0	78.9	93.5
Total	Count	763	924	440	2127

The main source of information for most individuals is neither the internet nor the newspapers, but television. More than 80 per cent of all respondents in the survey from all levels of education said they watch television, and most watch Egyptian and Arab satellite channels. Again, the most interest for all education levels was watching the news. Arab media, especially news channels like Al Jazeera and al Arabeya, have been influential throughout the past decade in disseminating knowledge about corruption, cronyism and abuse of political power in the Arab world. According to Lynch,[43] "one of the 2003 Al Jazeera talk shows addressed this question: Have the existing Arab regimes become worse than colonialism? The host, one of the guests, and 75 per cent of the callers said yes". Thus, information and communication is essential in the dissemination of knowledge, but not to develop trust towards the political system; rather, to show distrust in the prevailing political system.

Table 10.13: Television Watching

Do you watch TV?		Less Than Secondary	Secondary	Above Secondary	Total
Yes	Count	338	419	216	973
	% within education categories	44.3	45.3	49.1	45.7

No	Count	44	34	11	89
	% within education categories	5.8	3.7	2.5	4.2
Rarely	Count	104	82	24	210
	% within education categories	13.6	8.9	5.5	9.9
Total	Count	763	924	440	2127
	% within education categories	100	100	100	100

Conclusion

This research emphasises the importance of delinking social capital from democracy. The case study showed that social capital indicators as proposed by the World Bank and its development specialists, does not advance knowledge about the dynamics of citizens' behaviour in authoritarian regimes. It found out that civic and political engagement in Egypt is generally low. However, when they did prevail, especially among the higher educated individuals, they only did, to serve authoritarian purposes, rather than to develop democracy. Moreover, tolerance and knowledge prevailed among highly educated individuals, but did not transcend into trust for the social system at large. Very few individuals trusted the electoral institutions within the country, and lower educated citizens were more likely to trust other people than the higher educated ones.

Second, the study found a link in civic engagement and political engagement, amongst the higher educated people, which develops bridging within civic engagement and enhances bonding between the civic and political spheres. Nevertheless, this link was distorted, and rather than linking citizens to the political sphere, this link served patron-client relations and helped in the preservation of authoritarianism for more than four decades in Egypt. This is due to the fact that civil society and political party membership was mostly prevalent for ulterior motives of technocrats, and political participation was only to serve the interest of the authoritarian regime.

Looking in retrospect to the January 25 revolution, whose main slogan was to attain 'food, freedom and human dignity' and the findings of this study, it could be discerned that the social capital indicators of the World Bank, are not relevant in authoritarian regimes. Highly educated individuals, who have high levels of unemployment, have access to knowledge through the Internet, Arab and international media, instigated the uprisings. They had knowledge about the amount of corruption, available in the socio-economic and political spheres, and thus they abstained from civic and political participation. Thus their 'lower' levels of social capital, especially civic and political engagement, and trust were *deliberate*, yet also essential reasons behind their uprisings, which brought the issue of political democratisation in authoritarian regimes, especially Egypt and the Arab world back in.

Notes

1. J. Putzel, "Accounting for the "Dark Side" of Social Capital: Reading Robert Putnam on Democracy." *Journal of International Development*, 9 (7), 1997, 939-49.
2. J. Harriss, *Depoliticizing Development: The World Bank and Social Capital.* (London: Anthem Press, 2002); Jamal, A. *Barriers to Democracy: The other side of Social Capital in Palestine and the Arab World.* (Princeton: Princeton University Press, 2007).
3. This study is the result of previous empirical evidence concerning the socio-economic and political returns of education in Egypt based on a questionnaire conducted by an Egyptian private think tank, Partners in Development in partnership with Ford Foundation, with a sample of 3134 individuals. Of these individuals, 11.7 per cent were illiterate, 15.6 per cent attained primary education, 38.8 per cent had secondary education, and 29 per cent had higher education. Of these individuals, only 5.9 per cent were educated in private schools, while the rest was educated in public schools (Abdelfattah, 2011, p. 11).
4. P. Bourdieu, "The Forms of Capital" in Richardson, J. ed. *Handbook of Theory and Research for the Sociology of Education.* (New York: Greenwood Press, 1986).
5. J. Coleman, *Foundations of Social Theory.* (Cambridge: Harvard University Press, 1990).
6. R. Putnam, *Making Democracy Work: Civic traditions in modern Italy,* (Princeton: Princeton University Press, 1993); Putnam, R. *Bowling Alone: The collapse and revivial of American community.* (New York: Simon and Schuster, 2000); Putzel, J. "Accounting for the "Dark Side" of Social Capital: Reading Robert Putnam on Democracy." *Journal of International Development*, 9 (7), 1997, 939-49.
7. J. Farr, "Social Capital: A Conceptual History", *Political Theory,* February 2004, vol. 32, no. 1, 6-33.
8. M. Grenfell, *Bourdieu, Education and Training,* (London: Continuum, 2009), p. 20.
9. See for example the World Bank's website on Social Capital and its definition which concentrates mainly on Putnam and Coleman's definitions.
10. J. Coleman, *Foundations of Social Theory.* (Cambridge: Harvard University Press, 1990).
11. R. Putnam, *Making Democracy Work: civic traditions in modern Italy,* (Princeton: Princeton University Press, 1993); Putnam, R. *Bowling Alone: The collapse and revival of*

American community. (New York: Simon and Schuster, 2000).

12. J. Coleman, "Social Capital and the Creation of Human Capital." *American Journal of Sociology.* 94: Supplement, 1988, 95-120.
13. P. Paxton, "Social Capital and Democracy: An Interdependent Relationship", *American Sociological Review,* 2002, *67* (2), 254-277.
14. R. Putnam, *Making Democracy Work: Civic traditions in modern Italy,* (Princeton: Princeton University Press, 1993), p. 167.
15. Ibid., p. 174.
16. M.W. Foley, B. Edwards, Is It Time to Disinvest in Social Capital? *Journal of Public Policy* 19, 1999, 141-173.
17. A. Portes, Social Capital: Its Origins and Applications in Modern Sociology, *Annual Review of Sociology*, vol. 24, (1998), pp. 1-24.
18. M. Woolcock, "Social Capital and Economic Development: Toward a Theoretical Synthesis and Policy Framework." 1998, *Theory and Society* 27(2): 151-208.
19. A. Giddens, *The Third Way and it Critics.* (Cambridge: Polity Press, 2000), p. 78.
20. R. Putnam, *Making Democracy Work: Civic traditions in modern Italy,* (Princeton: Princeton University Press, 1993), p. 167.
21. P. Paxton, "Social Capital and Democracy: An Interdependent Relationship". *American Sociological Review, 67* (2), 2002, p.257.
22. R. Putnam, *Making Democracy Work: Civic traditions in modern Italy,* (Princeton: Princeton University Press, 1993), p. 167. Paxton, P. Social Capital and Democracy: An Interdependent Relationship. *American Sociological Review,* 2002, *67* (2), p.257. Almond, G. and Verba. *The Civic Culture: Political Attitudes and Democracy in Five Nations.* (Princeton: Princeton University Press, 1963).
23. Dewey in J. Farr, "Social Capital: A Conceptual History", *Political Theory,* February 2004, vol. 32, no. p. 18.
24. J.S. Dill, Preparing for public life: school sector and the educational context of lasting citizen formation. *Social Forces, 87*(3), 2009, 1265-1290.
25. G. Almond, and Verba. *The Civic Culture: Political Attitudes and Democracy in Five Nations.* (Princeton: Princeton University Press, 1963).
26. The social cohesion and inclusion indicator could not be measured in this survey because there was not enough information in the original questionnaire.
27. Evidence can be seen, in a previous study conducted by the author entitled: "youth political engagement and the persistence of authoritarianism in Egypt," paper presented at the Mediterranean Research Meeting, Montecatini, Italy, 2010. Here the majority of educated youth were not inclined to engage civically or politically for example. Yet during the January 25 revolution, new social movements were essential in mobilising middle class educated Egyptian citizens to demonstrate on the streets of Egypt.
28. In Upper Egypt, the governorates of Beni Suif and Aswan were sampled, and in Lower Egypt, the governorates of Beheira and Qaliubiyya were sampled. Here, both urban and rural sectors of society were sampled.
29. In Cairo, 746 families were sampled: in Beheira 520 families; in Qalyubiyya 435 families, in Beni Suif 440 families, in Asswan 223 families. 44.3 per cent of the respondents were

from rural areas, while 55.7 per cent were from urban areas.

30. In Cairo, 1087 individuals were sampled, in Beheira 981 individuals, in Qalyubiyya 692 individuals, in Beni Suef 825 individuals, and in Aswan 333 individuals. For further details about the sample, refer to Khalid Abdel Fattah, "Field Report" in eds. Feisal Yunis and Nadine Sika, *The Socio-Economic and Political Returns to Education in Egypt* (Cairo: PID, 2011) [Arabic].
31. J. Beall, "Valuing Social Resources or Capitalizing on Them? Limits to Pro Poor Urban Governance in Nine Cities of the South". *International Planning Studies, 6* (4), 2001, 357-375.
32. P. Evans, Ecologies of Local Political Actors and the Struggle for Livavility in Third world Cities. *International Conference on Democratic Decentralization.* (Kerala: State Planning Board, 2000).
33. Interviews conducted by the author during the period from September to December 2010. These included five masters students at the Faculty of Economics and Political Science at Cairo University; five members at the Heliopolis sporting Club, with Bachelors degrees from different Egyptian Universities.
34. M. Tadros, "The securitization of civil society: a case study of NGOS--State Security Investigations (SSI) relations in Egypt". *State, Security & Development* (11), 2011, pp. 79-103.
35. J. Brownlee, "Unrequired Moderation: Credible Commitments and State Repression in Egypt". *Studies in International Comparative Development* (45), 2010, 468-489.
36. This Table is from: Khalid Abdelfattah, "Background Results for the Survey Study," in Ola al-Khawaga, *The Issue of Education in Egypt: Economic and Social Returns to Education in Egypt* (Arabic), (Cairo: Partners in Development, 2008).
37. Al Masry al-Youm, 2010: http://www.*almasryalyoum*.com (Arabic)
38. E. Lust-Okar, "Elections under authoritarianism: preliminary lessons from Jordan". *Democratisation*, 2006, 13(3):456–71
39. E. Lust, Competitive Clientalism in the Middle East. *Journal of Democracy*, 2009, 20, 122-135.
40. Ibid.
41. R. Putnam, *Bowling Alone: The collapse and revival of American community.* (New York: Simon and Schuster, 2003).
42. E. Lust, "Competitive Clientelism in the Middle East". *Journal of Democracy (20)*, 2009, 122-135.
43. M. Lynch, "Taking the Arabs Seriously". *Foreign Affairs, 82* (5), 2003, 81-94.

11. The Muslim Brotherhood Movement Facing the Challenge of Democracy: Political Transition in Post-Revolutionary Egypt

Mohanad Mustafa and As'ad Ghanem

Introduction

The Arab Spring, which in effect began with the toppling of the authoritarian regimes in Tunisia and Egypt, has forced the Arab states to face many challenges even before democratic regimes replace the old authoritarian ones. In Tunisia and Egypt, the overthrow of the regime had the consensus support of the entire opposition, as well as the youth and other segments of society. However, the revolutions were followed by intense debates about the character of the new regime to be established. Even while the protests were in progress, the demonstrators called for the establishment of a civic democratic regime that would respect citizens' political freedoms and be based on equal citizenship, with no distinction of religion, sex, or class.

Against the backdrop of these discussions, various political groups, spanning the Egyptian and Tunisian political spectrum, emerged and sought to have a say in determining the nature and format of the new regime. As we know, events unfolded at different rates in Tunisia and in Egypt. In Egypt, new political movements were formed after the Military Council eased the restrictions on the formation of political parties; political figures began declaring their intention to run for president even before a date was set for the presidential elections. The Egyptian Military Council also introduced a number of amendments to the Egyptian constitution, with the focus on the sections related to the electoral process and election procedures. In a national referendum; 72 per cent of the voters approved the amendments.[1] Parliamentary elections were set for November 2011.

This process made the internal Egyptian debate about the future of the regime in post-revolutionary Egypt more acute; their position on these amendments divided the Egyptian political system into two main camps. The first camp included the various Islamist groups (the Muslim Brotherhood, the Salafi movements, both moderate and extremist, and other independent Islamist groups), while the second camp included secular movements, parties, and groups, left-wing liberals, and young leaders of the revolution, such as the 'Revolutionary Youth Alliance' and the 'Revolutionary Youth Union'. The first camp favoured the amendments, whereas, members of the latter voted against them.

The main argument advanced by those opposed to the amendments was that they did not meet the expectations raised by the 'successful Egyptian revolution'.[2] The opponents asserted that the amendments were based on the old Egyptian constitution, which was fundamentally undemocratic; likewise, the amendments were limited in scope and did not relate to the essence of the regime.[3] Moreover, they argued, the Egyptian constitution had 'fallen' with the regime; the proper course of action was to draft a new constitution instead of amending the old one. They maintained further that holding parliamentary elections in September 2011-January 2012 would not give candidates – especially those representing the Revolutionary Youth – sufficient time to prepare. This would significantly boost the traditional parties, especially those affiliated with political Islam, which was the dominant force with the best infrastructure for contesting the parliamentary elections, thanks to its social, organisational, and institutional network, and the large financial reserves at its disposal. The Revolutionary Youth, on the other hand, would not have enough time to gear up and establish themselves by September, especially because they were still focused on consolidating the achievements of the revolution.[4]

Those who favoured the amendments, primarily the Islamist camp, did so for two reasons – first, because the Islamist groups were already prepared to run for parliament and were sure that they would win a significant share of the vote, and the second reason was ideological, regarding the status of religion in the post revolution regime. Even before it was decided which articles of the constitution would be amended, a heated debate broke out in Egyptian societ – one that will continue until a new constitution is written – about the status of Article II: *The principles of Islamic law are the chief source of legislation*.[5] Because the Islamist camp wanted to keep this article in the constitution, they had a strong motivation to vote in favour of the amendments before the election of a new parliament that would draft a new constitution.

That is, the difference between the secular and Islamist camps was that the former wanted a new constitution before the elections, in order to define the state's religious neutrality, whereas, the latter wanted to defer the constitution-drafting process until after the September-January elections because they believed that their influence on the substance of the document would be much greater then.

This debate, which became increasingly fierce when the Islamist camp abandoned the street protests after the revolution, poses a major challenge for the democratisation of post-revolutionary Egypt. The way in which the Islamist current integrates into the new regime is one of the most important challenges for the establishment of democracy in Egypt. The Muslim Brotherhood, along with the other Islamic factions in Egypt, serves as a model for Islamic movements elsewhere in the Arab world. Egypt's willingness to make strides towards democracy could prove favourable to the Muslim Brotherhood and lead to their becoming part of the new regime. Thus, one might argue that how political Islam conducts itself in Egypt could well influence political Islam as a whole, especially in the Arab world.

At this point, it is very important to examine the challenge that political Islam poses to the establishment of democracy in Egypt. As a major force in the public arena, it is pertinent to ask whether political Islam will curb democratisation in Egypt and even try to confine it within limits that it can live with. Perhaps, though, political Islam has internalised the lessons of the Egyptian revolution and will favour the establishment of a fully democratic civic regime. Will political Islamic speak about the character it seeks for the new regime in terms identical to those employed by the secular movements and their advocates? Will political Islam be willing to accept separation of religion and state in Egypt? These are important issues, because this is the first time in Egyptian history that political Islam has had to address them as a serious contender for control of the state, with direct influence on its policies. In the past, the discourse about democracy conducted by political Islam, which was always an opposition force, existed in isolation from any real option of replacing the regime or even integrating into the power structure of the state; it focused, instead, on enhancing its image as freedom-loving democratic force.

Prior to the revolution, political Islam was never a viable alternative to the authoritarian regime, with a real possibility of gaining power through elections. After the regime was overthrown, however, and the preparations to determine the future of the Egyptian system began, political Islam could aspire to lead the state. The ambition to lead or at least be partners in the new regime had become realistic. This paper will analyse and discuss the Muslim Brotherhood's 2005 initiative for political reform, which marked the climax of its political development under the Ancien Régime, and compare it with its post-revolutionary political discourse (in February 2011).

This paper's primary assertion is that mainstream political Islam – the Muslim Brotherhood – has always attempted to find common ground between its fundamentalist ideology and democratic values; its chief goal, before the revolution, was to achieve political legitimacy and a political presence in the public sphere, both local and international.[6] The movement did not aspire to achieve power through elections, inasmuch as that was impossible under the authoritarian regime. Post-revolution, however, its participation in the new regime seems very realistic; that is, mainstream political Islam would be responsible for policy in practice, and not only for discourse on the theoretical plane. This has made it more conservative in its presentation of its political attitude towards democracy and the character of the state and led it to explicit highlight its support for retaining its Islamic character.

The paper is divided into three sections. The first presents political Islam's attitude towards democracy while it was in the opposition; that is, the Islamic rhetoric about democracy before the crumbling of the authoritarian regime. Our analysis will be based chiefly on the Muslim Brotherhood's political platform of 2005, the first such document in the movement's history. The second section will analyse the Islamic rhetoric about democracy after the revolution, based on an examination of its new political platform, which was published following the revolution, and in the third section, we will present our main insights on the topic.

Political Islam and Democracy in the Era of Authoritarianism

Democracy, in its modern sense, made its significant appearance in the Islamic discourse in the early 1980s. This was manifested in books, articles, and conferences and symposiums that grappled with the relationship between Islam and democracy, both from the historical and political perspectives and from that of Muslim religious law. Within Islamic thought, a broad array of literature on democracy has emerged. The subject has acquired increasing political, social, and economic weight and has influenced the agenda of the Islamic political movements.[7]

During the 1980s, there was an increase in the number of Muslim and Arab Scholars and writers who began to take an interest in the relationship between Islam and democracy. Some Islamic activists, too, began to demand that the regimes make political reforms and allow for democratic pluralism.[8]

Esposito and Voll[9] claim that, in the past few decades, Islamists have become interested in two important processes, Islamisation and democratisation, which they see as exerting a strong influence on the political development of the Arab and Muslim world. From the perspective of political Islam, not only are these two processes advancing in parallel; in fact, they need to converge. This is why some Islamic activists demand more democracy and push in this direction: they believe that democratisation and the incorporation of political Islam, as a popular stream, can assist the movement in its mission to Islamise society and the state.

Sadiki[10] argues further that according to political Islam, Islamisation is not meant to thwart democratisation; nor is democratisation supposed to prevent Islamisation. Rather, each process should strengthen the other. That is, as political Islam becomes stronger, it will demand increasing political reforms and democracy. And as democratisation spreads, Islamic political movements will be the main winner.

In his study, 'Democracy in Muslim Discourse in Modern Times', Zaki Ahmed[11] presents an anthology of Islamist writings on democracy. According to him, "Since the eighties ... the issue of democracy has been presented in loud and animated tones in the contemporary Islamic discourse, at a different rate of historical, philosophical, political, and linguistic understanding and analysis, in which one can see a change of direction in the Islamists' political views about this topic".[12]

Kramer counters, however, that even though Islamists have begun to espouse democratic dogmas, they remain faithful to the belief that Islam encompasses both religion and state. In other words, democracy must exist within the framework of this equation.[13]

El-Solh[14] categorises political Islam's attitude to democracy into three main groups. The first group is completely opposed to the democratic regime; the second group believes that Islam embodies democratic elements and they should be cultivated; they note in particular the concept of 'al-Shura' (consultation), and the third group is willing to adopt Western democracy and believes that the democratic theory that has been applied in other places can succeed in Muslim society as well.

In this section, we will focus on the Muslim Brotherhood's initiatives for political reform in Egypt in 2005. This initiative was the Egyptian movement's first political platform of its type since its founding; it reflects, among other things, the Brotherhood's tendency to increased integration with the existing regime. In March 2004, the movement's then–General Guide, Mohammad Mahdi 'Aqef, presented the Brotherhood's platform, with its proposals for political reforms in Egypt. In an interview, 'Aqef explained that the platform was intended to present the movement's nationalistic and Islamic views on the issues associated with political reform, such as democracy and elections and the status of the various branches of government.[15]

Through this proposal, the Muslim Brotherhood also wanted to present to the Egyptians with its general political perspective on the general state of the country in advance of the elections in 2005. The platform comprised an introduction and thirteen chapters, which discussed various issues and proposed improvements. These topics were not only political; they also included social, economic, and cultural issues, and, most importantly, reforms associated with democratisation and the essence and structure of the regime.

Areas for improvement included strengthening civic society; reforming the regime, the judicial system, and the election process; instituting reforms in education, scientific research, and at Al Azhar University; pursuing economic reform and battling poverty; introducing social reforms, including those linked with the status of women and the Coptic minority; introducing cultural reforms; and modifying foreign policy.[16]

According to the Muslim Brotherhood's platform, implementing the political reform project requires unification of all the political forces in Egypt. The government cannot carry out and lead political reform by itself, without the cooperation of the other political actors in the state.

Below we will present several sections of the Brotherhood's plan for political reform, which testify to their ideological evolution, adjustment to democratic values, and willingness to be involved in democratisation. The movement defined its ideal political regime in this way: *We favour a democratic, constitutional, parliamentary republic, within the framework of Islamic values.* This introduction is compatible with the Egyptian constitution's definition of the regime as a constitutional republic. The Egyptian constitution defines Muslim religious law as the chief source of state jurisprudence. That is, the Muslim Brotherhood concurs with the Egyptian constitution's definition of the regime – an important step in its adjustment to the values of the current system.

Democracy became a central issue in the Muslim Brotherhood's proposed political reform. The platform states that Egypt's independence, strength, international standing, and freedom to make political decisions cannot possibly be realized without a democratic regime. Furthermore, it calls on the political parties to sign a 'national covenant' in which they pledge their allegiance to a democratic regime and its values. In this program, the Muslim Brotherhood favours a direct form of democracy; instead of the Islamic term 'al-shura' (consultation), they demonstratively preferred 'democracy'.

The national covenant that the Muslim Brotherhood would have all political and ideological streams sign, was based on the following principles:

- 'The people are the source of authority for all branches of government in the country. No person or party, group or organisation has the right to claim exclusive authority unless it derives from the people by their free will'. Note that this section openly challenges Sayyid Qutb and his school of thought, which deemed Allah to be the sole source of authority (in the sense of hakimiya or divine sovereignty) and held that this role could not be delegated to other sources.
- A commitment to respect the principle of replacing the party in power by means of free and honest elections.
- A guarantee of freedom of conscience.
- A guarantee of freedom of religion for all recognised religions (meaning, the monotheistic faiths: Islam, Christianity, and Judaism).
- A guarantee of freedom of expression: Freedom of expression must be guaranteed as part of the general order and norms and according to the basic principles of society—guaranteeing freedom of the press and property as the way to achieve freedom of expression. The freedom of expression that the Muslim Brotherhood proposed was limited: this freedom must take account of society's basic principles—but the Brotherhood did not define these principles. However, it is clear that it refers to Egyptian society's religious principles, thereby restricting freedom of expression and setting basic principles and general norms of society, whether traditional or religious, beyond the pale.
- A guarantee of freedom of political organisation, including the establishment of parties, and denial to any authority or agency the power to interfere in a way that would obstruct or limit this right: The

independent judicial system is the only agency of government entitled to determine which organisations are opposed to the general order and norms and to the basic principles of society. This point is significant for the Muslim Brotherhood. The regime's refusal to recognise the Brotherhood as a political party, starting in the Nasser era, was one of the main factors that stymied the movement's political development and kept it from becoming a viable political alternative to the ruling party.

- A guarantee of freedom of assembly and of individuals' rights to participate in community activities, as long as they keep the peace.
- A guarantee of freedom of nonviolent demonstration and protest.
- A guarantee of the right of popular representation through a freely elected parliament, with a fixed term, and its replacement through free elections. Election laws must assure free and honest elections while ensuring the state's neutrality. The most efficient type of regime for state and society is a parliamentary regime, which gives the party that received the most votes' responsibility for forming the government and running the country.

Note that the Muslim Brotherhood focused on parliament and the cabinet, and did not mention the presidency; in other words, they preferred not to clash with this institution. This can be interpreted in one of two ways: first that the Muslim Brotherhood wanted to stay as far away as possible from any conflict with President Mubarak, at least for the time being, and hence declared that its maximum political aspiration was to form a government, which would deal primarily with domestic issues. The movement was not interested in running a candidate for president. According to the second interpretation, the Brotherhood was interested in a genuine parliamentary regime in which the president has only limited powers. The presidency is mentioned later in the platform, albeit in very general terms.

- Limitation of the powers held by president of the republic, which would turn him into a symbol for all of the Egyptians: the president would not be the head of a political party and would not have any executive responsibilities. He would be limited to two terms in office.[17] This section is very general and insufficiently detailed to reveal the Brotherhood's true view of where the presidency should fit in the Egyptian regime. The movement, though, did state its preference for a president who would not be associated with any political party. This notion was compatible with that of part of the Egyptian elite, who wanted to run famous Egyptians who were not associated with political parties as presidential candidates. Through this proposal, the Muslim Brotherhood attempted to neutralise the president's link with the ruling party and turn the presidency into a symbolic – rather than executive – institution.

- Removing the military from politics to enable it to focus on defending the country and to keep the government from exploiting the military, directly or indirectly, in order to tighten its control of society. The Minister of Defence would be a civilian politician like every other government minister.
- The police and security forces would be obligated to play civilian roles, as prescribed by law, and to limit their role to defending the security of society and state – not to take advantage of it in order to maintain the regime's dominance or to suppress the opposition. They would not be allowed to intervene in public activities or elections.
- Repeal of undemocratic laws, such as the Parties Law, the state-of-emergency regulations, the Trade Unions Law, and the Press Law. The movement suffered primarily from the first three laws, which limited its activities in all of its foci of power, especially the Trade Unions Law and the law that prevented it from becoming a political party.
- Release of political prisoners[18] and an end to the use of torture by the police and the security forces.

Regarding the proposed election reforms, the Muslim Brotherhood demanded that judges supervise elections by means of a special committee. The Supreme Judicial Council (a sort of constitutional court) would appoint judges to oversee elections, with no interference from the Minister of Justice. This proposal had been implemented by the regime in the 1990 elections; but the Minister of Justice and Minister of Interior, who were members of the ruling party, had their fingers in the pie and, according to the Brotherhood, influenced the results of the national elections.

With regard to the Christian Coptic minority, the Muslim Brotherhood reiterated the traditional nationalistic view that the Copts are an integral part of the Egyptian people. The platform put it this way: "We emphasise that our position regarding our Coptic brethren is fixed and unchanging, and is as follows: (1) they are part of Egyptian society, (2) they are partners in the homeland and in the collective national definition of all Egyptians, (3) their rights and responsibilities are the same as ours, (4) freedom of religion is guaranteed to all citizens, and (5) we must fortify national unity and prevent any activity that could endanger this unity.

This proposal was another step towards democratisation in the Islamic political discourse in Egypt; the 2004 proposal was essentially based on the political platform that the Muslim Brotherhood had published in the mid-1990s. What set the new platform apart, though, was its emphasis on freedoms rather than on the enforcement of Islamic law. This was because the Brotherhood believed that the implementation of these basic freedoms would eventually lead the Egyptian nation to choose shari'a as the law of the land. This point was emphasised by General Guide Mahdi 'Aqef in a newspaper interview:

> The advancement of freedoms must precede the implementation of shari'a. Therefore, I say, freedom before shari'a. Whoever studies the writings of Imam Hassan al-Bana, the movement's founder, can see that the issue of freedoms is fundamental for us, because it would be impossible to implement Islamic law in the absence of a free atmosphere and popular willingness. The alternative to freedom is to impose shari'a through force and repression. This, however, goes against the principles of Islam. The Prophet's biography and the history of the spread of Islam never recorded a precedent of the enforcement of religious law through brute force.[19]

Political Islam and Democracy after the Revolution

The Islamic camp's support for the amendments to the Egyptian constitution enacted in March 2011, and its support for the political changes led by the military hierarchy intensified the concerns of the Islamists' opponents. Their fears stemmed from the possibility that the Egyptian Islamists would win the first elections after the toppling of the Mubarak regime, because they were the best organised bloc and prepared for these elections. The winner of these elections, they knew, would exert direct influence on the nature of the new Egyptian constitution, because the parliament to be elected would appoint a constitutional council to draft it. A victory by the Islamic camp, therefore, would certainly influence the composition and nature of this council and its policy vis-à-vis the new constitution., They were concerned that the Islamists would opt for a more religious and less democratic system than it had always demanded under the old regime.

The concerns expressed by some of the revolutionary leaders and secular parties intensified after the final decision by the Brotherhood's Shura Council that the movement would contest fifty percent of the seats in parliament—

despite the fact that it had declared, on various occasions, that it would run for only 30 per cent of the seats. This quota, however, did not apply to other Islamist parties that declared their intention of running for parliament, such as the Islamic Group (*Al-Gama'a al-Islamiyya*) and the New Center Party (*Hizb al-Wasat*). This would result in Islamist control of the new parliament and influence the nature of the new regime to be established.

In what follows, we would like to present the Muslim Brotherhood's post-revolutionary political Islamic discourse (January-February 2011) and compare it to its discourse before the revolution. After the revolution, the Muslim Brotherhood declared the establishment of a political party, the Freedom and Justice Party, which would essentially serve as the Brotherhood's political arm but would also enjoy a large extent of organisational and even political autonomy vis-a-vis the mother movement.[20] Nevertheless, the party would be based on the Muslim Brotherhood's political, social, and cultural ideology and the movement would wield influence in certain areas connected to the party's activity.

The establishment of a political party separate from the Muslim Brotherhood can be seen as a compromise between the movement's two streams – the first wanted to turn the Brotherhood into a political party rather than leaving it as a voluntary association that promotes religion and engages in social and educational activities. The second and more traditional stream wanted the movement to remain an organisation of the type launched by Hassan al-Bana and was opposed to turning the movement into a political party. The tension between the two streams had accompanied the Brotherhood since the 1970s. The issue had never been settled, though, because there had never been an urgent need to do so; the movement had never before been a political alternative to the authoritarian Egyptian regime.[21]

The new situation in Egypt and the need to diffuse the tension within the Muslim Brotherhood led to the establishment of a political party that was separate from but affiliated with the movement. In this manner, the Brotherhood retained its status as a voluntary association while also establishing a party to satisfy the faction that sought greater involvement in the state's political life. Yet, by establishing this party the Muslim Brotherhood tacitly acknowledged that it was not interested in political power in its own right; the party would cater to all Egyptians who agreed with its platform. Moreover, its members would not have to undergo the Muslim Brotherhood's religious vetting. In other words, anyone who accepted the party's political platform could be a member – even if they were not Muslims, not religious Muslims, or not identified ideologically with the Muslim Brotherhood's fundamental principles. After the party's launch, its chairman announced that more than a hundred Christian Copts had joined, including the author Rafiq Habib.[22]

Following debates in the Muslim Brotherhood's Shura Council, the new party's political platform was approved. That is, the Brotherhood was responsible for drafting the party platform, for electing its chairman (who is, incidentally, a member of the movement), and for presenting the party's platform to the public. The platform comprises eight chapters; for our purposes, though, we will focus on the first two. The first article presents the party's values and vision while the second expounds the nature of the state and the regime.[23]

In the first chapter, which expounds the party's values and ideological basis, they note: *The principles of Islamic law are the chief source of legislation … though non-Muslims are granted the right to be judged in accordance with their laws in matters of marriage and divorce.*

The second political value was associated with the nature of the regime. This section stated: *Shura [an Islamic term that means consultation] is the essence of democracy and is the path to realizing the homeland's interests.*" In this section the movement attempts to attach religious overtones to the concept of democracy, tying the democratic regime to Islamic history's political and ethical value of shura. In the fourth section, the party attempts to link its political values with the social values that political Islam often exploits and takes pride in; that is, the association between political reform and moral reform: "The political and constitutional reform and moral reform are the springboards for reform in all areas of life.

In any case, the theoretical basis emphasises two political principles – justice and freedom; this explains the new party's name. The platform states: *Justice, freedom, and equality are man's God-given rights; therefore, they are to be considered natural rights for all citizens, regardless of religion, sex, and colour, on condition that the individual's liberty does not detract from the rights of others or those of the nation*. But the expression 'those of the nation' is never explained. Does it refer to the Egyptian nation or the entire Islamic umma? It is also unclear what these individual rights are that, according to the Muslim Brotherhood's understanding, could 'harm other people'.

With regard to the subsection that deals with the new party's objectives (13 in all), we will briefly review the elements relevant to our discussion:

achieving constitutional and political reforms and upholding general rights, especially the right of association, both to form political parties and to establish civil-society institutions. The nation, the platform asserts, is the source of governance. This principle is revolutionary for the fundamentalist school of political Islam, which staunchly maintains that Allah is the sole source of governance (*al- hakimiya l'allah*). The latter approach was advanced by Sayyid Qutb in his various books, where he stated that only Allah, and not the people, could be the source of governance. For this reason, he strongly objected to democratic or parliamentary regimes.[24]

The platform also discusses the party's mission to disseminate and internalise Islam's authentic values and morality as principles for organising the life of the individual and of society in general, while upholding the supremacy of the law and building a state based on modern democratic institutions.

In the second chapter, 'The State: Basic Principles', the platform details its vision of the character of the state and the regime. The concept of the state advocated by the platform is based on the Islamic understanding of the term. The chapter opens with the statement: *Islam has conceived a model for the state, its basic principles, and supporting pillars.* The platform does not differentiate between the concepts of state and regime, inexplicably interchanging the terms. For example, the following text appears under the rubric 'Type of State': *The Freedom and Justice Party maintains that the parliamentary regime is most compatible with Egypt's conditions, because this type of regime is based on a moderate separation of powers and on cooperation between the judicial branch and the executive branch.* The Muslim Brotherhood's support of a parliamentary regime sheds light on its decision not to put up a candidate for president: the movement believes that the Egyptian regime should be parliamentary and not presidential, as it has been up until now. This, of course, will influence Egypt's new constitution, now that the Islamic camp has won a majority in the first elections after Mubarak's fall.

Another sub-section, 'Characteristics of the State', list four of them: (1) The state upholds the principle of citizenship; this section states that 'Egypt is the state of all of its citizens ... who enjoy equal rights and obligations'. (2) It is a constitutional state that maintains a separation of powers. (3) It is a state based on Shura (consultation), which is a basic principle of the state, because democracy is the regime most compatible with the principles of Shura, and (4) It is a civil state. Under the fourth principle, the platform states: *The Islamic state is, in essence, a civil state and not a military state controlled and ruled by the military; a civil state is not a theocracy in which clergymen rule. There are no ordained clergymen in Islam; rather there are individuals who specialise in religion. There are no rulers by divine right and there are no persons who have the exclusive right to interpret the Qur'an and its religious precepts.*

The Muslim Brotherhood offers a different interpretation of the civil state than do the Egyptian liberals, as expressed by one of the latter's leaders, 'Amr Hamzawi.[25] That is, the Brotherhood refers to a 'civil state' as one that is not a military state or a theocracy; but it is not a liberal state in the sense used in secular Egyptian discourse, meaning a democracy in which there is a separation of religion and state.[26] In its platform, the Muslim Brotherhood expounds its concept of a state at the end of the subsection about the civil state: *The difference between an Islamic state and various other forms of government is its basis in the religious law that most of the Egyptian people believe in. This law, in addition to its ethical and religious dimensions, organises all aspects of Muslim life ... while safeguarding the right of non-Muslims to employ their own religious laws in matters of marriage and divorce.* That is, the Muslim Brotherhood's platform champions Islamic law as the theoretical basis for a civil state in all domains; non-Muslims must return to their own religious law only in matters of marriage and divorce, but not for issues linked with the public political, cultural, or social spheres.

In summary, the Muslim Brotherhood's political platform mentions equality, equal opportunity, citizenship, the supremacy of law, separation of powers, a democratic regime, and civil state; nevertheless, it states that the Egyptian state must be based on Islamic law, both as the chief source of legislation and as the principle that organises the private and public spheres.

The Debate

In this article, we addressed the issue of political Islam's challenge to democratisation in the wake of the January-February 2011 revolution. We built our argument on a textual analysis of two political platforms that the Muslim Brotherhood published, before and after the revolution. It is not the intention here to challenge the Brotherhood's platforms or their conceptualisations by means of political theory and democratic thought. Rather, we believe that the use of political concepts in the two platforms is not based on the political theory with regard to issues of democracy and citizenship. We will relate to this conceptualisation in the platforms from the perspective of their authors, and not the theoretical framework familiar from the literature.

There are a number of differences between the two platforms (published in 2004 and 2011). The first significant one relates to the essence of the state and not only to the political regime: in the first platform, the movement focused on its demand for more democracy and political freedom. After the revolution, though, it placed the state itself, and not only the regime, at the centre. It holds that the Egyptian state should become a civil state – not in the liberal sense of the word, but in the sense of a state run by civilians. This change is linked primarily with the goals of the two platforms. The first addressed political changes within an authoritarian regime; therefore, its demands for change were less extreme. The second platform, however, aims at the formation of a new regime after the fall of Mubarak's, when the movement identified its opportunity to influence the creation of a new polity in which Islamic law would be an element.

The first platform was a response to the movement's limited room for political manoeuvre, in the shadow of the authoritarian regime. The second was drafted with much more political leeway, in as much as the Muslim Brotherhood was aware of its new political opportunity, as a well-organised political force, following the revolution. The post-revolutionary platform placed greater emphasis on Islamic law as the legal basis for the emerging regime. This is also manifested in the Brotherhood's position in the political debate about the relative priority of holding elections or drafting a new constitution. The Islamist stream in general, and the Muslim Brotherhood in particular, considers elections to be a prerequisite for drafting a new constitution; the secular camp, on the other hand, would draft the constitution before holding elections. This stresses the greater politicisation of the second platform as opposed to the first.

One might argue that the first platform was directed more towards Egyptian society and less towards the regime; it was drafted in response to social unrest, at a time when people wanted to know where the Muslim Brotherhood was headed. In contrast, the second platform focused more on the state, because it was intended to influence the Egypt's future political and governmental structure; hence it was more practical and less polemical. The state was a main issue in the second platform, whereas society stood at the centre of the first. That is, in the first platform, the Muslim Brotherhood's sphere for political activity was primarily within society and the existing regime; in the second platform, however, its political activity also targets the regime and the very nature of the state. This is why the Muslim Brotherhood supported holding elections before drafting a new constitution, because the opposite sequence would diminish its ability to introduce political changes.

In conclusion, the Muslim Brotherhood in post-revolutionary Egypt found itself facing the challenge of democracy, but no longer as an intellectual exercise and not to gain public sympathy and support. In the wake of the revolution, there is a good chance that the Muslim Brotherhood will become part of the executive branch, not only the legislature. One of the movement's responsibilities, as part of the new regime that will emerge before our very eyes in the near future, will be to propose a model of a political party that is involved in the transition to a democracy and can live together under one roof, as part of the same regime, with streams that are politically and ideologically opposed to the Brotherhood's path. The discussions conducted to date, testify to the serious pragmatism of the Brotherhood's perception of the political world and of its opportunity to become part of a competitive system. Of course, we are now only at the beginning of the process; we must wait to see what eventuates, and whether the changes within the Muslim Brotherhood become permanent.

Notes

1. *Al-Shuruq Newspaper*, March 15, 2011
2. Sameh Rashid, "The Arab Spring: the first year". *Shoan Arabiya Journal*, 2008, 148, pp: 16-27. (In Arabic).
3. Interview with Tarek Al-Bishri, the chair of the constitutional amendment committee, "All the amendments that we have set are temporary", *Al-Shoruq Newspaper*, March 04, 2011, p. 6-7.
4. Tamim Ahmad, "The current constitution and reproduction of the tribal chief", *Al-Shoruq Newspaper*, March 12, 2011, p.13.
5. See the official English translation of the Egyptian constitution: http://www.egypt.gov.eg/english/laws/constitution/default.aspx
6. Hisham Al-Awadi, *In Pursuit of Legitimacy: The Muslim Brothers and Mubarak 1982-2000*. (London: Tauris Academic Press, 2004).
7. Ahmad Moussalli, "The Views of Islamic Movements on Democracy and Political Pluralism". In: *Islamic Movements: Impacts on Political Stability in the Arab World*. (Abu-Dhabi: The Emirates Center for Strategic Studies and Research, 2003), pp. 113-156.
8. Gudrun Kramer, "Islamist Notions of Democracy". In Joel Beinin & Joe Stork (eds.). *Political Islam: Essays from Middle East Report*. (Berkeley, CA: University of California Press, 1997), pp. 71-82.

9. John L. Esposito and John O. Voll, *Islam and Democracy*. (New York, Oxford: Oxford University Press, 1996).
10. Larbi Sadiki, *The Search for Arab Democracy: Discourse and Counter Discourse*. (New York: Columbia University Press, 2004).
11. Zaki Ahmad, "Democracy in the Modern Islamic Discourse". Al-*Mustaqbal Al-Arabi*, 1992, 164, pp. 112-122. (In Arabic).
12. Ibid., p. 115.
13. Martin Kramer, "The Mismeasure of Political Islam", in Martin Kramer (Ed.). *The Islamism Debate*. (Tel Aviv: Tel Aviv University, 1997), pp. 161-173.
14. Raged El-Solh, "Islamist Attitudes towards Democracy: A Review of the Ideas of Al-Ghazali, Al-Turabi and 'Amara". *British Journal of Middle Eastern Studies, 1993*, 20:1, pp. 57–63.
15. See the interview with Mohammad Mahdi 'Aqef on the Muslim Brotherhood's official site (Arabic): http://www.ikhwanonline.com/Article.asp?ArtID=5207&SecID=210
16. See the text of the Muslim Brotherhood's proposal for political reforms on its official website (Arabic): www.ikhwanonline.com/Article.asp?ID=5172&SectionID=356
17. While this paragraph really appears fourteenth on the list in the Muslim Brotherhood's plan, we placed brought it earlier in order to link it with the ninth paragraph about its demand to establish a parliamentary regime in Egypt.
18. The Muslim Brotherhood call members of the moment 'political prisoners' while the regime terms them 'security prisoners', that is, individuals imprisoned in light of their activities that were hostile to the state's security—not because of their activism or political views.
19. Supplement of *Ñawt al-Haq we-al-Hurriya*, October 23, 2009, pp. 3–4.
20. Look at the party political program in the website of the party: http://www.hurryh.com/Regulation.aspx
21. Lia Brynjar, *The Society of Muslim Brothers in Egypt: The Rise of an Islamic Mass Movement 1928-1947*. (England: Ithaca Press, 1998).
22. Habib is an Egyptian Christian intellectual with a doctorate in social psychology. He wrote many books on Egyptian society and on religiousness in Egypt. His books were critical of Mubarak's regime. He is one of the Christians who support the second article of the Egyptian constitution stating that religious Islamic law forms the basis for jurisprudence. Before joining the Muslim Brotherhood's party, he was one of the founders of the Egyptian Center Islamic Party (*al-Wasat*), a party with moderate Islamic leanings in relation to the Muslim Brotherhood (*al-Shorouq*, May 18, 2011).
23. See the party's full platform on the *Al-Masri Al-Yawm* (The Egyptian Today) website (Arabic) at: http://www.almasryalyoum.com/node/388019 (visited July 2011).
24. Sayyid Qutb, *Milestones = Ma'alim fi'l-Tareeq*. (Birmingham: Maktabah Booksellers and Publishers, 2006).
25. Amr Hamzawi, "The Liberty and Justice Party," *Al-Shorouq*, May 3, 2011, p. 5.
26. Ibid.

12. Debates on Transition and Democracy in Central Asia: The Post Soviet Experience

Sreemati Ganguli

The process of transition, that began in 1989, among the authoritarian Communist regimes in the Soviet bloc of Eastern European countries, faced its logical conclusion in the disintegration of the Soviet Union in 1991. The newly independent states of the erstwhile USSR had to confront the tasks of 'triple transition,' that is, managing democratisation, transforming centralised economies into market-economies and state-building in the modern sense of the term. This article concentrates, first, on some of the on-going academic debates about the process of transition and democratisation in post-Soviet states of Eurasia in general and then, to a brief study of the Central Asian scenario.

Debates

1. The study of transition from authoritarian Communism to democracy in Eurasia is approached by various scholars though a variety of methods and approaches. The collapse of the USSR, as some scholars analysed it, was brought about by a 'revolution' that was largely 'rejective' in approach, as Communism as a policy pursued by the state was rejected. But, at the same time, there was no definite perception about the transition to life beyond Communism. There was uncertainty about the goal to be reached as also about the process to reach it. And there was a simultaneous trend in academic discussions about the pattern of transformation in post-Soviet countries of the USSR and East Europe as well as comparisons of experiences in these regions and South Europe, South America and China. But, Leslie Holmes explained that the nature of transformation in these post-Soviet countries is far more comprehensive than the other states in contention: None of these countries (of South Europe, South America and China) has attempted a nationalised economy, a simultaneous and very rapid transition from a centralised and state-run and largely nationalised economy, highly centralised and relatively closed

polity, a society largely devoid of a bourgeoisie, and from long-standing military and trading blocs, towards a marketised and privatised economy and pluralist democracy and a society with a powerful capitalist class and to new military allegiances and trading blocs.[1]

Transition Debate

The debate centres around the process as well as the goal of transition to post-Communism would definitely lead to democracy, or another form of authoritarianism or a chaos-uncertainty. Transition has been defined by A. Jankauskas-L. Gudzinskas: "A distinctive moment in the political life and trajectory of a country – a period of unknown duration and extraordinary uncertainty that is generally initiated from the dynamics within the authoritarian regime. They commented, …… firstly, because of its inherent uncertainty, transition can lead either to democracy or to another type of regime, e.g., some kind of soft authoritarianism. Secondly, in such times of 'abnormal politics', structural preconditions matter less than short-term strategic calculations of elites, and if these calculations are positively interlinked with the isolation of hardliners of regime and the reached broad consensus on the change of regime, a new democracy can emerge".[2]

Vladimir Tismaneanu[3] analysed the process as "perhaps the only safe prediction is that some of the post-communist countries will develop stable democratic institutions and join the European and Atlantic political, economic and military structures. Others will persist in a hybrid semi-liberal, semi-authoritarian order that combines populism and nationalism as forms of expedient legitimisation based on mass enthusiasm". To Bill Lomax,[4] the transition in post-communist countries is "not the transition from one system to another, but the resolution of an intra-system crisis and the recuperation of a system of authoritarian power" and though changes occur, 'they are, more often than not, serving only to reproduce the very worst features of the old system'. Steven Fish[5] had an interesting observation – post-communist transitions start 'from backwards', that is, such states introduce free competitive elections before civil society institutions that could be developed into mass-based political parties. Ghia Nodia[6] emphasised on another very interesting and, important, phenomenon of 'post-communist mentality' to describe transition in post-communist societies. This mentality is also termed as 'mass infantalisation' – the result of total control by communist institutions and abolition of private property. Such a mentality was described as 'playful creativity without the ability of doing real things, abstract yearning for something without clear knowledge what it is and how it is to be obtained, fear of responsibility, expectation that somebody else will make ultimate decisions within the pre-given general framework'. Nicholas J. Lynn analysed that "systemic transition in the former USSR is an inherently spatial process. In the most general sense, marketisation, privatisation and internationalisation involve a reordering of the political space and the restructuring of the economic and the social landscapes of the former Soviet Union". To him, "transition needs to be seen as being driven by a range of different processes at a range of different levels of interaction, some of which will also act upon other places in other regions of the globe at different times.' He emphasised on the significance of the understanding of the variety of outcomes that might come out during the process of systemic change and concluded that in this way, 'transition is reconceptualised away from the idea of fixed paths toward a plurality of interdependent moments".[7]

Democratisation Debate

Samuel P. Huntington termed different phases of democratisation as 'waves' and categorised the process of democratisation engulfing Europe and Latin American countries in the 1970s and the Communist regimes of Eastern Europe in the late 1980s as the "Third Wave of democratisation", after the First wave of 1828-1926 in Europe and the Second wave of 1943-62 in the developing world. To him, "successful democratisation occurs in one country, and this encourages democratisation in other countries, either because they seem to face similar problems, or because successful democratisation elsewhere suggests that democratisation might be a cure for their problems whatever their problems are, or because the country that has democratised is powerful and/or viewed as a political and cultural model".[8]

Based on Huntington's thesis (1991), in mid-1990s a new model of universal understanding of democratisation was offered to analyse the process everywhere- in Eastern Europe, in post-Soviet States, in sub-Saharan Africa and elsewhere. Thomas Carothers offered a counter-analysis in his 'End of the Transition'[9] paradigm as, according to him, Reality is no longer conforming to the model, as the number of transitional countries, with different socio-eco-political background, reached nearly 100. He analysed 5 core assumptions of the so-called 'transition' paradigm: (1) this paradigm assumes that any country, in the process of moving away from dictatorial rule can be considered to be in transition towards democracy, (2) the paradigm offers a three-stage sequence of 'opening', 'breakthrough' and 'consolidation' for the democratisation process to unfold, (3) this model believes in the importance of elections as 'not just a foundation stone but a key generator over time of further democratic reforms', (4) it assumes that the existing conditions of transitional states like political history, institutional legacies, socio-ecopolitical conditions do not matter much 'in either the onset or the outcome of the transition process', (5) this paradigm 'rests on the assumption that the democratic transitions making up the third wave are being built on coherent, functioning states'. Carothers opined, on the contrary, that as 'democracy is not built in a day, it is too early to reach judgments' about the results of the transition processes. He argued that the notion that any state that moves away from authoritarianism is in transition to democracy is often 'inaccurate and misleading. According to him, most of the transitional states are neither dictatorial nor clearly democratic; he proposed the concept of a 'political grey-zone' to accommodate them. Such states do enjoy some attributes of democracy, yet they suffer from serious democratic deficits. And he identified two political syndromes – 'feckless pluralism' and 'dominant power politics'. In the first one, states have some kind of political freedom but democratic base remains shallow. Interestingly, no state in the post-Soviet space falls in this category, according to him. The second one is marked by most of the basic institutional forms of democracy, yet the system is dominated by only one political grouping or party or leadership. He put Azerbaijan, Georgia, Kyrgyzstan (before 2005) and Kazakhstan in this category, while other Central Asian states and Belarus are 'better understood as out-and-out authoritarian systems'.

Michael McFaul[10] categorised three 'democratic breakthroughs' in Serbia (2000), the 'Rose Revolution' in Georgia (2003), the 'Orange Revolution' in Ukraine (2004), and pointed out seven common factors that were crucial: (1) a semi-autocratic rather than fully autocratic regime, (2) an unpopular incumbent, (3) a united and organised opposition, (4) an ability quickly to drive home the point that voting results were falsified, (5) enough independent media to inform the citizens about the falsified vote, (6) a political opposition capable of mobilising tens of thousands or more demonstrators to protest electoral fraud, and (7) divisions among the regime's coercive forces'. To him, such a categorisation was the 'best method of predicting future democratic breakthroughs not only in this region but perhaps in others as well', and he employed John Stuart Mill's 'method of similarity' to put forward these similar or common variables, present in all these three cases of analysis.

Valerie Bunce and Sharon Wolchik[11] proposed the concept of international diffusion to analyse the electoral revolutions in the wide post-Communist region of East-Central Europe, the Balkans and the Soviet successor states during 1996-2005. They defined diffusion as 'a process wherein new ideas, institutions, policies, models or repertoires of behavior spread geographically from a core site to other sites, wherein within a given state or across states'. In the present context, diffusion is referred as 'an electoral model of democratisation' or a model of regime change, that is, transforming elections in authoritarian settings into genuinely fair and competitive processes with substantial involvement of people. The model was developed and applied, first, in the Presidential elections in the Philippines in 1986 and the Presidential plebiscite of Chile in 1988. In the post-Communist region, the model was applied in the electoral revolutions of Bulgaria, Romania and Slovakia during 1996-1998; and later, in Serbia, Georgia, Ukraine and Kyrgyzstan. The success for this model was categorised in three respects – first, the electoral model is easily amenable to diffusion because of its modular character: 'it is a compact package of detailed and inter-related tasks, such as forging cooperation among opposition groups, registering voters and getting out the vote, pressuring the government for reforms in electoral commissions, using the media (where possible) to counter the biases of the official media, running campaigns that provide voters with information and hope they need to take elections seriously and vote their consciences, monitoring elections, and preparing for protests', Second, the existence of similar conditions in the post-Communist region, like recent statehood or recently regained sovereignty; experience of earlier rounds of protests; heterogeneous population with cultural differences; hybrid forms of democracy that combines limited democratic opportunities with fragmented opposition and corrupt officials; and poor economic performance or a growing degree of economic inequalities., and third, the importance of collaborative networks that help to diffuse and promote democracy that include regional democracy promoters and local civil society members. The inclusion of the role of the United States to export democracy to these countries in the category of collaborative network is notable. Interestingly, the call by Paul Goble[12] for the Central Asian states to replicate the Arab Spring in the region and usher in a Central Asian Spring to allow 'the peoples of that region at last to gain what they were denied in 1991 – genuine freedom, real democracy, and the human rights that all peoples should enjoy' may become an interesting study in analysis of the collaborative network of the diffusion model.

Lucan Way, along with Steven Levitsky, presented a somewhat counter-analysis of the diffusion and electoral model. Lucan[13] argued that 'it is entirely possible that the post-communist opposition movements chose to use elections and protests – as opposed to armed rebellion – to overthrow dictators less because they had recently witnessed the use of such tactics in nearby countries and more because elections and protests have arguably been the easiest, most effective, and most internationally acceptable mechanisms for bringing down incumbents'. He also referred to the failure of this model to analyse the failed revolutions in Belarus (2006), Azerbaijan (in 2003 and 2005) and Armenia (2004 and 2008). Their study 'brings to light two key structural explanations for why some post-communist authoritarian regimes have been more vulnerable than others to opposition threats'. And the factors they found most crucial to affect the stability of authoritarian regimes are: the strength of a country's ties to the West; the strength of the incumbent regime's autocratic party or state; and the extent to which state leaders have discretionary control over wealth in society – whether through direct state control over the economy or through reliance on energy revenues that are relatively easy for even weak autocrats to capture.

Henry E. Hale's concept of 'Regime Cycles'[14] analysed the institution of 'patronal presidentialism' in the context of post-Soviet states and argued that 'such institutions tend to generate cyclical phases of elite contestation and consolidation that are defined by elite expectations about the future, in particular, a 'lame-duck syndrome' that precipitates elite defection from the incumbent president's team when elites believe the incumbent may leave office'. To Hale, such an approach 'helps us see how certain types of institutions can in fact lead to regular and reasonably predictable cycles of movement both toward and away from ideal types of democracy and autocracy. What may appear to be a country's strong shift from autocracy toward democracy at a given moment, therefore, may not be a part of transition or trajectory at all, because the observed shift may simply be just another swing in a fairly regular cyclical process'. The institution of patronal presidentialism is characterised by a directly elected presidency with relatively greater formal powers, as compared to other organs of the state, and a high degree of informal powers at the disposal of the president 'based on widespread patron-client relationships at the intersection of the state and the economy'.

The study discussed three sets of states: The first set consists of states (Russia and Azerbaijan) where incumbent presidents entered lame-duck periods but where their teams successfully installed hand-picked successors... The second set contains countries (Ukraine, Armenia, Georgia and Kyrgyzstan) where the incumbent presidents experienced the lame-duck syndrome and whose teams were ousted in the process... The third set includes those states (Belarus, Kazakhstan, Tajikistan, Turkmenistan and Uzbekistan) that appear not to have demonstrated any competitive phase since the establishment of the super-presidential institutions... Among the countries that have experienced the predicted cycles, what crucially distinguishes successful successions (set1) from unsuccessful ones (set 2) is found to be public opinion, although there is also a role for incumbent strategy.

The concept of Neopatrimonialism[15] has been applied by Andrea Gawrich, Inna Melnykovska and Rainer Schweickert to explain bad governance and more than that, the stability of autocratic regimes in Central Asian states, the factors that hinder the democratisation process in these countries. Neopatrimonialism means (according to Erdmann and Engel), A mixture of two co-existing, partly interwoven, types of domination: namely, patrimonial and legal-rational bureaucratic... the distinction between the private and the public, at least formally, exists and is accepted... two role system exist next to each other. The study focused on two criteria to explain the concept in the case study of Central Asia. The first is 'unexplained homogeneity' that is shared by all the Central Asian states – 'the obvious strong top' and 'systematic clientilism'. Regarding the first criteria, political power has been systematically concentrated at the hands of the Presidents. They usually enjoy permanency and formal accumulation of power (except in the case of Kyrgyzstan) through suppression of alternative candidates, fraudulent elections and subversion of original constitutional term limits by amendments of the Constitution and they rule with extensive use of informal power distribution. At the same time, they use 'ideological leadership' role through their personality cults and/or their image as 'Fathers of the Nation' to their advantage. According to the study, Turkmen President Niyazov has been the most successful in building up this image, with Presidents of Uzbekistan, Kazakhstan and Kyrgyzstan remaining distant followers. Secondly, clentilism is rampant in all these states-whether it is family connections in Kazakhstan, power circles around the President in Kyrgyzstan and Tajikistan, and clan relations in Turkmenistan and Uzbekistan. The second criterion is the 'unexplained heterogeneity' of different categories of neopatrimonialism in these states: Sultanistic variation of very strong concentration of power in an impermeable narrow circle of power elites, a model that is in vogue in both Turkmenistan and Uzbekistan; oligarchic variation, characterised by competition among patronage or rent-seeking cycles, a common feature of both Kyrgyzstan and Tajikistan; and the unique case of Kazakhstan that has changed its orientation from sultanistic to oligarchic version. The study concludes that the 'specific Central Asian forms of neopatrimonialism, are influenced by post-Soviet habits of hierarchy, non-transparency and informality. However, it is even deeper rooted in Central Asian historical experiences of group loyalty, group hierarchy, regional identities and historical forms of stateness'.

Judging from an economic perspective, Andreas Freytag-Jac C Heckelman[16] searched the correlation between the US Aid and democratic reforms in countries of East Europe and Eurasia. Promotion of democracy through foreign aid programmes has been declared as 'strategic pillars' of post –Cold War foreign policy agenda of the US government. And two new aid programmes – the SEED (Support for East European Democracy Act of 1989) and the FREEDOM Support Act (Freedom for Russia and Emerging Eurasian Democracies and Open Markets Support Act of 1992) were initiated to help these countries develop democratic institutions in the transition period. Freytag-Heckelman took into consideration 26 countries of East Europe and of FSU (Former Soviet Union), including Russia and five Central Asian countries, for the period of 1998-2007 and judged the effect of aid on six democracy categories of civil society, corruption, electoral process, local governance, judicial framework and independence of media. And they reached the conclusion that 'despite assistance from USAID, Eurasian and Eastern European countries are generally unable to maintain and improve their democratic environment in the years after 1998. The positive influence of US aid has mainly been limited to judicial framework, civil society, media independence, and electoral processes, but the US aid does not significantly affect governance and corruption….We also find that democratic freedoms are more strongly affected by aid if the recipient country suffered longer from central planning. In countries where central planning ended the longest time ago, aid is not helpful. Some have argued that focusing developmental aid on democratisation and institutional capacity building is necessary before directing aid flows into economic activity, because this sort of aid has been revealed to be growth enhancing, if at all, only in countries with better institutional settings. Thus, one modest lesson from the study can be that aid donors should concentrate aid flows on countries with low civil liberties and a longer history of central planning'.

Grigore Pop-Eleches emphasised on the factor of historical legacy and the 'powerful and temporally resilient influence of these overlapping social, economic and political legacies on post-communist regime trajectories'.[17] His argument is that 'no single legacy was either sufficient or necessary for post-communist democracy. Nor were the political preferences and choices of post-communist elites and citizens irrelevant'. He also claimed that 'the stark cross-national differences in the region's overlapping cultural, socio-economic and institutional legacies significantly shaped the preferences of political actors and the constraints on their choices. As a consequence, the prospects for democratisation and democratic deepening were significantly better in countries with favorable legacies (such as the relatively developed, ethnically homogeneous countries of East Central Europe with their longer histories of statehood, democracy, and bureaucratic competence) than in many of the fledgling new states emerging from the former Soviet Union and Yugoslavia'. He categorised five key legacy dimensions like geography, cultural/religious heritage, economic legacies, social conditions/modernisation and institutional legacy and discussed their impact on post-Communist democratisation. The study showed that countries like Moldova, Mongolia and Kyrgyzstan were more democratic than their legacies would have predicted, while Belarus, Croatia and Yugoslavia performed below 'legacy-based expectations' and this suggests that 'countries do not simply follow a deterministically preordained path towards a uniform endpoint'. He commented that the 17 years have not produced a Fukuyama-style 'end of history', but rather a return to historically rooted differences. And to him, 'History matters not only because some countries had a democratic head start, but because countries with different legacies experienced divergent trajectories over the course of the post-communist transition'.

The Central Asian Reality

Stephen Blank once commented that 'talk of prospects for democratisation in Central Asia appears to be either an exercise in mindless bravery or in futility. Nowhere in this region do the economic-political requirements for and understanding of genuine democracy exist nor will they soon either in elite or mass practice. Worse, both here and in the Muslim world generally, the transplantation of Western and/or democratic institutions has often paradoxically strengthened the forces of authoritarian rule, not liberalism or democracy'[18].

For the Central Asian states, the promises of building a democratic state, with a truly independent media, non-governmental groups and opposition parties are not yet fulfilled after nearly two decades of their independence. In these states, political power remains concentrated in the hands of the President, tolerance levels for opponent views are low and successive elections are used as tools for perpetuating the rules of the reigning authorities. And authoritarian rule is promoted as a viable model of governance, as citizens are fed with the warning that rapid democratisation would threaten political stability of the state and economic security of the population and would strengthen Islamic terrorism. Different socio-political patterns characterise the processes of establishing government set-ups: strong tribal identities form centres of power in the highly centralised governmental structures in Uzbekistan and Turkmenistan; whereas regional identities are a potent force in Kazakhstan, Kyrgyzstan and Tajikistan. Family connections also control decision-making in a significant way. And so, there is the trend that hinders the democratisation processes in these Republics and there is the suggestion that the variation in the region is different shades of authoritarianism, 'from the totalitarian dictatorship in Turkmenistan to the hard authoritarian regime in Uzbekistan and up to the more or less soft authoritarian regimes of Tajikistan, Kazakhstan and Kyrgyzstan'.[19]

In the 'Freedom in the World 2011',[20] the latest Report by the Freedom House on global political rights and civil liberties, the rankings for the Central Asian countries are mixed, depending on their performances on the freedom score in 2010. Freedom House categorises countries into three categories- Free, Partly Free and Not Free. A Free country is one where there is open political competition, a climate of respect for civil liberties, significant independent civic life, and independent media. A Partly Free country is one in which there is limited respect for political rights and civil liberties. These states suffer from corruption, weak rule of law, ethno-religious strife and single party- domination, though there remains a pluralist party structure. A Not Free country is one where basic political rights are absent and basic civil rights are systematically denied. Kyrgyzstan has moved from Not Free to Partly Free category, as the old authoritarian regime gave way to civilian rule, as determined by popular elections. Kazakhstan and Kyrgyzstan remain in the category of Not Free countries. And, Turkmenistan and Uzbekistan are rated in the lowest possible ranking of the Not Free category, along with seven other countries like North Korea, Sudan, Libya and Myanmar.

Kyrgyzstan's experiments with democratisation is unique in Central Asia – it got the title of 'the island of Democracy' in the early 1990s with the development of multiple political parties and a relatively free press. The Constitution was changed a number of times – in 1996, 2003, 2006, 2007 and again in June 2010. The reason might be to accommodate the interests of the ruling coterie or might be, in a very limited sense, to adjust to popular expectations. Kyrgyzstan is also the only Central Asian country to experience two revolutions within a short span- in March 2005 and April 2010. The last one may be called a reverse Colour Revolution as it toppled Kurmanbek Bakiyev – the leader of the 2005 Colour Revolution and who replaced Askar Akayev – by a popular uprising. But the Tulip Revolution leadership failed to meet demands of democratisation and of economic restructuring. Widespread corruption by the Presidential family, the use of organised crime gangs for short-term gains by the ruling elite (just as was in the Akayev era), nepotism, promotion of regional interests (while under Akayev, Northerners got favoured, Bakiyev regime was dominated by Southerners) and lack of socio-economic development (some 40 per cent of the population lives below poverty line, unemployment stands at 18 per cent) were enough for popular discontent. To make matters worse, taxes were raised and price of electricity was doubled in late 2009 and again in January 2010. The April Revolution was followed by bloody ethnic (Kyrgyz-Uzbek) clashes, putting into question the making of arbitrary inter-state borders by the Soviet authorities as well as the contemporary ethnic composition regional ethnic distribution of Kyrgyzstan.

Since then, Kyrgyzstan has, more or less successfully, held two more elections – the 2010 Parliamentary elections and the Presidential elections of October 2011. But the crisis in Kyrgyzstan is a pointed evidence to the challenges of transition that the post-Soviet states of Central Asia have been facing all along – it is not only about holding of free and fair elections, it is also about the true representation of the interests of all the clans, political groups and regions of the states; it is also about governance by not a coterie but by an administration, free from corruption and nepotism; and it is also about restructuring of the economy according to the rules and norms of market economy and distribution of the fruits of economic success even to the lowest strata of the population.

The kind of democratisation that is not forced upon, (as Joseph Nye suggested that the main lesson to be learned from the Iraq War 'is that while the development of democracy can be aided from outside, it cannot easily be imposed by force'[21]), and that includes all the ethno-religio-linguistic complexities of these Central Asian states is the only way for a stable polity. Because the promotion and consolidation of democracy is the determining factor in building sustainable human development and lasting peace, through enforcement of rule of law and protection of human rights. And also because in that sort of a polity, people get more choices to voice their grievances against authorities in a peaceful manner as otherwise, the lack of truly representative political institutions would result in more people turning to religious extremism as the last resort to register protests. The development of such political institutions will also have better opportunities to provide the political space needed for genuine public participation, to limit selective political exclusion (like in cases of ethnic communities or gender) and thus to initiate the process to build political pluralism (which allows each part of society to get involved in the political process) to thwart the sense of alienation on the part of any section of society – either ethnic, or regional or religious or gender. And that polity will then be able to confront the challenges of conducting viable economic reforms and establishing security within itself.

Conclusion

There are some points in this process of transition and democratisation that are worth-noting. First and foremost, this is the first experience of democratisation for the Central Asian states, as in the pre-Soviet era, they were under the rules of hegemonic and authoritarian Khanates where change in leadership followed either hereditary rules or through war and coup. And transition from authoritarian rule to democracy is not an easy task. As Pinar Akcali commented in the case of Kyrgyzstan, but it is true for all the Central Asian states that '...... the relationship between democratisation and political stability is complex, multidimensional and fragile... As such, political stability and democracy do not develop in tandem with each other, and in many cases they turn out to be mutually exclusive'[22]. The process of transition is an on-going one, with all the possibilities of twists and turns at every juncture. And the path does not always take the linear way to democracy- there always remains the practical possibility of turns to more authoritarian rule under the garb of democracy or, worse, to total authoritarianism. But the process does not end there. And, more significant, the process is not time-bound. The events of Arab Spring show years of authoritarian or semi-authoritarian rules can only delay the process.

Also, the rules and norms of democracy may be universal, but the process of the establishment of democratic system of governance is not so structured that it can provide one universal solution for every country or, for every region. The phase of transition or the era of post-Communism was termed by David Stark as a 'non-system',[23] while Leslie Holmes developed a 14-point formula that characterises this era of post-Communism, and the list includes the near-absence of a culture of compromise, cynicism towards political institutions, high expectations from rulers, the creation of an ideological vacuum and moral confusion, political dynamism and instability.[24] But, the process of democratisation has to be understood against this perspective, as Nicholas J. Lynn aptly commented, that 'It is within this general political context- of volatility, uncertainty, and flux – that competing strategies for implementing systemic change have to be seen.'[25] Relatedly, strategies or models analyse the events and processes in a state or a region in a given context of a particular time. And, these models, strategies and paradigms are also, as Carothers pointed out, are products 'of a certain time'. So, there always remains the need 'to move on to new frameworks, new debates and perhaps eventually a new paradigm of political change – one suited to the landscape of today, not the lingering hopes of an earlier era.'[26]

John O'Loughlin commented, while analysing the phenomenon of global democratisation, that 'In many respects, globalisation in the form of political democratisation is similar to globalisation in the form of economic liberalization. While the principles behind both trends can be welcomed, the reality is a lot far messier. Economic globalisation is now increasingly challenged by its supposed beneficiaries as attention turns to the institutions and powerful actors that guide the process to their own benefits and to its unequal impacts. Democratisation is also looked at more skeptically. What kind of democratisation and for whom? Who is promoting it and for what purposes?' He suggested that 'The debate about the process is not yet over and growing skepticism about the nature of democracy as applied in (heretofore) non-democratic states, despite the gloss and aura of this form of political structure' is continuing and growing and concluded that 'the match of ideal and reality will be continually under scrutiny'.[27]

The prospect of achieving the goal of 'genuine' or 'real democracy' is, to be practical, an impossible and unachievable dream, as there is no fixed tool to judge and authenticate the 'genuineness' of democracy anywhere in the world in a particular given time. More important, democratisation is an evolutionary process that must evolve from within a particular state, taking into account a lot of inter-connected factors – history, culture, development of national identities based on ethnic, linguistic, regional and religious preferences, socio-economic conditions, political culture, structural formation of the ruling elite and so on. The particularity and uniqueness of each society is the key deciding factor in the nature of the evolution process and of the democratic set-up that gets evolved. The countries of Eurasia, particularly, the Central Asian states are not even mid-way through this process of democratisation or transition to post-Communism as only twenty years have passed after the disintegration of the USSR. Also, the history of the process of democratisation worldwide shows that the success of this process does not depend on any time-bound formula.

Notes

1. Leslie Holmes, *Post-Communism: an Introduction*, (Oxford: Polity Press, 1997, p.19 (emphasis by the author).
2. A. Jankauskas and L. Gudzinskas, "Reconceptualizing Transitology: Lessons from Post-Communism", www.isn.ethz/ch/isn/Digital-Library/Publications
3. Vladimir Tismaneanu, *Fantasies of Salvation: Democracy, Nationalism and Myth in Post-Communist Europe*, (Princeton: Princeton University Press, 1998), p. 19.
4. Bill Lomax, "Impediments to Democratisation in Post-Communist East-Central Europe" in Gordon Wightman (ed) *Party Formation in East-Central Europe: Post-Communist Politics in Czechoslovakia, Hungary, Poland and Bulgaria*, (Vermont: Edward Elgar, 1995), p. 179.
5. Steven Fish, *Democracy from Scratch: Opposition and Regime in New Russian Revolution*, (Princeton: Princeton University Press, 1995), p.66
6. Ghia Nodia, "How Different are Post-Communist Transitions?", *Journal of Democracy*, 7(4), 1996.
7. Nicholas J. Lynn, 'Geography and Transition: Reconceptualizing Systemic Change in the Former Soviet Union', *Slavic Review*, 58(4), winter 1999, pp. 824-840.
8. Samuel P. Huntington, *The Third Wave: Democratisation in the Late Twentieth Century*, (Norman: University of Oklahoma Press, 1991).
9. Thomas Carothers, 'The End of the Transition Paradigm', *Journal of Democracy*, 13(1). January 2002, pp. 5-21.
10 Michael McFaul, 'Transitions from Post-communism', *Journal of Democracy*, 16(3), 2005, pp. 5-19.
11. ValerieBunce-Sharon Wolchik, ' International Diffusion and Post-communist Electoral Revolutions', *Communist and Post Communist Studies*, 39(3), September 2006, pp. 283-304.

12. Paul A. Goble, Testimony for a hearing of the U.S. Commission on Security and Cooperation in Europe o 'Central Asia and the Arab Spring: Growing Pressure for Human Rights?', *www.iwp.edu/news../prof-goble-testifies-at -the-helsinki-commission.*
13. Lucan Way, 'The Real Causes of the Color Revolutions', *Journal of Democracy*, 19(3), July 2008, pp. 55-69.
14. Henry E Hale, 'Regime Cycles: Democracy, Autocracy, and Revolution in Post-Soviet Eurasia', *World Politics*, 58(1), October, 2005, pp. 133-165.
15. Andrea Gawrich-Inna Melnykovska-Rainer Schweickert, *'More than Oil and Geography-Neopatrimonialism as an Explanation of Bad Governance and Autocratic Stability in Central Asia'* Paper presented at 'Neopatrimonialism in Various World Regions', GIGA German Institute of Global and Area Studies, Hamburg, August 23, 2010.
16. Andreas Freytag-Jac C Heckelman, 'Has Assistance from USAID been Successful in Promoting and Sustaining Democracy? Evidence from the Transition Economies of Eastern Europe and Eurasia', JENA Economic Research Papers, #2011- 017, *www.jenecon.de*, accessed on October 25, 2011.
17. Grigore Pop-Eleches, 'Historical Legacies and Post-Communist Regime Change', *The Journal of Politics*, 69(4), November 2007, pp. 908-926.
18. Stephen Blank, 'For a Transition to Democracy in Central Asia', in Birgit N. Schlyter (ed), *'Prospects for Democracy in Central Asia'*, Swedish Research Institute, Istanbul, 2005.
19. Eugheniy Zhovtis, 'Democratisation and Human Rights in Central Asia', *CEPS Policy Brief*, no. 134, July 2007.
20. Freedom in the World: The Annual Survey of Political Rights and Civil Liberties 2011, www.freedomhouse.org, accessed on November 02, 2011.
21. Joseph S. Nye Jr., 'Does Increasing Democracy Undercut Terrorists?', *The Christian Science Monitor*, September 22, 2005.
22. Pinar Akcali, 'Democracy and Political Stability in Kyrgyzstan', in Birgit N. Schlyter (ed) '*Prospects for Democracy in Central Asia*', Swedish Research Institute, Istanbul, 2005.
23. David Stark, 'The Great Transformation? Social Change in Eastern Europe?', *Contemporary Sociology*, 21(3), 1992, pp. 299-305.
24. Leslie Holmes, *'Post- Communism'*.
25. Nicholas J. Lynn, 'Geography and Transition'.
26. Thomas Carothers, 'The End of the Transition Paradigm'.
27. John O' Loughlin, 'Global Democratisation', *www.colorado.edu/IBS/PEC/johno/papers/Global%20Democratization*, accessed on October 20, 2011.

13. Russia: From *Demokratizatsiya* to *Suverennaya Demokratiya*

Susmita Bhattacharya

Over the last two decades, *democratisation* and *democracy* have been the most widely debated and central organising concepts in the context of political evolution of the post-socialist and post-communist regimes, and the world in general. "Yet it has proved to be maddeningly elastic and nuanced".[1] Though the evidence suggests that the Russian President, Vladimir Putin could not really succeed in ensuring an adequate transition towards liberal democracy rather reflects a trend toward consolidation of Federal executive power in the Russian Federation, still there is no simple answer to the question whether Putin's Russia is a democracy. While there is no disagreement among the scholars in admitting that Russia is not yet a democratic nation, at the same time, in no way could it be referred to as an undemocratic one either. In fact, at some quarters Kremlin's efforts in favour of achieving the democratisation of the country have been appreciated.

There are international and Russian observers who view the contribution of Putin to the development and democratisation of the Russian Federation in a positive light. For instance, Tom Bjorkman, the former Russian analyst at the Central Intelligence Agency, stated that Russia under Putin was ready for a new wave of democratic reforms to engage a population that Bjorkman claimed was 'committed to democratic values'.[2] Andranik Migranyan, Director of the Institute for Democracy and Cooperation, New York, argues that the Putin regime has restored what Migranyan believed were the natural functions of a government after period of the 1990s, when Russia was allegedly ruled by oligopolies expressing only their narrow interests. Migranyan wrote, "If democracy is the rule by a majority and the protection of the rights and opportunities of a minority, the current political regime can be described as democratic, at least formally. A multiparty political system exists in Russia, while several parties, most of them representing the opposition, have seats in the State Duma".[3]

However, there are numerous others, who do not share this view, express concern that the path to democracy made possible by the collapse of the Soviet system has been derailed, by all indications, due to the federal reforms put forward by Putin during his two terms of presidency 2000–2008. For example, Michael McFaul suggested that Russia, as of 1996, was as democratic as it could be reasonably expected.[4] Larry Diamond, a political science professor University of Stanford noted in 2003, "… at the third wave of world democratization which began in 1974, there were 41 democracies among the existing 150 states. Of the remaining 109 states, 56 (more than half) of them subsequently made a transition to democracy, and of those 56, only Pakistan, Sudan, and Russia are not democracies today".[5] Pierre Hassner commented that Putin "has led Russia into a harsh brand of authoritarianism with some fascist features..."[6]

In the late 1990s, there was a wide speculation about the developments in the domestic political arena followed by the disintegration of the Soviet Union; it was said that post-Soviet Russia was going through a transitional phase toward democracy. But after the changes that took place in the political system of the Russian Federation as a consequence of the federal reforms launched by Putin soon after becoming the president of the country in 2000, the euphoria was over. There were plethora of writings which suggested that the democratisation process that started under Yel'tsin was derailed by Putin's reforms, and the country was heading towards 'soft autocracy'.

This paper attempts to trace the course of the democratisation process in the post-Soviet Russia and explores the impact of the federal reform policies during Putin's presidency on the transitional democratic process of the Russian Federation from a totalitarian state to a democratic polity, and on the matters relating to the regional governors, the Federal Legislature and electoral politics, human rights, and media, in particular. This would also touch upon the questions: how far was Boris Yel'tsin's period really close to democracy; how did it get derailed during 2000-08, the period of Putin's two terms of presidency; and whether the predictions in the 1990s about the political direction that Russia might take were premature or had been misjudged.

The structure of this paper includes two parts. The first part is fact-based and the second part is analytical. The facts begin with a brief overview of the situation prior to Putin's presidency; then the phases of Putin's administration and transition of power described in different terms crafted by the political advisers and Kremlin ideologues, as well as a more detailed discussion of the

Putin administration's policies and reforms that have contributed in shaping Russia's political system and impacted it.

The second part would provide an analysis of the current political scenario by focusing on the institutions that are necessary for governing modern democracies according to Robert Dahl and the actual situation prevailing in today's Russia.

Before Putin

The transitional process of democratisation of the Russian Federation of today has its root in the erstwhile Soviet Union. Before analysing Russia's current political system, it is necessary to briefly highlight some of the significant events that culminated in President Putin's presidency.

In his 'Report to the Central Committee of the CPSU' Moscow, January 27, 1987, Gorbachev had declared, "...we need democracy like air. If we fail to realise that, or if we realise it but make no real serious step to broaden it, to advance it and to draw the country's working people extensively into the reorganisation process, our policy will get choked." Again in his speech to the 27th Party Congress of the CPSU in 1986 he had stated, "...democracy is the wholesome and pure air without which a socialist public organism cannot live a full-blooded life".[7]

'*Demokratizatsiya*' or democratisation, was one of the four basic campaigns – others being '*perestroika*' (restructuring), '*glasnost*' (public discussion of issues, transparency), and '*uskorenie*' (acceleration),[8] launched in the late 1980s and early 1990s by Mikhail Gorbachev, who assumed the position of General Secretary of the Communist Party in March 1985. '*Demokratizatsiya*' was a significant part of his political reform aiming at greater participation by citizens and different interest groups of the country in the political processes. As part of its programme of *demokratizatsiya*, the Supreme Soviet amended Article 6 of the Constitution on March 14, 1990, which abolished the 'leading and guiding role in the Soviet society' of the CPSU and permitted the existence of other parties.

Glasnost', usually translated as an openness or transparency, was neither the same as freedom of press nor the right to information nor was it original to Gorbachev (it figured, for instance, in the constitution adopted under Leonid Brezhnev, in 1977). It did, however, reflect Gorbachev's belief that without a greater awareness of the real state of affairs and of the considerations that had led to particular decisions, there would be no willingness on the part of the

Soviet people to commit themselves to his programme of *perestroika*. He told the Central Committee meeting that elected him, "the better the people are informed the more consciously they act, the more actively they support the party, its plans and programmatic objectives".

Influenced by considerations such as these the Gorbachev leadership made steady and sometimes dramatic progress in broadening the scope of public debate and exposing the Soviet past as well as the Soviet present to critical scrutiny, such as lacuna of the Brezhnev era, Stalinism and repression of 1930s', restoration of the forgotten leaders like Bukharin, reappraisal of contribution of personality like Trotsky.[9] *Glasnost*' led to further changes in the quality of Soviet public life, from literature and arts to statistics, and a wide-ranging discussion of myriads of subject unmentionable before. The new law, adopted in June 1990, abolished the censorship entirely.

The 'democratisation' of Soviet political life was an associated change, and one that was intended to unlock the human energies that, for Gorbachev, had been choked off by the bureaucratic centralism of the Stalin and Brezhnev years. He told the 19th Party Conference in the summer of 1988 that the political system had undergone 'serious deformations', leading to the development of a 'command-administrative system'. The role of party and state officialdom had increased out of all proportion, and a 'bloated administrative apparatus' had begun to impose its own priorities in political and social matters. Those who were elected to the soviets or commissions that advised them rarely had no influence as such over the decisions taken by their executives. Social life, as a whole, had become 'straitjacketed' by controls of various kinds, and ordinary working people had become 'alienated' from the system that was supposed to represent their interests. It was this 'ossified system of government, with its command-and-pressure mechanism', that had become the main obstacle to *perestroika*.

Glasnost was a policy aimed at creating greater transparency in the workings of the Soviet government, thus, creating the necessary conditions for successful economic reform. Then, in his first official statements as General Secretary, he emphasised the need for transparency (*glasnost*) in the work of Party, Soviet, state and public organisations. Regarding *perestroika*, he also stressed the importance of 'upgrading the economic mechanism and the system of management in its entirety'. Though Gorbachev's reform gave birth to the multiparty system and openness, Brian Crozier suggested, that "*Glasnost* released a 'genie' from a bottle and followed the examples of unprecedented freedom of speech".[10] However, it is believed that while Gorbachev wanted to reform the Soviet system, he aimed at maintaining the Union and the Communist Party's control over it.[11] However, Gorbachev's reform agenda could not attain its desired goals. The state itself disintegrated and fifteen of its constituent republics became independent states after the collapse of the attempted coup in August 1991 that intended to preserve a viable union.

Gorbachev resigned as Soviet President and Yel'tsin took over the Kremlin as the President of the newly independent Russian Federation, the largest post-Soviet republic. Nonetheless, the reforms "unleashed a drive for enhanced sovereignty spearheaded by the Baltic republics, a process that grew into a tidal wave of demands for devolution of power and responsibilities dubbed the 'Parade of Sovereignties'".[12]

By 1990, the constitutional amendments set the stage for what would be the final attempt by the Communist Party to maintain total control over the Soviet Union. On March 13, 1990, the Congress of People's Deputies amended Article 6 of the Soviet Constitution to strip the Communist Party of its 'monopoly of vertical power'. A proposed amendment that would have removed all mention of the Communist Party from the constitution barely failed. Additionally, the Congress of People's Deputies established a presidency of the Soviet Union, to which Gorbachev was elected. Meanwhile, Boris Yeltsin won election as the chairman of Russia's Supreme Soviet on May 29, 1990, effectively becoming Russia's first President.

With Yel'tsin as the President of Russia and Gorbachev as the President of the Soviet Union, the stage was set for a struggle between the Soviet Union and its constituent Republics. As Kempton and Clark note, while Russia was just one of the fifteen Soviet republics, its size and location made its struggle with the Soviet government "a struggle between two contenders for the center".[13] Yel'tsin employed the strategy of encouraging the Russian regional governments to 'take all the sovereignty they could swallow,'"[14] which helped him gain popular support in Russia.

In March 1991, the plans for a New Union Treaty were made public and an All-Union Referendum was held to determine the future of Soviet federalism in which 76.4 per cent of soviet voters sought to preserve the union, though six of the Soviet Republics[15] boycotted the poll.

Ultimately, the Soviet Union's fate was sealed by a failed coup attempt in August 1991. The Soviet government structure and the Republics negotiated a New Union Treaty during the summer of 1991, which would have established a looser federal relationship between the Soviet government and the Republics.[16] Before the Treaty could be signed, however, the conservatives within the Communist Party attempted to oust Gorbachev and regain their strangle hold on the Soviet Union.

The coup attempt that was to save the Soviet Union and push the Communist Party back into control, led Gorbachev to resign as President and the official dissolution of the Soviet Union in December 1991. In the following years, an independent Russia attempted to strengthen its independent political system, and a new Russian Constitution was adopted in 1993 that remains in force till date.

New Russia: New President

The plethora of writings suggests that the democratisation process thrived under Yel'tsin and has been derailed by Putin's reforms, and the country has been heading towards 'soft autocracy'. It is no denying the fact that there existed some important elements of democracy under Yel'tsin, above all, the freedom of the media and wide-ranging public debate. But an analytical study provides evidence that there was actually no equality and no real rule of law. The power and corruption of the Yel'tsin's family turned the pretence of democracy into a farce. Pierre Hassner, while viewing the future of Russia's transition to be toward autocracy, has remarked, "Russia's progress toward democracy began going off the rails even before Putin came to power."[17] Lilia Shevtsova in her *Russia – Lost in Transition*, dates back the crisis to Russia's progress towards democracy from 1993, when Yel'tsin ordered troops to fire on a rebellious parliament.[18] The crisis of democracy under Yel'tsin culminated with his re-election in 1996, which was manipulated by the oligarchs to give him a victory in spite of his disastrous standing in the opinion polls.

Yeltsin's Presidency profoundly influenced the course of current state of Russia's political system. The three most important aspects of the Yeltsin Presidency, in terms of their influence on the current political system were (1) his handling of Russia's fledgling capitalist economy, (2) his stance against the Chechen separatist movement, and (3) his instalment of Putin as Prime Minister, and later Interim President in 1999.

The effects of early post-Soviet privatisation to a great extent moulded the future political environment. Yel'tsin undoubtedly deserves credit for taking the country away from the planned economy of the Soviet times. The first set of economic privatisation, known as 'shock therapy', included 'abrupt deregulation of prices, privatisation of state-owned enterprises, and the shift to a market economy'. But on the other hand, rapid privatisation caused the accumulation of public wealth in very few hands of oligarchs. Putin found uneasy relations with a handful of politically influential businessmen, created by Yel'tsin, who wielded tremendous power and helped selecting the country's new leader, but then found themselves struggling to maintain influence and redefine their role under the new regime. They symbolised a very curious, Russian-style form of capitalism. They were forces of growth and progress, but also actively meddled in politics and tried to impose a highly monopolised form of development.[19] The rapid privatisation has also been blamed for causing extreme levels of poverty. That poverty has resulted in a depressed social climate as evidenced by the rise in alcoholism and suicide rates, and the drop in length of life expectancy.[20]

Chechnya, the small region in southern Russia is of particular importance to Russia because of its oil pipelines and rail links. The Chechnya war during Yel'tsin's presidency and Putin's role in dealing with the second round of armed conflict between the Russian government and Chechnya cast a long shadow on the subsequent development of the Russian political system at the later phase. By 1994, the inability of the weakened Russian state to exert its control over Chechnya led to armed conflict. What started as a proxy war against the regional governor's regime became a full-scale military campaign by that summer. The insurgents were led by Chechnya's Djokar Dudaev, who declared Chechnya's independence from Russia and violated the Russian Constitution by basing his regime on Islam. The war lasted until 1996, when President Yeltsin's administration negotiated a cease-fire and pulled out its troops. The result was practical autonomy for Chechnya, with final status to be postponed for five years.[21] Before those five years elapsed, however, Chechen separatists forcefully attempted to merge Chechnya with neighbouring Dagestan, another Russian region, hoping to combine the two Islamic regions into one independent state.[22] Thus, began the second round of armed conflict between the Russian government and Chechnya.

In the last part of the 1990s, Yel'tsin started promoting Putin all the way to the presidency. In 1998, Yel'tsin appointed him to head the KGB's successor, the FSB. Then, on August 09, 1999, Yel'tsin introduced Putin as his new Prime Minister. As Prime Minister, Putin gained authorisation from Yel'tsin to dispatch troops to Chechnya in response to the Chechens' move against Dagestan. On December 31, 1999, Yel'tsin resigned from the presidency. Under the Russian Constitution's succession of power provisions, Putin became the Interim President and in 2000, he was elected as the Second President of the Russian federation. Putin was re-elected as President for the second term in 2004 and remained in office till 2008. On May 7, 2008, Dmitry Anatol'evich Medvedev became the third President of the country and Putin became the Prime Minister. Putin once again has been elected for his third term at the March 04 Presidential elections with 63.64 per cent of the total votes by defeating his nearest rival, the Communist Party leader Gennady Zyuganov, who managed to get hold of 17.18 per cent. Putin will take the oath during the inauguration to be held on May 7, 2012 and continue for six years, till 2018.

Currently, Russia is undergoing triple transition and its prime task of the hour consists of simultaneously reforming its (1) economy, (2) polity, and (3) configuring the centre-local relations by creating a stable and viable form of federalism. Building a new federal democratic system along with privatising economy and attempting to radically overhaul the political system have made the job for Russia even tougher.

The reforms that Putin initiated after becoming the president in 2000, ostensibly aimed at creating a more rationally structured federalism, turned out to be more narrowly focused on enhancing the power of the centre. Under both Yelt'sin and Putin, political manoeuvrings aimed at consolidating the power of the president took the prime position than building democratic institutions.

Putin's Federal Reforms

Regional Governors

Putin appears to believe that reforming the economy to modernise the country is a far more urgent priority than building democracy that bears more than a superficial resemblance to the variants recognisable in the west.

Throughout his administration, Putin has set forth policies and proposed legislation[23] that have shaped Russia's political system. He justified his moves to centralise more authority in the federal executive branch of government, at the expense of the federal legislature and the regions to counteract the influence of corrupt business owners or oligarchs and protect the country from terrorist threats,. The Beslan school hostage crisis of September, 2004[24] reiterated Putin's concerns over national security, giving him a reason to impose further reforms on the Russian political system.[25] In the wake of the Beslan school tragedy, Putin announced a series of proposed changes to the political system as a way to strengthen Russia's unity and fight against terrorism. Putin's plans proposed to end the direct election of regional governors and candidates nominated by the President to be elected by the regional assemblies, and announced to do away with first-past-the-post elections to the Duma, the lower house of parliament, so that delegates are elected only on the basis of party lists.

Structurally, Russia's political system is set up as a federal system. Of the numerous benefits of federalism, one relates particularly to minority groups within a country. It allows a minority group 'to preserve itself by allowing it to control the cultural and educational policy within a set territory'.

Putin's reform got a blow after the July 2002 verdict by the Constitutional Court allowing regional leaders to run for more than two terms. With such leaders left in place, allowed to flout or undermine the federal laws on their own territory, the law-based division of powers between centre and periphery made no sense. In 2000, Putin had already altered the national executive branch's control over the regional governors, by appointing special envoys to oversee the governors. Most of these envoys were 'siloviki', the former military or security service personnel.

By the end of his first term, on December 11, 2004, a law vested the Russian president with the authority to nominate the regional governors. According to the law, the President would nominate a candidate thirty-five days prior to the end of a sitting governor's term in office. The regional legislature then must vote to approve the nominee by a simple majority. Should a regional legislature reject two nominees, however, the President can dissolve that legislature and simply appoint an acting governor. Additionally, the President may dismiss governors in whom the President loses confidence, or who improperly fulfil their duties.

This scheme was designed to create a single chain of command for purposes of addressing national security concerns exposed by the Beslan school hostage crisis. It has also been justified by the need to combat corruption. At the time the new law came into being, however, State Duma, the lower house of the Russian federal legislature, Sergei Glazev, a deputy explained that President Putin had misjudged the effect the centralising authority would have on the country. Others have argued that this law violated the Russian Constitution;

Nonetheless, Russia's Constitutional Court declared the procedure to be valid under the Constitution.

The Federal Legislature and Electoral Politics

Putin's initiatives regarding Russia's federal legislative branch have been intended to solidify support for his administration. Changes to the way the members of both the Federation Council and the State Duma are selected has made it easier for the current majority party, United Russia, to maintain control of the legislature.

The Federation Council

The upper house of the Russian legislature, called the Federation Council, is composed of two members from each region. Article 96 of the Russian Constitution leaves the particular method of selecting members of the both Federation Council and the State Duma up to the federal law.[26] At its inception in 1993, a presidential decree established that members were to be popularly elected by the regions. That changed in 1995 when a federal treaty called for the heads of the regions' legislative and executive branches, who were elected by the regions, to sit as members of the Federation Council. The system changed again on August 8, 2000. The Federation Council members are now either elected by regional legislatures or appointed by the regional executive branch. If appointed by the executive, the legislature must approve the nominee.

The State Duma

Federal Law of May 18, 2005, No. 51-F3[27] drastically changed the way the 450 members of the State Duma would be selected, starting from December 2007. A mixed-member system was used from 1993 through 2003, whereby half the seats were filled by single-constituency districts and the other half were filled on a party-proportionality basis. According to this law, from December 2007 elections, all members were to be selected proportionally along party lines.[28] Also, the threshold for winning seats would increase from its previous level of 5 per cent of the total seats won to 7 per cent of the total seats won.

Additionally, under Federal Law No. 51-F3, political parties must have a membership of at least 50,000 to register and get onto the ballot. Election officials can petition the Supreme Court to dissolve parties failing to meet the requisite registration numbers. Such was the fate of Russia's Republican Party in March of 2007, which was shown to have only 40,000 members. Though the Republicans never won State Duma seats, some members won election as independents from single-constituency districts in the past. The justification for the 50,000 member requirement was to improve electoral efficiency by ridding Russia of the numerous small parties that formed in the 1990s.

Critics of Federal Law No. 51-F3 have voiced concern that the new scheme allows for the majority parties to eliminate any remaining opposition.[29] In addition, reports tell of parties selling spots on their party lists. The current majority party, United Russia, was reported to have placed popular governors at the top of its party list for the 2003 State Duma election, only to assign seats to other candidates after the election.

Putin defended the change in the same way he defended his new power to appoint regional governors. He viewed the law as necessary for combating terrorism and corruption. The critics argued that the reforms were merely an attempt to gain total control cloaked in national security concerns.

No denying the fact that Putin has brought some significant changes in the arena of political system of Russia, including tough restrictions on media analysis and reporting of elections under a law passed in 2002 and a law on political parties applicable from 2007. And these initiatives were portrayed by critics as backward steps for democracy, cutting down the number of smaller and regionally based parties. But with 29 movements that stood for election in 1999 election, and 23 in 2003, this was perhaps an attempt by the Kremlin 'to tweak a party system that many argued was far too fragmented and ineffective'.[30]

Human Rights

The Russian Constitution explicitly protects free speech and incorporates international law to protect other human rights. Article 17 states, "The basic rights and liberties in conformity with the commonly recognized principles and norms of the international law shall be recognized and guaranteed in the Russian Federation and under this Constitution."[31] Article 29 expressly protects 'the right to freedom of thought and speech'.[32] Article 31 protects freedom of assembly, stating, Citizens of the Russian Federation shall have the right to gather peacefully, without weapons, and to hold meetings, rallies, demonstrations, marches and pickets.[33]

In practice, however, these constitutional provisions mean nothing if the Russian government refuses to respect them. The government exercises control over non-governmental organisations. Individuals wishing to voice dissent against their government's policies and practices have been stifled. Each of these categories deserves a more detailed examination.

Non-governmental Organisations

The Federal Law No. 18-FZ, commonly known as the Russian NGO Law, significantly expands government control over NGOs and considerably restricts the right to association and the right to privacy of NGOs and NGO members. President Putin signed the law on January 10, 2006, and it went into effect on April 18, 2006., Julie Finley, the US Ambassador to the Organisation for Security and Cooperation in Europe (OSCE) expressed specific concerns over the law. According to her, the law 'authorises' the Federal Registration Service 'to initiate a judicial process to close down foreign NGOs if they 'threaten the sovereignty, political independence, territorial integrity, national unity and self-identification, cultural heritage and national interests of the Russian Federation'. It also 'gives extensive powers to the Federal Registration Service to refuse registration of Russian and foreign NGOs and to monitor and control their activities'. Finley ultimately concluded that"Given the use of vague criteria, there is a real risk that the law could be applied selectively for political purposes'.[34]

Freedom of Speech and Assembly

Recently, activists have pointed to a continued increase in 'Soviet-style restrictions on freedom of speech and expression'.[35] In a handful of separate instances within just a few months, police have forcefully shut down anti-government protests. The US described one of the crackdowns as 'Russian government's heavy-handedness' against people trying to exercise democratic rights'.[36] Two protests, one in Moscow and one in St. Petersburg, resulted in numerous arrests and allegations of police brutality.[37]

When hundreds of protesters tried to march on the Moscow landmark of Pushkin Square, many, including the former World Chess Champion Garry Kasparov, were arrested. Others who fought with police were beaten.[38] At one of the St. Petersburg protests, participants claimed riot; police became physically violent towards peaceful protesters.[39]

Independent Media

The evolution of the Russian media after the end of Communist state censorship has been a sad saga. Instead of becoming an important counterbalance to the authorities and the basis for establishing democracy and civil society too often got corrupted by mercantilism and pride, and a tool in the hands of competing business clans. Putin's clampdowns cowed it and restored television in particular to its traditional role as a mouthpiece for the authorities. Television has arguably overtaken print media in terms of how the average person receives news and information about his or her government. Putin has taken steps to assert control over Russian television stations. A state-controlled company called Gazprom took over Russia's only independent television station on April 14, 2001, thus granting the government greater control over television's ability to influence the public.

Print media, while more independent than television, thanks to the Internet, faces an entirely different threat. According to the Committee to Protect Journalists, over the past fifteen years, Russia is the third most dangerous country for journalists, behind only Iraq and Algeria.[40] As the Committee to Protect Journalists communications director Abi Wright noted, there have been thirteen 'contract-style killings since Vladimir Putin took office'. Wright calls this a 'major indicator of the kind of press freedom climate that you find today in Russia'.[41]

Definitional Democratic Framework: Putin's Reforms

According to Article 1 of the Russian Constitution of 1993, the Russian Federation 'is a democratic federative rule of law state with a republican form of government'. Before going into the issue of the impact of Putin's federal reforms, one needs to understand the prevailing system of the post-disintegration Russia.

In the contemporary political theory, great controversy has been going on over the meaning and definition of democracy, and hence, the literature attempting to define democracy is far from unanimous.[42] There exist many competing definitions of democracy. Even restricting to modern representative democracy there is a broad distinction within the existing literature between formal and substantive democracy, between a more 'minimalist' definition and a more 'maximalist' definition. The concept of democracy may indeed be defined much more broadly, but the logic behind selecting this definitional framework lies in the fact, that for a country like Russia, which is still passing through transitional phase, it is first and foremost needed to develop a more 'minimalist' democracy to achieve a more substantive democracy at a later stage. Moreover, given the fact that Russia has been experiencing difficulties in providing even the minimal condition for democratic rule, a more exhaustive set of criteria would make the issue of democratisation nothing better than a mere academic exercise.

For this purpose, the starting point of this study is a core, minimalist definition, something along the lines of Robert Dahl who lists the following eight 'institutional guarantees' which citizens must enjoy before a country can be classified as a democracy: (1) Freedom to form and join organisations; freedom of expression; (2) right to vote; (3) eligibility for public office; (4) right of political leaders to compete for support and right of political leaders to compete for votes; (5) alternative sources of information; (6) free and fair elections; (7) institutions for making government policies depend on votes, and (8) other expressions of preference.[43]

Dahl groups these eight factors into the three essential attributes of a democratic polity: (1) Meaningful and extensive competition among individuals and organised groups (especially political parties) for all effective positions of government power, at regular intervals and excluding the use of force; (2) a 'highly inclusive' level of political participation in the selection of leaders and policies, at least through regular and fair elections, such that no major (adult) social group is excluded, and (3) a level of civil and political liberties – freedom of expression, freedom of the press, freedom to form and join organisations – sufficient to ensure the integrity of political competition and participation.

Dahl argued that there was no country where all of his eight conditions were fully satisfied thus; he preferred to call such states 'polyarchies', leaving the term democracy for the non-existent, ideal types.[44]

The facts, and the framework within which to analyse the facts, are clear. The appointment of regional governors, the practical limitations on dissent, the situation with the media, and the new legislative election procedures all impact Russia's ability to govern within the framework of Dahl's polyarchy. What follows is the analysis of these issues against the backdrop of elections, elected officials, freedom of expression, alternative sources of information, associational autonomy, and inclusive citizenship. Let us now analyse how Putin's reforms have impacted on the institutions necessary for governing modern democracies, and whether that would really help perceiving Russia's current status as either democratic or non-democratic, one must work within a definitional framework. As mentioned above, according to Robert Dahl, large-scale, modern representative democratic (polyarchal) governments are characterised by the use of six political institutions. The six institutions of polyarchal governments include (1) entrusting power in elected representatives, (2) free, fair, and frequent elections, (3) freedom of expression, (4) access to independent sources of information, (5) associational autonomy, and (6) inclusive citizenship.[45] A closer look at each of Dahl's institutions reveals why they help to define modern democracies.

Pure democracy, in which every citizen has a chance to voice concerns and exercise control, simply cannot work on a large scale. This is where elected representatives come in. By concentrating governmental authority in public representatives, democratic government allows the masses to have a say in what policies the government chooses, at least in the most practical way possible.

Free, Fair, and frequent elections are a corollary of the use of elected representatives. If people are to choose government officials, and entrust them with the power to enact and administer laws, those officials must be the candidates the people actually want to elect. Dahl defines a free election as one in which people participate without fear of reprisal, and a fair election as one in which all votes are counted as equal.[46] He further explains that frequent elections are necessary for people to maintain control over their government.[47]

Elected Representatives

On both the national and regional level, Putin's reforms led Russia away from polyarchy's institution of governance by elected officials. As one of the most basic requirements of a democratic system, elected officials serve the vital purpose of holding policymakers accountable to the true power holders, the public. There is room for improvement in the use of elected representatives at the regional governor level and in the federal legislative branch.

While the president and local legislatures are still elected, regional governors are now appointed by the president. This was the latest step in Putin's quest to gain more control over the regions. His appointment of the seven envoys early in his presidency was just the beginning. While the regions' legislatures have a say in approving or disapproving the president's appointment, they do so at their own peril. In effect, the president has near total control over the regional executive branches.

The federal legislative branch is also insufficiently composed of elected officials. Much of the blame goes to the Federal Law No. 51-F3. Granted, the proportional representation scheme the Duma has been employed since December, 2007 still relies on elections to choose legislators. Unfortunately, without single-constituency districts, Russian citizens will no longer be able to point to a particular Duma member and know whom to hold accountable for government policies. In this way, the new scheme removes one of the main benefits of government by elected representatives.

Additionally, the use of a purely proportional system in the Duma harkens back to the days when the Communist Party controlled all facets of government. Instead of appealing to the needs of the local voters, politicians looking for a Duma seat will need to work their way up the party hierarchy. This system has already proven highly susceptible to corruption in Russia, and the reports of bait and switch tactics in the elections showed it still is. An example of this bait and switch tactic occurred in the 2003 State Duma election when United Russia placed popular governors atop its party list, thus enticing voters' support, only to award seats to other party members later.[48]

The Federation Council can be considered an even less democratic body than the State Duma. Since 2000, regional elites, and not voters, choose the two representatives who sit in Moscow. With the president now appointing regional governors, a president can exert control over the very regional elites who pick the Federation Council members. Thus, the Federation Council has now become a mechanism whereby the president can exert further control over lawmakers.

Free, Fair and Frequent Elections

One thing that can be said in favour of Russian elections is they are frequent. Since 1990 six Presidential elections and six State Duma elections have been held in Russian Federation.[49]

With election cycles at intervals similar to the world's healthiest democracies, frequency is not the problem. Successful democracies however, must utilise frequent elections that are also free and fair. In Russia the elections have come under severe criticism both within the country and abroad as far as the terms 'free' and 'fair'. But this problem is not isolated characteristic of Russia alone, even the acknowledged democracies cannot escape allegations in this context. At the same time, it is a fact that the appointment of regional governors, the media problem, and the new system for electing the State Duma all impact Russia's ability to utilise free, fair and frequent elections.

Appointing regional governors is perhaps the clearest example of Russia's failure to use elections. No longer will citizens of the various regions have a direct voice in choosing their governors. Instead, they will be forced to rely on their legislature to approve or deny the president's appointments. While this offers some regional control over the choice of governor, it is likely that the regional legislatures will be wary of defying an ever more powerful president, considering the president can dissolve the legislature if it rejects two consecutive nominees.

The media must be allowed to cover all sides to the issues and all candidates for Russia to run fair elections. Likewise, candidates must have access to media outlets in order to get their messages across to voters. The dwindling number of independent news agencies in Russia poses the prospect of abusive campaign tactics going unreported. The total lack of independent television stations is, perhaps, the greatest risk factor for misuse of mass media by the majority. Ultimately, the government can use state-run television and print media as a way of monopolising the attention of the voting public.

Federal Law No. 51-F3 determines how the Duma is to be elected in the future. Hopefully, voters will be able to discern which party best promotes their interests. Unfortunately, the proportional system does not seem as capable of creating a connection between would-be legislators and the voting public. Coupled with the majority's hold over the media, this system is less capable of establishing a successful institution of elections than elections via single-constituency districts.

Freedom of Expression

Freedom of expression is necessary for people to participate in the democratic process.[50] To run a successful democratic government, people must have a chance to persuade others of their views. Moreover, freedom of expression allows people to influence elected officials. When people are free to express their opinions, the decisions and actions of elected officials can more closely reflect the will of the public.

The centralisation of authority in Moscow, justified by a need to combat terrorism, has had obvious lasting effects on freedom of expression. The right to protest government actions peacefully is essential to freedom of expression. Unfortunately, the majority's unrelenting drive to maintain authority has led to crackdowns on free expression. Individuals' rights to free speech and assembly have not been respected.

When police violently stifle protesters, the effect is twofold – first, an individual protester who is beaten or arrested is effectively silenced at that moment, and second, and arguably more damaging to free expression, is the chilling effect on other would-be protesters. It is clear that for Russia to satisfy the requirement of free expression, people must be allowed to gather together in public and express discontent with their government's policies.

Additionally, it is alleged that journalists who criticise the government might face serious consequences. Though it would be an exaggeration to agree with the extreme view that Putin has a hand in the violence against journalists in Russia, but perhaps he could take up measures for their greater protection. Vulnerability and lack of insecurity, first of all silences individual journalists who fall victim to the violence and secondly, the frequency of the killings and their continued status as unsolved mysteries dissuade others from covering stories that might expose the government's flaws.

With all its flaws, today, most critics of the Russian authorities can talk openly on the telephone, meet with foreigners in Moscow's plentiful cafes without fear, and usually live without repercussions when their comments are published.[51]

This is no less achievement that after centuries of authoritarian rule, the Russian people experience glimpse of self-governance. They now know what it means to live in an open and free society.

Availability of Independent and Alternative Sources of Information

Next important precondition is the availability of independent sources, which is closely linked to freedom of expression. In order to share their ideas with others people should have access to the information they need to formulate those ideas in the first place. That information must come from some source other than the government if society is to form accurate opinions of the government, taking into account criticism of the government's policies and conduct.

Russia has not fully met polyarchy's requirement of alternative sources of information. Granted, this aspect of polyarchy is better developed than some of the others, thanks to the Internet. But, the prevailing state of affairs indicates governmental control over both television and print media. In 2001 Russia's last independent television station, NTV was taken over by the Russian state-run oil company, Gazprom. In 2005, Gazprom also purchased over half the shares of Izvestiya, one of Russia's largest general circulation newspapers.[52] The endangered journalist situation also comes into play here.

When state-backed Gazprom bought Russia's only independent television station, the most influential source of mass media fell under the control of the national government. State-run and state-influenced television stations only cater the information the government wishes them to do, or at times, ignoring stories that an independent station would like to air. For instance, Kyrill Dissanayake of BBC Monitoring reported that Russian television stations ignored the story of poisoned ex-FSB agent Alexander Litvinenko after a radio station first broke the story. Even with the best of intentions, the ability to disseminate any message over television airwaves creates too strong a temptation to use control over television for political gain.

It is indeed a fact that the diversity of media ownership and output has undoubtedly declined under Putin "but Russia also remains a country in which editor of an extremist newspaper can publish 'Mr. Hexagon', a book which clearly alleges the complicity of special services in the 1999 apartment bombings as a prelude to the Chechen campaign. Or where the weekly paper, Novaya Gazeta lambasts the authorities, and the internet site kompromat.ru spreads salacious rumours on public figures with impunity".[53]

Associational Autonomy

Dahl explains that for elections to succeed, people must be free to join into groups for the furtherance of their ideas.[54] Moreover, when a group is formed, people opposed to that group must be free to join together to form another. Modern democratic governments rely on political parties to entice the electorate, to educate it as well as to persuade it to support. Trade associations, professional groups, trade unions, and NGOs also play an essential role in political mobilisation.

The reforms, particularly those related to the federal legislature and non-governmental organisations, have curtailed the level of associational autonomy in Russia. The Federal Law No. 51-F3 has restricted associational autonomy in two ways. On the one hand, it restrains the would-be legislators' abilities to associate with the party of their choice, and on the other hand, it makes it almost impossible for smaller political organisations to survive.

Whereas single-constituency district Duma seats left open the possibility of independent and minority party candidates winning elections, the only way to win election now is by becoming a member of one of the main political parties. The only option left with the aspiring legislators is to join up with one of the larger political parties to acquire any opportunity of earning a seat in the State Duma. While a small number of large political parties are the norm in even the healthiest democracies, the fact that seats are chosen only on party lines means a would-be legislator does not have the option of associating with no party at all. The chance of being elected now appears bleak for any independent and minority party, but this matter does not lie with the public or lack of their support for them. They will not be able to contest simply because the changes in the rules of the electoral system shunt them away from elections.

Secondly, the Federal Law No. 51-F3 affects the associational autonomy of even a larger number of people. With the requirement that political parties have a registered membership of at least 50,000 people, even parties with no chance of meeting the 7 per cent threshold to make an entry into the State Duma may be stamped out by Supreme Court. This makes it nearly impossible for new political parties to grow from minority opposition voices to viable alternatives to the majority.

The Russian NGO Law also has negative impact on associational autonomy. With the Federal Registration Service empowered to monitor the activities of NGOs, people may be dissuaded from entering into civil society to begin with. The government's power to initiate proceedings to ban foreign NGOs deemed harmful to Russia means an organisation someone wants to join may not even exist in Russia. If an organisation is really a threat to the public, the government must have the authority to ban it. But the concern with the Russian NGO Law is that it has the provision to be applied for political purposes. And once it is applied this way specify the type of limit on associational autonomy that should not exist in a healthy democracy.

Judging from D. Beetham's excellent studies of democracy, it becomes apparent that Russia indeed lags behind as far as 'political equality' and 'popular control' are concerned. 'Political equality' means equality of votes among the electors, and equal right to stand for public office as well as an equality in the conditions for making one's voice heard and in treatment at the hands of legislators'.[55] Beetham's 'popular control' basically reflects many of Dahl's original eight pre-conditions for polyarchy: (1) the popular election of the parliament or legislature and the head of government, (2) open and accountable government, and continuous direct political, legal, and financial accountability of government to the electorate, (3) guaranteed civil and political rights or liberties: freedoms of speech, association, assembly and movement, and the right to due legal process, and (4) a lively civil society.[56]

Inclusive Citizenship

According to Dahl, the notion of inclusive citizenship was the last institution to form in modern democracies.[57] Inclusive citizenship means that virtually all adult citizens must have the right to participate in the political process and they must have the opportunity to vote and to run for political office.

Historically, the institution of inclusive citizenship was the last to develop in modern democracies and it is already well established in Russia. But, in spite of no official barrier on the right to vote, the 7 per cent threshold implies that some voters are deprived of expressing their choice. On this point, certain section of electorate even in the healthiest of democracies is often left without a viable option supporting their ideals and goals. At some point, the desire to give everyone a voice must give way to the practical requirement that government be capable of functioning day to day. In these terms, Russia has struck a good balance.

Conclusion

Many of Putin's actions during his presidential two terms that were criticised abroad were popular and more comprehensible at home in the context of the Russia that he had inherited. His achievements have been mixed. The economy has been in much better shape, but there was also a shift away from western-style democracy that suggested he had created a very specific form of 'liberal authoritarianism' with an inclination to 'soft autocracy'.

The Russia that Putin inherited was a country severely weakened and demoralised, riddled with corruption and sharply divided between rich and poor, old and young. The bloody repressions and miserable living conditions of totalitarianism had been replaced by a limited democracy or better to say 'liberal anarchy' and a painful economic transition to wild capitalism in the 1990s that left some freer and richer than they had ever been, but others abandoned, embittered and nostalgic for the past. As a consequence the political institutions suitable for a democracy had already been very fragile. Moreover, the Beslan school hostage crisis along with the ongoing situation in Chechnya gave President Putin the motive for scaling back democratic reforms achieved in the early post-Soviet era. Under the shroud of national security, even healthy democracies can begin to chip away at democratic political institutions. When viewed against the standards of polyarchal governments, today's Russia is far from deserving the designation of a democracy. Despite Putin's outward expressions in favour of a democratic Russia, in practice, the country is less democratic now than it was just a few years ago.

However strongly the Yel'tsin period is praised, in particular, by a group of Western as well as Russian scholars for initiating democratisation process, the existing volumes suggest that despite some formal democratic institutions being established, it in fact led to 'liberal anarchy' and not really any trend toward a healthy polyarchal government was in sight.

In short, Russia has met the formal criteria of democracy. Its president, parliament, and regional leaders are subject to popular elections involving more than one candidate and with results that are not a foregone conclusion. However, it is also apparent that the presidential elections are basically a process of legitimating an incumbent and not the freely contested selection of a leader from a range of alternatives. And the parliamentary elections, though regular, lively and contested, do not really count because the parliament does not form the government and is limited in its capacity to hold the president and government accountable.

The Russian constitution limits presidents to serving two successive terms.[58] Putin nominated Dmitry Medvedev as the next incumbent and Medvedev proposed Putin's name as the next prime minister and hence in Russia ushered a new era of 'tandem or tandemocracy'.[59]

Despite being criticised for his controversial role in the development of democratisation in many circles, Putin also could claim support behind him within and without the country. The Former President Mikhail Gorbachev, the man who set Russia's transformation from communism to capitalism in motion, expressed his perception about Russia under this way:

> "Under Putin's governance, Russia got out of a chaos and can proceed along the path of democratic reforms. Today, Russia is being often criticized and accused in exerting pressure on the media and diverging from democracy. At the same time, only few admit that during the Yeltsin's epoch the country was falling apart while the west was applauding. It was the time of the shooting down the parliament in 1993, the time of the 'elections without a choice' in 1996, the time of oligarch-bureaucratic control over media, growing poverty etc. The critics became sharper when Russia began getting up from the knees. These critics were sometimes relevant, but often too hasty and unacceptably knocking. They tell us that Russia in its very nature

> is unable to adopt democratic principles and procedures as well as to create civil society and give in its 'imperial ambitions'. I cannot agree with this. Russia is a country in transitional democracy".[60]

Vladimir Vladimirovich Putin, currently the Prime Minister of the Russian Federation, has once again been elected for his third term at the March 04 Presidential elections with 63.64 per cent of the total votes, while his nearest rival, the Communist Party leader Gennady Zyuganov, got hold of 17.18 per cent. He will take the oath during the inauguration to be held on May 07, 2012 and continue for six years, till 2018. On the other hand, Putin's party United Russia won 238 seats with 49.32 per cent of votes in the elections to the Russia's State Duma or the lower chamber of the legislature, held on December 04, 2011, in which 60 per cent of the electorate turned out to vote under a proportional representation system.[61]

In the eyes of many Russian and some Western scholars, Putin's popular support among the majority of Russian people is sufficient to make the regime a kind of democracy in line with Russian traditions. Perhaps the secret of Putin's popularity consists of the fact that Russian society is tired of the political and economic reforms, the unfulfilled promises. If we compare the situation that prevailed in the USSR merely twenty years ago one can say that 'the fledgling Russian democracy is still, of course, far from perfect, but its existence and its successes cannot be denied'.[62]

Following Beetham one can say that Russia is perhaps going through 'the process of consolidating democracy which [began] where the transition to democracy [ended], that is, with the inauguration of a new government at the first free and fair elections', but the country has to go through a 'much more lengthy and difficult process [of consolidation] than the transition itself'.[63] It has taken the first of many essential steps on the path to consolidation by installing democratic institutions and ratifying a democratic constitution.[64]

Putin's Russia is not a trivial authoritarian state. It is not 'Soviet Union lite' It is not a liberal democracy either. It has been a 'managed democracy'. The term captures the logic and the mechanisms of the reproduction of power and the way democratic institutions are used and misused to preserve the monopoly of power. Putin engineered certain changes to the political institutions during his first term, establishing a form of 'managed democracy' designed to tame the regions and the parliament to his will. It explains the limitations of the previous very imperfect system he inherited from Yel'tsin, and its changing role in pushing through the new president's economic and other policy initiatives, crafted by Putin's political advisors, to tandem or tandem-ocracy.

According to the Kremlin ideologues Putin is not hostile to pluralism as such but merely claims the right to choose a different model, more suitable to Russia's present circumstances. Putin on his part has always insisted on his commitment to 'democracy' but made clear that it would be a particular kind of democracy, compatible with Russia's distinctive geography and culture. Putin explained in his address at the turn of the millennium, it would not be a 'second edition of, say, the US or the UK, where liberal values [had] deep historic relations', but one that was better suited to a country in which 'the state and its institutions and structures [had] always played an exceptionally important role'.[65] During his first term, the Kremlin's ideologues described Russian system as a 'managed democracy', which means a form of government that was more appropriate, in the view of Kremlin advisers, to a country that was undergoing far-reaching social and economic change and in which Western-style institutions – such as political parties – had not yet established themselves.

During Putin's second presidential term, a more considered response began to emerge: the notion of sovereign democracy,[66] that took account of universal values but at the same time, in Putin's words, allowed Russians to find their 'own path to the construction of a democratic, free and fair society and state'. Putin told the Russian Parliament, that he was 'convinced that in contemporary Russia the values of democracy [were no less important than the aspiration to achieve economic success or social wellbeing'. But he rejected the attempt that was being made to, for transparently political purposes, to represent the strengthening of Russian statehood as some kind of 'authoritarianism'; on the contrary, a commitment to democratic values was 'dictated by the will of our people and by the strategic interests of the Russian Federation itself'. The essence of 'sovereign democracy',[67] in this interpretation, was that states should be able to make their own decisions in any matters of this kind, and not have them imposed from outside.

Putin has neither been the beginning nor the end of the story of democracy in Russia, but he undoubtedly played a crucial role. In fact, the economic crisis of 1998, the rebellious oligarchs and defiance of some of the federation's constituent units to follow the federal laws and refusal to pay taxes to the federal coffer, anarchy at the regional level, Chechnya war, Beslan school hostage crisis, development of terrorism, the huge increase in economic inequality through the enrichment of some and impoverishment of most, the enlargement of NATO, the presence of US troops in Central Asia, and the talk of Ukraine and Georgia joining NATO – all these created impediments to the democratisation process of Russia. One cannot ignore his popular support among the majority of the Russian people, despite allegations of rigged elections, which is common even for acclaimed democracy, the improvements that he has achieved in certain areas as compared to the catastrophic situation he found when coming to power and the fact that his authoritarian rule has stopped well short of totalitarian terror.

Some Putin-era reforms were based simply on federal laws. Others were merely practices without the backing of formal authority. And the very fact that Putin did not go for amending the Constitutional provision on presidential term to pave the way to contest for the consecutive third time is probably a source of optimism that the future presidents will push for new laws and carry out different policies that would favour democratic government.

At present, even the staunchest critic cannot imagine in Russia that there might come a time when any form of freedom of speech, private initiative or liberal thinking would be prohibited and punished; when the Russian citizens would be denied of the most fundamental freedoms; and freedom of movement beyond the frontiers of the Russian Federation would be virtually non-existent; and opportunities to travel abroad would be limited to a very few and that only a few organised groups would be able to do so, and even then prospective travellers would have to endure the humiliating procedures involved in obtaining authorisation. But this was the situation just a couple of decades ago in the same space bearing a name Soviet Union.

Finally, following Gitelman one can say that 'democracy should not be seen as an absolute, but as a spectrum'. Some states are more democratic than others 'and the same system may vary over time in the extent to which it is democratic'.[68] Therefore, all is not lost for Russian democracy. If left free from the type of top-down meddling that has exemplified the past decade, post-Soviet Russia has the potential to grow into a healthy democracy.

Notes

1. Peter Rutland, Introduction " What comes after socialism?", Yitzhak M. Brudny, Jonathan Frankel, Stefani Hoffman, (eds.), *Restructuring Post-Communist Russia*, (Cambridge: Cambridge University Press, 2004)

2. Tom Bjorkman, *Russia's Road to deeper democracy,* (Washington, D.C.: Brookings Institution, 2003).
3. "Shto takoe putinizm?", *Strategiia Rossii*, No.3, March 2004.
4. Michael McFaul, *Russia's Unfinished Revolution: Political Change from Gorbachev to Putin,* Ithaca, (New York: Cornell University Press, 2001).
5. Larry Diamond, "A Universal Democracy", *Polity Review*, June/July 2003, p. 3.
6. Pierre Hassner, "Russia's Transition to Autocracy", *Journal of Democracy*, vol.19, no. 2, (April 2008) p. 7.
7. *Sobranie sochinenii , Tom 2-7,* (Mart 1984 –Oktyabr'1987), Gorbachev-Fond, Moscow: Ves' Mir, 2008.
8. See for details, Mikhail Gorbachev, *Memoirs*, (New York: Doubleday, 1995); Mikhail Gorbachev, *Izbrannye rechi i stat'i,* (vol.1-7), Moskva: Izd.vo Politicheskie literatury, Mikhail Gorbachev, *Zhizn' i reformy , Kniga 1,* Moskva: Izd.vo Novosti, 1995; *Sobranie sochinenii , Tom 2-21,* (Mart 1984 –Avgust 1990), Gorbachev-Fond, Moscow: Ves' Mir, 2008-2012.
9. Stephen White (ed.), *Understanding Russian Politics*, (Cambridge: Cambridge University Press), pp. 18-19.
10. Brian Crozier, *The Rise and Fall of the Soviet Empire*, (Rocklin, CA: Forum, 1999), p. 409.
11. D.R. Kempton and Terry D Clark (eds.), *Unity or Separation: Centre-Periphery Relations in the Former Soviet Union*, (Westport, Connecticut, London: Praeger, 2002), p. 102.
12. D.R. Kempton and Terry D Clark (eds.), *Unity or Separation: Centre-Periphery Relations in the Former Soviet Union*, (Westport, Connecticut, London: Praeger, 2002), p. 170.
13. D.R. Kempton and Terry D Clark (eds.), *Unity or Separation: Centre-Periphery Relations in the Former Soviet Union*, (Westport, Connecticut, London: Praeger, 2002), p. 32
14. On August 05, 1990, during a speech at Kazan, Tatarstan.
15. Georgia, Armenia, Moldova, Lithuania, Latvia, and Estonia.
16. Mikhail Gorbachev, *Memoirs*, (New York: Doubleday, 1995), pp. 626-627.
17. Pierre Hassner, "Russia's Transition to Autocracy", *Journal of Democracy*, vol.19, no. 2, (April 2008) p. 8.
18. Lilia Shevtsova, *Russia –Lost in Transition*, (Washington, D.C.: Carnegie Endowment for International Peace, 2007).
19. Andrew Jack, *Inside Putin's Russia: Can There Be Reform without Democracy?* (New York: Oxford University Press, 2004), pp. 33-34.
20. Andrew Jack, *Inside Putin's Russia: Can There Be Reform without Democracy?* (New York: Oxford University Press, 2004), p. 34.
21. Peter Baker, Susan Glasser, *Kremlin Rising: Vladimir Putin's Russia and the End of Revolution*, (New York: A Lisa Drew Book/Scribner, 2005), p. 103.
22. Peter Baker, Susan Glasser, *Kremlin Rising: Vladimir Putin's Russia and the End of Revolution*, (New York: A Lisa Drew Book/Scribner, 2005), p. 54.
23. During his presidency, Putin proposed 227 legislative acts.
24. Khronika zakhvata zalozhnikov v shkole goroda Beslana v Severnoi Osetii accessed at http://www.nbuv.gov.ua/polit/04nrbso.htm

25. *Russia: Putin Seeking Government Changes to Strengthen Fight Against Terror, Reuters*, September 13, 2004, accessed at http://www.rferl.org/content/article/1054826.html
26. *Konstitutsia Rossiiskoi federatsii* stat'ya 96, accessed at http://constitution.kremlin.ru.
27. Federal'nyi zakon No. 51 F3 "O vyborakh deputatov Gosudarstvennoi Dumy Federal'noi Sobraniya Rossiiskoi Federatsii".
28. *Duma Election Law: Details,* accessed at http://www.russiavotes.org/duma/duma_electoral_system.php.
29. Daisy Sindelar, *2004 And Beyond: In Russia, Tragedy Furthers Kremlin Vision of Centralized State*, RADIO FREE EUROPE/ RADIO LIBERTY, December 15, 2004, accessed at http://www.cdi.org/russia/johnson/8505-4.cfm.
30. Andrew Jack, *Inside Putin's Russia: Can There Be Reform without Democracy?* (New York: Oxford University Press, 2004), p. 226.
31. *Konstitutsia Rossiiskoi federatsii,* stat'ya 17, accessed at http://constitution.kremlin.ru; For details on the Russian constitution A. Umnova, *Konstitutsionnye Osnovy Sovremennovo Rossiiskovo Federalizma*, Moscow: Delo, 1998.
32. *Konstitutsia Rossiiskoi federatsii,* stat'ya 29, accessed at http://constitution.kremlin.ru.
33. *Konstitutsia Rossiiskoi federatsii,* stat'ya 31, accessed at http://constitution.kremlin.ru.
34. Jeffrey Thomas, "US says Russian NGO Law does not meet Human Rights Commitments", *NCSJ Weekly News Brief*, Washington, D.C., February 03, 2006
35. Maria Danilova, "Activists Say Russia Stifling Dissent", *The Associated Press*, March 27, 2007, accessed at http://www.pressmon.com/cgi-bin/press_view.cgi?id=527592
36. Maria Danilova, "Activists Say Russia Stifling Dissent", *The Associated Press*, March 27, 2007, accessed at http://www.pressmon.com/cgi-bin/press_view.cgi?id=527592
37. *Police beat anti-Putin protesters in Russia*, Reuters, April 14, 2007, accessed at http://uk.reuters.com/article/2007/04/15/uk-russia-protest-idUKL1444695920070415
38. *Chess champion detained at Moscow march, The Associated Press*, April 14, 2007, accessed at http://www.msnbc.msn.com/id/18096644.html).
39. *Police beat anti-Putin protesters in Russia, Reuters*, April 14, 2007, accessed at http://uk.reuters.com/article/2007/04/15/uk-russia-protest-idUKL1444695920070415
40. Joel Simon, *Who will be Russia's conscience? Murder of crusading journalist spotlights dangers of the profession*, Committee To Protect Journalists, October 22 October, 2006, accessed at http://www.cpj.org/op_ed/Simon22oct06.html.
41. Claire Bigg, *Russia: Two Journalists Die in Contract Killings a Year*, Radio Free Europe/ Radio Liberty, October 10, 2006, accessed at http://www.rferl.org/featuresarticle/2006/10/135abf80-8e82-4cb9-b150-af4236f3874e.html.
42. Schmitter, Philippe C. and Terry Lynn Karl, "What Democracy Is... and Is Not.", *Journal of Democracy* 2.3 (1991): 75-88
43. R. A. Dahl, *Polyarchy: Participation and Opposition,* (New Haven: Yale University Press, 1971), p. 3.
44. See, Robert Dahl, *On Democracy*, (New Haven, Connecticut : Yale University Press, 1998); G. Sorensen, *Democracy and Democratisation,* (Boulder: Westview Press, 1993), p.12.
45. Robert Dahl, *On Democracy*, (New Haven, Connecticut : Yale University Press, 1998), p. 85.

46. Robert Dahl, *On Democracy*, (New Haven, Connecticut : Yale University Press, 1998), p. 95.
47. Robert Dahl, *On Democracy*, (New Haven, Connecticut : Yale University Press, 1998), p. 96.
48. Peter Baker, Putin moves to centralize authority, *Washinton Post*, September 14, 2004, accessed at http://www.washingtonpost.com/wp-dyn/articles/A17838-2004Sep13.html
49. Presidential elections in 1991, 1996, 2000, 2004, 2008, 2012 and State Duma Elections in 1993, 1995, 1997, 1999, 2003, 2007, 2011. Accessed at http://www.vybory.izbirkom.ru.
50. Robert Dahl, *On Democracy*, (New Haven, Connecticut : Yale University Press, 1998), p. 96.
51. Andrew Jack, *Inside Putin's Russia: Can There Be Reform without Democracy?* (New York: Oxford University Press, 2004), p. 298.
52. See for details, Peter Baker, Susan Glasser, *Kremlin Rising: Vladimir Putin's Russia and the End of Revolution*, New York: A Lisa Drew Book/Scribner, 2005, pp. 78-79; Claire Bigg, *Russia: State-Controlled Gazprom Buys Leading Independent Daily 'Izvestiya'*, Radio Free Europe/Radio Liberty, June 3, 2005, accessed at http://www.rferl.org/featuresarticle/2005/06/46087eca-0e7a-4c1c-8e22-1e96ee664cd2.html.
53. Andrew Jack, *Inside Putin's Russia: Can There Be Reform without Democracy?*, New York: Oxford University Press, 2004, p.299.
54. Robert Dahl, *On Democracy*, New Haven, Connecticut :Yale University Press, 1998, p. 98.
55. D. Beetham, *Democracy and Human Rights*, Cambridge: Polity Press, 1999, pp. 154–5.
56. D. Beetham, *Democracy and Human Rights*, Cambridge: Polity Press, 1999, pp. 154–5.
57. Robert Dahl, *On Democracy*, New Haven, Connecticut :Yale University Press, 1998, p.
58. *Konstitutsiya Rossiiskoi federatsii*, stat'ya 81, accessed at http://constitution.kremlin.ru.
59. 'Tandemocracy has nothing to do with democracy, it is tandem-ocracy. It indicates Putin-Medvev style of functioning in tandem.
60. Mikhail Gorbachev, "About Pluralism and Glasnost in the New Russia," *Rossiiskaia Gazeta*, Moscow, September 06, 2006.
61. Source: Central Election Commission of the Russian Federation, accessed at http://www.vybory.izbirkom.ru
62. Alvaro Gil-Robles, the Commissioner for Human Rights, the Council of Europe, in his report on visits to the Russian Federation from July 15-30, 2004 and September 19-29, 2004 for the attention of the Committee of Ministers and the Parliamentary Assembly accessed at https://wcd.coe.int/ViewDoc.jsp?id=846655.
63. For details see, D. Beetham, *Democracy and Human Rights*, (Cambridge: Polity Press, 1999), pp. 154–155.
64. For Democratic consolidation see, Andreas Schedler, "What is democratic consolidation?" *Journal of Democracy*, vol. 9, no. 2 (April 1998), p. 91; D. Beetham, *Democracy and Human Rights*, (Cambridge: Polity Press, 1999), pp. 69–70; G. O'Donnell, 'Illusions about consolidation', *Journal of Democracy*, vol.7, no. 2 (April 1996), pp. 34–51; J. J. Linz and A. Stepan, *Problems of Democratic Transition and Consolidation*, (Baltimore: Johns Hopkins University Press, 1996); J. J. Linz and A.

Stepan, "Toward Consolidated Democracies", *Journal of Democracy*, vol.7, no. 2 (April 1996), pp. 14–33; S. Mainwaring, G. O'Donnell and S. J. Valenzuela (eds), *Issues in Democratic Consolidation* (Indiana: University of Notre Dame Press, 1992), p. 70; S. Huntington, *The Third Wave: Democratisation in the Late Twentieth Century*, (Norman: University of Oklahoma Press, 1991), p. 263; Z. Gitelman "The Democratisation of Russia in Comparative Perspective", in S. White, A. Pravda and Z. Gitelman (eds.), *Developments in Russian Politics – 4,* (Basingstoke: Macmillan, 1999).

65. Stephen White, *Understanding Russian Politics*, (New York: Cambridge University Press, 2011), p. 323.
66. Introduced by Kremlin ideologues, particularly by Gleb Olegovich Pavlovskii, the head of the Effective Policy Foundation, a Kremlin-funded think tank, says that "a regime of managed democracy had to be established [after Putin came to power] in 2000, in order to counter real threats from shady groups who had seized power in Moscow and in the regions. That task has been accomplished now. Today, Putin's power is based on the moral authority of a leader of civil society and not upon an authoritarian dictatorship."
67. Vladislav Surkov, "Suverenitet- eto politicheskii sinonim konkurentosposobnost'", in Polyakov, ed. *Pro suverennaia demokratiiu*, pp. 33-61, p.58; Vyacheslav Nikonov, *Suverennaia demokratiia: ot idei -k doctrine*, Moscow: Yevropa, 2006, pp. 21-25, p. 23; Vladislav Surkov, 'Natsionalizatsiia budushchego', *Ekspert*, no.43, 20 November2006, pp.102-108, pp. 102-104; Extract also appeared in *Rossiiskaya gazeta*, November 21, 2006, and in *Izvestiya,* November 22, 2006, p. 4.
68. Z. Gitelman, "The Democratisation of Russia in Comparative Perspective", in S. White, A. Pravda and Z. Gitelman (eds.), *Developments in Russian Politics – 4,* (Basingstoke: Macmillan, 1999).

14. ISLAM AND DEMOCRACY: A CONCEPTUAL ANALYSIS

Abhik Samanta

Democratic Law

This paper is based on my perception of the contradictions that arise when we see democracy both as an ethical and political concept. Democracy can be interpreted as a form of law that gives precedence to individuality. The political empowerment of the individual is the basis of state law in a democracy. However, enlightenment rationality, on which the ethical value of a democracy is based, betrays a contradiction when put into the ideal political framework of a democratic polity.

The history of the liberation of man from subjection to the church and feudal state is the basis for the establishment of the rule of the self-evident human truth which a human being embodies. Social inequality based on collective law is thus eradicated and replaced by social equality based on the universal internal truth about the goodness of man. The discourse of Enlightenment thus connects the internal world of thoughts, feelings and desires with the external world of action – both individual and collective – through a fundamental notion of the purity of expression. Universal Law or the Law of the Ideal Collective is, thus, an example of this expression, which serves the purpose of eternally facilitating action, which is the goal of human life. Law is thus ideally conceived as an agency of the manifestation of a human quality rather than a definer and demarcator of absolutes, for instance, the definition of good and evil. This conception of Law, as changeable through popular will, is central to the ethical configuration of a democracy, which in turn is the key to its institutionalisation.

The contradiction in the ideal framework of a democratic polity that is posited by the West today stems from this formulation of law as an expression of human will, which, by definition primarily through historical narrative, knows no boundaries. I mention the historical narrative here because the discipline of history is the site where the political achievements of the European social movements are construed as internal or individual achievements of the Europeans. This is implicit in the use of the word Enlightenment for the events of a particular time period in human history, which by virtue of this term comes to embody both internal qualitative achievement as well as external achievements of social action. Thus, the notion of a history of the Enlightenment is at odds with the way the discipline of history functions. Historical inquiry is conceived of as an exercise in understanding the co-relation of thought and practice. But a historical work becomes meaningful in the ideal democratic society, that is, in a society that sees democracy as the means to inculcate the values of the Enlightenment on the principle that human expression can be replicated as law. Thus in the process of constitution of the polity through law the particularity of political actions impinge on all other actions. Thus, the advocacy of democracy as an ideal form of government is actually a process whereby a political colour or a legal perspective is constituted. Herein lies the contradiction mentioned earlier, that although modern democracy is based on the liberating principle of human will which allows it to ideologically sustain various disciplines of action at its service like the discipline of history, the way it functions actually privileges political action over all other action. In this, the act of power is not the evident capacity to control an action which is the purpose of law but to constitute actions themselves. In this sense, it is the conception of action or thought, which is controlled in a democracy. This is the nature of law in a modern democracy. Law is subject to change through human will as human expression is supremely valued but the power of law is first felt in the framing of human expression itself as will. So, the practice of the discipline of history, as a manifestation of human expression, is actually divorced from the process where history is used through the legal process in everyday life.

Let us try to understand this by positing two poles of thought and their relationship to democratic law. One pole is this – man is incomplete by nature and needs laws to protect itself from itself, and the other pole is man is complete by nature and needs no laws, that is, there is no necessity of protecting man from man. Are these the two poles of thought that guide the institutional working of a democracy? No, because it is resolved that man is complete by nature, and yet, there is need of law to protect man from man. Institutional interaction takes place on the basis of absolute equality where each has a chance to express an opinion. All opinions are valued but it remains an opinion. What is sought is a resolution or a decision, which is a process of the accumulation of opinions. The decision being the law is no longer an opinion but something radically different, the opposite of opinion. If opinion can be regarded as thought, then, law is action.

The process of a democracy is designed to straddle these worlds of thought and action, which it does by the process of training. Again, in the institution building of a democracy, thought and action are separated as disciplines of their own. It is in this sense that political science is distinguished from the practice of law. Hence, the process of training cannot be conceived of without an impersonal body of knowledge, which would serve to guide action.

Here, it is important to understand the relationship between religious law and democratic law. Religious law deals with strictures, which are by definition absolute. The act, which is forbidden, is not separated in the utterance of religious law from the thought which preceded it. Therefore, there is the necessity of theology in order to interpret the notion of causality between thought and action embodied in a religious stricture. It is to be understood here that the premise for a theological perspective is to treat religious law as external to man. Interpretations of law are distinct because of their admittedly human origin and are as in Islam as much explorations of cultural practice as they were an exercise in verification of the temporality of the prophet. Thus, since conformity to Islam is acceptance of the Qur'an as proof of the existence of God, the act of interpretation is also an act of deliberation on the nature of the divine being. It has to be noted here that it is a deliberation on the commandments that have been given from before rather than a deliberation leading to commandments as in a democracy. But in Islamic polity, theologians are an institution distinct from the monarchy since in social practice as well as in theory, both are regarded as separate vocations. Thus, separate disciplines are maintained in an ideal Islamic polity, even on the basis of acceptance of law as divine will.

Let us clarify this perspective further with reference to the constitution of a modern discipline. The example cited here again is the discipline of history. In the 18th century, Enlightenment thinkers such as Voltaire used irony and skepticism as the means to uphold the idea of progress as a part of the self-evident spirit of man. The notion that there is a possible structure of truth, that is, the truth about man can be realised by virtue of following certain principles is conceived of through the discipline of history.[1] Hence, although facts are consciously used to construct a skeptical narrative, it is stressed that there is a self-evident truth that must come forth from the method of adherence to facts. This is how the discipline of history gets constituted. The structure of a discipline is born with the essential distinction between the means and a goal. However, it is important to understand that this was essentially a process of the formation of practice whereby the truth about human nature could be depicted. Thus, the ethic which gives form to the discipline is that expression is a means of living the truth about man. Here, in the distinction between the means and goal, the modern discipline becomes similar to the one based on religious law.

Islamic Law

In order to understand the difference between a democratic polity and an Islamic one in terms of ideal conceptions it is necessary to have a perspective on the historical evolution of Islamic Law. Let us start with an observation on the nature of Islamic law by Nasim Ahmad Jawed:

> The distinction between what can stand a legal test (e.g. soundness or impairment of the senses) and what can only be a matter of subjective judgment (wisdom) is often not made in classical Islamic literature on this subject, nor always by the contemporary Ulama (Ulema) of Pakistan. This is of course partly a reflection of the general character of Islamic law, in which religio-moral values imposed by one's Islamic conscience and rules of law enforceable by an Islamic state were in some cases discussed together within the same chapters of the legal treatises. Such treatment of the law is in itself a reflection of the fact that the real validity of Islamic law – as of laws in several other religious traditions – is seen by the believer as resting on Gods own commands, irrespective of whether a state enforces it or not and even whether it is enforceable by the state or not. In this sense, all religious norms are, from the standpoint of the faithful, essentially the same, whether they are observed by conscience alone or enforced by the state as well.[2]

This phenomenon can be seen as a strategy to accommodate the fact of dynastic kingship as the prevailing norm in society. This can be seen as a means of overcoming an essential contradiction which is to formulate a body of laws to which both the person of the king and the person of the subject must confirm but done in a polity where all laws emanate from the will present in the body of the king. Here is the basis for individuality in Islam. The laws of Islam are composed on the basis that all are equal before

God. Since it is God's law and God is inherently distinct from man, the 'other' vis-a-vis which individuality is framed, is not another man but something or someone distinct from all men.

Democracy, which is based on the distinctiveness of each individual preserved through a notion of equality before law can do so only with a definition of rights. Right or empowerment means that the 'other' vis-a-vis which individuality is defined, is actually the state. The principle of individuality is thus a collectively defined space for the individual. The state as the embodiment of collective will in a democracy is thus absolute vis-a-vis the particular which is the individual. The fact that in Islamic tradition laws are framed to mask the arbitrary authority of the ruler's dynastic will implies the construction of a realm of laws which regulate a person's relationship to God and other men as well as the states regulation of men.

It is this mask which is important here because it provides the occasion for the altercation between the stateless submission of the individual before God's law, and the complete submission of the individual before the state. It is between these two poles of thought that notions of rationality and temporality are framed. The construction of what I call a mask is not intended to deceive or be apologetic about the fact that it is the dynastic will of the ruler that will make the laws of God operational. Rather, the aim is to use the principle of dynastic will or the arbitrary authority of the ruler. The essence of the unequal relationship between the king and his subjects is that the body of the king is considered the sole embodiment of justice. The fact of the monopoly of justice holds together both the material and the spiritual worlds or the inner world of thoughts and the external world of actions. In other words, the singularity of the monarch is indicative of the totality of his or her law. The logic of materiality of the state expressed in the form of collection of taxes and the allocation of resources is not seen as an exchange in the form of a payment for the maintenance of justice and the judicial system. Rather it is the right of the ruler following from the fact that he has the power to compel his subjects to act according to his will. There is thus no conceptual separation of the duality of thought and action. The arbitrariness of the law emanating from the will of the ruler is the basis for its totality. For law in this pre-modern state by refusing to distinguish between the inner and outer or public and private or spiritual and material addresses existence in its totality.

It is here that we must locate Islam as positing a completely antithetical notion. The laws of Islam are the laws of God. It begins with the assertion that there is only one God, and an individual becomes a Muslim only by accepting this proposition as a reality. The ritual of acceptance which is what the word Islam or submission intends to convey is actually conceived as an act. As an act it is conceived in a manner which straddles the worlds of thought and action. Mental acceptance of the oneness of God is coupled with the acceptance of the Qur'an as proof of this oneness. Thus, to think that God is one, enables one to act according to the precepts of the Qur'an. There is a certain circularity here. Acceptance of the oneness of God actually tantamount to distinguishing between God and man, whereas, acceptance of the Qur'an is the affirmation of the relationship between the two. Revelation being the phenomenon which sets a time and space to this entire exercise makes this an essentially unequal relationship. This is because the fact of revelation is depicted essentially as an incident where it is the arbitrary will of God which is the constituting agent of the narrative. Thus, two aspects of Islam stand out – one, it addresses both realms of thought and action, and the other, it posits an essentially unequal relationship characterised by a tie of dependence. Here, it can be seen that Islam actually replicates the substance or principle on which the notion of kingship is based but with a fundamental difference. The monarch is replaced by the figure of God.

It is important to understand here that this replacement neither means that Islam was opposed to what I have called the pre-modern polity, nor does it mean that Islam upheld it as it effectively provided a check on the principle that the ruler was distinct from his subjects. What it did was – it provided a dialectical principle based on two poles. On one end was the stateless submission of the believer before God's law, which essentially meant that each individual was empowered by God to listen to his commands alone which is the basis for individuality in Islam; at the other end, the community of believers or the Qur'an as determining relations between people as the absolute law of the community, which is the defining principle of the Islamic umma or community of the faithful. It is important to understand that this dialectic is only possible because Islam emphatically seeks to retain the absolute nature of monarchical law. Thus, the totality of submission to law is central to Islam. Hence, the reality of monarchic rule is undermined even as the nature of monarchic law is written. This is the basic pattern of medieval Islamic jurisprudence as the work of the jurist Abul Hasan al Mawardi (died 1058 AD) shows. A quote from his work 'Ahkam al-Sultaniyya' is cited below:

The first duty of the ruler, described by Al Mawardi, reads:

> He must maintain the religion according to the principles established and agreed upon by the earliest Muslims (Salaf al-umma), and if an innovator appears, or someone with dubious opinions who deviates from those principles, then he must clarify matters by logical proofs, and show him the correct way, and finally apply the rules and punishment to which he is bound – that religion may be preserved from disorder and the community from stumbling.[3]

In this tract, which is popular even today, Mawardi is thus constructing a state out of the dialectical relationship that Islam posits. This is done through the exercise of reason, components of which are temporality or sense of time and logic, which are both important in determining a judicial decision. Power emanates from the body of the ruler but not from his or her arbitrary will, since he has to perform certain prescribed tasks before he can deliver a judgment and preserve the community. But it is only the king who can do this because this dialectical relationship has also to be located in the body of the ruler. The singularity of the monarch is the basis for the state and preservation of order. For the act of law to embody its absolute nature it is, thus, necessary that the singularity of the head of state be preserved in a single person.

Let us now look at a commonly perceived contradiction in Islamic polity:

> All (Muslims) would accept that the divine will is supreme and, in theory, that God's law is immutable and cannot be altered by human desire or whim. Yet, at the same time, by the insistence on the need of rulers to consult and to rule on the basis of consensus, they effectively concede that some form of popular participation is required.[4]

This principle is instrumental in attaching judgment to knowledge. Thus, the contradiction implied in the above observation does not arise. It is precisely because of this acceptance that God's law is immutable and cannot be altered by human desire or whim that rulers are asked to rule on the basis of consensus. The manner in which law is conceived in an ideal Islamic polity moves as a dialectic between the totality of individual submission before God as a stateless phenomenon, and individual submission to the law of the state as the law of God. This dialectic arises out of the need to preserve the finality of law. This is also the need felt in the lawmaking of a modern democracy. The means or knowledge that a modern democracy uses to preserve the finality of law is actually a process of attaching judgment to knowledge but it is a human judgment that knowledge is attached to by the defining principle of a democracy since it is imperative in principle as well as in practice that justice be embodied within the body of man. Thus, the logic of practice of finality in a modern democracy has to concede that its laws are partial and subject only to humanity, but only if it refuses to consider that, there can be a completely stateless yet law-bound existence of a human being.

Only if we understand that Islam considers the existence of dialectic between the totality of the two submissions between God and the state, can we seek to understand the formation of oppositional categories in the history of Islamic polity. One such oppositional category is the distinction that is commonly made between the Sufis and the Ulema. The Sufi is generally seen as a figure that embodies the principle of a personal relationship with God, while the Ulema are seen as the embodiment of the collective will of the Umma in their effort to dispense justice on the basis of the interpretation of the law of God. They are, thus, polar opposites; one operating on a personal basis making the laws of God explicable to the individual and the other seeks to establish order on a communitarian basis. This has generally been the secularist view of Islam, which essentially implies that Islam functioned as a polity with justifiable laws on this basis. The Sufis mediated with the non-Muslims, while internally, Islam was administered by the Ulema. This view actually does not deny that there was a community of Islam or the notion that these two spheres of historical institution making were connected by the same spirit. But the greatest lacuna of this view is that it does not fully explain the existence of monarchy as an institution. Secular historians have extensively depicted the monarchic state as the centrepiece of their argument that syncretic Islam or forms of Islam that sought to display their association with non-Islamic forms of behaviour or belief was the basis of a state that existed to procure resources for an elite that was also significantly non-Islamic in social composition.[5] The problem with this depiction is that it doesn't account for the connection between these two wings of Islamic polity, for it is with the historical depiction of secular monarchy and its association with syncretic culture that the secular narrative begins. Hence, it has to resort to a notion of monarchy where the ruler himself embodies the spirit of mediation. Let us take an example – in the case of a ruler like Akbar, the choice is between a divine right theory derived from his ancestors as the basis for unity or the pattern of a syncretic Sufi which means conformity to Islam. Thus, Akbar, in order to be a syncretic ruler while conforming to Islam, had to be a Sufi or the mediating face of Islam or rule on the basis of the authority of his dynasty, which we know to be the basis of his kingship. If the latter is accepted to be the case then, Akbar's state or the Mughal state did not merely have an un-Islamic character but violated the very logic on which the law of Islam was formulated.[6]

The secular and its mirror, the communal, are thus locked over the identity of the monarch as the key to his laws while overlooking the fact that it was by the very manner in which God's laws were conceived in Islam that allowed the co-existence of the Sufis and the Ulema as two polar principles of Islamic polity in the Indian sub-continent. From Al-Mawardi's tract, it is evident that the body of the ruler is crucial in the way the dialectic that Islam embodies the functionality of an ideal Islamic polity. It is not that Al-Mawardi conceived of rationality and the spirit of temporality in the spirit of his times; nor did he do it because kingship is a pre-given structure on which Islam is superimposed but because the individuality promised by the laws of God thrives only in a monarchy. The ruler must preserve the dialectic himself or the basis of the Islamic polity does not exist since its laws cannot be absolute.

Conclusion: Modern Islam

It is important to note the manner in which the modern notion of Islam, as a sociological phenomenon, locates the questions of human will, law and discipline. A quotation from Allama Iqbal is analysed below:

> It is the same reality which appears as the church from one point of view and the state from another. The essence of *tawhid* (monotheism) as a working idea is equality, solidarity and freedom. The state from the Islamic standpoint is an endeavour to transform these ideal principles into space time forces, an aspiration to realise them into a definite human organisation.[7]

The essence of Islam is embodied in the historical reality of the laws of Islam as they operate in an Islamic state if a certain principle is said to function. The principle here is that 'tawhid' is based on equality, solidarity, freedom as a 'working idea'. Iqbal is saying that the essence of the history of the Islamic state is located in a general sociological principle that holds true for all religions that monotheism or *tawhid* is based on this 'working idea'. Thus, Iqbal implies that the monarchic Islamic state is a part of Islam not from his individual experience of *tawhid* as a working idea to which he must also be subject, but from the fact that he can see through the contradictions that arise in the sociological view of Islam viz. whether it is a church or a state. Thus, Iqbal affirms the position that there are laws over and above Islam through which Islam can be understood but he does not say that it is he who understands them alone. They are essentially meant for everyone because the notion of understanding Islam is actually conceived as part of a wider understanding of how ideal principles are realised as 'space time forces' and 'definite human organisation'. The rational perspective, thus, operates on the principle that what should be and what is understood by everyone is the same. It can thus be seen as a principle on which the notion of the study of human will is based. It is a study of the 'reality' of human will. Hence, from the point of view of discipline, Iqbal makes a postulation. Therefore, two things coincide in this statement – assertion of individuality outside Islam and conformity to the notion of a modern discipline.

It can be seen from Iqbal's perspective that the principle of monotheism is central to the understanding of Islam as a sociological phenomenon. It is asserted that an individual's understanding of the world around is actually mediated by following the logic of a discipline. It actually stresses that through concepts, the world is comprehended by human beings. Thus, the notion of human will as both what is and what should be is not violated but seen to operate only within the logic of a discipline. The question of the operation of power is left out in this consideration.

The growth of republican spirit and the gradual formation of legislative assemblies in Muslim lands constitute a great step in advance. The transfer of the power of 'ijtihad' from individual representatives of schools to a Muslim legislative assembly, which in view of the growth of opposing sects, will secure contributions to legal discussions from laymen who happen to posses keen insight into affairs. In this way alone we can stir into activity the dormant spirit of life into our legal system and give it an evolutionary outlook.[8]

There is also a contrasting perspective on the notion of human will expressed through the spirit of the reform of Islam. Here Iqbal gives not a postulate of a discipline but one of social action. Here too the path of action is conceived on the basis of human will as embodying both what is and what should be since it is on this principle that laymen are justified for their inclusion into the 'legal system'. This is the transfer of power of ijtihad from those individuals who are nominated by and who represent schools of Ulama to a Muslim Legislative Assembly. The logic of inheritance or the principle of the transmission of qualities through birth is opposed by a 'transfer of power' to an institution which embodies human will. The description 'keen insight into affairs' as the qualifying category embodies the conception of a notion of reform as embodied in social practices. But it is specified that it is specifically a reform of the 'legal system' rather than a general notion of social practice.

Thus, what comes out of these observations is that an individual perspective outside Islam is essentially mediated through the notion of a discipline whereas the question of law is located firmly within Islam. Modern Islam, as reflected in the writings of Allama Iqbal, accommodates the notion of human will but maintains a firm duality with respect to the discipline and the configuration of the legal system. Hence, the very principle of human will as both what is and what should be in the form of the basis for the operation of power seems to be at odds with Islam but only if a democracy violates the logic of a discipline on which it is ultimately based.

It would be worthwhile to note that although no region has been specified as the site for the conceptions analysed in this paper, it is in fact, the Asian experience of Islam as well as of democracy that the paper broadly addresses. The historical backdrop from which the examples have been cited are all located in Asia, and the concern about democracy seen as 'ideal ethical configuration' is also very much a part of the contemporary Asian political experience.

Notes

1. Hayden White, *Meta-history: The Historical Imagination of Nineteenth Century Europe*, (Baltimore and London: The John Hopkins University Press, 1975), p. 47.
2. Nasim Ahmad Jawed, *Islam's Political Culture: Religion and Politics in Pre-divided Pakistan*, (Austin: University of Texas Press, 1999), p. 82.
3. Al-Mawardi, "Ahkam al-Sultaniyya", excerpt in John Alden Williams, *Themes of Islamic Civilization*, (Berkeley: University of California Press, 1971), pp. 86-87.
4. John L Esposito and James P. Piscatori, "Democratization and Islam," *Middle East Journal* 45, Summer 1991, p.439.
5. By secular historians I refer to two broad categories of views, the primarily cultural and political works of historians such as Satish Chandra and Tara Chand as well as the economic accounts of the Mughal Empire by historians such as Irfan Habib.

6. The exemplary analysis of this viewpoint is to be found in various works of the Pakistani historian Ishtiaq Husain Quraishi.
7. Sir Muhammad Iqbal, *The Reconstruction of Religious Thought in Islam*, (Lahore: Sh.Muhammad Ashraf, 1962), p. 154.
8. Sir Muhammad Iqbal, op.cit. pp. 173-174.

15. MAULANA ABUL KALAM AZAD: THE PROPHET OF DEMOCRACY

Safoora Razeq

National solidarities were constructed often by vigorous contestation because there were various voices, various contradictions and various forms of consciousness. It is democracy which gives power to all but authority to none in this sea of variations. Democracy literally means 'rule by the people' and this distinguishes it from any pattern of governance not deriving its legitimacy from the people's choice while the core principle in democracy is 'equality and freedom of expression and thought'.

Culture is an expression of human experiences; each culture speaks of its own experiences in the history of human evolution. Humans even subscribe to their language, culture and records to reflect upon a particular experience that might be expressed in a different way because culture has its own language. But the facts remain that human experiences in each culture are to some extent same as far as the relation of power is concerned with the suppression of human freedom. Therefore, the struggle for human freedom is a universal truth since time immemorial. History has witnessed different forms of struggle. Democracy has often emerged as a common tool to establish the right of the people. Religion had been a source, and at times, the cause for such struggle. In the past, prophets were not only messengers of God, they were also the leaders of mankind in their struggles against injustice, oppression and lawlessness. Tocqueville citing the American experience proposed that democracy can indeed become a friend to religion and may be crucial to its future. I would like to argue that leaders like Gandhi had successfully used religious vocabulary and idioms, in constructing the nationalist trajectory, in their struggle against the World's greatest colonial power.

He [Allah] claims that His wisdom resides with the community and collective. To Him, only that Government can be legitimate which is not autocratic but is in the hands of a nation (its people). Accordingly He commands that there be a mutual consultation, hereby establishing the principles of democracy, as an obligatory duty of every pious Muslim. It is in accordance with the religious duty that a Muslim should not rest until the parliamentary Government has been established.

> atar bashart-e adab geer, chun ke ba tarbee bash
> az kash-e Jamshed wa Behrman -act wa Qubad.

(Pick up the cup but respectfully:
For it is made from the cup of Jamshed and Behman and Qudad,
It reflects the Universe.[1]

The concept of 'ahimsha' and 'satyagraha' were religious connotations appropriated by Gandhi as the nationalist cultural idiom. For centuries, striving for the cause of Human freedom has united Men from different walks of the life, in this shared responsibility. In India the most important imaginings of the nation continue to be religious,[2] aspiring from its multi –religious and multi-cultural origins. The role of the state in the formation of nationalism, deserve to be the central issue because the nation aspires to control the state. The Indian reality had the 'colonial state' as the catalyst, through the tyranny and oppression it unleashed, provoking the resistance movement. The reactions at various quarters shaped the multitude of imagination.

Each effort of defiance crystallised into a specific expression of resistance. Since each had been the result of its own understanding of history and society, there were multiple conceptions of the notion of nationhood. Thus each religion has been appropriated in its own capacity by the champion of democracy to establish the lost ground on human rights. Through these different constructs, the Indian nation came into its lofty existence.

Charles Kurzman elaborately discusses how the liberal Islamic reformers of the early twentieth century, in other parts of the world were working on the idea of 'freedom of thought, envisaged in the Holy Qur'an, to emphasis the concept of 'Shura' or consultation, which is taken as an expression of popular will in secular matters.[3] Therefore 'freedom of thought' emerged as the focal point of the emerging debate on democracy in the Muslim World at this time because the Muslim World from West Africa to East Asia was tightly under the grip of Colonial and Imperialist regimes. Since freedom of thought and expression has been the founding stone for the working of any democratic system, they made the most of the 1300 years of struggle within Islam for the establishment of individual freedom against tyrannical regime. Men who worked within the tradition of Islam for the establishment of democracy saw the 'Right of Man' fundamental to the concept of (faith) Iman. Because the Qur'an mentions 'Shura' as a principle governing the public life in the society of the faithful rather than a specifically ordained system of government[4].The principle of 'Shura' does not differ from democracy because both strive to establish the central argument, that is, collective deliberation is more likely to lead to a fair and sound result for social good than individual preference.

The traditional Islamic concept which was utilised by the liberal Islamic reformers of the twentieth century to establish the idea of 'jamhuriah' or democracy was the tool of 'ijtihad' (independent judgement). The conditions that religious scholars have established for ijtihad are:

- In condition to the knowledge of Qur'an a person should be familiar with literature also. He should have complete knowledge of the text of the Qur'an; he should know when every verse was revealed and what the circumstances of its revelation were; he should be well acquainted with the literal meaning of every word in the Qur'an; and besides this, he should know what connotations are hidden within these words
- He should have memorised the entire Qur'an
- He should have complete mastery of the science of hidith and command of at least 3000 major hidiths
- He must be very devout and pious
- He must be completely familiar with the science of Islamic jurisprudence (that is, with all five branches of fiqh)[5]

Historical Background for the Rise of Democratic Ideas among the Liberal Islamic Reformers

Democracy lay at the root of the various conceptualisation of the nation-state which emerged in the teleology of the nationalists. Individual freedom was the founding stone for the nationalists, to construct the basis for the notion of peoples' democratic rights against colonial atrocities. The decision to put up a challenge against the colonial state had been precipitating within many circles of the Indian Muslim, especially the 'Wahabis' from the 19th century. They had put up a tough resistance against the atrocities of the colonial regime. But, they had failed to synergise the same with the modernist version of revolt, empowered by the right of the right of the people. Their obscurantist ideas were bound to suffer. The revolt of

1857, and the leadership of Sir Syed Ahmad Khan had made the Muslim community subservient to the British Raj and this made them indifferent to any political participation. In fact in their desperation for survival had taken the face of loyalty to the Raj. This is because existence of the feeling of 'distinctive as a community' as envisaged in the elitist politics, reflected in the elements that sustained the politics of Muslim representation. Ayesha Jalal feels that the Muslim identity in the subcontinent cannot be reduced to a mere rationalization of the normative of Islamic discourse.[6] The Muslim voice of disaffection against the colonial rule reflects the historiographical narrative of Hindu-Muslim relations that does not harp on the fault line of enmity, conflict and tension but, on the effort to project the 'will' of inter-community, together with that of the multitudes within the community, as a reality in its tussle to establish the democratic ideals within the realm of society and polity.

Maulana Azad's argument for democracy was an effort not only to establish the right of the Indian nation to rule its own independent state but it was through democratic ideals that Azad argued the right of the individual in relation to the community and the state should reign supreme. In doing so, he accepted the multiplicity of religion within a state and multiple interpretation of a single religion (Islam) as an accepted social and political reality. Arguing against the demand for separate electorates by Muslim League, Azad exhorted that such an argument only weakens the logical demand for a democratic government, whereas the right of the people of India against the colonial government is reduced to a lesser platform.

This understanding of new social and political unity among the Muslim leaders was to some extent influenced by the British policy of oppression. The Muslim community negotiated the new situation by extending their hand of friendship towards the Hindu nationalists. In India, Lord Curzon had proved to be a denigrator to the cause of British Imperialism. It was during his viceroyalty, that the Indian nationalism got its first fillip. The Bengali nationalists seriously took Lord Curzon's University Act, 1904 as an attempt by the Government to establish its stringent control over the system of education. Similarly, the Calcutta Corporation Act of 1899 was interpreted as the Government's show of power. The worst was the Partition of Bengal into two provinces in 1905. Bengali nationalism was working to make itself felt at all levels but, the Muslims in Bengal and Calcutta were still unperturbed. The need to build up a liaison, between the two major communities, was felt by both.

While the colonial knowledge system boldly wiped out the longstanding Muslim political, social and religious institutions, declaring them as citadels of superstitions, despotism and irrationality, the ideas of European renaissance hit hard every citadel of culture and knowledge. And the answer to it required the restoration of Muslim self confidence, which had much eroded. This encounter with the more vibrant cultural values of the West was at a time when the Muslim world was at its weakest – economically and militarily – and at its least dynamic intellectually and scientifically. Hence, the need of the tradition was to acquiescence themselves with what seemed to be their own storehouse of knowledge, and harness its strength.

The logic of appropriating the ideal of Islam to feed the need for a struggle against the unjust and tyrannical colonial Government was perceived by many but it was Azad who projected it as the sacred duty of individuals and the community. Azad argued, "Islam has taught us both to bestow freedom and to obtain it...we believe it is in consistence with God's will, that nations and countries should be granted the freedom to rule over themselves."[7] Maulana Azad the 'mujaddid', as the 'renewer', argued for the reinterpretation of the Qur'an in the light of the present situation. He, as the leader of the new millennium, brought revolution changes to the Muslim political, cultural and social ideas. The spirit of Islam – the concept of equality and brotherhood, humanity and liberty, became the clarion call of the Islamic democrats in India, for the cause of India's freedom. The new Islamic democrats formulated their ideas from the Islamic perspective, the role of the community and the freedom of the individuals in the context of the on-going struggle for democracy.

By turning their back to the cause of representative politics, the community had been actually denying the guidance of God, argued Azad in the pages of Al Hilal. "This defiance of God's command had come as a curse to the community in the shape of its misfortunes and miseries."[8] Maulana Azad's argument for democracy highlighted that consultation should not be restricted to the realm of religion alone, but should be extended to matters of education, society and politics too. He explicitly argued that the guidance of the Qur'an, is for the establishment of Human freedom and democracy. So, it was from 1912 onwards, that Maulana Azad had been advocating for the cause of Parliamentary democracy in India, and the cause for single nationhood, that is, 'Umaah i –Ummah-e Wahida'. Still more significantly, Maulana Azad had been promoting the cause for 'freedom of thought' from as early as 1910 as the foundation for such representative politics, from the time he published his article on *Sarmad Shaheed*, at the request of Khwaja Hasan Nizami. It is with this essay that his ideas of democracy and liberal Islam comes into play. Azad, henceforth, is a democrat within the realm of Islam.

Why did Maulana Azad use the Martyrdom of Sarmad Shaheed?

Maulana Azad based his information for Sarmad on two authoritative sources, that is, *Miratul Khayal* by Sher Khan Lodi and Riaz-ul-Shuara by Ali Quli Valeh Daghistani. He traces Sarmad's origin among the Jews of Kashan, who had come to India as traders. And in India, it was the divine glance of a Hindu boy, which turned him to the mystic path of search for the truth. Sarmad was in close touch with Dara Shikoh, the sufi prince. In Alamgir's eyes, Sarmad's greatest crime was his closeness to Dara Shikoh but Aurangzeb executed him on the pretext of his heresy or misinterpretation of Islam.

Aurangzeb's order to execute Sarmad has been interpreted by Maulana Azad, as an example, of interference in matters of private concern. To Maulana Azad, religious faith is a matter of individual freedom of thought. Maulana Azad, being a Sufi by birth, upholds mysticism as a particular method of approach to Reality (Haqiqah). That the intuitive and emotional spiritual faculties, which are generally dormant and latent, is brought to play through training under guidance, hence, it is meant as 'travelling the path' (salak at-tariq). To Azad, it is as relevant a part of the Prophetic tradition as the Shari'ah. Aurangzeb, as the torch bearer of canonical Islam, failed to see the manifold path of reaching to God. Aurangzeb, being a 'shuhudi' by persuasion, upheld the Shari'ah, or the canonical law, as the pillar of faith, while Sarmad as a Wujudi, knew no bound in his love for God, and thus, he upheld freedom of expression and freedom of thought more holy and pious, than the rule of the land and the rule of the Shari'ah.

That 'Shari'ah' and 'Tariqa' are the only two different means of reaching God. But, what Maulana Azad wanted to emphasise through his article on Sarmad, was his belief that each individual has his own 'freedom of thought', 'to decide the path' he will take to reach to his creator. And Aurangzeb, by executing Sarmad, had actually given the greatest blow to the basic concept of Islam, which has granted individual freedom of thought as a rational being. Every act of individual is supposedly to be exercised by virtue of Man's own reason of judgement, and for which he and he alone is answerable to God.

Thus, on his return to India from his Middle East sojourn in 1908, Maulana Azad took upon himself to teach his community the lessons of democracy, with its inception in the concept of freedom of thought. Although Azad read Arabic fluently, it was the writings of Abduh and Rashid Rida in Al Manar, which had actually inspired him. He was aware of the tendency of the Arabic language press which was most articulate in its anti-British and anti-Ottoman sentiments. But it was his visit to the Middle East (which Azad himself emphasised) was a decisive factor because it was in Egypt that he must have met the Egyptian nationalist, the followers of Mustafa Kamil. Douglas rightly points out that the year Azad landed in Egypt, the idea most prevalent was not that of Abduh, which was in favour of educating the Egyptian society in political virtue (which bear some resemblance to Sir Syed's ideas) but that of Kamil. He was an anti-colonialist, who envisaged co-operation of Muslims and non-Muslims compulsive to achieve the target of independence from the domineering effect of the colonial rule. It was in Egypt that he met the Lebanese writer who produced the newspaper *al-Muqattam* and the monthly *al-Muqtataf*; these were the papers, which he had been reading in the Calcutta office. In 1908, the argument they put forward in their struggle against the Ottoman Sultan was impressive to Azad because they were based on the pages of the Holy Qur'an.

It was here that these Arab and Turkish nationalists posed a question to him, and this made him conscious of the fact that although the Indian Muslims were under the oppressive rule of the colonial regime, they would not enter into an understanding with the Hindu nationalists in India to achieve their freedom. This aspiration for national freedom among the Arabs and the desire for constitutional government among the Turks, developed the cravings in Azad to launch a movement for national freedom. On his return from Middle East in 1908, he fired this passion of cooperating with 'others', that is, the Hindu Nationalists, in the struggle for freedom.

Thus, Azad used martyr Sarmad to base his argument first for freedom of expression in matters of religion, and then, extend the same argument to the other arena of human life, that is, political question. How holy was Azad's mission for freedom in the days when the Muslim community failed to recognise the need for freedom! He bothered not whether the road to his passion made him look unreligious or a heretic. And as he had quoted Sarmad:

Az saqi-e-kausar mai-e-gulfam talab
Dar peeri-o-zof jam-e-aaram talab
Ta chand griftar-ba duniya basti
Az fazl-e-Khuda nijat z-ein daam talab
From the Saqi of heaven
Ask for the blushing wine,
A soothing goblet for your advanced years.
No matter how entangled are you in this world,
From the grace of God
Ask for freedom from the snare

The freedom denoted here is not the political freedom but the spiritual freedom to which Azad had laid his actual focus because the freedom to think for ourselves gives us the right to decide what is good for ourselves in the context of our society. So, the question of freedom is related in more than one way to our capacity as the decision-maker. And no decision is a decision unless the decision-maker has the freedom to decide. Blind faith has no place in the contestation for freedom, be it the religious, political or social arena.

The Qur'an (x:8-10) says:

Have we not made
For him a pair of eyes?
And a tongue,
And a pair of lips?
And shown him
The two highways?
Of Guidance and of errors[9].

Maulana Azad explicitly chose to project in the pages of *Al Hilal*, his argument that there is no greater enemy of the divine qualities of human beings, than the evil of 'taqlid' or blind imitation. All the deviations and error committing to human actions have their seeds in the soil of imitation. Hence, the first stage on the way to 'freedom of thought' is to free oneself from the shackles of 'taqlid'.[10] The special quality of a human being, his distinctiveness consists of his intellectual, his capacity to think, his mental endeavour, and his inquisitiveness. The development of sciences and arts, discovery of divine laws and knowledge of nature, the knowledge of the properties of things in the universe, the entire progress of civilisation and manufacture, and all the inventions of new instruments and new means of comfort and welfare – in short, all the miracles of the mental and intellectual growth of human beings that can be observed today, are the outcome of the intellectual endeavour and the working of the human mind. The message which the Holy Qur'an brought to humanity, according to Maulana Azad, has the real objective of delivering man from the fetters of 'taqlid' and intellectual oppression.[11]

Maulana Azad, when arguing the case of Sarmad Shaheed against Emperor Aurangzeb, was actually advocating his idea of popular sovereignty against autocracy, despotism and intellectual oppression. To him, the ideas of democracy should prevail in the avenues of society, polity, and religion. Again, to Azad, the common man was shackled not only politically by British Imperialism, but socially under the grip of the misguided leadership, which claims to talk for the community but suppresses the need and the voice of the community. Finally, the realm of religion was in the hands of half-learned qazis. During the 1300 years, since the advent of Islam, the instrument of the fatwa has been a sword without a sheath. During any given period of Islamic history, there are examples of kings who made equal use of both the pen of the qazi and sword of the general in bleeding to death whoever threatened their supremacy...Sarmad was executed by the same sword.[12]

To Azad, Sarmad did not believe in blind imitation, so he had set for the search of truth, his intense love for God, is in itself the answer for his call. Sarmad's truthfulness in reciting the 'kalima' partially that is 'la ilaha', which is a negative statement proved his denial of the faith. Azad pointed out that Sarmad was truthful to his own understanding because the 'Kalima-e shahadat' testifies and certifies the existence of God. Since witness (shahadat) in the true sense is the appearance of truth itself and Sarmad was aware that the truth had not been unveiled to him so he could not certify to it. Maulana Azad's accusation against Emperor Aurangzeb in executing Sarmad was based on an understanding of Islam, where Islam itself grants freedom of thought and expression to its followers. Maulana candidly expressed that the voice of Sarmad was a reflection of popular will. When they [the Mughal authority] led Sarmad to the place of martyrdom, the whole Shahjahanbad accompanied him. Here Maulana Azad was logically promoting the idea that the popular voice and freedom of expression were sacrificed at the altar of the Mughal state. The Alamgiri state used religion and the religious men (ulema) to suppress the freedom of expression granted by Islam. Since such freedom not only questioned the existence of God but hit hard at the foundation of states denied of popular will.

Christian W. Troll [13] argued that Azad's essay on Sarmad Shaheed reflected Azad's religious world view, removed from any direct political engagement. But I would prefer to argue that Azad's article on Sarmad was basically the starting point of his greater political argument on democracy. By arguing the case for individual freedom, in matters of religion, Azad was actually promoting the right of the ruled, to have a voice of its own. It was the time when Maulana was trying to formulate a discourse on democracy based on religion.

It was not the Western Enlightened ideas of individual freedom, which must have inspired him but it was his reading of the Arab nationalists, the Iranian and the Turkish constitutionalists which made his faith on tradition and Qur'an stronger. He built his testament on the bases of Islamic liberal tradition. The concept of individual freedom and liberty in Muslim society is very different to the Western concept. A Muslim links true freedom to his submission to God, His Prophet and community. Roger Garaudy has observed that the Islamic 'whole' and the place of the individual within it is comparable neither to Hegel's notion of the state and society as an 'organic reality', nor akin to the totalitarianism postulated by Fascism.

By 1910, the question of faith (mazhhab) in term of politics and society had emerged to be the greatest enemy to the unity of the freedom movement for India; elsewhere, it might be the strongest force to bring about the social dichotomy. In Iran, the orthodox Ulema and the modernist made up their differences to bring the autocratic regime of the Shah under control by constitutional checks. They used religion as the cementing force. In Bengal, increasing number of riots and political tussle became evident with the birth of the Muslim League in 1906. Azad, at this time, did not know the implication of the Muslim League as a political force. It is better to argue that Azad, at this time, was not involved with a political programme of his own except that he found in the Colonial government a good patron for western learning. On his return to Calcutta in 1908, he could find the revolutionaries as a good partner in his struggle for freedom. He thought it necessary to provide deep-rooted doctrinal argument to his community, against the communal strive so that a strong base could be built on which the issues for democratic struggle and setting up of democratic government could be argued through.

Azad's Influences from other parts of the Islamic World

The historical background for the rise of democratic ideas, in the Muslim political thought in the last two centuries, can be traced back to the socio-political milieu of dual challenges to the Muslim societies. It was perceived to be a combination of the two. The first was the external threat by a more vibrant cultural force of the west. And the second, assumed to be more serious in nature, was the actual departure from the moral and the religious teaching of the Qur'an.

The defeat of the Ottoman Empire at the end of the first great Balkan crisis in 1876-78, after the French occupation of Tunisia in 1881, the British conquest of Egypt in 1882 and the first Armenian revolt in Istanbul and in Anatolia in October 1895 and in the winter of the same year resulting in the general belief that the Ottoman sultan had lost its sovereignty over the Islamic 'ummah' for good. Following these military defeats, Muslims became painfully conscious of their scientific, technological and military shortcomings compared to the Europeans.[14] A major shift in power occurred as declining Muslim fortunes reversed the relationship of the Muslim world to the west, from that of ascendant expansionism to one of defensiveness and subordination. By the 19th and early 20th century, Europe (in particular, Great Britain, France, and Holland)had penetrated and increasingly dominated much of the Muslim world from North Africa to Southeast Asia(the French in North Africa, the British and French in the Middle East and South Asia, and the Dutch and British in Southeast Asia).[15]

The major outcome of the West's success in this part of the world was the erosion of the 'cultural confidence' of the Muslim Community. Muslim intellectuals or 'muhadith'/scholars of religion in this part of the Islamic world started working on a new Islamic theory of modernism, which had its logical roots in the Islamic Prophetic tradition and Qur'an. Their major emphases were to establish a dialogue between Modernity and Islam. They pressed for an internal reform, through a process of reinterpretation (ijtihad), so that they could formulate their own ideological bases, to fight back the twin evils of colonial rule and autocratic regimes near home. Inspired by the hope of establishing a democratic society, the intellectuals quite logically traced back their ideals to the period of great Islamic humanism of the 10th and 13th century.

The modern world no doubt promises progress, emancipation, justice and liberty – a guide to continuous human development. The Muslim democrats, of the early 20th century, argued that Islam too posses the potential for human development in its concept of liberty, rationality and justice. They postulate that ideal society had already been realised at the time of Prophet, which promoted democratic and humanist ideal as the basis of all governance and society.

The new 'muhaddithun', the leaders for Islamic democracy in this part of the world, took 'ijtihad' as the ideal pillar within Islam to install the concept and logic for democratic society. Maulana Azad was impressed by the idea of popular sovereignty right from 1904, when he had personally interacted with the Arab revolutionaries, on his visit to Iraq. Although he was in touch with their ideas, as he regularly read the Al Manar and Al Hilal, he frequented the reading room library of Maulvi Ahmad Hussain in Calcutta. When he was in Bombay, such journals were easily available.

In their struggle against the colonial rule, the Muslim democrats made use of the basic law of God and the source of Law –the Qur'an, as their guide to establish justice and democracy. The democrats not merely re-appropriated past solutions, but carefully mapped the future Muslim polity and society in the light of the establishment of nation-states.

Reformers feigned foreign conquest as the cause for the erosion of religious and moral standard and ensuing decline of Muslim societies.[16] The decline of the Muslim society was morally and spiritually resulting in loss of humanity. Depending on the specific geopolitical, social and political conditions and their own historical experiences in the field of politics made individual Muslim societies tailor its own answer to these new challenges. But, what remain common to all such societies were their doubts on the potency of their own cultural and religious value. Thus, when their leaders accepted the western concept of modernity, it was mainly taken as a compromise of the very basis of the social and religious value. The compromises of such values were of defensive character. They were meant to acquire the superior technology and science, economic and military know-how of the Europeans only to resist them in the end.

While the reaction to the spiritual and moral decline of the community was met with the most important effort of reintroducing a broad notion of rationalism to the interpretation of Islamic sources, including the Qur'an. While leaders like Jamaludin Afghani (1838-97) and Sir Syed Ahmad Khan (1878-98) stressed the point that Islam and science were not only compatible, Islam, of all religions, was the friendliest to science. In fact Afghani stretches it further to argue that Muslims had lost their rationalist and scientific spirit, or more accurately, had passed it on to the Europeans.[17]

Since the middle of the 19th century, efforts by different Muslim society to break through the shackles of political domination, of Imperialist rule or colonial domination effecting economy and society forced Muslim thinkers to repeatedly challenge the classical Islamic ideas about religious authority and the role of the individual and community. Muslim thinkers during this time had rationally used 'tradition' both to change and to justify the change of government, in favour of 'the People'. Daniel Brown argues how tradition is frequently appealed to as a way of defending against perceived innovation, as a way of preserving threatened values.[18]

Politics and participation in the formation of government became a part of the religious duty of the faithful because it is the media of establishing the good and eradicating the evil. It goes by way of misconception that there is always a fusion of religion and politics in the Islamic culture. Often it was the reverse, the majority of Muslims, for the greater part of their history, lived under regimes which had only provided an outward allegiance to the observation of Shari'ah. Thus the movement for democracy, pointed to the fact that these regimes had openly flouted the democratic ideal, which seemed to be the bases of Islam.

In Islam, the duty of the government is not only to establish the physical wellbeing of its citizens but to create an environment to observe spiritual needs too. To a student of political thought, the political ideas prevalent in the first six and seven centuries, of the Islamic history, is a fascinating mosaic of competing schools, who argued for monarchy as well as against it, upholding the right of the individuals and the community.

According to al Kawakibi[19] and some others, the 'despotism' of the Ottoman Empire was, above all, responsible for this general misery. Kawakibi saw himself exposed to persecution by secret agents of the empire who belonged to a countrywide network of spy against Arab intellectuals. Ibrahim al- Muwailihi (1846-1906) had, under a pseudonym and after his appointment by order of the Ottoman Sultan in 1994 as the under-secretary of the State to the Ministry of Culture, reflected that Aba al Hamid II, was not a real sultan, but an effeminate tyrant addicted to pleasures and women.[20]

The 20th century saw the rise of a new understanding of Islam in the context of colonial realities. The optimism of the years before 1870, when Islamic intellectuals still believed that they could participate in modernism precisely because of their Islamic tradition, (which had a rational past and was akin to Science) was turned down by the new intellects. In India the ideologies of the great Islamic Modernist – Sir Syed Ahmad Khan was turned down by the new leadership.

Schulze has correctly pointed out that there were no casual relations established between the Russian Revolution of January 1905, the Persian constitutional Movement of 1906, the nationalist propaganda in Egypt in 1906 and the Young Turk coup in Istanbul of July 1908. It was definitely the critical period, before the First World, which marked the end of the 'golden decade' of colonialism (1896-1906).

While the nationalist in this part of the world, who fought against the Colonial regime, belonged to the Islamic tradition, they created their own Islamic conceptual world, where rebellion against the colonial oppressive regime was considered as a religious duty, while the establishment of Peoples' democracy became their sacred mission. The constitutional movement marked its first success in Persia in 1906, on June 05, a year after the revolution in Russia. The oppositional movement led by the liberal Ihtisham al Sattaneh, carried through its proposal for a Constitutional assembly.[21] In Turkestan too, the 1905 revolution established the foundation for a new political culture shared by liberals, nationalist and Islamist. The triumph celebrated by the Constitutionalists of the Ottoman Empire marked the stage set by the Iranian constitutionalists. It was the economic crisis of 1905-07 that set off agitation against the government, when Greek and Bulgarian rebels increasingly became active in Macedonia. In June/July of 1908, armed conflict over Macedonia threatened to break out between the committee and official Ottoman troops; it resulted in the re-establishment of Constitutional Government in 1908-23.[22] The greatest victory was of the constitutionalist Revolution in Iran in 1906 because it had removed the distance between the orthodox Ulema and the modernist in their urge to bring about the constitutional revolution. It ended the rule of the autocratic regime.

Maulana Abul Kalam Azad as Liberal Islamic Democrat

Azad was the pioneer in British India among the 'Mujaddid', who unwaveringly purported the belief that democracy is the essence of Islam, and the establishment of the same is the pious duty of all Muslims. It has been pointed out by all thoughtful leaders of the Muslims, in the late 19th century that there exist dual problems for Muslim backwardness and political decadence – the presence of colonial rule and the waywardness of the faithful. But it was

Maulana Azad who actually pointed out the apathy of the community towards the concept of democracy, which had drifted them away from the guidance of God and bereft them of their own wellbeing. Maulana Azad wrote, No community by its evil deeds can stop the inevitable. A day will come when the final political revolution of India would take place. The shackles of slavery which it had dragged for centuries will be broken into pieces, as the tide for freedom will set in. When the history of this great success story will be written, what will it reflect on the contribution of the seven hundred millions of its inhabitants? As ' Muslim' they are duty bound to raise the banner of revolt, against the colonial rule and fight for India's independence and progress, with all the other communities of India, and even follow their footsteps.[23]

Maulana Azad, who hoped to be the 'mujaddid' of the new millennium, upbraided his community for its departure from the basic Islamic rationality, scientific spirit and traditions to fight for the cause of humanity and freedom. According to Schulze, the impact of nationalism on Islamic countries was, however, primarily confined to domestic politics and largely concerned the question of who had the right to wield power in the modern state.[24] Thus it was the struggle for democratic power. Azad based his logic to rebel only to regain power for the people.

In most parts of the Muslim world, the nation state identity of the elites had become self-evident by 1900. The focus of political conflict was the colonial state, for hardly any of the nationalist movements had irredentist tendencies. The impact of nationalism on Islamic countries was, however, primarily confined to domestic policies and largely concerned the question of who had the right to wield power in the modern State. In this context, constitutionalism stood at the heart of nationalist demands; it was mainly directed against the European rule, whose power was compared with the power of autocratic monarchs. Thus, the nationalist intellectuals first sued for their right to participate in decisions and institutions but in the course of time radicalised their position, and finally, demanded the abolition of the European rule.[25]

Maulana Azad's Argument for Political Sovereignty

When Maulana Azad returned to Calcutta in 1908, he was overwhelmed by the constitutionalist ideology put forward by the Turkish nationalist, based on Islamic ideals and Qur'anic dictums. His familiarity with the Arab nationalist and their argument for democracy made Azad work for a theoretical base for democracy within the realm of Islam. He consciously built up his case for democracy within the historical tradition of Indian Islam so that he could relate the concept of democracy as internal both to the Islamic tradition and to the Indian socio-political scenario. An article on Samad Shaheed was published in 1910 to promote the concept of freedom of thought, while his writing in Al Hilal overtly argues for political democracy. His acquaintance with the greater Islamic world made him consciously aware of his own responsibility in awakening the masses for popular participation. It has been wrongly read that the Muslim consciousness against the Imperialist and the colonial regime of the West was an assertion of the Islamic force to regain its hold over the lost political ground. A close reading of the situation would definitely reflect a different picture. It was during this time that colonial force had hit the lowest point. Right for self-determination and the desire for nationhood, which had touched Europe in the 19th century reached this part of the world. The nations who were subjugated as colonies of the Western democratic nations were no longer ready to live in servitude. To the extent that they demanded their own right to rule from the Muslim Imperialist (Ottoman Turks) and the Western colonial regimes, because freedom was in the air. In India, the Muslims were still not aware of the new era of revolution which had swayed half the globe. Azad used Qur'anic injunctions to enforce his argument for popular democracy from 1912 onwards. To Azad, democracy not only speaks of political participation but it builds in the right of all – the weakest and the strongest – on the same ground. Through democracy, the greatest hurdle of communal politics could be put to rein, not to talk of the great social disparity which exist in the social milieu in context of ownership of resource. Hence, it was not Western democracy for which Azad was championing but it was the freedom through which social, economic and political imbalances could be corrected by popular participation. Like many other enlightened democrats, Maulana Abul Kalam Azad felt that democracy was the answer to our long years of suffering.

Notes

1. Maulana Azad, *Gubar-e-Khatir*, Letter No. 18.
2. Peter van der Veer, *Religious Nationalism: Hindus Muslims India,* (New Delhi: Paul Press, 1996), p. 22.
3. Charles Kruzman, ed *Liberal Islam, A Source Book*, (New York: O.U.P., 1998), pp. 19-20.
4. Sadek J. Sulaiman, Democracy and Shura, in Charles Kurzman, ed, *Liberal Islam; A Source Book,* (New York: O.U.P., 1998), p. 94.

5. S.M. Zafar, Accountability, Parliament and Ijtihad in C. Kurzman ed, *Liberal Islam: A Source Book*, (New York: O.U.P., 1998), p. 70.
6. Sugata Bose and Ayesha Jalal, ed, *Democracy and Development; State and politics in India*, (Delhi: O.U.P., 1998), p. 80.
7. Maulana Abul Kalam Azad, Al Hilal, vol. 1, no. 15, December, 1912.
8. *Al Hilal*, vol.1, no.12, November, 1912.
9. *Al Hilal* vol.1, no.11, September 22, 1912.
10. *Al Hilal*, vol. 1, no.11, September 22, 1912
11. *Al Hilal*, vol. 1, no.11, September 22, 1912
12. *The Rubaiyat of Sarmad*, Translated by Syeda Saiyidain Hameed, (New Delhi: ICCR, 1991), p. 34.
13. Christian W. Trall, "Abdul Kalam Azad's Sarmad the Matyr" in Christopher Shaclke, ed, *Urdu and Muslim Asia*, (London: SOAS, 1998), p.124.
14. Hunter T. Shireen, ed, *Reformist voices of Islam, Mediating Islam and Modernity*, (New Delhi: Pentagon Press, 2009), p. 13
15. Esposito L. John, *ISLAM: The straight path*, (New York: O.U.P., 1991), p. 125.
16. Esposito L. John, *ISLAM: The straight path*, (New York: O.U.P., 1991), p. 6.
17. See Nikkie Kaddie, *Sayyid Jamal ad—Din al Afghani: A Political Biography*, (Berkeley: University of California Press), 1972. (for a comprehensive view of Afghani on anti-imperialism)
18. Brown Daniel, *Rethinking tradition in Modern Islamic thought*, (U.K.: Cambridge University Press, 1996), p. 3.
19. Abd al-Rahman al-Kawākibī (1849–1902) was a Syrian author and Pan-Islamic Arab solidarity supporter from Aleppo. He was one of the most prominent intellectuals of his time; however, his thoughts and writings continue to be relevant to the issues of Islamic identity and Pan-Arabism. His criticisms of the Ottoman Empire eventually lead to Arabs calling for the sovereignty of the Arab Nations, setting the basis for Pan-Arab nationalism. Al-Kawakibi was influenced by the teachings of Jamal al-Din al-Afghani as well his disciple Muhammad Abduh. Al-Afghani preached Pan-Islamic identity - with this as his basis, Al-Kawakibi went one step further, incorporating Al-Afghani's theories into Pan-Islamic Arabic solidarity. Another one of Al-Kawakibi's contemporaries was the Salafiya thinker, Rashid Rida who lived in Egypt at the same time. Rida and Al-Kawakibi discussed ideas of Islamism and Pan-Arabism as well as Qur'anic interpretations. Al-Kawakibi believed that Arabs should be representatives of Islam, not the Ottomans. Rida believed that imitations (taqlid) was the reason for downfall of Islam and Muslims. They both believed in the resurgence of independent thinking (ijtihad).
20. Reinhard Schulze, *A Modern History of the Islamic World*, (New York: I. B. Tauris, 1988), p. 20.
21. *A Modern History of the Islamic World*, p. 35.
22. *A Modern History of the Islamic World*, p. 36.
23. *Al-Hilal*, vol.1, no.23, December 18, 1912.
24. *A Modern History of the Islamic World*, p. 29.
25. *A Modern History of the Islamic World*, pp. 28-29.

16. Ulan Ude and Ulaan Baatar: The Mongol space re-visited

Suchandana Chatterjee

Inner Asia-the Spatial Turn

Since Soviet disintegration new historical enquiries about Asiatic Russia have generated interest in regional studies (*kraievedenie*)[1] and spatial categories like *Inner Asia.* In perceptions about a spatial turn,[2] interdependent and interactive moments in Inner Asian history have acquired significant attention. Referring to the region's spatiality—that is, the interior of the Eurasian landmass with Turko-Mongol affiliations that belonged to the Yenisei Kyrgyz 'kaghanate' and the Chingizid Empire, experts have not only applied the geographical-historical determinant but also the cultural determinant. The region corresponds (1) to the south-east Siberian environs that were reconstituted in the 20th century as autonomous regions, Soviet satellites or independent republics, and (2) the Mongolian plateau that was colonised by the Qing Chinese and Russians and split up into Inner and Outer Mongolia in the 20th century. In ecological terms, the region also includes Tibet. In cultural terms, the term applies to nomadic people who inhabit the region from the China Sea to Eastern Europe, including parts of the former Soviet Union and their interaction with surrounding sedentary cultures. The Turko-Mongol-Tungusic ethnic communities of this region include the Buryats, Khalkh Mongols, Kyrgyz, Oirots, Zhungars, Tibetans, and the Uyghurs. Due to the contiguity of borders and overlapping identities, the region has historical links with Central Asia and Mongolia besides direct links with metropolitan Russia or China. To deal comprehensively with either of these regions of Inner Asia is a formidable task and would require extended forays into the history not only of the Chinese and Russian empires but also of the Siberian khanates on the Irtysh as well as the Zhungar khanate of the western Mongols.[3] Such details of intertwined histories are beyond the scope of a single project. But what has been attempted here is a comparison of varied approaches towards the study of Inner Asia as a spatial and cultural unit. Turko-Mongol affiliations and religious affinities (Buddhist and Islamic) make Inner Asian 'crossroads culture' an interesting study, though on the whole, there seems to be the dominant rhetoric of a Mongol 'pax'. In post-Soviet assessments of Mongol history, there is an attempt not only to revive the Chingizid past but also to review the Russian and Chinese analytical frameworks and re-assess the Mongolian worldview. This engagement with the inner and outer world of the Mongols gives a perspective of the local and the global contexts of the Mongol domain. But, there are also various opinions that look beyond the Mongol prism and express diverse sentiments. For instance, the Buryat mentalite is expressed through such self-definitions as 'We-Buryats'.[4] Such reconsiderations are growing in number and some of these were experienced during my research trips to Ulan Ude and Ulaan Baatar in 2009-11. As an outsider who had walked into the field, I was trying to come to terms with multiple representations of that 'we' factor. The primary aim of the research trips was to understand the manifestation of 'the local' and the intersection of global trends. This was primarily done by (1) collecting primary and secondary research material about historical developments in Buryatia centered round Ulan Ude that evolved as an administrative and intellectual centre since the Tsarist period,[5] (2) interacting with Buryat scholars to get an idea about their transcendental awareness on aspects as ethnicity and nationalism, Buddhism, integration and development,[6] and (3) witnessing the spectacle of the Mongol space, demonstrated through festivals, gatherings, congresses and celebrations. The images of Verkheudinsk and the twin rivers, Selenga and Uda as leftovers of an imperial setting, Ulan Ude as the urban Soviet planned city symbolised by the giant bust of Lenin in the central square of Arbat Street and neighbourhoods dotted with Buddhist 'datsans' and 'dugans' were part and parcel of that cosmopolitan space. In the next few sections, some of these encounters with Inner Asia's cosmopolitanism will be narrated.

The 'Spectacular'

Surkharban

Surkharban is a summer festivity in Buryatia in which the central event is sports but also includes music and dance that are ingredients of what may be considered to be popular culture. I witnessed the spectacle that was held in July 2010 during the weeklong 4th Annual Mongol Convention in Ulan Ude. Held in a national stadium that was situated at a distance from the city centre of Ulan Ude, this is an ancient form of Buryat-Mongol festivity of sports and games that comprise of wrestling, horse riding, archery contests in which Buryatia's 16 districts participated in traditional clothes. It is an event that evokes nationalistic pride among the Buryats, and includes a repertoire of performances beginning with the formal inaugural of the ceremony by the chief guest who is usually the Buryat sports minister, march-past of the contesting groups in their traditional clothes who carry the national flag as well as the 'team flags' that represent the Buryat districts, the display of horses, the parade of the 'national champions' who have participated in district-level, state-level and international wrestling, judo or karate competitions. The 'strength sports', that is, wrestling and power-lifting, a visual display of Mongol heroic traits, were conducted in a special stage or in a sand pit and spectators cheered the participants. The field and track contest was carried on simultaneously in which archers proved their skills with the bow and the arrow and jockeys with their speeding horses thrilled the spectators. The event, is generally considered to be a show of the three traditional games of men (archery, wrestling and horse riding), but according to the western ethnographer Stefan Krist, has been 're-traditionalised'.[7] Sometimes, there have been induction of new games like volleyball competition into the event but that comes as an add-on component of the main event. Due to additional features like jugglery, kickboxing and pop music the event has become more of an annual extravaganza and a show rather than a national competition. 'Surkharban' means archery-but today it has a collective meaning whereby it relates to a series of other games and gaming skills. The event in Ulan Ude is an urban one, whereas in the rural areas there are other levels of 'competition', for example in the domain of music whereby the people compete by singing or reciting Buryat compositions (portions from the Geser epic, for instance) or even in the field of cooking by competing in the preparation of the traditional noodle soup. Buryats and Russians participate together in dumbbell lifting, rifle shooting and baseball. The audience and participants reflect the co-existence of the two communities in Buryatia. Buryatia, a society of integrated Russian and Buryat cultures, has moved with time and this synergy is reflected in music, dance, festivity and competition during 'Surkharban'.

Noch Ekhor

In the new age research on Eurasian religiosity, shamanism is perceived as cultural heritage and a new form of shamanic narrative has crept into the discourse.[8] This may have called for a revival of shamanism in Siberia in general and Buryatia in particular. But in the changing social context in Eurasia, shamanism is considered to be woven into the overall matrix of ethnic belonging. So, shamanic spiritual revival, wherever it has occurred, is part of a desperate, uneven ethnic revival.

In Buryatia, Buryatness was represented by offerings made at the shamanic sites on the banks of Lake Baikal. Such offerings, conducted by the tour groups, have become a major touristic attraction in Buryatia. They are accompanied by music and dance (e.g. 'Noch Ekhor', a rhythmic dance by groups of young girls who are dressed in blue and white costumes and stand in lines facing the sun). The tourists are greeted by these young girls with their hands outstretched. It is performed in a clockwise direction with incantations and accelerating movements. 'Tailagan' (shamanic offering) by standing around a metal casket was made by two or three priests, which was watched by the tourists. This is a sort of purification ritual that is practised in the Olkhon region, but has been revived on both sides of the Baikal and has tremendous touristic appeal. Similar offerings to the gods of nature were made on the way to the Baikal as well as on the river banks of the Selenga and Onon (during the trips by bus that I made to the Baikal and Gorkhi Terelj National Park that is situated in the outskirts of Ulaan Baatar).

Buddhism as Tradition-Ivolga Datsan and Gandan Monastery

The long history of association between Buddhist lamas of Russia, Mongolia and Tibet and the history of Buryat Buddhist pilgrimages to the seminaries and *datsans* of Mongolia and Tibet feature prominently in the post-Soviet writings on Buryatia. The tourist wish list of visiting Buddhist pilgrimage sites in southern Siberia and Mongolia is probably being well publicised. There have been strong assertions of Buddhist pilgrimage tradition as an integral part of Buryat heritage and discussions on this tradition play a prominent role in contemporary Buryatia's cultural policies, especially in the regions east of Lake Baikal. From this perspective, visits to the Ivolga Datsan, 'datsan' of Rinpoche Bagsha and Gandan Monastery have been a learning exercise.

The grandeur and historical memory of the monastery of Khambo Lama in Ivolginsky, about 50 km from Ulan Ude, is unmistakable. This is a huge complex of Buddhist monasteries that were built over five decades. The Buddha, Bodhisatvas and images of Buddhist reincarnation, for example, Avalokiteshwara and Arya Baala are prominent features in this quiet complex.

Monks' quarters are spread over the complex. This place is like a pilgrimage site for practitioners of the Buddhist faith who believe in the eternity of souls who have dedicated their lives to the practice of Buddhism. Khambo Lama, a Buryat Buddhist monk, is God to the Buddhists. He went into hiding in 1927 when the Bolsheviks raided the Buryat city of Ulan Ude. For almost 50 years, the lama was 'forgotten'. He was revived from a cave in a meditating posture in the 1980s. According to Buryat nationalists and believers, the lama is still alive. Today he is seen in a huge glass box in the same sitting position, head drooping and monk's clothes draped over his body.

The story about the lama in Ivolginsky 'datsan' is shrouded in mystery. But it is a place where the Soviet and post-Soviet realities intersect. It is a site of Soviet repression and is also the icon of post-Soviet Buddhist revival. In Gandan, close to Ulaan Baatar's city centre, the experience of being a visitor to the citadel of 19th century Buddhist learning was truly enchanting. Here too, like Ivolginsky, the story of Stalinist repression cast its gloomy spell. Originally situated in the centre of Ulaan Baatar, Gandan Monastery was moved to another location in the city in 1838 by the 5th Bogd Jebsundamba. Over the next century, the monastery grew to include nine datsans, a library and housed a community of 5,000 monks. Gandan became an important centre of learning and practice of Buddha's teachings, not only in Mongolia but also in the entire Mahayana Buddhist community. In 1938, Communist suppression of religious institutions resulted in the destruction of several Buddhist temples including Gandan. Only a few of its temples were saved to accommodate Russian officials. It came under strict supervision of the government officials in 1944. The restoration programme of the temple started after the Democratic Revolution in Mongolia in 1990. The central building is a symbol of independence for the Mongolians. It was built in 1911 at the time of Bogd Khan, the 8th Jebsundamba (Mongolia's last spiritual and temporal ruler). The towering statue of the Bodhisattva of Compassion (26.6 m high gilded in gold) is located inside the building. It was destroyed in 1938 but restored with donations from Buddhist devotees in 1966. In the same altar of the main building is the Gandantegchenling, where the Buddhist texts scripted by Mongolian masters of the 14th century are preserved. There is a statue of Buddha in a central glass case made by Mongolian lamas in 1956. There is a portrait of Zanzabar, the 1st Jebsundamba. Surrounding these are small statues of the succeeding Jebsundambas. Gold-plated figures of Bodhisattvas and 'thangka' paintings commemorating Buddha's life and the

Bodhisattvas are seen in the colourful walls. There is a great 'ger' and a pigeon square facing the main building in the 'datsan' complex.

Buddhism as Art-Bogd Khaan Palace Museum

The Bogd Khaan Palace compound (consisting of summer and winter palaces) in Ulaan Baatar was built during 1893-1924. The creative works of Mongolia's first Bogd Khan Gegen Zanzabar (1635-1723), a master sculptor who belonged to the Khalka noble family and followed the canons of Buddhist iconography are displayed here in the Lavran temple. His summer palace had several temples and pagodas, which are fine structures of woodwork and Buddhist art. The winter palace is a European style architecture where the last Bogd Khan of Mongolia lived. This palace now exhibits the personal belongings of the ruler (examples being the leopard skin ger presented to him or the 'elephant house' that sheltered the brown elephant that was brought for him from Russia) and his wife. As per record, he spent twenty winters here. In the summer palace, unique works of Buddhist art are displayed. Also, royal proclamations (example the declaration of independence from Manchurian Empire) written on papyrus are displayed here. The various temples in the complex have an extraordinary display of silk embroidery and religious painting (thangkas) as well as a rich collection of 'sutras' (engraved on printing blocks and clay icons). Some of these sutras are preserved in the State Central Library in Ulaan Baatar. Extensive restoration work of the palace compound began in 2004 with support from the World Monuments Fund.

Hero Memory

A synonym for contemporary Mongolia can be 'Chingiz Khan Solo'. It is amazing to see the country's identification with the personality of the empire builder. Exclusive importance is given to the performance of the Mongol warrior tribe and the military order of the 'zhuz' or the Horde. The cosmopolitan urban space in Ulaan Baatar not only showcases the Chingizid regime and the Chingizid era but also gives attention to the multiethnic tribal groupings within the Golden Horde. The principal sites of this heroic domain are the following:

I. Chingiz Khan Statue Complex

The Chingiz Khan Statue complex is located 54 km from Ulaan Baatar, and about 20 km from Gorkhi Terelj National Park which was the venue of the second day of the conference. Situated on the bank of the Tuula River, this was legendary place where Chingiz Khan found his golden whip. In memory of the 'man of the millennium', a 40 m high stainless steel statue of the great Khan on horseback has been built to commemorate 800 years of Chingiz Khan's empire. The massive complex, spread over 100 hectares of steppe land, is being developed as a recreation area. Visitors can actually climb up to the neck of the horse from where they can have a panoramic view of the complex. The complex was inaugurated on September 26, 2008.

II. The National Museum of Mongolia

The National Museum of Mongolia, established in 1924, is a storehouse of records and artefacts of Mongolia as a tribal and nomadic entity and a long history spread over more than 3000 years. Apart from the usual display of artefacts on the character of dispersal of Mongol tribal groups that we also see in similar historical museums in Ulan Ude, there is an unusual section on the Mongolian Empire and the character of political authority in Mongolia. The section on Chingiz Khan was closed due to reconstruction work at the time of my visit. But there were other sections like the halls on the Manchu rule (17th to early 20th century) and the Bogd Khan state (1911-20) which portray Mongolia's path to self-determination. The exhibits on Socialist Mongolia (1921-90) explain the milestones of socialism in Mongolia and the personalities associated with Communist ideology and action. But the posing of questions like 'Why the Purges'? surely strikes a different chord. Noteworthy is the sub-section 'Sukhbatar and the Revolution' eulogising Sukhbatar as the leader in action against Chinese occupation. The foundations of the Mongolian People's Party, the National Democratic Revolution are other important categories of this hall and the hall depicting 'Democratic Mongolia'. The year 2008 is portrayed as the marker of a historical era: showcasing the completion of 800 years in the history of the Mongolian empire. Mongolia's entry into the international arena through foreign relations and market economy and democratic pluralism are other attributes of the new age that has begun in 1990. Interesting are some of the powerful quotes—He Who Keeps His Word Has a Strong Mind. In the Sukhbatar Square, Chingiz Khan's grand statue has replaced the memorials of the revolutionary leaders Choibalsan and Sukhbatar.

Interaction

The interactive meetings were held in the usual style of commemorative gatherings that were hosted by the republican governments of Buryatia and Mongolia in collaboration with Buryat Scientific Center and Institute of Mongolian, Buddhist and Tibetan Studies (IMBT, Ulan Ude), Institute of History SBRAS (Novosibirsk), Mongolian Institute of Science and Technology (Ulaan Baatar). Buddhist culture in the Trans-Himalayan region, the variety of Buddhist art forms in Russia and India, the ambience of a trans-Himalayan Buddhist space and the use of metaphors like 'Brand Buddha' and 'Buddhist traffic' signifying linkages between South Asia and Central Asia were highlighted.

The Fourth All Mongol Convention, a republican commemoration of unity of the Mongol world, held in Ulan Ude on July 15-17, 2010 was a four-day national festival including both academic programmes and cultural festivities like 'Surkharban' and 'Noch Ekhor'. The Convention itself was a gathering of high profile dignitaries and was represented by a high level presidential delegation of the Buryat republic followed by plenary meeting and six sectional meetings of the international conference 'Globalisation and the Mongol world'. Presentations were premised on global projects as Mongolovedeniya and Buddhology with a projection of Chingiz Khan's world vision and ideal of connectivity that would be re-enacted through new age contacts and economic integration with East Asia. The policy interest for countries like South Asia, South East Asia and the Asia Pacific was reiterated. Migration and demography are the two principal subject areas that have sensitised an entire generation of scholars and activists in Russia, Central Asia and India.

Voices of concern have been raised about the fast pace of a changing demographic space of Asia, whether it was South Asia, Central Asia or the Far East, that affected inter-relationships among resident communities. The perspectives of migrant communities in Central Asia are crucial to the discourse of migration and displacement. These perspectives were juxtaposed to the voices of migrant communities in South or South East Asia who played an important role in resource generation in their places of settlement. Literature is the key tool for understanding the dialectics of migrant activities. There are interesting case studies of the Chinese community as a community in motion since the time of the Russian revolution especially in the Siberian enclaves of Khabarovsk and Irkutsk (research of I.V. Kuras). Home-grown scholars have sometimes challenged the hypothesis that Russia-Central Asian 'integration' has been affected by uncontrolled Central Asian migration to Russia. According to Viktor Dyatlov, 'migrantophobia' is not restricted to

Central Asia, but is also seen in the Caucasus. The role of rural communities as independent actors in Siberia's Tunka region has been pointed out by Russian ethnographer Sergei Panarin. Marina Baldano emphatically argues about the historical and contemporary dilemmas of Siberian communities like the Shenekhen Buryats residing in Mongol-Chinese borderlands. The ways in which their fortunes changed as their fate got entangled with historical developments in Mongolia and China since the 1911 Revolution in China reflect the versatile nature of this borderland community.

Trajectories about Eurasia's cross-cultural contact in the Mongol and Qing periods have been indicated. The extent of nomad polities from Iran in the west to Manchuria in the east and Baikal in the north to Tibet in the south indicates the inner dynamism not only of a Mongolian template but also of a series of templates representing connected histories of Russo-Chinese-Mongol borderlands. In such discussions about regional specifics, East Siberia's Baikal specifics have gained attention. Bashkuev's projections of Baikal as an ethnosphere and a civic sphere are unique. The dynamics of Eastern Siberia is also visible in the contemporary period. Vladimir Malov, an economist in Novosibirsk's Akademgorodok, made a prognosis about the Siberian 'prostor' and its prospects about its incorporation into a system of international transport corridors. His hypothesis is based on the creation of standby modes of transport networks bypassing conventional routes (Trans-Siberian Railway) and channelling transport via the northern sea route and the western and Far Eastern ports (viz. Suez Canal and Nakhodka). If Siberia has such options, can Mongolia be far behind? This was another related question about Mongolia's multi-vectored foreign policy.

Language preference (especially Chinese, Korean and English) in Mongolia is sector-specific. Mongolia's new rich are projecting a pro-western link and the country has tried to emerge from the shadows of an ex-Soviet satellite to a globalised environment with investment opportunities for foreign investors in metallurgy, mining (coal and gold mainly). To showcase this global environment in Mongolia, cosmetic changes like bilingualism based on promotion of English, Chinese, Korean and Russian as second languages have been introduced.

Conclusions: a Reality Check

My impression of the visits to Buryatia and Mongolia is that there are diverse opinions about identity and history that have not always been part of the broader narrative about social change. These are subplots and sub-narratives in a space that has its own tradition of syncretism, reflected in its relationships with the dominant ethnic group, the Russians. It is also a space that has its own sacred tradition symbolised by shamanism and Buddhism. These multiple narratives explain the shifting character of Buryat identity.

The contemporary reality of Mongolia is that it has a definite agenda for garnering international support as a country with Buddhist heritage. Tibetan Buddhist tradition in Mongolia is visible. The Dalai Lama is the symbol of tolerance and has attracted an international audience to Mongolia. In politics, a permissive environment prevails and the new rich and the educated elite are conscious about the constraints and challenges of a mobile labour force, especially the Kazakhs in Mongolia. The issue of migration also evokes multiple responses among other nationalities like the Russians and the South Koreans who also feel the pressure of competition from another community, the Chinese. There is evidence of pent-up emotions about the long period of historical domination of Mongolia by the Qing Empire. Intra-regional tensions are reported by the media in Inner Mongolia which is under Chinese influence.

Notes

1. The revival of regional studies in Russia has been indicated by Susan Smith-Peter, 'How to Write a Region-Local and Regional Historiography' (Review article) in *Kritika: Explorations in Russian and Eurasian History*, 5, 3, Summer 2004.
2. Malte Rolf, "Importing the Spatial Turn to Russia: Recent Trends in the Spatialization of Russian History", *Kritika: explorations in Russian and Eurasian history*', vol. 11, no. 2, Spring 2010.
3. Introduction by Christopher Kaplonski in David Sneath and Christopher Kaplonski eds *The History of Mongolia*, vol. III-*The Qing period-Twentieth century Mongolia*, Folkstone, (Kent: Global Oriental, 2010), p. 637.
4. See conclusion of L.L. Abaeva and B.V. Bazarov in L.L. Abaeva and H.L. Zhukovskaya eds *Buryaty*, (Moscow: Nauka, 2004), p. 588.
5. The early Soviet journal *Zhizn Buryatii* (1924-1930) and the compiled material in *Buryativedenie* are useful because of the series of writings on the following themes: (a) territoriality of Buryatia and *raionirovanie* of the 1920's (b) interpretations of Buryat intellectuals M.N. Bogdanov and G. Ts. Tsybikov about Buryat-Mongol Buddhist space (d) ethnographic case studies about Selenga Buryats, Khorinski Buryats and others.
6. The fluid and changeable nature of Buryat discourses have been indicated by new-age historians in Institute of Mongolian, Buddhist and Tibetan Studies (IMBT). For Marina Baldano, the Buryat literary tradition was nurtured and respected during the Soviet period

and was repressed during the Stalinist era but was never lost. For Darima Amogolonova, ethnic resurgence is a process of cultural identification.

7. Stefan Krist, 'Kickboxing, Break Dance and Pop Music versus Wrestling, Folk Dance and Round Music?-Popular Culture in Buryatia Today', [http://www.folklore.ee/folklore/vol41/krist.pdf].
8. Series of writings in Mihaly Hoppal ed *Shamans and Traditions*, [Bibliotheca Shamanistica], (Budapest: Akademiai Klado, 2007).

17. Mass Attitude in Democracy Sustainment: A Case Study of Public Perceptions of Democracy in Afghanistan

Arpita Basu Roy

The idea that mass attitude affects a society's chances to attain and sustain democracy is the central argument of an entire school of thought in political culture.[1] Despite this argument, empirical evidence about variation in mass attitude in varied forms of democracy is surprisingly rare.[2] Most of the literature on democracy, in fact, ignores this aspect of mass attitude. In contrast, socio-economic and socio-structural factors are the pivotal themes of research on democracy and democratisation.[3] Variable factors like economic prosperity, world market position, dispersal of resources, and dependence on oil and ethnic factions are considered to be the best indicators of a society's democratic standards.[4] In the past, the unavailability of survey data made it impossible to include mass attitude as a factor in country studies. But there is no substantive reason to ignore mass attitude now that adequate data is available. The most comprehensive study on this aspect is the one by Inglehart and Welzel.[5] Their major finding is that, among a number of supposedly pro-democracy attitude, a syndrome of 'self-expression values' is most conducive to democracy. This syndrome combines attitude that share an emancipative thrust in pursuing the freedom of ordinary people, involving an emphasis on people power, tolerance of non-conforming people, and trust in people. The hypothesis that a combination of emancipative attitude affects democracy more than other factors is a strong element in this research. Findings by Inglehart and Welzel indicate that emancipative mass attitude has a positive effect that can make democracy sustainable. There are further arguments showing that emancipative attitude motivates mass action that demonstrates people's willingness to struggle for democratic achievements. Implicitly, most scholars interested in the relation between mass attitude and democracy assumes that when pro-democratic attitude is more widespread in a society, the society is more likely to attain and sustain high levels of democracy.[6]

Democracy is often considered to be an advantage for the political, social and economic development of states and as such, democratisation is regarded to be internationally acceptable. This has been the case of Afghanistan, where post-conflict democratic trends have been the key focus of national and international actors. However, little attention has been paid to the meaning of the term in the Afghan context. The process of democratisation in Afghanistan has involved the re-establishment of a presidential system of government, a bicameral parliament, provincial councils and an electoral cycle which has seen two rounds of elections. However the existence of these institutions alone does not constitute 'democratic politics'[7], but the process of improving their performance is in itself a central component of democratisation.

Afghanistan's post-2001 democratic experiment has been a combination of imported democratic institutions with a range of other power structures, networks of allegiance, and methods of negotiating power. Some of these are rooted in tradition, while others have emerged as a result of conflict dynamics and new opportunities. Representative governance in the country is, thus, an evolving hybrid of democratic procedures and existing practices that interact in diverse and at times, unexpected ways. It is unrealistic to expect democracy in Afghanistan to resemble Western-style, liberal democracy with social freedom in the near future. Nor is there much local desire for it to do so. However, if supporters of democratisation continue their efforts based on a realistic understanding of how representation functions in practice, a space is created for the emergence of a political system that conforms to the basic norms of a democracy.

The present study tries to assess whether pro-democratic attitude and the 'self-expression values' are becoming widespread in Afghan society, and whether a correlation can be drawn between mass attitude and democracy sustainment in Afghanistan. It would be premature to predict or discredit a democratic future for Afghanistan-however the attempt here is to understand which way the process might move. Assuming that Afghanistan has embarked on the technical and political process of democratisation[8] since 2001, it focuses on the perceptions of the Afghans and analyses the findings of three synthesis and policy papers published by the Afghan Research and Evaluation Unit[9] in Kabul to find out whether mass attitude is tending to be pro-democratic. Public perceptions on various issues have been discussed in the following sub-sections. The focus has been to understand whether a pro-democratic mass attitude can be conducive to democracy because such attitude can increase public support for pro-democratic forces and distract support from anti-democratic forces. Mass support is a central element in the power balance between political forces.

Definitions, Perceptions and Interpretations of 'Democracy' in Afghanistan:

Anna Larson's 2009 Study

The discussion paper of Anna Larson[10], the first of its kind on Afghanistan, explores different perspectives of democracy and democratisation held in three provinces of Afghanistan – Kabul, Balkh and Parwan – in both rural and urban areas.[11] It provides a brief background to democracy as a global movement, and to its origins in Afghanistan, before focusing on two key areas: definitions, perceptions and interpretations of the term 'democracy', and respondents' experiences of representative processes.

The most common association made by respondents of all backgrounds was that of democracy with 'freedom'. This association was often discussed in terms of the 'freedom to' participate in elections, and to choose and criticise one's own government, alongside the concern that (other) people's freedom to 'misuse' democracy, or condone any kind of behaviour in the name of democratic freedom, might result in social problems. These respondents see western forms of democracy as opposed to Islamic norms of democracy.[12] Respondents referring to this dichotomy were numerous, and reflected an array of social backgrounds, indicating that this way of conceptualising democracy in Afghanistan is not uncommon. Western democracy was generally associated with immorality and secularism, and therefore, was rejected, while Islamic democracy was considered to encompass positive values that would be acceptable in an Afghan context. A third key trend noticeable in interviews was the association of democracy with security. This was often expressed from a negative perspective, indicating that the situation now in Afghanistan is not democratic due to the lack of security. Evidently, the concepts of free and fair elections and universal suffrage are called into question when votes are gained (or at least perceived to be gained) by force, and when polling stations could not be established in various insecure parts of the country. Democracy was associated with poverty reduction, economic development and equality. The perception that many Afghans (and particularly those in rural areas) would prioritise short-term economic gains over the prospect of being able to vote freely, was common. Urban respondents in particular perceived that rural poverty was engendering the use of potential votes as a means to extract monetary or material payoffs, indicating a preoccupation with short-term, practical and localised needs as opposed to long-term, strategic interests at the national level.

General comparison between Afghanistan's economic status and that of established democratic states revealed that a predominant perception among respondents was that given the conditions of unemployment, poverty and corruption, Afghanistan could not be classified as a democracy, to the extent of assuming that 'real' democracies do not have these kinds of economic problems. There was scepticism about parliament as an institution for voicing citizens' concerns, and it is not surprising given the fact that it had been functioning only for four years; it is indicative of the unrealised expectations of parliamentarians concerning their own potential achievements, and of citizens concerning the potential parliamentary outcome. Provincial councils were prescribed in Afghanistan's constitution as a means to bridge the gap between national and local level politics in the country, but have developed a reputation as relatively worthless institutions, whose political clout is dependent on their relationship with provincial governors and which have been systematically overlooked by international development actors. According to common belief, parties are unpopular in Afghanistan due to their association with civil warfare and ethnic identities.[13] Having said this, a more subtle perspective on party politics is evident throughout most of the data collected on this subject – a general sense of the potential utility of parties as political actors is common, albeit followed by the caveat that, in Afghanistan, parties are too flawed to take up this role.

However, this brings into question the assumption that democratisation will be a stabilising force in post-conflict situations. Encouraging multi-party competition may well be considered the best way to bring about democratic representation, modelled on political systems in established democracies, but this does not take into account the fact that parties emphasise divisions between groups and thus potentially fuel underlying identity politics and tensions. Initial qualitative research suggests that there is a decreasing level of acceptance of the current democratisation process among citizens for a number of reasons. Firstly, democracy is increasingly associated with the individual liberal freedoms of the West, and thus, distanced from Afghan religious and cultural norms. If liberal values continue to be considered 'imposed' in Afghanistan, the result may be rejection of the democratic process entirely as a reaction against a perceived Western cultural 'invasion'. Secondly, there is widespread disillusionment about the benefits that 'democracy' can bring, due to an expectation that is lacking regarding the improvement of the rule of law and economic development combined with a hopelessness brought about by deterioration of security. This is heightened by concerns that encouraging multi-party competition and political opposition could 'contribute to insecurity' rather than promote peace and stability. Thirdly, democratic representation is seen as inherently flawed, due to the inefficacy and fraud perceived to infiltrate formal representative processes and the lack of performance of elected representatives. Finally, there is a fundamental disconnect between people and government, which has not been addressed by the formation of formal democratic institutions.

In spite of these factors, the study showed that there was a clear and widespread desire for a public role in the political process in the three provinces studied. The ideal of democratic participation and self-determination of government was held in high regard. This may seem unbelievable in the aftermath of the 2009 elections, notorious for low voter turnout and allegations of corruption. But people's desire to take part in choosing their government cannot be measured by turnout for an election in which outcomes were widely considered pre-determined, and in which for many, voting was a life-threatening exercise. Indeed, for many Afghans these elections did not represent a 'test' of democracy or democratic principles at all. A number of those interviewed for this study expressed the belief that the development of democratic systems of government takes time, and that this process cannot be implemented quickly.

Deconstructing 'Democracy': Anna Larson's Findings, 2011

Anna Larson's second study shows that 'democracy' and 'Afghanistan' do not match.[14] This report is based on two years of research in six different provinces, and explores Afghan perspectives on democracy and their possible implications for the future. Larson's research shows that many Afghans are disappointed with the country's 10-year process of democratisation – it has proven to be 'bitterly disappointing in its failure to deliver justice, equity or services, while the term itself has become increasingly associated with the unwanted imposition of Western values. This also indicates a sense of fatigue among members of the donor community, who have promoted the rhetoric of democratisation and paid for election cycles, yet have seemingly little to show to their increasingly war-weary and impatient public'.[15]

However, in tune with her previous studies, Larson reports on Afghan perspectives of democracy and democratisation in rural and urban areas to show that there is still space for the development of democratic politics in Afghanistan. Her report claims that democratisation is a process, without an end-point – and a process that is constantly shifting between poles of 'more' or 'less democratic'. In this respect, democratisation in Afghanistan has the potential to move in either direction. The report also asserts that if the process of democratisation is to last in the country, it needs to be situated firmly within Afghan priorities, many of which may not necessarily overlap with the principles enshrined in western models of liberal democracy. Therefore, there is a definite eagerness for democratic representation with apprehension about corruption and foreign interference. However, Larson argues, this must be centred firmly on their own priorities. Her research brought together the opinions of men and women from diverse social backgrounds, living on both sides of the rural/urban divide and in areas with varying levels of security. Different levels of hopes, expectations and concerns have been revealed, and this has created awareness about the existing realities.[16]

There seems to be a disconnection between Afghan principles and foreign notions of democracy. People are hostile to the term 'democracy' which is regarded as a symbol of Western domination and was related to the widespread acceptance of elections and the institution of the parliament as a way of making the government more inclusive and accountable. In contrast to immoral, unfettered 'freedom' in liberal democracies, many people have supported the implementation of democracy within an 'Islamic framework'. However, what this might entail was hardly explained, and there seems to be some scope for negotiation. Democracy and democratic participation were also viewed as a distant second priority to ensuring security and stability. Immediate concerns over the threat of violence that political engagement often entails were framed against a more general call for a 'politics of consensus' and a deep suspicion of political parties. Larson's findings revealed that there were sharp contrasts in people's perspectives on the nature of equality and representation, specifically regarding who should be represented, and how. However, there was an almost unanimous call for greater equality of access to decision-making, service provision and resources, and in this respect many saw Afghanistan's current 'democracy' as little more than a front for the powerful to accumulate wealth and extend their reach.

Perceptions, Parliament and Elections: Oliver Lough's Findings, 2011

Research shows that there are certain identifiable trends in the views of the Afghans surveyed but they vary largely from western ideals of democracy and normally have a strong interest in how their country is and should be governed[17]. Olivier Lough's findings, in consonance with other studies mentioned above show a strong support among many Afghans for people's right to select their representatives through elections. In many people's minds, these desirable aspects of representation are distinct from wider connotations of democracy, which is often seen as an import of Western social values and ideals that threatens people's identities as both Afghans and Muslims. Afghans often expressed that democratisation should take place within an 'Islamic framework', where people's behaviour conforms to an acceptable – though rarely defined – set of Islamic norms and values.

Lough's work indicates that Afghans stress the importance of consensus when describing what politics should ideally look like. People consider local methods of community governance such as 'shuras' or 'jirgas' as more effective for consensus-building and a more predictable, stable and inclusive way to make decisions rather than competitive individualism typical in the West. Similarly, political parties are often viewed as potentially destructive forces that exacerbate divisions and heighten the risk of conflict, due in part to their destructive role during the jihad and civil war periods and the violent competition between different groups they are seen to represent. Especially in less secure areas, many people ultimately prize a basic level of security above all else, and are reluctant to involve themselves in politics of any kind should it threaten to disrupt this.

There is a general demand for equal access to political influence and economic resources. In this respect, many see Afghanistan's current system as little more than a front for existing power holders to enrich themselves at the expense of the population at large. However, there is a lack of consensus over exactly how representation should work in Afghanistan and views often differ according to people's backgrounds. For example, there is often a sense that the right to represent should somehow be tied to a person's level of education or capacity, and there are competing opinions on whether and how power should be allocated among Afghanistan's different population groups.

In many instances, voters equate MPs with other community leaders such as 'maliks', who have traditionally served as a point of contact with the state. This can lead to the view that they are bound by similar norms of reciprocal obligation; rather than serving as representatives, they are expected to provide services and political connections in exchange for community support. In a similar vein, there is a sense that only someone familiar with a given community can represent it and be held to account if promises of service provision go unmet. These factors can ultimately lead to the expectation that MPs will primarily represent communities with which they are associated (rather than the entire population of their home province, which is their actual electorate). These understandings can lead to disillusionment when people's high expectations of service provision are not met by MPs, as well as feelings of disenfranchisement among communities without 'their own' parliamentarian.

Concluding Observations

The studies reviewed here illustrate democratic aspirations despite frustrations about the process and personalities. Democracy and democratisation in Afghanistan will be drawn out on volatile but valuable processes, which urgently need redefining according to Afghan perspectives. The conclusions of Welzel's study on pro-democratic effect of emancipative attitude show that this effect is of a twofold nature – emancipative mass attitude helps both to sustain democracy in more democratic societies, and to attain democracy in less democratic societies. Addressing the mechanism by which emancipative attitude does this, the evidence suggests that the attitude motivates mass actions aiming at democratic achievements. Welzel also argued that emancipative orientations can operate as a force to attain democracy only in democratisation cases of the 'societal-led' type. This has been the dominant type of democratisation in the recent decades. But it is not the only type, as there also exist 'externally-induced' democratisation. This type applies to post-war democracies such as Germany, Italy, and Japan after the Second World War. He emphasised that in the future, Afghanistan and Iraq might also fall into the category of externally-induced democratisation following wars. Still, even in the externally-induced type of democratisation, emancipative attitude becomes relevant: the extent to which this attitude takes hold in the population is a major factor of democratic consolidation. This is where the research on public perception of democracy in Afghanistan becomes relevant. The findings mentioned above reflect an apparent desire for liberal democracy notwithstanding concerns about corruption, foreign interference and inefficiency. People have strong opinions on their political system and representatives. Therefore, sustaining it for a considerable length of time would be imperative for sustaining democracy. Given the linkage between emancipative attitude of people and democracy sustainment, this emancipative approach would play a significant role for promoting sustainability. In some way, this is relevant to democracy, confirming the emancipative theory of democracy proposed by Inglehart and Welzel.

Notes

1. G.A. Almond and S. Verba, *The Civic Culture*, (Princeton, NJ: Princeton University Press, 1963) and H. Eckstein, *A Theory of Stable Democracy*, (Princeton, NJ: Princeton University Press, 1966).
2. Christian Welzel, "Are Levels of Democracy Affected by Mass Attitude? Testing Attainment and Sustainment Effects on Democracy", *International Political Science Review/Revue internationale de science politique* 28, no. 4 (2007): 397-424.
3. This is true of modernisation theory, world system theory, resource distribution theory, resource curse theory, and cultural fragmentation theory.
4. The most recent studies in this tradition include: C. Boix, *Democracy and Redistribution*, (New York: Cambridge University Press, 2003); R. Doorenspleet, "The Structural Context of Recent Transitions to Democracy", *European Journal of Political Research 43, May (2004): 309-36*, and T. Vanhanen, *Democratisation: A Comparative Analysis of 170 Countries*, (London: Routledge, 2003).
5. R. Inglehart and C. Welzel, *Modernization, Cultural Change, and Democracy*, (New York: Cambridge University Press, 2005), pp. 254-271.
6. Christian Welzel, "Are Levels of Democracy Affected by Mass Attitude? Testing Attainment and Sustainment Effects on Democracy", *International Political Science Review/Revue internationale de science politique* 28, No. 4 (2007): 397-424
7. R. Luckham, A-M. Goetz and M. Kaldor, "Democratic Institutions and Democratic Politics," in S. Bastian and R Luckham, eds., *Can Democracy be Designed? The Politics of Institutional Choice in Conflict-torn Societies*, (London: Zed Books, 2003).
8. "Democratisation" as a term can signify the process begun after a given country (or its government) shifts from alternative means of governing (authoritarian or totalitarian regimes, for example) or a period of civil conflict towards a democratic politics. This often involves the establishment of democratic institutions, which include but are not limited to 'free and fair elections', a national assembly, local governance structures and other methods of linking citizens to the government, such as political parties.

9. The Afghanistan Research and Evaluation Unit (AREU), established in 2002 with the assistance of community working in Afghanistan, is an independent research institute based in Kabul. AREU's informs and influence policy and practice through conducting high-quality, policy-relevant research and actively disseminating the results, and to promotes a culture of research and learning. Supposedly it is an impartial Afghanistan-based voice dedicated to research excellence; AREU aspires to contribute to the development of inclusive and transparent policymaking processes, driven by the priorities of the Afghan people, which give rise to better informed policies and programmes that improve Afghan lives. They have representation from donors, the United Nations and other multilateral agencies, and non-governmental organisations.
10. Anna Larson, *Toward an Afghan Democracy: Exploring Perceptions of Democratisation in Afghanistan*, Discussion Paper, (Kabul: AREU, September 2009).
11. Data was collected over six months. A total of 69 qualitative semi-structured interviews were conducted, both with individuals (36) and focus groups (33, of 3-15 respondents in each), with a sample of men and women of different ethnicities and social backgrounds. Respondents interviewed included teachers, students, religious scholars, civil society representatives, traders, community leaders and political party members.
12. Anna Larson, n.8, p. 9.
13. International Crisis Group. *Political Parties in Afghanistan*, Asia Report No. 39, June 02, 2005(cited August 10, 2008). Available from www.crisisgroup.org
14. Anna Larson, *Deconstructing "Democracy" in Afghanistan*, Synthesis Paper Series, (Kabul: AREU, May 2011).
15. Anna Larson," Ibid., Afghan Research and Evaluation Unit (AREU) Synthesis Paper Series, May 2011.
16. Ibid., p. 1.
17. Oliver Lough, *Practicing Democracy in Afghanistan: Key Findings on Perceptions, Parliament and Elections*, AREU Policy Note Series, May 2011.

18. Koh Kim Seng, *Misunderstood Myanmar: An Introspective Study of a Southeast Asian State in Transition*

Swapna Bhattacharya (Chakraborti)

In presenting me a copy of his publication, Koh Kim Seng wrote: "In consonance with a like minded scholar whose search for the truth is quite insatiable, but who fortunately is endowed with an alimentary canal which is robust enough to digest and assimilate the toughest of material, devoid of any indigestion – age notwithstanding." I am not sure whether my alimentary canal is really robust enough, or whether through this review I would be doing justice to his scholarship. But, I have no hesitation to add that I took a very long time to read the book of nearly 300 pages, and then digest the materials presented quite skilfully in this extremely provocative book. Therefore, I feel extremely obliged to the Maulana Abul Kalam Azad Institute of Asian Studies, Kolkata and my former colleague Priya Singh for giving me the time.

The book is divided into 8 chapters – (1) Toward an 'insense' of Myanmar, (2) Misunderstood Myanmar, (3) The *Milieu Interieur* Part I, (4) The *Milieu Interieur* Part II, (5) The *Milieu Exterieur*, (6) Reeling under a colonial past, (7) Myanmar: International Relations Calculus, and (8) Epilogue. The subject covered by the annexes range from a facsimile of an inscription from early medieval Myanmar, to international narcotics strategy report to the texts of the US and the EU sanctions on trade with Myanmar. But, the most valuable part of this annexe is the series of letters written by Davis O. Abel, one of the author's key respondents. These letters cover subjects as wide as the Communist infiltration, Renationalisation of assets by General Ne Win, LDC status, the Bloodless Coup of 1962, etc. The book has an updated bibliography. The author belongs to those very few fortunate souls who had the opportunity to go to Myanmar even during the time when the country was partially closed for outsiders. He is from the world of business. But, did his Ph.D work from the National University, Singapore. The book is the outcome of his painstaking research. I can only congratulate my friend Koh Kim Seng for this extremely valuable contribution – full of honest submission, very rare in the world of knowledge today.

After having watched the politics of Myanmar over the last two decades and also having visited the country 6 times over the last 15 years or so, I may be allowed to add that Singapore has remained a very trusted partner in many ways. Singapore stands firmly, helping Myanmar to overcome some of the most formidable challenges caused by western sanctions, for example, while other ASEAN partners occasionally expressed dissatisfaction over the slow progress of political and economic reforms in Myanmar. For us, Indians, Singapore is a country of business and trade, a country of good governance, and a country where your professional expertise counts above everything. That such a country would follow a well-thought policy with regard to a neighbourly country, which never turned aggressive to her neighbours – is most expected. This phenomenon of regional integrity has been repeatedly highlighted in this work. On November 30, 1988, the Foreign Investment Law became effective. The law allowed foreign investors to establish either wholly foreign-owned enterprises or joint ventures in which the foreign partner would be required to take a 35 per cent equity stake. The first industrial joint venture established under the new law is in the field of woodworking, with a partner from Singapore. Singapore's advantage is its strong economic base and pluralist civic composition. Every time I go to Myanmar, I hear that Singapore has become a 'second home' for the people of Myanmar.

In Myanmar, Koh Kim Seng had the privilege to interact with a number of people from various fields: policy making, business, government, military, academic institutions, etc. Indeed, the major portion of the book is a critical reproduction of his interviews. It is quite exciting for me to read such interviews, as quite a few of these high profile personalities are also known to me for many years. For example, the First Lady Daw Ni Ni Myint, the eminent historian and the author of the book 'Burma's Struggle against British Imperialism 1885-1895'. It was quite interesting to follow the interview where Daw Ni Ni Myint, a Professor at Yangon University and former Director of Universities, Historical Research Centre, Yangon University, spoke about General Ne Win's understanding of colonialism and neo-imperialism of the West.

The author's visits to the Golden Land, in connection with FDI projects were utilised to understand the mindset of the people of Myanmar – a country which he described as having fallen into a time warp. Throughout the length and breadth of his investigation he was in search of finding for himself a 'peace' by virtue of achieving which, he could do justice to Myanmar, for he really loves the country. The 'Myanmar Exceptionalism' persisted throughout the period of parliamentary democracy (1948-62), military socialism (1962-88) and stratocratic rule (from 1988 to the present). He keenly aspires to prove that one has to go back to history and history alone to understand the self-imposed isolation of the Myanmar people. He argues that the western world, the US in particular, never tried to understand the mind of the people of Myanmar. In his list, Europe is also included, the UK in particular, though for Germany he seems to have a soft corner. Throughout the book one can trace numerous examples of constant tension between these two uncompromising forces. The style of communication is unnatural. Koh Kim Seng speaks through his 'friends', 'brothers' and 'cousins' – for whom he used the term 'key respondents'.

The themes for discussion are (1) Historical-political, (2) Economic and Developmental, (3) Drugs and Narcotics problem, (4) International repercussions of the events played in Myanmar, (5) Myanmar's capability of strategising the regional potential, and (6) Myanmar's own way of adjusting her history and the present.

Seeing from a particular angle, the book can be interpreted as a metaphor of a conflict between two parties: milieu exterieur and milieu interieur. Under the first, he brought the Myanmar diaspora, living in various western countries, who, according to the author, were by no means, concerned about peace and prosperity in their country. On the other hand, under the term 'milieu interieur' he means the people of Myanmar who have served the country, defended their motherland from various formidable challenges. Of course, under this grouping he places the Myanmar Army in the higher platform. Aung San Suu Kyi can be placed, as far as I see, between these two parties. She, being the daughter of the father of the Myanmar Nation, Aung San, certainly cannot be grouped as 'milieu exterieur'. On the other hand, her long stay outside Myanmar and the US backing she enjoyed somehow made things difficult for her.

Koh Kim Seng has discussed a wide number of issues, but has also maintained a chronological order: (a) The colonial experience of the Myanmar people and the trauma of subjugation, (b) Influence of Buddhist morale and Buddhist rationale on the society, (c) the experience of civil rule under U Nu with special reference to the 18 months caretaker Government, (d) General Ne Win's rise to power in 1962, end of the Ne Win era and also the end of the isolation period, (e) Immediate (1988-89) ups and downs with a view to the struggle within the army, (f) Presence of US Navy on the Indian Ocean: in the Andaman Sea, (g) Short interim period of civil rule under President Dr. Maung Maung, (h) Khin Nyunt and his 7 point roadmap to democracy, (i) Fall of Khin Nyunt, (j) Aung San Suu Kyi's withdrawal from the Convention, and (k) the acquired stability through the passing of the Constitution, ethnic rehabilitation through cooperation of the neighbouring countries. Unfortunately, neither India nor Bangladesh found any importance for their valuable contribution towards a peaceful and bloodless transition. China and the ASEAN are his major focus, though the author mentions Jawaharlal Nehru, Zhou En Lai, U Nu, and the Five Principles of Peaceful Co-existence. But, India has come a long way since Nehru, though as regards foreign policy, I have no problem in accepting that the spirit of 'Panchsheel' is still very central. Thus, India, not having shifted from the firm stand of promoting a democratic form of Government across the world, has engaged herself intensively with Myanmar. Indeed, in dealing with Myanmar, the present Government under Prime Minister Dr. Manmohan Singh has shown a path, which could have been followed by many countries. Some of the most remarkable achievements are visible in the progress of the Kaladan Multi Modal Project, linking Mizoram with the Rakhine (Arakan) coast, reconstruction of Sittwe port on the principle of Built, Operate and Transfer (BOT), etc. A wide range of cultural, academic and religious activities, along with defence collaboration are going on between Myanmar and India. I have experienced it during my last visit to Myanmar in August 2011, during the celebration of Rabindranath Tagore's 150th Birth centenary. China's achievement in getting/buying the major share of Myanmar gas may be seen as an economic victory of China over India. As the author has the prudence to link the present with the past, I humbly suggest him to read my book 'India-Myanmar Relations 1886-1948' (Kolkata 2007).

The author spoke about a vacuum that was created in the minds of the people of Myanmar, as the royalty (the last dynasty) was the protector of the Buddhist clergy and Buddhist order. The 'dhamma' was attacked with arms. Therefore, the answer should be to build a strong 'Tamadaw'. As such, this argument is not new, already addressed by a number of scholars. But, the distinct character of his book lies in the throbbing spirit of Asian neo-nationalism, which I salute. Yet, it is quite interesting to note that the author has completely ignored the name of Frank Trager, father of Myanmar Studies, and the leading figure in Cornell School of Southeast Asian Studies.

In Trager's vision, Myanmar and India had the great potential to contain the emerging challenge of communism in post-colonial Asia. Three countries – India, Indonesia and Myanmar – were of immense strategic importance in the perception of many schools of thought during the 1950s and 1960s.

On various topics the author exchanged his views with Brig. Myo Thant (p.61 ff), former Minister of Information. What comes up goes to argue that there has been a tremendous progress in the area of infrastructural development in various parts of Myanmar from the 1990s onwards. The subject of border trade has not been adequately dealt with. Upon a question about State-Sangha relationship, the answer given was that the relation was excellent! Only a few militant Pongyis (monks) were behind the outbreak of the September 2007 Saffron Revolt on the street of Yangon. Brig. Myo Thant saw foreign involvement in this event, but did not disclose the name of the country or 'elements' originating from the country concerned (see p. 91). Brig. Bo Myo Thant saw the root of the authoritarian tradition in the style of functioning of Prime Minister Dr. Ba Maw, who happened to be the *Anashin* (Dictator) of Myanmar during the time of the Japanese awarded 'independence' (April 1943). We know that Aung San also had his concept of free Burma with a strong state: federal, but with a centralised structure. Very little has been spoken about Aung San and his unique role in the history of Freedom struggle, especially in the most constructive phase between 1943-1947.

The author made no secret of the fact that (see p. 194) opium trading in Myanmar, especially along the eastern and northern borders, increased from 40 tons to 300-400 tons over the period from 1945 to 1962. The American backed KMT forces, cooperated with the Kokangs, Kachin Independent Army (KIA) and Shan United Revolutionary Army (SURA). All benefited from this formidable illegal trade. Trade (teak, gas) with Thailand brings a considerable amount of foreign exchange for Myanmar. But, about Thailand's role in harbouring a large number of dissidents (milieu exteriuer) on its soil we don't hear much from the author.

Rapid burning of poppy fields under the supervision of the UNDP, and in collaboration with the local administration, has changed the scenario considerably. I have no trouble in accepting the fact of the government's constructive role. But, I strongly believe that the civil society movement (NGOs, religious institutions, Buddhist and Christian, the Israel backed Shalom foundation) also played quite an impressive role in this sector of rehabilitation of drug addicts, the cease fire and the peace process in general. Nevertheless, the author should be congratulated for having taken up boldly a subject, like Narcotic trade that scholars working on Myanmar otherwise avoid. Also I greatly admire the author's courage in criticising, quite legitimately, some of the western scholars' views on Myanmar.

For all the governments, starting from SLORC, (State Law and Order Restoration Council) SPDC, (State Peace and Development Council) and USDA (Union Solidarity and Development Association), the primary focus has been ensuring of law and order, public livelihood, non-disintegration of the Union, nation's sovereignty and solidarity. All these should be observed juxtaposed with the event of joining of two erstwhile close associates of Ne Win, U Aung Gyi and Tin Oo in NLD (Daw Aung San led National League for Democracy). The situation got complicated when in August 1988; the US war vessels were seen in the Andaman Sea. The US Ambassador was summoned by the then Myanmar Government to explain, and to take back the vessels.

It is said by the author that a student from the years 1987-1988 had to look in to the dictionary for the meaning of the word 'Democracy' (see p. 125). In the backdrop of all these, it is understood why Daw Aung San Suu Kyi, in spite of her undivided victory in the election of 1990, could not be handed over power. It has been argued that Daw Aung San Suu Kyi's free movement would have caused a greater damage to the country; it could even have led to large-scale disturbances and disintegration. In the entire book, the rondo has been repeated again and again, arguing that there was no other way for Myanmar to go than the one she has come all along from 1988 up to now. But, who can deny the fact that the credit of opening the country to the outside world should in major part go to Daw Aung San Suu Kyi?

On page 217-218, quoting the view of 'brother', the author of the book under discussion said and I quote with the author's permission, "From this point of view, it appears that Myanmar draws inspiration from many states in the same straits such as Cuba, North Korea and above all China. Brother's perception is that China was likewise in slumber for many years but by its slow and systematic appraisal of local conditions it effected a gradualist policy of change and flourished yet again". Just like Deng's visit in the late 1980s to Southeast Asia and coastal China brought changes within the Chinese economy, Myanmar's opening and integration with ASEAN during the 1990s should bring economic spin offs for Myanmar. In the context of this argument, it is remarkable how Myanmar, which refused to join ASEAN in 1967, smoothly got integrated within ASEAN, and how China, along with Japan and South Korea emerged as the Group called 'ASEAN plus 3' in the mid-1990s. I would like to remind the author humbly that Myanmar has over the last few years gained confidence from two of her most important neighbours, Bangladesh and India. Thus, Myanmar, instead of China, has been given an observer status in the SAARC. As much as India and Bangladesh look East, Myanmar also looks West for her own security and prosperity. Myanmar is also a trusted partner for India, in the regional forums such as BIMSTEC, Mekong Ganga Cooperation, etc.

The book should be read and reviewed widely to clear up many misconceptions about Myanmar and her people, though the style of writing may appear extremely difficult for some readers.

APP. No 304
21112

121